Russian Silver Age Poetry

TEXTS AND CONTEXTS

CULTURAL SYLLABUS
SERIES EDITOR — MARK LIPOVETSKY (UNIVERSITY OF COLORADO, BOULDER)

Russian Silver Age Poetry

TEXTS AND CONTEXTS

Edited and introduced by
Sibelan E. S. Forrester
and
Martha M. F. Kelly

BOSTON / 2015

A catalog record for this book as available from the Library of Congress.
Copyright © 2015 Academic Studies Press
All rights reserved

ISBN 978-1-61811-352-8 (hardback)
ISBN 978-1-61811-363-4 (electronic)

Book design by Ivan Grave
On the cover:
"Romantic Landscape," by Wassily Kandinsky (2011), a fragment.

Published by Academic Studies Press in 2015
28 Montfern Avenue
Brighton, MA 02135, USA
press@academicstudiespress.com
www.academicstudiespress.com

Contents

Preface	x
How To Use This Book	xi
Some Issues in Translating Russian Poetry into English	xv
Several Different Versions of the Same Russian Poem	xx
Acknowledgments	xxviii
Sources and Permissions	xxx
Introduction: Poetry of the Russian Silver Age ***Sibelan Forrester and Martha Kelly***	xxxviii

SECTION I: THE POETS

Biographies and Poetry	3
Anna Akhmatova	5
Innokenty Annensky	22
Nikolai Aseev	28
Konstantin Balmont	32
Andrei Bely	38
Alexander Blok	44
Valery Bryusov	58
Sergei Esenin	64
Zinaida Gippius	68
Nikolai Gumilyov	74
Vyacheslav Ivanov	80
Velimir Khlebnikov	83

Vladislav Khodasevich	94
Nikolai Klyuev	101
Alexei Kruchonykh	107
Mikhail Kuzmin	110
Mirra Lokhvitskaya	120
Osip Mandelstam	126
Vladimir Mayakovsky	147
Dmitri Merezhkovsky	166
Sofia Parnok	171
Boris Pasternak	176
Igor Severyanin	190
Maria Shkapskaya	193
Fyodor Sologub	198
Vladimir Solovyov	204
Marina Tsvetaeva	210
Maximilian Voloshin	237
Selected Bibliography of Poetry Translations	240

SECTION II: BEYOND POETRY

Essays	247
From Poetry as Enchantment (1915) **Konstantin Balmont**	248
Symbolism and Contemporary Russian Art (1908) **Andrei Bely**	251
Keys to the Mysteries (1904) **Valery Bryusov**	269

A Holy Sacrifice (1905)   284
  Valery Bryusov

Symbolism's Legacy and Acmeism (1913)   290
  Nikolai Gumilyov

Nietzsche and Dionysus (1904)   294
  Vyacheslav Ivanov

The Precepts of Symbolism (1910)   304
  Vyacheslav Ivanov

Thoughts on Symbolism (1912)   321
  Vyacheslav Ivanov

The Morning of Acmeism (1913)   329
  Osip Mandelstam

The Word and Culture (1921)   334
  Osip Mandelstam

From The Apocalypse of Our Times (1917)   340
  Vasily Rozanov

Poets' Demons (1907)   343
  Fyodor Sologub

Criticism   349

Innokenty Annensky (1963)   350
  Anna Akhmatova

From "On Contemporary Lyrism" (1909)   353
  Innokenty Annensky

In Memory of Vrubel (1916)   366
  Alexander Blok

Chertova kukla (The Devil's Doll): *A Novel by Z. N. Gippius* (1911)   370
  Kornei Chukovsky

Reviews of Works by Blok, Klyuev, Balmont, and Others (1912)   382
  Nikolai Gumilyov

Review of Akhmatova's Beads (1914) 391
 Nikolai Gumilyov

Foreword to Evening by Anna Akhmatova (1912) 395
 Mikhail Kuzmin

Review of Igor Severyanin's The Thunder-Seething Goblet (1913) 398
 Osip Mandelstam

On Contemporary Poetry: Almanac of the Muses (1916) 399
 Osip Mandelstam

V. V. Khlebnikov (1922) 402
 Vladimir Mayakovsky

In Quest of a Path for Art (1913) 409
 Sofia Parnok

On Symbolists and Decadents (1901) 415
 Vasily Rozanov

Reviews of Russian Symbolists (1894) 430
 Vladimir Solovyov

Downpour of Light: Poetry of Eternal Courage (1922) 443
 Marina Tsvetaeva

The Horoscope of Cherubina de Gabriak (1909) 464
 Maximilian Voloshin

Memoirs 472

Reminiscences of Alexander Blok (1955) 473
 Anna Akhmatova

From "Osip Mandelstam" (1964) 477
 Anna Akhmatova

Bryusov (1925) 483
 Zinaida Gippius

The End of Renata (1928) **Vladislav Khodasevich**	485
From The One and a Half-Eyed Archer (1933) **Benedikt Livshitz**	497
From On the Banks of the Neva (1967) **Irina Odoevtseva**	499
On Vladimir Mayakovsky (1931) **Boris Pasternak**	508
From a review of Kuzmin's Alexandrian Songs (1906) **Maximilian Voloshin**	521

Other Prose Works 523

Letter to Alexander Blok (1907) **Innokenty Annensky**	524
Letter to Maximilian Voloshin (1909) **Innokenty Annensky**	525
Futurist Manifestos (1912, 1913)	527
Letters to Vyacheslav Ivanov (1909) **Osip Mandelstam**	531
Quote about the Stray Dog cabaret (no date) **Viktor Shklovsky**	535
The Demonic Woman (1913) **Nadezhda Tèffi**	536
Thematic Index	541
Index of Poem Titles and First Lines (Russian)	546
Index of Poem Titles and First Lines (English)	551

Preface

Why do we want to draw your attention to the poetry of the Russian Silver Age? For us, it is the most fascinating period in Russian culture: an era of brilliant poets, vivid personalities who had important intellectual as well as aesthetic gifts, and who plunged into creative life with all their energy—to produce what is simply some of the sexiest, most gripping *writing* to come from any time or place in the world. Poetry is only one of the era's many cultural achievements, but it is one of the most exciting—and the Silver Age produced the first body of poetry that grabbed and kept the attention of readers, not just scholars and specialists, outside Russia. This attention points to its quality, its high status in both the East and the West during the Soviet period, and its provocative dialogues with various non-Russian literatures and cultures. Russian Silver Age poetry engages with Classical Antiquity and Western European writings, of course, but also with Africa, the Far East, and the Americas. The Silver Age witnessed an unprecedented degree of collaboration of writers with visual artists, musicians, dancers, and other creative individuals. Many of the poets included here also wrote plays, memoirs, fiction, literary criticism, and publicistic articles. The personal idiosyncrasies, friendships, and entanglements of the poets themselves can be quite interesting, and they offer some insight into the poems—as well, perhaps, as some warning about the possible side effects of such an all-consuming artistic program on the lives of real human beings.

How To Use This Book

This collection is intended for readers of many kinds: for undergraduate and graduate students who are still learning the Russian language and starting to explore Russia's poetry, or who want to add a sense of Russian poetry to their more specialized knowledge of other literatures; for comparativists who work with literary texts in translation, at least in some stages of their research; for general readers who are curious about Russian poetry, who have seen some of the names mentioned, or who just love good poetry; for poets who learn by reading about the vibrant cultures of other times and places; for people of Russian heritage who find it easier to read in English, or who want to introduce Anglophone friends to some of the riches of the Russian Silver Age. This collection contains some rudiments of a reference book, and it may point the interested reader to other materials, though it concentrates on the poetry of the time, supplemented with indicative prose writing by contemporaries about these poets and poems.

Because we are aiming for broad usability, the introductory material is not written in steep scholarly language; the suggested additional sources for each poet and for the era in general point readers to serious academic publications. We are also convinced that some of the best, most exciting scholarship on Russian literature deals with the Silver Age, reflecting the period's special features.

After this preface, an introduction (which includes some lists of recommended reading), and a short discussion of the issues raised by translations of Russian poetry, this book falls into two main parts. Section I gives the poetry, with some information about the poets' biographies and other published resources, and Section II provides various supporting materials. The book closes with three indices: an abbreviated thematic index (for readers looking for poets belonging to particular groups or engaging with certain issues), an index of first lines in Russian (for readers who want to compare a translation to the original poem or to use these materials in comparative translation studies), and an index of first lines in English (meant to help find a poem whose author has temporarily been forgotten).

The poets in Section I appear in alphabetical order, rather than chronologically or (as is often the case for presentations of the Silver Age) according to their poetic affiliation. This makes it easier to find a particular poet, and the poets' brief biographies open each selection for readers who need to know their dates, group affiliations, or theoretical positions. The list is in English alphabetical order, since readers may not know Russian, and because in North American libraries even Russian books are catalogued as they happen to fall in the Latin alphabet. (Once you are searching online, of course, it doesn't matter what order the poets are in, and their names may be spelled in a variety of ways in English.) We have tried to use the most common spellings of the poets' names and those that make the pronunciation more evident ("Bely" rather than "Belyi," "Gumilyov" rather than "Gumilëv"), to help the reader who does not know the Russian pronunciation.

The poetic translations themselves include some of the best existing versions we could find and, in places, our own translations (along with some work by talented and generous friends). We consider fidelity to the original meaning of the poems extremely important: the reader should be able to get an accurate sense of what the poet is writing about—especially considering the importance of specific themes and key terms to the Silver Age. Beyond that, though, the most essential thing for translations is to be persuasive signs of poetic value. In other words, we strive to provide translations that are *adequate* from every aspect of the reader's experience, and that make clear why this or that poet is a big deal in Russian culture. For each poet, we offer a list (sometimes much abbreviated) of available translations into English, for readers who want to explore further. The brief bibliographies that follow each selection of poems likewise offer a selection of scholarly or biographical sources available in English (some translated from Russian); we suggest those that we have found most informative and enjoyable.

Section II includes a variety of texts from and about the Silver Age: criticism and memoirs by the poets themselves or by others, and stories or essays meant to convey the atmosphere of the time, such as Nadezhda Tèffi's humorous story "The Demonic Woman." As a self-respecting demonic woman in the Russian Silver Age, the title character writes poetry, of course. Other texts in Section II are deeply serious: the Silver Age poets were in it for real, profoundly concerned with philosophy, religion, and spirituality as well as with the nonverbal arts and various amusements. The reader will notice that the works in different prose sections often do similar things: they cite copiously from the work of a poet or a school, and they often make important programmatic assertions. In some cases the prose works blur generic boundaries, as in Maximilian Voloshin's critical article on the poetry of Cherubina de Gabriak—a poet who never existed, or rather the *nom de mystification* of Elizaveta Dmitrieva, whose poetic career more or less ended after her cover was blown. Within the four generic parts of the prose section (essays, criticism, memoirs, and other texts), the texts are arranged alphabetically by author; dates of composition or first publication are given in the table of contents for those who prefer to read chronologically.

This coursebook is primarily intended for learning about Russian poetry, but it may be adapted to many kinds of courses as well as to self-directed study. It can serve as a beginning reference work for the poetry of the period, and (we hope!) for pleasure reading.

The huge body of poetry written in the Silver Age means that we can offer only a taste of what is there. Most of the poets are represented in many versions, and the reader should head to the library to explore further.

Many of these poems have been recorded, sometimes by the authors themselves. For audio versions, along with more information of all kinds, we recommend Northwestern University's website From the Ends to the Beginning: A Bilingual Anthology of Russian Verse, at http://max.mmlc.northwestern.edu/~mdenner/Demo/.

We have included a few notes on the prose pieces. Like readers and scholars of Russian literature in general, we owe a debt of gratitude to Ardis Publishing and all who were involved in the endeavors of that visionary press. Ardis, founded in Ann Arbor, Michigan by Carl and Ellendea Proffer in 1971, was for nearly two decades a central place to publish Russian literature that could not be published in the Soviet Union. It was through Ardis that the first relatively complete publications of poets like Osip Mandelstam and Marina Tsvetaeva saw the light of day. And for many years Ardis served as a major venue for English translations of key Russian texts—poetry and prose alike—as well as for literary and critical anthologies that helped shape the English-language canon of Russian literature. We have included relatively few poem translations from Ardis publications, but a number of our prose pieces are taken from Ardis anthologies, with the permission of Overlook Press, who currently holds the rights to Ardis volumes.

Some of the prose translations we selected contained a rich array of footnotes in their original editions. While we have not added informational footnotes to any of the prose pieces, we did decide to include a few of the footnotes provided by other translators. The footnotes we reproduce include basic information that we thought might be helpful for readers, especially those less familiar with the Russian literary tradition. We chose not to include many footnotes that contained more specialist knowledge, but we encourage more knowledgeable readers to consult the original publications in which the translations appeared. (This information can be found in the "Sources and Permissions" section at the front of the book.) We also excerpted some footnotes so as to present only what seemed to us the most essential information for our readers. To distinguish notes by original authors from translators' notes, we have placed the translator's initials before footnotes the translator composed. Footnotes without initials were composed by the original author.

Some Issues in Translating Russian Poetry into English

Over time there have been many marvelous translations of Russian poetry into English. At the same time, translating poetry from or into any language is never a simple thing, and there is no single correct way to do it, though individual translators may have strong feelings (and that is all to the good). Russian and English poetry offer a special case for the study of translation: they are similar in many ways—much more so than many possible translational pairs—but their different historical development and the different prosodic structures of the two languages (naturally reflected in the poetry) complicate a translator's choices interestingly. It is no surprise that various translations of the same poem can look quite dissimilar.

Different Literary Histories

The different histories of Russian literature and English literature (meaning literature written in those languages, whether or not by authors who were themselves ethnically Russian or English) have led to different results. The tradition of English poetry is today generally traced back to Geoffrey Chaucer, and so has been developing along that path since the fourteenth century (very roughly speaking), with occasional important influences from earlier works, such as *Beowulf*. By the twentieth century, when Modernism made a decisive break with traditional rhyme, meter, and poetic genres, English poetry had been chugging along for six centuries. Modern Russian poetry (as opposed to the earlier, unrhymed epics such as the twelfth-century *Lay of Igor's Campaign* or the first appearance of rhyme in Simeon Polotsky's seventeenth-century *virshy*) got going in the eighteenth century, and by the Silver Age (when, we would argue, it was brought completely up to date with the rest of Europe) it had been going for about two centuries. The poems people still really *read*, though, dated from a mere 120 or 130 years before the Silver Age (Derzhavin, Batyushkov, Zhukovsky). Both English and Russian poetry were decisively shaped by other literary traditions, though Russian readers, writers, and scholars generally do a better job of remembering this. Most of Chaucer's works were translations, and Elizabethan poets kept busy adapting poetic genres from Italian or French to their own language. (Indeed, French literature, as Russians came to know it, was decisively formed in the seventeenth and eighteenth centuries: Ronsard looks very different from Corneille and Racine.) Modern Russian poetry stuttered to life by imitating the form of Polish *wierszy*, then got on track with Lomonosov's recommendation of syllabo-tonic verse (that is, verse with both regular stress patterns and a regular number of feet per line), with various rhyme schemes. Like French poetry, which incorporated many of the lessons of Neoclassicism, Russian poetry used terms from Classical Antiquity, reformulated by Boileau (Nicolas Boileau-Despréaux) in *L'Art poétique* (1674), a treatise on verse that was itself written in verse. No doubt like Boileau and his peers, Russian poets of the Silver Age deplored the bad verse their predecessors had written, considered it their duty to clean up Russian poetry—and succeeded magnificently.

If the situations in English and Russian poetry in the early twentieth century had grown (at last) largely similar, the same cannot be said of the next several decades. As this volume's introduction mentions, the Soviet period was not an easy time for literature. The impact of government literary bureaucracy and censorship, obligatory Socialist Realism, and all kinds of self-preserving moves by writers sent most poets back to more traditional genres and metrical forms; those who had experimented with unrhymed or slant-rhymed verse tended to leave those experiments in their past, perhaps retaining Mayakovskian "stair-step" format as a gesture toward the revolutionary avant-garde. (Some Russian poets, of course, did not self-preserve in these ways; look up the OBERIU, if you have not read them yet. Poetry was a surprisingly high-stakes game in the Soviet period.) Some of the more traditional-looking poetry of the Soviet era was still great—the late Akhmatova, the late Pasternak, not to mention the work of younger poets—but it was no longer in step with prosodic and generic developments in England, France, or the countries of Central and Eastern Europe that were geographically nearer to Russia. The "freeze" imposed on the many Silver Age poets who were politically unacceptable meant that both their works and the innovations they embodied could not be part of public discourse; few Soviet readers had access to their work, and it was risky to be caught with a forbidden book while trying to enjoy that access, never mind to bring innovations into one's own poetry. In the late Soviet period, the cost of writing in different forms was not so high, but it still meant writing for an underground and self-publishing in *samizdat*. Russian poets write and publish today in all kinds of forms, but forms other than syllabo-tonic verse still feel innovative against that recent background; many significant poets continue to write in the forms that shaped the tastes and aesthetic responses of Soviet readers. Therefore, we would argue, many of the issues that translators of Russian poetry into English now face were shaped by the decades *after* the Silver Age, not by the Silver Age itself.

Besides the different political situations and the historical timing, two big additional reasons help explain why Russian and English poetry are different now: one is the arsenal of rhymes and perception of rhyme, and another is the different word length and stress patterns of the languages themselves, with their consequences for poetry written in those languages.

Rhyme in Russian and English Poetry

Neither Old Russian (Rusian) poetry nor Old English (Anglo-Saxon) poetry used rhyme; in both traditions rhyme came in "from outside," borrowed from other literary traditions and generally described with terms taken from Classical Greek via Latin in the Renaissance and beyond. The possibilities for rhyming became evident once poets (be they Chaucer or Lomonosov) began writing rhymed poetry and others followed them. It is certainly true that some Russian rhymes were already "tired" by the Golden Age; Pushkin made fun of the rhyme "*morozy/rozy*"—literally "frosts/roses," but translatable as "moon/June"—in 1824-25, in the fourth chapter of his novel in verse *Eugene Onegin*. Nevertheless, Russian grammar and word forms still offer more possibilities for rhymes in Russian, with not only feminine rhymes (where the stressed, rhyming syllable is followed by another syllable that also fits the rhyme) but even dactylic and hyperdactylic rhymes (where the stressed syllable is followed by two or more syllables that also fit the rhyme). English poetry had shifted to using predominantly masculine rhymes by the seventeenth century, neglecting the longer rhymes. Due to shorter word length (about which more below), many exact rhymes in English are now hackneyed (though they live on in popular songs, rap music, and spoken word poetry, where moreover feminine rhyme sounds incisive and clever rather than merely amusing). It is telling that Mayakovsky's play with rhyme and meter closely resembles the work of Ogden Nash, a well-known comic poet writing in English. Both stretched the rules for verse composition to humorous effect for readers who were accustomed to versification that was essentially syllabo-tonic.

Word length and stress patterns conditioned the shift of English-language poetry away from strict metrical forms. The average length (in syllables) of a word in an ordinary prose text in English is a bit over one syllable, while the average length of a Russian word in an analogous text is over two syllables. English does have plenty of long words, but words of more than three syllables tend to have secondary stresses, and very long words will have more than one secondary stress. (Most of these long words are "twenty-five-cent words," which will also affect the stylistic level of a poem where they might be used.) Any Russian word—even a very long one (unless it compounds two words)—has only one stress, and the many unstressed syllables in these words (which, again, are already longer on the average than English words) allow a skillful poet to write regular metrical verse (especially trimeter verse, fully represented in the Russian tradition by all three variants: dactyl, amphibrach, and anapest) more easily without becoming rhythmically monotonous. For more discussion of the differences in rhyme and word stress between English and Russian, see Vladimir Nabokov's famous article "Problems of Translation: *Onegin* in English."[1] Nabokov took these difficulties as sufficient reason not to make a rhyming and scanning translation of Pushkin's *Eugene Onegin*.

An additional factor impacting all of this is the fondness of most English-language literary traditions for "domesticated" translations, discussed

---

1 Vladimir Nabokov, "Problems of Translation: *Onegin* in English," in *The Translation Studies Reader*, 3rd edition, ed. Lawrence Venuti (London and New York: Routledge, 2012), 113-125.

in detail by Lawrence Venuti in his book *The Translator's Invisibility*.[2] People who read poetry in English are often very fond of the rhymed, metered work of earlier generations, but those who read contemporary poets are used to poetry that signifies its aesthetic value in different ways. A translation that rhymes and scans can sound like bad Tennyson, and that might fit a late nineteenth-century Russian poet like Nadson but most assuredly does not suit the best writers of the Silver Age. Readers accustomed to English-language poetry are likely to prefer verse that feels more like what most English-language poets are writing today—which is for the most part not rhyming, scanning poetry.

Some translations in this collection scrupulously reproduce the meter and (as much as possible) the rhyme scheme of the original poems. We have also included some very free translations, and then a number that shift between the two positions, drawn away from reproduction of meter and rhyme when those exigencies force too much padding, require too many syllables, or make it impossible to convey the meaning of the original. (Because we don't read a Russian poem just to enjoy it, right? We also want to see what these certified great poets are writing ABOUT.) More than one approach to formal equivalence can result in a meaningful translation, and we would argue that there is no "right way" to do it: different approaches to translation will get different results, each with its particular values. To close this brief discussion we offer several versions of a poem for the reader to compare. Reading multiple translations is the richest and most informative way to approach a poem from a foreign literature, and if you are drawn to any of the poems in this anthology we strongly recommend looking at multiple versions. Each will offer a particular angle or window on what the original does. This is one reason why we list the collections where you might find more translations of a particular poet, under each poet's individual selection of poems.

As you read the following versions of the same poem by Anna Akhmatova, you will notice that some are stricter in reproducing the rhyme and meter, while others are less strict. If you know Russian, you will see where the translators have kept unusual turns of phrase, or added new turns of meaning in pursuit of similar effects.

---

2   Lawrence Venuti, *The Translator's Invisibility: A History of Translation*, 2nd edition (London and New York: Routledge, 2008).

Several Different Versions of the Same Russian Poem

A much-translated early poem by Anna Akhmatova:

Все мы бражники здесь, блудницы,
Как невесело вместе нам!
На стенах цветы и птицы
Томятся по облакам.

Ты куришь черную трубку,
Так странен дымок над ней.
Я надела узкую юбку
Чтоб казаться еще стройней.

Навсегда забиты окошки:
Что там, изморозь или гроза?
На глаза осторожной кошки
Похожи твои глаза.

О, как сердце мое тоскует!
Не смертного ль часа жду?
А та, что сейчас танцует
Непременно будет в аду.

1 января 1913 г.

Translations:

We are all carousers and loose women here;
How unhappy we are together!
The flowers and birds on the wall
Yearn for the clouds.

You are smoking a black pipe,
The puff of smoke has a funny shape.
I've put on my tight skirt
To make myself look still more svelte.

The windows are boarded up forever.
What's out there—hoarfrost or a storm?
Your eyes resemble
The eyes of a cautious cat.

Oh, I am sick at heart!
Isn't it the hour of death I await?
But that woman dancing now
Will be in hell, no doubt.

January 1, 1913

Judith Hemschemeyer, *The Complete Poems of Anna Akhmatova: Expanded Edition*, ed. Roberta Reeder (Boston: Zephyr Press, 1992), 135-136.

Several Different Versions of the Same Russian Poem

We are heavy-drinkers and whores,
What a joyless, miserable crowd!
There are flowers and birds on the walls
And the birds all grieve for a cloud.

You are smoking your old black pipe,
And the smoke looks strange over it.
The skirt that I'm wearing feels tight,
But I hope that it makes me look fit.

What's the weather—thunder or ice?
Here, the windows are all boarded shut.
I examine your face and your eyes
Have the look of a sly cautious cat.

Ah, what sadness I'm feeling inside!
Am I waiting for death's solemn bell?
And that girl, who's been dancing all night,—
She will surely end up in hell.

January 1, 1913

Andrey Kneller, *Final Meeting* (Boston: Kneller, 2008), 31.

Several Different Versions of the Same Russian Poem

"We're All Drunkards Here…"

We're all drunkards here, and harlots:
how wretched we are together!
On the walls, flowers and birds
wait for the clouds to gather.

You puff on your burnished pipe,
strange shapes above you swim,
I have put on a narrow skirt
to show my lines are trim.

The windows are tightly sealed.
What brews? Thunder or sleet?
How well I know your look,
your eyes like a cautious cat.

O heavy heart, how long
before the tolling bell?
But that one dancing there
will surely rot in hell!

— 1 January 1913

Stanley Kunitz and Max Hayward, *Poems of Akhmatova* (Boston and New York: Houghton Mifflin Company, 1973), 51.

We're harlots here and carousers,
How unhappy are we all!
On the walls the birds and flowers
Are homesick for the clouds.

The black pipe you are holding—
So strange the puffs of smoke.
To appear even more slender
I put on my narrow skirt.

Blocked forever are the windows.
Is there frost or a storm outside?
But the eyes of a wary house cat
Are not unlike your eyes.

Oh, how my heart is aching!
Do I wait for the hour of death?
But the woman who now dances
Will surely be in hell.

January 1, 1913

Frances Laird, *Swan Songs: Akhmatova and Gumilev* (© Frances Laird, 2002), 218-219.

All of us here are hookers and hustlers.
We drink too much, and don't care.
The walls are covered with birds and flowers
that have never seen sunshine or air.

You smoke too much. There's always a cloud
of nicotine over your head.
Do you like this skirt? I wore it on purpose.
I wanted to show lots of leg.

The windows here have been covered forever.
Is it snowing out? ... maybe it's rain.
You've got that look in your eyes again,
like a cat in a crouch for a kill.

Sometimes I feel this awful pain,
as if someone were breaking a spell.
Take a good look at that one over there!
She's dancing her way into hell!

January 1, 1913

Paul Schmidt, *The Stray Dog Cabaret: A Book of Russian Poems*, eds. Catherine Ciepiela and Honor Moore (New York: NYRB Classics, 2006), 6. (This poem is included in the section of works by Akhmatova, below.)

Several Different Versions of the Same Russian Poem

We're all drunkards here. Harlots.
Joylessly we're stuck together.
On the wall, scarlet
Flowers, birds of a feather,

Pine for clouds. Your black pipe
Makes strange shapes rise.
I wear my skirt tight
To my slim thighs.

Windows tightly shut.
What's that? Frost? Thunder?
Did you steal your eyes, I wonder,
From a cautious cat?

O my heart, how you yearn
For your dying hour…
And that woman dancing there
Will eternally burn.

D. M. Thomas, *Anna Akhmatova: Selected Poems* (London: Penguin Books, 1985), 22-23.

For more information about the history of Russian poetry, we suggest these books, some of which are mentioned elsewhere in this volume:

Obolensky, Dimitri, ed. *The Heritage of Russian Verse* (formerly *The Penguin Book of Russian Verse*), with plain prose translations. Bloomington and Indianapolis: Indiana University Press, 1976.

Scherr, Barry. *Russian Poetry: Meter, Rhythm and Rhyme*. Berkeley: University of California Press, 1986.

Wachtel, Michael. *The Cambridge Introduction to Russian Poetry*. Cambridge, UK and New York: Cambridge University Press, 2004.

Acknowledgments

We would like to express our appreciation to three colleagues who contributed brief biographies on poets they specialize in: Judith Deutsch Kornblatt (Vladimir Solovyov), Timothy Langen (Andrei Bely), and Jenifer Presto (Zinaida Gippius), all experts in the Silver Age and other topics whose work we can always recommend. Ellen Chances, Robert Chandler, Boris Dralyuk, Peter France, Alyssa Dinega Gillespie, Judith Kornblatt, Andrey Kneller, Pola Lem, Irina Mashinski, Kevin Reese, Margo Rosen, and Lisa Woodson offered advice on selection and translation of poems, or generously shared wonderful translations they had made, sometimes unpublished until now. Robert Chandler, translator extraordinaire, also gave us details regarding the important new anthology of Russian poetry that he is preparing for Penguin, with Boris Dralyuk and Irina Mashinski as co-editors.

We wish to thank Mark Lipovetsky, who helped initiate this project, and Sharona Vedol and Meghan Vicks at Academic Studies Press for a great deal of patient assistance. The anonymous reader for the press gave helpful and much appreciated suggestions, which have especially benefited the clarity of this work's presentation. Any remaining infelicities, of course, are ours alone.

Sibelan Forrester would like to express gratitude to Swarthmore College for faculty research and travel support, and for a George Becker Faculty Fellowship (funding a second semester of sabbatical leave) during the year this manuscript was completed. The Swarthmore College Libraries have been a vital and much appreciated resource. We were able to find essential original Silver Age publications with support from the incomparable Slavic Bibliography Service at the Library of the University of Illinois in Urbana-Champaign. I could not have attempted a project like this without the knowledge of Russian poetry I gained from Anna Borovkova, Sergei Davydov, George Pahomov, and Vadim Liapunov; Maria Stepanova has been an important interlocutor about what it all means and where it is headed. For their patience with my various struggles with creative writing, I express gratitude to my children, Yelena, Mislav, and Raian, and to the Critique Circle of the Mad Poets Society.

Martha Kelly would like to thank the University of Missouri Arts & Humanities Small Grants Program for research and travel support, and also the University of Illinois Russian, East European and Eurasian Center for research support (both funding and expertise!) in the Summer Research Lab. I extend particular thanks to Gregory Freidin for his in-depth work with me on Russian Modernist poetry, and to Jim East for first drawing my attention to Modernist traditions and helping me navigate its often difficult texts. Thanks to Rose, Allison, Jen, and Anne for kindly and productively vetting my fledgling translations. Heartfelt gratitude to Gabriel for kindness and wisdom cosmic, lyrical, and practical.

SOURCES AND PERMISSIONS

In order to offer the finest possible versions of the work of these poets, we have selected some translations that were first published elsewhere. Sources and details of copyright permission for these reprinted works are listed below.

We have made every effort to contact holders of rights for poets whose work is still under copyright protection—some, though far from all, of the big players in the Silver Age.

We thank the following for permission to reprint material first published elsewhere, or in some cases indicate the original sources for the texts we used to make our own translations in cases where they are not widely available or differ among various editions.

Anna Akhmatova: "Reminiscences of Alexander Blok," translated by Ronald Meyer; excerpts from "Osip Mandelstam," translated by Anna Lisa Crone and Ronald Meyer; and "Innokenty Annensky," translated by Mary Ann Szporluk, from *My Half Century: Selected Prose* by Anna Akhmatova, edited by Ronald Meyer. Copyright © 1992 by Ardis Publishers / The Overlook Press. Published in 2013 by Ardis Publishers, an imprint of Peter Mayer Publishers, Inc. www.overlookpress.com. All rights reserved.

["A memory / Is in me,"], ["At my neck, small rosary beads,"], and excerpt from *Poem without a Hero* in *Poem without a Hero and Selected Poems*. Copyright

© 1989 by Oberlin College. Edson. Reprinted with the permission of Oberlin College Press.

["I pray to the light in the window"], "Song of Our Last Meeting," ["I went to visit the poet"], ["I hear the oriole's voice. It sounds as sad as ever"], ["Just for this I used to carry you"], ["No, not with those who left their land"], ["The city I have loved since childhood"], and ["Lot's Wife" are translated with permission of Margarita Novgorodova.

Innokenty Annensky: "On Contemporary Lyrism," from *The Russian Symbolists*, edited and translated by Ronald E. Peterson. Copyright © 1986 by Ardis Publishers. Published in 1986 by Ardis Publishers, an imprint of Peter Mayer Publishers, Inc. www.overlookpress.com. All rights reserved.

Konstantin Balmont: excerpts from "Poetry as Enchantment," 1915, pp. 18-19, 34-35, and 52-53.

Andrei Bely: "Symbolism and Contemporary Russian Art" and "A Wreath or a Crown," from *The Russian Symbolists*, edited and translated by Ronald E. Peterson. Copyright © 1986 by Ardis Publishers. Published in 1986 by Ardis Publishers, an imprint of Peter Mayer Publishers, Inc. www.overlookpress.com. All rights reserved.

Valery Bryusov: "A Holy Sacrifice" and "Keys to the Mysteries," from *The Russian Symbolists*, edited and translated by Ronald E. Peterson. Copyright © 1986 by Ardis Publishers. Published in 1986 by Ardis Publishers, an imprint of Peter Mayer Publishers, Inc. www.overlookpress.com. All rights reserved.

Kornei Chukovsky: review of *The Devil's Doll* by Zinaida Gippius, text from www.chukfamily.ru/Kornei/Critica/Gippius, consulted August 10, 2010. Translated with gracious permission from Elena Tsezarevna Chukovskaya.

Futurist manifestos translated by Boris Dralyuk were originally published as an edition on the Manifestoh! imprint (series editor David Shook), reprinted with gracious permission from Insert Blanc Press.

Nikolai Gumilyov: Review of Blok, Klyuev, et al. First published in *Apollon*, 1912, no. 1; translation made from http://dugward.ru/library/gumilev/gumilev_rec_blok_brusov.html, consulted August 10, 2010.

"Symbolism's Legacy and Acmeism" and "Review of Akhmatova's *Beads*," translated by Robert T. Whittaker, Jr. from *The Silver Age of Russian Culture*, edited by Carl Proffer and Ellendea Proffer. Copyright © 1971, 1972, 1973, 1974, 1975 by Ardis Publishers. Published in 1975 by Ardis Publishers, an imprint of Peter Mayer Publishers, Inc. www.overlookpress.com. All rights reserved.

Vyacheslav Ivanov: "The Precepts of Symbolism," from *The Russian Symbolists*, edited and translated by Ronald E. Peterson. Copyright © 1986 by Ardis Publishers. Published in 1986 by Ardis Publishers, an imprint of Peter Mayer Publishers, Inc. www.overlookpress.com. All rights reserved.

Excerpts from "Thoughts on Symbolism" and "Nietzsche and Dionysus," from *Selected Essays*, edited by Michael Wachtel and translated by Robert Bird. Northwestern University Press, 2001. Translation, introduction, and notes copyright © 2001 by Northwestern University Press. Published 2001. All rights reserved.

Velimir Khlebnikov: Excerpt from *Zangezi* reprinted by permission of the publisher from *The King of Time: Poems, Fictions, Visions of the Future* by Velimir Khlebnikov, translated by Paul Schmidt, edited by Charlotte Douglas, pp. 212-213. Cambridge, MA: Harvard University Press, Copyright © 1985, by the Dia Art Foundation. Translations of lyric poems reprinted with permission of the publisher from *The Collected Works of Velimir Khlebnikov: Vol. III—Selected Poems*, translated by Paul Schmidt, edited by Ronald Vroon, pp. 30-32, 37-38, 50, 56, 58-59, 121. Cambridge, MA: Harvard University Press, Copyright © 1997 by the President and Fellows of Harvard College.

Vladislav Khodasevich: "The End of Renata," from his *Necropolis* (translation made from http://silverage.ru/hodkonren/, consulted July 11, 2012). (We have not included the notes and the helpful commentary by N. Bogomolov, E. Ben', I. Bocharova, and A. Lavrov included in this online version.)

Mikhail Kuzmin: "The Third Thrust," from *Mikhail Kuzmin: Selected Writings*, edited by Michael A. Green and Stanislav Shvabrin (Lewisburg, PA: Bucknell University Press, 2005). Reprinted here with gracious permission from Associated University Presses.

["Not for nothing did we read the theologians"] and ["Today's a holiday"], from *Wings. Prose and Poetry*, edited and translated by Neil Granoien and Michael Green. Copyright © 1972 by Ardis Publishers. Published in 1972 by Ardis Publishers, an imprint of Peter Mayer Publishers, Inc. www.overlookpress.com. All rights reserved.

Benedikt Livshitz: *The One and a Half-Eyed Archer*, translation, introduction, and annotations by John E. Bowlt (Newtonville, MA: Oriental Research Partners, 1977). Excerpts from pp. 55 and 125. Used with permission from ORP.

Osip Mandelstam: "Hagia Sophia," #3 ["There are orioles in the forests and the only real measure"], "The Twilight of Freedom (An Anthem)," #18 ["In Petersburg we'll meet again"], #41 ["We live without feeling beneath us firm ground"], and #49 ["I'll say it in draft in a whisper"], translated by Bernard Meares, from *Osip Mandelstam: Fifty Poems*. Copyright © 1977 by Bernard Meares. Reprinted with the permission of The Permissions Company, Inc., on behalf of Persea Books, Inc (New York), www.perseabooks.com

"Leningrad," "Flat," and "Rough Draft," from *Stolen Air: Selected Poems of Osip Mandelstam*, selected and translated by Christian Wiman. Copyright © 2012 by Christian Wiman. Reprinted by permission of HarperCollins Publishers.

["There: the Eucharist, a gold sun."] Reprinted with the permission of Scribner Publishing Group, a division of Simon & Schuster, Inc, from *The Selected Poems of Osip Mandelstam*, translated by Clarence Brown and W. S. Merwin. Copyright © 1973 by Clarence Brown and W.S. Merwin. All rights reserved.

"Silentium," translated by Robert Chandler and Boris Dralyuk in *The White Review* (http://www.thewhitereview.org/poetry/poems/). Reprinted here with gracious permission from Robert Chandler and Boris Dralyuk.

"Solominka," translated by Robert Chandler in *The White Review* (http://www.thewhitereview.org/poetry/poems/). Reprinted here with gracious permission from Robert Chandler.

"Morning of Acmeism," "Igor Severyanin. *The Thunder-Seething Goblet (Gromokipiashchii kubok)*. Poems. Introduction by Fyodor Sologub. Moscow: "Grif" Publishing House, 1913.," "On Contemporary Poetry: *Almanac of the Muses (Almanakh muz)*. Petrograd: Felana, 1916. 192p.," "The Word and Culture" and "Letters to V. I. Ivanov," from *Critical Prose and Letters by Osip Mandelstam*, edited by Jane Gary Harris, translated by Jane Gary Harris and Constance Link. Copyright © 1979 by Ardis Publishers. Published in 2003 by Ardis Publishers, an imprint of Peter Mayer Publishers, Inc. www.overlookpress.com. All rights reserved.

["Heaviness, tenderness—sisters—your marks are the same"], "Black Earth," and ["Armed with the eyesight of thin-waisted wasps"], from *Poems of Osip Mandelstam*, translated by Peter France (New York: New Directions, 2014). Reprinted here with gracious permission from Peter France.

Vladimir Mayakovsky: "V. V. Khlebnikov" (obituary), from Mayakovsky, *Polnoe sobranie sochinenii v 13-i tomakh* (Moscow: Gos. izdatel'stvo khudozhestvennoi literatury, 1955-1961), vol. 12.

Poems from Vladimir Mayakovsky, *Listen! Early Poems 1913-1918*, translated by Maria Enzensberger, foreword by Elaine Feinstein, San Francisco: City Lights Books, 1991, reprinted with gracious permission from Red Stone Press.

Vladimir Mayakovsky and El Lissitzky, *For the Voice*, translated by Peter France (Cambridge, MA: MIT Press, 2000), reprinted with gracious permission from Peter France.

The Stray Dog Cabaret, translated by Paul Schmidt, ed. Catherine Ciepiela and Honor Moore (New York: New York Review Books, 2007), reprinted here with permission from NYR Books.

Irina Odoevtseva: excerpts from *On the Banks of the Neva*, translated from *Na beregakh Nevy* (Moscow: "Khudozhestvennaia literatura," 1988), pp. 16-20 and 65-67.

Sofia Parnok: "In Quest of a Path for Art," first published in *Severnye zapiski* [Northern Notes], 1913, May-June, pp. 227-32, under the pseudonym Andrei Polyanin.

Boris Pasternak: "Spring," "My Sister, Life," "To Anna Akhmatova," ["If I had known that this is what happens"], "Fresco Come to Life" and ["In everything I want to reach"], from *Selected Poems*, translated by Jon Stallworthy and Peter France. Copyright © 1982 by Jon Stallworthy and Peter France. Published in 1983 by W. W. Norton. All rights reserved. Reprinted here with gracious permission from Jon Stallworthy and Peter France.

Excerpts from "Safe Conduct," in *The Voice of Prose: Vol. 1, Early Prose and Autobiography*, edited and translated by Christopher Barnes. Copyright © 1986 by Christopher Barnes. Published in 1986 by Polygon Books, an imprint of Birlinn Limited. Reprinted here with gracious permission from Birlinn Books.

["It's February. Grab the ink and weep!"] translated with permission of the Pasternak Estate.

Vasily Rozanov: excerpt from *The Apocalypse of Our Times*, translated by James M. Edie with James P. Scanlan, in *Russia Philosophy* in three volumes, eds. James M. Edie, James P. Scanlan, Mary-Barbara Zeldin, and George L. Kline (Knoxville, TN: The University of Tennessee Press, 1976), vol. II, pp. 296-98. Reprinted with permission of The University of Tennessee Press.

"On Symbolists and Decadents," translated by Joel Stern, from *The Silver Age of Russian Culture*, edited by Carl Proffer and Ellendea Proffer. Copyright © 1971, 1972, 1973, 1974, 1975 by Ardis Publishers. Published in 1975 by Ardis Publishers, an imprint of Peter Mayer Publishers, Inc. www.overlookpress.com. All rights reserved.

Viktor Shklovsky: Quotation about the Stray Dog, in his *Poiski optimizma*, Moscow, 1931, p. 100. Cited in Benedikt Livshits, *The One and a Half-Eyed Archer*, translation, introduction and annotations by John E. Bowlt (Newtonville, MA: Oriental Research Partners, 1977), note 19, p. 232. Reprinted with permission from ORP.

Fyodor Sologub: "Poets' Demons," first published in *Pereval*, 1907, No 7.

Vladimir Solovyov: "Russian Symbolists.—Summer, 1895. (Moscow, 1895, 52pp)," from *The Russian Symbolists*, edited and translated by Ronald E. Peterson. Copyright © 1986 by Ardis Publishers. Published in 1986 by Ardis Publishers, an imprint of Peter Mayer Publishers, Inc. www.overlookpress.com. All rights reserved.

["My tsaritsa appeared to me"] in Judith Deutsch Kornblatt, *Divine Sophia: The Wisdom Writings of Vladimir Solovyov* (Ithaca, NY: Cornell University Press, 2009). Reprinted by gracious permission from Judith Kornblatt.

Nadezhda Tèffi: "The Demonic Woman," with permission from Agnès Szydlowski.

Marina Tsvetaeva: "Downpour of Light," from *Art in the Light of Conscience: Eight Essays on Poetry by Marina Tsvetaeva*, translated by Angela Livingstone with verse excerpts translated by Donald Davie (Cambridge, MA: Harvard University Press), pp. 21-38. Reprinted with permission from Bloodaxe Books.

"Appointment," "Rails," and "To Mayakovsky," from Marina Tsvetaeva, *Bride of Ice*, translations by Elaine Feinstein from literal versions by Daisy Cockburn, Valentina Coe, Bernard Comrie, Simon Franklin, Jana Hewlett, Angela Livingstone, Cathy Porter, Tatiana Retivov, Maxwell Shorter, and Vera Traill (Manchester, UK: Carcanet Press Limited, 2009), with permission from Carcanet Press Limited.

Poems from Andrey Kneller's translation of Tsvetaeva, *My Poems* (Boston, 2008), reprinted with gracious permission from Mr. Kneller.

Marina Tsvetaeva, *To You—in 10 Decades. Selected Russian Poetry Rendered in English*. Verse translations from Russian by Alexander Givental and Élysée Wilson-Egolf. (El Cerrito, CA: Sumizdat, 2012), reprinted with gracious permission from Dr. Givental and Ms. Wilson-Egolf.

Sibelan Forrester's translation of "Harder and harder" first appeared in *Cardinal Points*, No. 12 (Spring 2010), (http://www.stosvet.net/12/forrester/index.html).

Marina Tsvetaeva, *Milestones: A Bilingual Edition*, translated, introduction and notes by Robin Kemball (Evanston, IL: Northwestern University Press, 2003), reprinted with permission from Northwestern UP.

Poems by Tsvetaeva from *The Stray Dog Cabaret: A Book of Russian Poems*, translated by Paul Schmidt, edited by Catherine Ciepiela and Honor Moore (New York: NYRB Classics, 2006), reprinted with permission of NYR Books.

Maximilian Voloshin: "The Horoscope of Cherubina de Gabriak" was translated from "Liki tvorchestva. Goroskop Cherubiny de Gabriak" (*Apollon* No. 2, 1909, in the section "Khronika").

Introduction: Poetry of the Russian Silver Age

Sibelan Forrester and Martha Kelly

Poetry is only one of the exciting cultural achievements of the Russian fin-de-siècle, which has come to be known as the Silver Age. Along with the *Ballets russes*, the music of Alexander Scriabin or Igor Stravinsky, the avant-garde painting of Kazimir Malevich or Marc Chagall, and the philosophical writings of Lev Shestov or Nikolai Berdyaev, poetry is one of the era's most precious treasures. The Silver Age witnessed an unprecedented and fruitful interaction between Russian literature and the other arts, sometimes within the same person: several of the major poets were (or could have been) musicians and composers; others were painters, important literary critics, religious thinkers, scholars, or philosophers. The culture of book illustration and graphic presentation of poetry rose to new heights, from Mstislav Dobuzhinsky's gorgeous initial letters in the Acmeist journal *Apollon* to the Cubist-tending images in Futurist publications.

The Silver Age also saw the emergence of a much wider range of poets than earlier periods: the poets in this collection represent a striking variety of class, gender, religion, ethnicity, and sexuality. There were plenty of aristocratic writers, of course (like Count Leo Tolstoy, the moral and literary giant whose importance continued right up to his death in 1910). The aristocrats had a better education, access to foreign languages and travel, and money to self-publish when publishers weren't biting. But there were also *"raznochintsy"* (figures of mixed social background, like Valery Bryusov or Marina Tsvetaeva—though in early Soviet literary surveys Tsvetaeva called herself, perhaps as a matter of provocative principle, a member of the nobility). Several of our poets are Jews. Even though Boris Pasternak's father Leonid had converted to Christianity, and Sofia Parnok and Osip Mandelstam themselves converted, Judaism still remained important in their writings: they were part of a generation of assimilated Jews in the Russian Empire with highly sophisticated literary knowledge, eager to shape the literary culture of the time. Several of our poets are women (you can tell by the -a that ends most Russian women's surnames). There had been prominent and successful female poets before—Karolina Pavlova (1807-1893), Evdokia Rostopchina (1811-1856)—but the Silver Age was the first era when Russian women writers not only became prominent, but *stayed* prominent. Perhaps it was the crashing disruption of the 1917 Revolution, which put Silver Age poetic achievements into a kind of deep freeze, fixing the fame of its best-known women writers in a way that had not occurred earlier in Russian literary history. Two of our poets are peasants (Sergei Esenin, fairly well known in the West, and Nikolai Klyuev, less well known), and genuine peasant speech became more of a factor in the writings of non-peasant poets even before the 1917 Revolution. Our poets often express great interest in religious variety, sometimes springing from their own backgrounds: Klyuev and Mikhail Kuzmin describe Old Believer communities; Andrei Bely, Alexander Blok, and Tsvetaeva are interested in the Khlyst ("flagellant") sect; Vyacheslav Ivanov is a specialist in Classical Antiquity, particularly drawn to Greek mystery religions not only as a literary source but also as models of behavior for his own life; Zinaida Gippius and Dmitri Merezhkovsky were prominent creators or theorists of new religious rites; and we have already mentioned Jewish voices such as those of Mandelstam or Nikolai Minsky (pseudonym of Nikolai Vilenkin, 1855-1937), whose poetic and publicistic activity still awaits scholarly treatment in English. The writer and philosopher Vasily Rozanov also engaged, imaginatively and sometimes problematically, with Judaism. Last, but far from least, the Silver Age saw both a relaxation of censorship and a growing interest in alternative theories and models of sex and gender, so it is no surprise to find in the Silver Age the first open, published writing about gay and lesbian topics (by Kuzmin, Klyuev, Parnok, and others), and intense interest in sexuality on the part of other poets, many of them bisexual in theory if not in practice.

This quick survey of "identity politics" does not limit the area these various poets covered—on the contrary, it broadens it significantly. In some cases the Silver Age began to talk more openly and transformatively about difficult topics (sexuality, religion, the implications of gender—and of course economic and social class, always a Russian specialty) than our own society has been prepared to do until much more recently (if, indeed, it has reached that level of willingness today). In many cases, the poets combined interests or concerns that may not seem harmonious at first glance, but that add particular angles to their work—for example, Kuzmin, whose homoerotic verse and powerful religious impulse came together in a spiritualization of aesthetic values that resonates with Russian Orthodox traditions as much as it does (though differently) with Classical and Hellenistic Greek culture.

You can expect that variety in this collection, embodied in some of the most wonderful poetry in the world. The collection includes the names anyone would look for in an anthology of the period (Akhmatova, Blok, Mandelstam, Mayakovsky, Pasternak, Tsvetaeva), while also selecting some (though far, far from all!) poets who are less well-known or well-studied but nonetheless talented and fascinating, and who added to the diversity and energy of the era. These poets are valuable parts of the cultural landscape of Russia, and they are also writers who can still shake you with their raw energy and the passionate conviction of their aesthetic seeking. They are excellent pretexts to inspiration.

Why Is It Called the Silver Age?

The cultural era from about 1890 to about 1925 is known in Russia as the Silver Age because it followed the Golden Age, the era of Alexander Pushkin (1799-1837) in which Russian poetry first reached great heights of creativity, philosophical depth, and aesthetic value. (One could expect a Bronze Age any time now...) Indeed, the Silver Age was largely oriented towards the Golden Age, and the Silver Age bestowed on the Golden Age of Russian poetry its status, confirming the installation of Alexander Pushkin as primary deity, but also giving more attention to poets such as Evgeny Baratynsky (1800-1844), Fyodor Tyutchev (1803-1873), and Mikhail Lermontov (1814-1841), whose works had been neglected in their own times. After several decades during which the Russian Realist novel was the genre of highest prestige and influence, the poets of the Silver Age returned to what the Golden Age had most prized, learning their craft both from Russian poetry and from earlier and contemporary foreign poetries. They also paid new attention to more recent predecessors such as Pavlova or Afanasy Fet (1820-1892), whose works had been overshadowed earlier by the prominence of the novel. Poetry was more prized in the Russian Silver Age than it had been for several decades before; Ivan Bunin (1870-1952, winner of the 1933 Nobel Prize in Literature) wrote a sizable body of poetry, and his translation of Henry Wadsworth Longfellow's *The Song of Hiawatha* won a Pushkin Prize in 1903. In the next generation Ilya Ehrenburg (1891-1957), whose novel *The Thaw* gave its title to the cultural relaxation of repression and censorship in the Soviet Union under Nikita Khrushchev, also began literary life as a poet.

Though we call the early nineteenth century the Golden Age, the name implies that it was much better than the Silver Age, and that was not the case. The scholar Simon Karlinsky has pointed out that the Golden Age had four poets who would merit top rankings from any fan of poetry, whereas "around 1910 there lived and wrote in Russia no less than nineteen poets who easily fit into the 'major-to-great' category."[1] (Not to mention the gender homogeneity of the poets who formed the Golden Age, and the relative uniformity of their class background.) This volume gives at least a taste of the work of twenty-eight poets, plus texts from critics, memoirists, and prose writers (many of these, in fact, the very same poets) who analyzed or exemplified the spirit of the age.

The importance to these poets of Western literature (written by predecessors and contemporaries), and of West European culture in general, makes many of these poets more "relatable" for Western readers than earlier Russian writers—although Silver Age writing can nevertheless often satisfy a taste for the "exotic." Unlike Pushkin, who was never allowed to cross the borders of the Russian empire, many Silver Age poets had profound and prolonged experience in Western Europe, traveling there while reading the best literature of the past and present. Many spent a significant amount of time in the West (sometimes using honeymoons as a pretext for extended voyaging—e.g., Andrei Bely,

---

1 Simon Karlinsky, *Marina Cvetaeva: Her Life and Art* (Berkeley: University of California Press, 1966), 4.

Marina Tsvetaeva—and other times fleeing there for political or personal reasons—e.g., Konstantin Balmont, Maria Shkapskaya), and this assumes a significant place in their writing. The poets knew and read foreign authors, translated them, and reviewed them for the press, and Silver Age journals included regular sections describing the latest publications and all kinds of cultural happenings in other countries. Like their contemporaries in ballet, music, and the visual arts, the poets participated fully in the cosmopolitan literary culture of Europe before and even during the First World War. This ability to have it both ways would change with time. After the 1917 Revolution, our poets met a variety of fates, but these came down essentially to three: death, emigration (usually to Western Europe, where they might have visited before), or remaining in the USSR.

The liveliness of the period, and the large number of people who were writing great poetry then, let things develop very quickly. Scholars have pointed out that, in these years, new books could be published so quickly (often helped by the poet's own financial contribution) that a writer could more easily move from one stage of creative development into the next. Thus, there are two generations of Symbolists (the older Symbolists born before or around 1870, and the younger born around 1880). A "crisis of Symbolism" took place in 1910, around the time when still younger poets, born in the late 1880s and early 1890s—and many of whom had played a role as minor Symbolists themselves—were starting to make waves. That younger generation—the Acmeists, Futurists, or the many poets outside of the schools—includes some of the world's great Modernist poets, amazingly talented creators who often faced deeply tragic fates. These are the poets that many readers in the West have heard of, and may already have read.

The Schools

Scholars and literary historians can find it useful to look into the past and impose the name of a movement on what might in fact have been a less formal group, less organized and coherent, or what began as a group of friends who met to write and discuss literature (like the Arzamas circle in Pushkin's time), with some members emerging as very important, while others are recalled as friends of the important ones. Russian writers of other eras participated in cross-cultural literary movements like Neoclassicism, Romanticism, or

Realism, which may also look more coherent after the fact. Many poets consciously joined, organized, and belonged to groups, naming them and creating statements of purpose, manifestos, and all manner of shared enterprises. Again, the writers of the Russian Silver Age were closely connected with the rest of Europe: they had read all the Western philosophers and visited the major European cities. Anna Akhmatova, for example, met Amadeo Modigliani in Paris; Andrei Bely spent years away from Russia, and his novel *Petersburg* is closer to Austrian Expressionism than to anything going on in Petersburg at the time. They quickly became aware of similar groups and ideas in the European metropoles, and vice versa.

The groups did a number of important things for their members: they focused literary discussion, sometimes sponsored formal lectures by poets with a theoretical or pedagogical bent (Bely), or organized tours in which poets performed (the Futurists). After 1917, a number of these poets taught literary courses (Gumilyov) or worked as government censors (Bryusov). The groups offered a fertile mix of support and criticism, encouraging or sponsoring one another's work, inviting participation in almanacs or debates, and reviewing one another's writings for publishers or (once published) in journals. Members would travel together, or meet by chance or agreement, to perform at the famous Stray Dog basement café in St. Petersburg (Acmeists, Futurists, even some Symbolists). Literary friends and allies regularly attended literary and cultural salons in one another's homes (such as Ivanov's famous "Tower" apartment in St. Petersburg), and would visit one another's dachas or country houses (such as Blok's family estate Shakhmatovo, where the famous mystical love triangle of Bely, Blok, and Lyubov Mendeleeva formed). The Cubo-Futurists began as a group called "Hyleia," largely oriented toward the visual arts and named for the estate in Ukraine where they met, and Maximilian Voloshin's house in Koktebel', Crimea functioned as an unofficial writer's colony for many years before its status was made official in the Soviet period. Even poets who did not join a group, like Parnok or Tsvetaeva, might attend lectures by Bely or spend time at Voloshin's house.

Just as important, if not more so, were the groups' joint and competing publishing enterprises. A surprising number of important works were self-published, but having a journal or a publishing house made a stronger impression, helped better advance a literary program, and worked to spread the wealth from older, richer, or more famous poets to newer or poorer ones. Many important Silver Age poets began their careers by asking the older ones for advice, and the older generation on the whole loved to play the role of mentor. This volume offers just a few of the letters poets exchanged, seeking or offering advice and commenting on writing. Changes in the Russian censorship laws for all kinds of publications after 1905 (with its failed revolution) made a huge difference in what poets could do; the number of periodicals and other publications rose sharply for some years after the new legislation was passed. Reviewing submissions for publication, and reviewing publications once they appeared, developed poets' critical senses and sharpened their opinions on what was happening (and, what should be happening) on the Russian literary scene, and suggested what they might want to do in imitation or in contrast with their own poetry. Once the Symbolists had established a serious literary system of poetry and a lively poetry *scene*, there could be reactions and rebellions by others, and this is where the discourse of the Silver Age gets especially interesting. Many of the poets and critics took a very dark view of what was going on, and this negative, cautionary attitude is represented both in the poetry and in the prose works in the second section of this volume.

Symbolism, Acmeism, Futurism

SYMBOLISM was the biggest, broadest, most general, and longest-lasting literary school of the Russian Silver Age. Our selection includes relatively few of the many Symbolists, though the big names are here. The Symbolists are commonly described as forming two generations: an older one (Balmont, Bryusov, Gippius, Ivanov, Merezhkovsky, Sologub, and many others) that began to write in the early- to mid-1890s, forming the school itself and its strong decadent wing, and a second one (Bely, Blok, and others) that began to write around 1900. Literary critics used the name by analogy with the French *symbolistes*, though it was not fully accepted until after the end of the Silver Age: even in the mid-1920s it was often still written in quotation marks by critics or scholars, with a lower-case letter; perhaps it was the younger poets (Tsvetaeva, Khodasevich) who firmly established it as a term of definition. On the other hand, any of those poets would have agreed that symbols were essential in the quest they had undertaken. Although the Symbolists and especially the Decadents often advanced the idea of art for art's sake, they never doubted the importance of a writer's civic mission and, therefore, of writing *publitsistika* (passionately committed journalism) for various media outlets: newspapers, journals, almanacs. This kept them intimately engaged in discussion of the big cultural and political issues of the day, and it continued the Russian tradition of using literature as a venue for political debate (though their *publitsistika* is less widely read today than their poetry). Many Symbolist poems addressed class enmity or cultural decline *à la* Oswald Spengler, themes that had been important in Realism, with fresh aesthetic power.

While writers in every era are drawn to other arts and disciplines, the Symbolists (and many "nonaligned" poets of the Silver Age as well) saw particular importance in dance, music, religion, theater, and philosophy. Meanwhile the typical Modernist quest for transcendent meaning sometimes led to interest in the occult sciences, such as astrology, palmistry, or Tarot. (The title of the Symbolist journal *Vesy* is usually translated as *The Scales*, but it also means Libra, and the publishing house Skorpion means both the creature and the astrological sign Scorpio.) Theosophy stimulated interest in various Eastern religions; Bely and apparently also Voloshin were deeply interested in Anthroposophy as propagated by Rudolf Steiner; Parnok makes poetic reference to palm reading; Tsvetaeva refers to fortune telling with playing cards and to astrology; Pasternak's complex lyric poems of the early 1920s make passing reference to homeopathy and astrology. These systems of symbols—esoteric languages that naturally attracted artists who were striving to "read" earthly reality for its ultimate significance—enriched the references to Classical Antiquity (often mediated by the scholarly Ivanov, who translated and wrote about Classical tragedies) and the approaches to more modern writers from all countries. Vladimir Solovyov's poetry and religious philosophy (some samples of which are included here) helped set the tone for the period's explorations of sex, love, and beauty.

Some relatively older poets (Annensky, Kuzmin, Voloshin) formed living links between their Symbolist peers and the younger poets and new movements who emerged around and after 1910. As Symbolism matured and then approached its "crisis" after 15-20 years of writing and publishing, it also began to serve as the background for younger movements who might reject Symbolist habits, but who depended on readers' familiarity with the Symbolists to shock and impress by doing something different.

The Symbolists themselves reacted in a variety of ways to the newer movements. It is striking, for example, that Blok thought highly of the Futurists but was irritated by the Acmeists, whose poetry one might consider closer to his. (Rather: he was irritated by the Acmeists with the exception of Akhmatova, whom almost everyone seemed to like, even when they envied her.) The Symbolists were very self-conscious as a movement, concerned with defining and developing what they stood for as well as with the meaning of various currents within the movement, and many of them strove to advance programs or beliefs about society (in their *publitsistika*) or about poetry (e.g., Bely's lectures and essays on poetics). The social and political atmosphere in the decades that followed the great Emancipation of 1861, familiar to readers of the great Realist novels, gave many Symbolists both the desire to define a holistic vision with programmatic writing and a sense that it was their duty to do so. At the same time, they drew on many other literary and cultural sources, from ancient Greece to Russian folk and sectarian traditions.

Another crucial contribution of Symbolism was the practice of life-creation (in Russian, *zhiznetvorchestvo*), which focused on the aesthetic qualities and trajectory of the individual's biography and arc of experiences as an aesthetic work. (This is depicted from a critical angle by Vladislav Khodasevich in "The End of Renata," in Section II.) As they observed scholars and editors studying earlier generations of writers, they began to take genres such as diary writing more seriously, so that in time almost everything written in the Silver Age was composed with an eye to the eventual reader. The Symbolist poets recognized the importance not only of writing in solitude for eventual publication, but also of meeting, debating, and collaborating, as well as founding cultural and publishing enterprises. A huge variety of poets participated in these; many of them were friends with Symbolists or moved in the same circles but did not particularly think of themselves as part of the school.

Although many Symbolists did not like the name the critics had given them (whether or not they admired Charles Baudelaire and other French poets), their attitude towards the symbolic function of poetry made the name a suitable choice. As their more theoretically oriented members wrote, the point of the movement was to move towards deeper and more important layers of reality, or *ab realibus ad realiora:* in essence, from everyday reality to the ultimate reality.

Brief Bibliography of Scholarly Works on Russian Symbolism:

Davidson, Pamela, ed. *Russian Literature and Its Demons*. New York: Berghahn Books, 2010.

Kalb, Judith E., J. Alexander Ogden, and I. G. Vishnevetsky, eds. *Russian Writers of the Silver Age, 1890-1925*. Dictionary of Literary Biography 295. Detroit and New York: Gale, 2004.

Green, Michael, ed. *The Russian Symbolist Theatre: An Anthology of Plays and Texts*. Ann Arbor: Ardis, 1986.

Grossman, Joan Delaney. *Ivan Konevskoi, Wise Child of Russian Symbolism*. Brighton, MA: Academic Studies Press, 2010.

Maslennikov, Oleg. *The Frenzied Poets: Andrei Biely and the Russian Symbolists*. New York: Greenwood Press, 1968.

McMillan, Arnold, ed. *Symbolism and After: Essays on Russian Poetry in Honor of Georgette Donchin*. London: Bristol Classical Press, 1992.

Morrison, Simon. *Russian Opera and the Symbolist Movement*. Berkeley, CA: University of California Press, 2002.

Peterson, Ronald, ed. *The Russian Symbolists: An Anthology of Critical and Theoretical Writings*. Ann Arbor: Ardis, 1986.

Pyman, Avril. *A History of Russian Symbolism*. New York: Cambridge UP, 1994.

West, James. *Russian Symbolism: A Study of Vyacheslav Ivanov and the Russian Symbolist Aesthetic*. London: Methuen & Co Ltd., 1970.

ACMEISM, also known as Adamism (see Parnok's skeptical review in Section II of this volume), is known today primarily because of the poets involved: Nikolai Gumilyov was the main critic and theoretical mover, while Akhmatova and Mandelstam became the most famous members of the movement. The group was strongly influenced by Innokenty Annensky (who died before the Poets' Guild was formed) and Kuzmin (himself not a member of any school), while Voloshin collaborated significantly in the journal *Apollon* and elsewhere. As in all the literary movements, there were interesting secondary poets among the Acmeists—we regret not being able to include more of them, such as the prolific Sergei Gorodetsky (1884-1967), or Vladimir Narbut (1888-1938). To some extent, the terms explain themselves: "Acmeist" refers to the "acme" of poetic aspiration, and "Adamist" to the freshness of newly given names in the Biblical story, as well as to the members' innovative attention to origins and cultural palimpsests. The name "Poets' Guild" was chosen to emphasize the down-to-earth craft of their poetry, in contrast to the sometimes vague philosophy of the Symbolists, but also to recall the medieval and Renaissance periods, in which they were interested. The Acmeists were organized in 1911; they published most frequently in the journals *Apollon* and *Giperborei*. According to members or friends of the Guild, Acmeism stood for "beautiful clarity" (Kuzmin), "a nostalgia for world culture" (Mandelstam), and the concrete thingness of things, expressed in poetry of high technical artistry. As the brief biographies of the individual poets in this book's first main section below will suggest, the Acmeists too were a varied group. The Poets' Guild never actually came to a formal end, and some of its surviving members considered themselves Acmeists to the end of their lives.

Brief Bibliography of Scholarly Works on Acmeism:

Cavanagh, Clare. *Lyric Poetry and Modern Politics: Poland, Russia and the West.* New Haven: Yale University Press, 2009.

Doherty, Justin. *The Acmeist Movement in Russian Poetry: Culture and the Word.* Oxford and New York: Oxford University Press, 1995.

Painter, Kirsten Blythe. *Flint on a Bright Stone: A Revolution of Precision and Restraint in American, Russian and German Modernism.* Stanford, CA: Stanford UP, 2006.

Strakhovsky, Leonid I. *Craftsmen of the Word: Three Poets of Modern Russia: Gumilyov, Akhmatova, Mandelstam.* Westport, CT: Greenwood Press, 1949, 1969.

FUTURISM in Russia was perhaps the most ramified of the movements, involving various, often competing groups of poets and visual artists. The best-known branch of the movement is Cubo-Futurism, named for its members' attention to modern art of the time: some of them (David Burlyuk, Mayakovsky) began as visual artists. Vladimir Mayakovsky had done time in jail for smuggling a gun as a very young member of the Bolshevik Party and was therefore banned from most other institutions of higher education, so enrolled in the Moscow School of Painting, Sculpture and Architecture, where he met Burlyuk. This group included Viktor (Velimir) Khlebnikov and

Alexei Kruchonykh, as well as several others. Khlebnikov in particular was almost a "language poet" before there was such a term; to the Western eye the work of the Cubo-Futurists may look postmodern before the era of postmodernism. The Ego-Futurists were headed by Igor Severyanin, pseudonym of Igor Lotaryov; other shorter-lived or more peripheral Futurist or Futurist-ish groups drew in the peasant poet Esenin and (more in character) Nikolai Aseev and Pasternak.

All the Futurists to some extent practiced the art of épatage; the Cubo-Futurists painted flowers on their faces, tucked a dead fish or a wooden spoon into their vest pockets in place of a handkerchief, or, in Mayakovsky's case, went about for some time in a yellow shirt his mother had made him, though he also appears in pre-Revolutionary photographs in elegant black evening wear with a top hat and a long cigarette holder—a devastating dandy. He and other Futurists toured, performed, and published outrageous collections and handmade volumes (printed on wallpaper and the like).[2] The Cubo-Futurists especially came to be known for their manifestos, some of which are included in the second section of this volume; like much of their published poetry, these texts demonstrate a keen sense for publicity and certainty that there is no such thing as bad publicity. Not unlike their Western counterparts, some of them were eventually drawn into unsavory alliances with political authorities—though the two best-known, Khlebnikov and Mayakovsky, died before the highly compromising era of Stalinism began.

Their avant-garde outrageousness, their pugnacious sensibility, and their closeness to abstract and poster art make the Futurists—although loosely focused as a movement—one of the most exciting Silver Age schools. Like the Acmeists, they have been marvelously translated, and sophisticated scholars have been drawn to their work and its implications for literature and linguistics almost from the inception of the movement, when members of the Russian Formal School (Formalist critics) such as Viktor Shklovsky and Roman Jakobson admired and analyzed their writings.

---

2 An impressive online collection from an exhibit of these materials at the Metropolitan Museum of Modern Art can be found online at <http://www.moma.org/russian/>.

Brief Bibliography of Scholarly Works on Futurism:

Barooshian, Vahan. *Russian Cubo-Futurism, 1910-1930: A Study in Avant-Gardism.* The Hague: Mouton, 1974.

Erlich, Victor. *Modernism and Revolution: Russian Literature in Transition.* Cambridge, MA and London: Harvard University Press, 1994.

Jakobson, Roman. "The Generation that Squandered Its Poets." Translated by Dale E. Peterson. *Yale French Studies*, no. 39 (1967): 119-125.

Lawton, Anna and Herbert Eagle, eds. and trans. *Russian Futurism through Its Manifestoes, 1912-1928.* Ithaca: Cornell University Press, 1988.

Lifshits, Benedikt. *The One and a Half-Eyed Archer.* Translated, introduced, and annotated by John E. Bowlt. Newtonville, MA: Oriental Research Partners, 1977.

Markov, Vladimir. *Russian Futurism: A History.* London: MacGibbon & Kees, 1969.

Proffer, Ellendea and Carl Proffer, eds. *The Ardis Anthology of Russian Futurism.* Ann Arbor: Ardis, 1980.

Although almost everyone had some connection with one or another of the schools—were friends with Futurists, attended "the Tower" in St. Petersburg or Bely's lectures in Moscow, or published a few poems in *Apollon*—many important poets were not affiliated with any of the three main movements. Given the legal reforms following 1905, it became possible to found and belong to a political party—or open a journal or newspaper—and participate in more open political debate. This change and the resulting political ferment could help explain both active, vocal participation in various schools at the time *and* the reluctance of some other poets to sign on, whether or not they respected the movement's poets and program. (Akhmatova's memoirs suggest that many more people were interested in politics than poetry at the time.) Taking account of movements helps a reader or scholar to keep straight some of what was going on, what the big debates or ideas were at certain moments, but in fact the arrangement was never as clear-cut as it might look now, in aesthetic and historical hindsight. See, for example, Parnok's article on the Acmeists: she was not herself a Symbolist, but she was friendly with a number of the Symbolists, a summer visitor of Voloshin, and very close to Adelaida Gertsyk and other less well-known poets whom we now view as Symbolists, not to mention her affair with the non-aligned Tsvetaeva, or her unfriendly relationship with the Acmeist Mandelstam. Barbara Heldt has pointed out that women were less likely to claim membership in the Silver Age schools—whether because they felt less welcome there, or because they were less eager to join, or even because other obligations kept them from attending meetings or events where groups were formed and cultivated. Women who were members of this or that school were typically married to one of the men involved.[3] Some of the "marginal" figures (Kuzmin, Parnok, Tsvetaeva—"marginal" in the sense of their positioning vis-à-vis the groups, not in their poetic importance) also explored alternative sexualities and interrogated the boundaries of gender. As the brief biographies for the poets suggest, however, gender was a popular

---

3   Here Heldt is worth quoting at length:

> It must be understood that the nature of these groups was social as well as poetic. There was a felt kinship among members for however brief a time. The names the groups bear helped win publicity for their members during their lifetimes, as they help the subsequent student of Russian poetry begin to understand a past age. However, the real history of poetry must begin with the actual poetry written, not with labels like symbolist, acmeist, futurist or imagist. Critics have been saddled with these labels, but, interestingly, they have found women poets less classifiable—with the exception of poets whose husbands belonged to a group, as did those of Gippius, Akhmatova and [Elena] Guro.
>
> A large anthology of twentieth-century poetry, *Russkaia poeziia XX veka*, published in Moscow in 1925 by I. S. Yezhov and E. I. Shamurin, groups poets according to schools, but nearly all the women poets included are in a category called 'poets not connected with definite groups.' These are: Lokhvitskaya, L'vova, Parnok, Shaginian, Stolitsa, Tsvetaeva, Pavlovich, Shkapskaya, Volchanetskaya, Butiagina, Odoevtseva, Inber, Polonskaya, Radlova, and Barkova, or sixteen of the thirty-five poets in that category. Of poets listed as belonging to groups, women comprise two out of nineteen symbolists (Gippius and Solov'eva), one out of ten acmeists (Akhmatova), one out of twelve futurists (Guro), and no peasant poets or proletarian poets (twelve and thirty-four males are listed, respectively). Whatever the reasons for the existence of groups, and however little they mean in terms of the actual poetry written, the independence of women is striking here. It may have been forced on them by exclusion: the tone of male assertiveness in the poetry of futurists like Mayakovsky or the quintessential imagist/peasant poet Esenin, as well as the flamboyantly male-oriented activities of their group, must have been a discouraging factor." Barbara Heldt, *Terrible Perfection: Women and Russian Literature* (Bloomington and Indianapolis: Indiana University Press, 1987), 116-117.

Though Heldt is citing from a publication at the very end of the Silver Age, the list of "non-aligned" women poets could be stimulus for further interesting reading.

place for exploration—and this element, too, makes the Russian Silver Age fascinating for readers in our own time.

The Big Topics

The Silver Age poets, and many of their readers, engaged with a number of topics: sex, sin, religion, divinity (both Russian Orthodox and other), ritual, suicide, ecstasy, inspiration. Merezhkovsky described the idea of a sacralized materiality, or "holy flesh" (*sviataia plot'*), in a talk he gave at the Religious-Philosophical Meetings, and both Symbolists and others brooded over the relation of body or flesh and spirit. Female and male poets picked up discourse about gender roles (from authors such as Otto Weininger)[4] and engaged with ideas of female and feminine creativity—noticeably unlike the Russian Romantics' appropriation of feminine discursive space while mocking actual women writers or preemptively placing them on pedestals during the Golden Age of Russian poetry.

Another striking element of the era was decadence, which accompanied a pervasive sense that culture was in decline—perhaps a well-deserved decline in the eyes of those upper-class poets who were wracked with guilt about the unfortunate position of peasants and workers in the Russian Empire. (See Gumilyov's grateful comment in the review in Section II on Klyuev's poetic offer, on behalf of Klyuev's fellow peasants, to welcome the upper classes into a new community.) The decadents (Bryusov, Sologub, sometimes Gippius) could toy with piquant depictions of sin, or they could raise fundamental questions of morality. Poets shared a widespread interest in the convergence of arts and the senses, exploring synaesthesia and attempting to construct new cultures, new worlds, while drawing on old cultures and traditions. The Futurists (as their name suggests) were taken with new technology, planes, fast cars, and urbanism, though these elements also show up in the work of other poets of the period. At the same time, the arche-Futurist Khlebnikov drew on archaic Slavic culture, its pagan gods and natural symbols, and on ancient Slavonic word roots in his poetic compositions. In their prose as well as their poetry, these poets imagined new religious communities and rituals; in this too they were not unlike West

---

4 Otto Weininger, *Geschlecht und Charakter* (Sex and Character), 1903, was translated into Russian before the First World War, though many educated Russians knew German and could read the influential book in the original.

European and American Modernists. Even as the past seemed a vanishing source of authenticity and of closer connections between language and reality, now tragically lost, and as contemporary civilizations showed signs of decline, the poets built new edifices with thoughtful reference to the past. As mentioned before, the Silver Age poets attentively read the European Modernists and philosophers contemporary to them, along with their own idiosyncratic selections of earlier poets, such as François Villon (a favorite of Mandelstam) or Walt Whitman (translated by both Balmont and Kornei Chukovsky).

Before and After: A Brief History

After the Golden Age of Russian poetry in the early nineteenth century, according to the then-émigré scholar and critic D. S. Mirsky, the level of poetic craft declined terribly while the novel became the most prestigious literary genre. The last of the big Realists who began his writing life as a poet was Ivan Turgenev, a friend of Henry James and George Sand, born in 1818. Poetry was often denigrated in the era of Realism, coded as feminine (read: effeminate) and aristocratic (read: effete), especially by Russia's leftist positivist critics (Nikolai Chernyshevsky, Nikolai Dobrolyubov, Dmitri Pisarev). The most famous poets of the era after the Golden Age were mainly marginal figures: Lermontov was killed in a duel in 1841, at the age of twenty-six; Tyutchev spent most of his life abroad as a civil servant; Fet was admired by authors such as Leo Tolstoy, but his impact was delayed until the Silver Age, when he was seen as exemplarily musical and had many of his lyrics set as art songs. Pavlova spent the last decades of her life in emigration in Germany, and almost everything she wrote there was lost. The exception to this neglect of poetry was the civic poet and journalist Nikolai Nekrasov (1821-1878), best known now for his long poems with sometimes tendentious subject matter, though some of his love poetry resonates with that of Blok and other Symbolists. Russian poets who immediately preceded the Silver Age have not fared well with later critics: Semyon Nadson (1862-1887) in particular was scorned by Silver Age poets for his pathos-ridden verse and poor technique, as well perhaps as for his popularity with less sophisticated readers. It may be typical for a new poetic era to begin by denigrating everything it objects to in the preceding one and (as it were) jumping over the heads of the "parents" to the "grandparents," the poets of the Golden Age.

The Silver Age began as the great Realist era was coming to an end: Fyodor Dostoevsky died in 1881, Ivan Turgenev in 1883, Nadezhda Khvoshchinskaya in 1889, Nikolai Leskov in 1895, and although Leo Tolstoy lived until 1910 he was now active as a moral teacher and thinker, having rejected his own fiction decades before. The early Symbolists gained energy partly from discovering and rediscovering poets of the nineteenth century who had not been properly appreciated: Vladimir Benediktov (1803-1873), Karolina Pavlova, and Konstantin Fofanov (1862-1911). The new school of poets was seeking elevated craft (Pavlova), verbal music and exotic language (Benediktov, Fofanov, and also Mirra Lokhvitskaya, who belongs here in the Silver Age but died young of tuberculosis, in 1905). At the same time, authors of the Silver Age by no means shirked the writer's authority and even duty to comment on social issues, which the poets had inherited from previous decades. They were eager to write for the "thick" journals of the late 1800s and the early 1900s, and these journals were full of articles by Gippius, Blok, and other Symbolists. The achievements of Russian Realism continued to some extent in shorter prose forms, by brilliant authors such as Anton Chekhov, Maxim Gorky, and Ivan Bunin. Leo Tolstoy remained a real and continuing reference point for Silver Age writers thinking about civic engagement—the pages of the journal *Mir Iskusstva* (World of Art) are full of references to him. This legacy endured in the Silver Age for years after his death. Scholars have also agreed with Mandelstam's comment that Russian novels of the nineteenth century lived on as the psychological underpinnings of Akhmatova's understated early poems.

Almost all the poets of the Silver Age welcomed the tsar's abdication in early 1917, but their culture was fatally ruptured by the October 1917 Revolution: some of our poets died much too young (Gumilyov was shot in 1921; Blok and Khlebnikov died in 1921 and 1922, both of a combination of starvation and illness); some emigrated and continued to work in smaller communities and increasing poverty, often growing more conservative in their writing (though Khodasevich, Severyanin, Tsvetaeva and others did their best work in emigration, after 1917); some remained in Russia, now the Soviet Union, and adapted in one way or another. For a few years the borders remained open, and many poets traveled back and forth from the USSR to Western Europe or published both in Berlin and in Moscow. Some were eventually unable to adapt as the new situation began to harden: Esenin and Mayakovsky committed suicide, and Mandelstam (who had tried in some ways to accommodate himself to the new situation) was arrested twice and died on his way to a prison camp in 1938. Some of Klyuev's major works were preserved only in a secret police archive, after his final arrest. Pasternak survived and even enjoyed some fame under Stalin, but his lover Olga Ivinskaya was arrested and sent to a camp to keep him in line, and the end of his life was darkened by scandal; after *Doctor Zhivago* was published abroad, he was awarded the Nobel Prize for Literature but not allowed to travel to receive it. Kuzmin and Parnok died sooner than they should have, of malnourishment and ill health. Women were often taken less seriously by the Soviet regime and thus were more likely to survive, though that imposed a new set of obligations: to fall silent as a poet, like Shkapskaya, in order to protect her family, or to represent the Silver Age itself in a later era, like Akhmatova. Tsvetaeva, whose life story is unusually full of incident, returned to the USSR in 1939, not long before the Second World War began, and committed suicide in 1941 under circumstances that are still murky but seem to implicate the literary establishment and/or the secret police. A new set of literary groups formed in the early Soviet period, some of them fascinating and very much worth reading (such as the Leningrad absurdists of OBERIU), but independent groups were quickly smacked down by the newly formed All-Soviet Writers' Union. (Many authors at first saw the Union as a good development, since some early Soviet literary groupings had been aggressively unpleasant to anyone who disagreed with their programs.) A few of our poets outlived Stalin: Pasternak died in 1960, Aseev in 1963, Akhmatova in 1966, and Kruchonykh in 1968—and we could argue that their work after the 1920s belongs to and reflects a different era and poetic moment, even when it harkens back to the Silver Age: Ahmatova's *Poem without a Hero* can serve as a primer for understanding this period. In hindsight, the many personal losses lend a tragic tinge to the Silver Age, even for the poets who did survive beyond it. A reader cannot help thinking: what would have developed out of this amazing ferment, if war and revolution hadn't intervened?

Silver Age poetry enjoyed an odd afterlife in Russian literature: the Soviet period imposed a sort of cultural deep freeze that kept many of its voices out of public discourse but thereby preserved and even increased its importance, especially for readers who trusted poetry more than political parties. Meanwhile, the conformist literary establishment rolled back some Silver Age poetic innovations and kept much of the best poetry under wraps (especially the poets who were under thirty in 1917, whose development was both intensified and made more difficult by the rapidly changing conditions of their lives). A new flare-up of great Russian poetry in the 1960s—a cultural marker of the Thaw period that was never quite squashed when Leonid Brezhnev came to preside over the so-called era of Stagnation—in many ways advanced the achievements and importance of the Silver Age. Some poetry of the Thaw grew into an avant-garde underground that was not cut off by arrests and prison sentences, though it was available only in *samizdat*, unofficial self-publication, and still carried certain risks. Because the development of Russian poetry in the Soviet Union was artificially slowed, the Silver Age's poetry felt truly vital and contemporary until the 1990s. It is no accident that one of the most prominent late-Soviet poets, Joseph Brodsky (1940-1996), carefully read Akhmatova (whom he knew personally), Mandelstam, and Tsvetaeva, composing insightful essays about their writing and lives. Poets who had suffered and died acquired a moral authority that also heightened their aesthetic importance (see Bella Akhmadulina [1937-2010] writing about Mandelstam or Tsvetaeva). Even now, the great Silver Age poets are loved by Russian readers around the world.

Recent Russian poetry is moving in a variety of new directions, and the status of the Russian poet has changed to become more like that of Western analogues: the loss of state sponsorship has meant both freedom (from censorship and Socialist Realism) and exposure to new and often unhelpful forces in the literary marketplace. "Being a famous poet isn't the same as being famous," as one (famous) American poet declared. Nevertheless, today's Russian poets know their Silver Age predecessors excellently, and some (Olga Sedakova, Vladimir Gandelsman, Maria Stepanova, Polina Barskova, or the late Elena Shvarts) consciously and overtly draw on and refer to the Silver Age tradition in their work and their thinking.

The Russian Silver Age in the West

The poets of the Silver Age had the benefit of being introduced to Anglophone readers by D. S. Mirsky in his survey of modern Russian literature, published in 1925, around what we might call the end of the Silver Age. By 1925, Akhmatova was no longer able to publish much poetry; Mandelstam had entered a five-year hiatus in his writing; Blok and Khlebnikov were dead; Shkapskaya was soon to stop writing poetry (at least, any that has survived). For many reasons, the story of the Russian Silver Age was only partly told for a time in the West: émigré poets were often taken less seriously, seen as a lesser cultural phenomenon or as representatives of an obsolete social class, while poets who remained in the USSR were eventually enclosed by the Iron Curtain. For a time Anglophone publishers favored Silver Age prose writers—Merezhkovsky's novels, for example, were translated early and fairly often retranslated, as was Fyodor Sologub's *Petty Demon*. After Stalin's death, during and after the Thaw, Western readers made a series of discoveries that each quickly reverberated in scholarship: Pasternak became famous when he was denied access to the Nobel Prize; Akhmatova, when her poetry began to appear in more complete Soviet editions and she was invited to be honored in Britain and Italy; Mandelstam, when his widow managed to get his manuscripts out of the country for publication; Tsvetaeva, when her daughter had some of her poetry published and then more copiously republished in the USSR. The Futurists, especially Khlebnikov and Mayakovsky, have always appealed to both scholars and readers with a taste for the avant-garde. Because Soviet censorship made it difficult for scholars to access the complete collections of some Silver Age poets, and potentially dangerous for a scholar to probe too deeply in a poet's work and career, Western scholarship on the Silver Age was as likely to be cutting-edge as work published in the USSR—and the presence of many important Russian or former Soviet scholars in emigration also helped to establish high-quality traditions of interpretation. Scholars such as Italian critic Renato Poggioli helped give a sophisticated introduction of the poets and their importance to readers in the West. Not only are the most famous of the Russian Modernist poets now available in many very effective translations into English, they have also significantly influenced and impacted poets in other traditions. (Looking at a poem by Irish poet Nuala Ni Dhomhnaill, dedicated to Tsvetaeva, one need not posit a very long series of connections: Joseph Brodsky was a good friend of Seamus Heaney.)

For those who would like to read and explore more, the select bibliographies below include translations of our poets (sometimes, only part of the cited work is from the Silver Age) and scholarly books on Silver Age topics larger than just one writer or poetic school. Some of these books have helped to shape our own approach to the period, and the most recent books on the list (such as those by Colleen McQuillen and Sara Pankenier Weld) show that the poetry and culture of the Silver Age continue to attract and fascinate some of the best scholars working on Russian literature.

SELECTED BIBLIOGRAPHY: THE RUSSIAN SILVER AGE

Translations

Chandler, Robert, Irina Mashinski, and Boris Dralyuk, eds. *The Penguin Book of Russian Poetry*. London: Penguin Classics, 2015.

Glad, John, and Daniel Weissbort, eds. *Russian Poetry: The Modern Period*. Iowa City, IA: University of Iowa Press, 1974.

Kazakova, Rimma, ed. *The Tender Muse*. Moscow: Progress Publishers, 1976.

Kelly, Catriona, ed. *An Anthology of Russian Women's Writing, 1777-1992*. Translated by Catriona Kelly, Sibelan Forrester, Diana Greene, Elizabeth Neatrour, Brian Thomas Oles, Marian Schwartz, and Mary Zirin. Oxford and London: Oxford University Press, 1994.

Mager, Don, ed. and trans. *Us Four Plus Four: Eight Russian Poets Conversing*. New Orleans, LA: UNO Press, 2009.

Markov, Vladimir, and Merrill Sparks, eds. *Modern Russian Poetry*. Indianapolis and New York: Bobbs-Merrill Company, Inc., 1967.

Muchnik, Slava, ed. *Salt Crystals on an Axe/Как соль на топоре. Twentieth-Century Russian Poetry in Congruent Translation. A Bilingual Mini-Anthology*. Translated by Alex Shafarenko. Godalming, Surrey, UK: Ancient Purple, 2009.

Nabokov, Vladimir, trans. *Verses and Versions: Three Centuries of Russian Poetry*. Edited by Brian Boyd and Stanislav Shvabrin. Orlando: Harcourt, Inc., 2008.

Natchez, Meryl, trans., with Boris Wolfson and Polina Barskova. *Poems from the Stray Dog Café: Akhmatova, Mandelstam, Gumilev*. Hit & Run Press, 2013.

Obolensky, Dimitri, ed. *The Heritage of Russian Verse*. Bloomington & Indianapolis: Indiana University Press, 1976.

Pachmuss, Temira. *Women Writers in Russian Modernism: An Anthology*. Urbana: University of Illinois Press, 1978.

Peterson, Ronald E., ed. and trans. *The Russian Symbolists*. Ann Arbor, MI: Ardis Publishers, 1986.

Proffer, Carl, and Ellendea Proffer, eds. *The Silver Age of Russian Culture.* Ann Arbor, MI: Ardis Publishers, 1975.

Schmidt, Paul, trans. *The Stray Dog Cabaret: A Book of Russian Poems.* New York: NYRB Classics, 2006.

Tomei, Christine, ed. *Russian Women Writers.* New York: Garland, 1998.

West, Thomas G., ed. *Symbolism: An Anthology.* London & New York: Methuen, 1980.

Yarmolinsky, Avrahm, ed. *Two Centuries of Russian Verse: An Anthology, from Lomonosov to Voznesensky.* Translated by Babette Deutsch. New York: Random House, 1966.

Yevtushenko, Yevgeny, ed. Translated by Albert G. Todd and Max Hayward (with Daniel Weissbort). *20th Century Russian Poetry: Silver and Steel.* New York: Doubleday, 1993.

CULTURE AND SCHOLARSHIP

Bowlt, John E. *Moscow & St. Petersburg, 1900-1920: Art, Life, & Culture of the Russian Silver Age.* New York: Vendome Press, 2008.

Crone, Anna Lisa. *Eros and Creativity in Russian Religious Revival: The Philosophers and the Freudians.* Leiden and Boston: Brill, 2010.

Gasparov, Boris, Robert Hughes, and Irina Paperno, eds. *Cultural Mythologies of Russian Modernism: From the Golden Age to the Silver Age.* Berkeley, CA: University of California Press, 1992.

Greenfield, Douglas, ed. *Alter Icons: The Russian Icon and Modernity.* University Park, PA: Pennsylvania State University Press, 2010.

Grillaert, Nel. *What the God-Seekers Found in Nietzsche: The Reception of Nietzsche's Übermensch by the Philosophers of the Russian Religious Renaissance.* Amsterdam and New York: Rodopi, 2008.

Hingley, Ronald. *Nightingale Fever: Russian Poets in Revolution.* New York: Knopf, 1981.

Kelly, Catriona, and Stephen Lowell, eds. *Russian Literature, Modernism, and the Visual Arts.* Cambridge, UK: Cambridge University Press, 2000.

Loewen, Donald. *The Most Dangerous Art: Poetry, Politics and Autobiography After the Russian Revolution.* Lanham: Lexington Books, 2008.

Matich, Olga. *Erotic Utopia: The Decadent Imagination in Russia's Fin-de-Siècle.* Madison, WI: University of Wisconsin Press, 2005.

McQuilllen, Colleen. *The Modernist Masquerade: Stylizing Life, Literature, and Costumes in Russia*. Madison, WI: The University of Wisconsin Press, 2013.

Mirsky, D. S. *Modern Russian Literature*. London: Oxford University Press, 1925.

Paperno, Irina, and Joan Delaney Grossman, eds. *Creating Life: The Aesthetic Utopia of Russian Modernism*. Stanford, CA: Stanford University Press, 1984.

Rylkova, Galina. *The Architecture of Anxiety: The Russian Silver Age and Its Legacy*. Pittsburgh: University of Pittsburgh Press, 2007.

Weld, Sara Pankenier. *Voiceless Vanguard: The Infantilist Aesthetic of the Russian Avant-Garde*. Evanston, IL: Northwestern University Press, 2014.

SECTION I: THE POETS

BIOGRAPHIES AND POETRY

Poets are listed here alphabetically, rather than chronologically or by affiliation (if any), to make it easier to find the one you want. Before each selection of poems, there is a brief biography (including how to pronounce the poet's name, and the Library of Congress spelling, useful in looking their work up in libraries). Why do we include the whole three-part Russian name? Many Russians have similar names, and in some cases you need all three names—first, patronymic, and last name—to distinguish different individuals. The poet Vyacheslav Ivanovich Ivanov, whose last name is the Russian equivalent of "Johnson," is not the same as the prominent later scholar Vyacheslav Vyacheslavovich Ivanov. They are listed according to the English alphabet, which will look peculiar to a Russian reader.

One way you can tell that Andrei Bely (like Maxim Gorky) is a pseudonym is that there is no patronymic: anyone who did not know him well would have called him "Boris Nikolaevich," his birth name and patronymic. (Close friends would have called him "Borya.") Some other poets essentially changed their names, rather than writing under pseudonyms, out of personal taste or family preference.

A few of the brief biographies here (Bely, Gippius, Solovyov) were written by scholars who specialize in the study of those poets; the authors' names follow these entries.

Some biographical data recurs in many of the entries: for example, many poets attended *gimnazia*, the elite Russian high school where children studied foreign and sometimes classical languages and literatures as well as other liberal arts and sciences. The *gimnazia* was a high school of a distinct type (and you will notice that the peasant poets, Esenin and Klyuev, did not attend *gimnazia*—nor did many of the women). Access to education after high school depended not only on social class (financial support and family expectations) but also on a poet's political affiliations, as "undesirable" elements were prevented from enrolling in a university.

The best-known poets are represented here by larger selections; less famous poets by fewer poems. Each set of poems closes with a select bibliography of translations and biographical or scholarly sources in English, for further reading and exploration. For some major anthologies of translations, we include only the name of the collection's editor; these anthologies are identified in the bibliography at the end of this section. The best-known poets have attracted more attention from scholars and translators into English, so they also have lengthier bibliographies. The bibliographies are not complete, but they offer good places to start; just reading the titles gives an idea of the poet's reputation and importance in literary studies. Some of the poets listed here are now considered more significant for their critical, theoretical, or prose writings than for their poetry, and many are represented at greater length in the second large section of this book.

Some poets did not date their poems; some (like Akhmatova) might change a date in order to get past censorship; some (Blok, Tsvetaeva) date their poems with great precision, suggesting that they are meant to be read in a context of life-creation. When possible, we have dated the poems included here even if the original publications did not include dates.

Anna Akhmatova

Anna Andreevna Akhmatova (akh-MAH-tuh-vuh, born Górenko, 1889-1966). Akhmatova (a pseudonym taken from her Tatar great-grandmother) was born near Odessa in 1889; she later liked to describe it as the same year T. S. Eliot, Charlie Chaplin, and Adolf Hitler were born. Her father was a naval engineer, her mother an aristocrat with a radical political past. Akhmatova grew up in Tsarskoe Selo, near St. Petersburg, a great reader of poetry from childhood. The family moved to Kiev, where she finished *gimnazia* and studied law at the Kiev College for Women, without completing a degree. She married Nikolai Gumilyov in 1910 (he had been courting her for years), and they became both a glamorous couple on the St. Petersburg cultural scene and founding members of the Poets' Guild or Acmeist school. Her first poem was published in 1907, and her first collection in 1912. Her next collection, *Rosary* (1914) became tremendously popular, and fans could buy her photographs (alongside Blok's) in bookshops, signaling their status as best-loved poets of the time, something like rock stars today: personal attractiveness always helps to bolster a creative person's popularity. By 1917 Akhmatova was one of the best-known poets in Russia; Bolshevik feminist Alexandra Kollontai praised her sensitive treatment of women's issues, especially problematic aspects of love and sex. Not long after, however, Akhmatova was banned from publication, and the ban lasted until the beginning of WWII (when censorship of all kinds was relaxed and churches reopened to encourage Russian citizens to contribute to the war effort). Meanwhile, Gumilyov had been shot (1921); their son Lev was arrested several times as punishment for having the wrong father or to keep his mother in line. In the darkest days of Stalinist repression, Akhmatova continued to write poetry, asking friends like Lidia Chukovskaya to memorize and thus preserve her new compositions. Her cycle *Requiem* is one of very few works about the Great Terror that was written as the Terror occurred. Akhmatova had a second life as a literary translator (which for a poet, she said, was like "eating your own brains") and also wrote significant scholarly works, especially on the Golden Age poet Alexander Pushkin. After Stalin's death, and especially in the 1960s, Akhmatova emerged as the *grande dame* of Russian letters. Her vision of the Silver Age, expressed in *Poem without a Hero*, shaped later readers' views of the period and its writers. She also mentored young Leningrad poets such as Joseph Brodsky. She died in 1966 near Leningrad.

[Молюсь оконному лучу]

I pray to the light in the window—
It's pale, poised and slight.
Today I've been silent since morning,
And my heart is split in two.
The copper basin of my wash-stand
Has started turning green.
But watching how light plays on it,
I feel joyful again.
So innocent and simple
In the evening hush,
But in this empty dwelling place
It's like a golden holiday,
The comfort that I need.

1909

TRANSLATED BY Martha Kelly

Song of Our Last Meeting
[Песня последней встречи]

Though a chill spread through my helpless breast,
Still my steps were as light as ever.
Onto my right hand I pulled
The glove from my left hand.

There seemed to be so many steps,
Yet I knew there were only three!
Autumn moving amongst the maples
Whispered, "Come, die with me!

"My mournful fate has deceived me—
It's a changeful and evil companion."
I answered, "My dear one, my dear one!
Me, too. I will die with you . . ."

Here's the song of our last meeting.
I glanced up at the darkened house.
In the bedroom alone burned candles
With indifferent yellow flames.

1911

TRANSLATED BY Martha Kelly

[Все мы бражники здесь, блудницы]

All of us here are hookers and hustlers.
We drink too much, and don't care.
The walls are covered with birds and flowers
that have never seen sunshine or air.

You smoke too much. There's always a cloud
of nicotine over your head.
Do you like this skirt? I wore it on purpose.
I wanted to show lots of leg.

The windows here have been covered forever.
Is it snowing out? . . . maybe it's rain.
You've got that look in your eyes again,
like a cat in a crouch for a kill.

Sometimes I feel this awful pain,
as if someone were breaking a spell.
Take a good look at that one over there!
She's dancing her way into hell!

January 1, 1913

TRANSLATED BY *Paul Schmidt*

[На шее мелких четок ряд]

At my neck, small rosary beads,
My hands are hidden in a wide muff,
My eyes look out distracted
Unable to cry.

In the shadow of purpling silk
My face pales,
Straight bangs
Brush my eyebrows.

And this is nothing at all like flight,
This slow and uncertain walking
As if there were a raft under my feet
And not the squares of the parquet.

My mouth is slightly open,
My breathing difficult and uneven,
And at my shoulder flowers tremble
The flowers of an unconcluded rendezvous.

1913

TRANSLATED BY Lenore Mayhew and William McNaughton

[Я пришла к поэту в гости]

to Alexander Blok

I went to visit the poet.
Sunday at midday. Right at noon.
It was quiet in the spacious room,
And beyond the windows, freezing.

And the sun hangs raspberry
Over shreds of blue-grey smoke . . .
And my host—how clear his gaze!—
Looks at me without a word.

His eyes are such that each who sees them
Never ever should forget them.
As for me, I'm very cautious
And would do best to avoid them.

But I'll remember all we said,
The hazy midday, Sunday noon
In the building high and grey
Where the Neva meets the sea.

1914. January.

TRANSLATED BY *Martha Kelly*

[Как белый камень в глубине колодца]

A memory
Is in me,
A white stone
At the bottom
Of a well.

I can't
Struggle with it,
I don't want to:
It is gaiety.
It is suffering.

And if someone
Looks in my eyes,
He will see it.
He'll become sad
And thoughtful
              Like someone
Who listens to old stories.

They say the gods,
In changing men
To things,
Leave the mind.
To give life
To my miraculous
Sadness
You have become

Memory.

Summer, 1916, Slepnyovo

TRANSLATED BY Lenore Mayhew and William McNaughton

[Я слышу иволги всегда печальный голос]

I hear the oriole's voice. It sounds as sad as ever.
I welcome splendid summer's disappearance,
While ears of grain crowd up against each other,
The sickle severs with a snake-like whistle.

The short skirts of the slender reapers fly
In the wind like festival-day flags.
All we need now is the jingling bell,
The lingering gaze through dusty eyelashes.

I'm not looking for love's caress or flattery
In this foreboding of relentless darkness,
But come behold the paradise where we
Together once were innocent and blessed.

1917

TRANSLATED BY Martha Kelly

[Для того ль тебя носила]

Just for this I used to carry you
Back then in my arms,
Just for this strength used to radiate
From your sky-blue eyes!

You grew up tall and comely,
Sang songs, drank Madeira wine,
Went off in your torpedo boat
To far-off Anatolia.

On the Malakoff-Kurgan ridge
They gunned the officers down.
Just a week away from twenty
He looked down on God's good earth.

1918

TRANSLATED BY *Martha Kelly*

[Не с теми я, кто бросил землю]

No, not with those who left their land
For enemies to tear apart.
I will not heed crude flatterers,
I'll never give my songs to them.

The exile, though, I pity ever,
Like prisoners and invalids.
Wanderer, your road is dark,
And foreign bread tastes like wormwood.

But here in fire's voiceless fumes
That ruin what remains of youth,
We've never moved to shield ourselves
From any harm that struck at us.

We know that in the final judgment
Each hour will be justified;
Yet in this world no one is simpler,
Calmer, haughtier than us.

1922

TRANSLATED BY Martha Kelly

Lot's Wife
[Лотова жена]

> But Lot's wife looked back from behind him,
> and she became a pillar of salt.
> *Book of Genesis*

And the righteous one walked down the black mountainside
Behind God's envoy, large and shining.
But alarm spoke in strident tones to his wife:
It's never too late to look back
On your native home, on Sodom's red towers,
On the square where you sang, the courtyard where you spun,
On the empty windows of that tall house,
Where you once bore your sweet husband children.
She looked back—and mortal pain seized her,
Her eyes could no longer look on;
Her body transformed into transparent salt,
Her swift feet grew into the earth.

Who then will weep for this woman?
Surely she is the least of our losses.
My heart alone will never forget
One who gave up her life for a final look.

1922-1924

TRANSLATED BY *Martha Kelly*

[Тот город, мной любимый с детства]

The city I have loved since childhood
Because it's silent like December
Appeared to me today, an image
Of my squandered heritage.

Of all that gave itself to me,
That I so blithely gave away;
The soul's own fire, the sounds of prayer,
The abundant grace of that first song—

Transparent smoke bore all away,
All rotted in the mirror's depth . . .
The noseless fiddler has struck up
His tune about what's lost forever.

But like a curious foreigner
Who's charmed by every novelty,
I watched how sleighs rushed swiftly past
And heard my native language spoken.

And, wildly fresh and powerful,
The wind of happiness brushed my face,
As though a friend I've long held dear
Walked out with me onto the porch.

1929

TRANSLATED BY *Martha Kelly*

From *Requiem*
[Из *Реквиема*]

They took you at dawn, I remember,
As though to the wake, I trailed,
Children wept in a darkened chamber,
By the icon, the lamp grew frail.

Your lips kept the icon's chill.
The deathly sweat—I remember it all!
Like the wives of the Streltsy,* I will
Moan for you by the Kremlin Wall.

1935

TRANSLATED BY Andrey Kneller

---

* MK: In the year 1698, the Russian palace guard, or Streltsy, mutinied against the policies of Peter the Great. Those involved were subjected to brutal executions, including being broken on the wheel and buried alive. As in the time of Stalin, the cities were filled with destitute wives and children of the regime's victims.

From "Three Poems"†
[Из "Трех стихотворений"; Он прав — опять фонарь, аптека]

The poet was right: once again—
lantern, side-street, drug store,
silence, the Neva and its granite . . .
A monument to our century's
first years, there he stands, as when,
waving goodbye to Pushkin House,
he drank a mortal weariness—
as if such peace
were more than he deserved.

1960

TRANSLATED BY *Robert Chandler*

---

† RC: Homage to Alexander Blok, whose last poem is addressed to Pushkin House in Petersburg.

From *Poem without a Hero* (1940-1963)
[Из Поэмы без героя]

You have come to Russia out of nowhere,
   My blond marvel,
        Columbine of the 1910s!
Why the veiled and hawkish stare,
   Petersburg doll, little actress,
       You—one of my doubles.
We must add this title, too.
   Oh friend of poets,
       I, heiress to your glory,
Here, in the shade of the cedar tree of Kellomiage
   To that music in magic meters,
       The furious wind of Leningrad,
          See a dance of courtly bones ...
The wedding candles melt,
   Under the veil "the kissable shoulder,"
       The church thunders with "Enter, dove!"
Mountains of Parma violets in April—
   And the rendezvous in the Malta Chapel
       A curse in your heart.
A vision of the golden age
   Or a black crime
       From the fearful chaos of the past?
At least tell me now:
            is it possible
That once you really were alive
   And that you stamped the pavement of the squares
       With your dazzling little foot? ...

TRANSLATED BY Lenore Mayhew and William McNaughton

Translations:

The Complete Poems of Anna Akhmatova. Translated by Judith Hemshemeyer and Roberta Reeder. Somerville, MA: Zephyr Press, 1990.

My Half Century: Selected Prose. Translated by Ronald Meyer. Ann Arbor: Ardis, 1992.

Poem without a Hero and Selected Poems. Translated by Lenore Mayhew and William McNaughton. Oberlin, OH: Oberlin College Press, 1989.

Strong Words: Poetry in a Russian and English Edition. Translated by Vladimir Azarov and Barry Callaghan. Toronto, Canada: Exile Editions, 2014. (Also includes poems by Alexander Pushkin and Andrei Voznesensky)

The Word that Causes Death's Defeat: Poems of Memory. Translated by Nancy K. Anderson. New Haven, CT: Yale University Press, 2004.

You Will Hear Thunder: Akhmatova, Poems. Translated by D. M. Thomas. Athens, OH: Ohio University Press, 1985.

In Chandler/Mashinski/Dralyuk; Glad/Weissbort; Kazakova; Kelly; Mager; Markov/Sparks; Muchnik/Shafarenko; Natchez; Obolensky; Schmidt/Ciepiela; Tomei; Yarmolinsky/Deutsch; Yevtushenko.

Biography:

Driver, Sam. *Anna Akhmatova.* New York: Twayne Publishers, 1972.

Haight, Amanda. *Anna Akhmatova: A Poetic Pilgrimage.* New York: Oxford University Press, 1976.

Naiman, Anatoly. *Remembering Anna Akhmatova.* Translated by Wendy Rosslyn. New York: Henry Holt, 1991.

Bibliography:

Amert, Susan. *In a Shattered Mirror: The Later Poetry of Anna Akhmatova.* Stanford, CA: Stanford University Press, 1992.

Chukovskaya, Lydia. *The Akhmatova Journals.* Translated by Peter Norman. New York: Farrar, Straus and Giroux, 1994.

Harrington, Alexandra. *The Poetry of Anna Akhmatova: Living in Different Mirrors.* London, New York: Anthem Press, 2006.

Polivanov, Konstantin. *Akhmatova and Her Circle.* Translated by Patricia Beriozkina. Fayettevillle, AR: University of Arkansas Press, 1994.

Reeder, Roberta. *Anna Akhmatova: Poet and Prophet.* New York: St Martin's Press, 1994.

Rosslyn, Wendy. *The Prince, the Fool, and the Nunnery: The Religious Theme in the Early Poetry of Anna Akhmatova.* Aldershot, UK/Brookfield, VT: Avebury, 1984.

———. *The Speech of Unknown Eyes: Akhmatova's Readers on Her Poetry.* Cotgrave, Nottingham, UK: Astra, 1990.

Innokenty Annensky

Innokenty Fyodorovich Annensky (AHN-nin-sky, LoC Innokentii Annenskii, 1855-1909) was born in Omsk, Western Siberia, in the family of a high-ranking official. When he was six, his family moved to St. Petersburg. He was educated first at home, then at the Philological Faculty of St. Petersburg University, graduating in 1879. He taught Russian language at the Bychkov *Gimnazia* and lectured at the Bestuzhev Courses, which opened higher education in Russia to women. In 1896-1906 he was director of the *gimnazia* in Tsarskoe Selo, and in 1906 he was appointed inspector of the entire St. Petersburg educational region. He was a member of the scholarly committee of the Ministry of People's Education and a lecturer in the history of Classical literature at the Raev Women's Advanced Courses. Annensky died of a heart attack on November 30, 1909. He was an outstanding pedagogue and a reviewer of educational books in Russian. His final, posthumous collection of poetry surprised many readers and was a particular inspiration to the Acmeists, one of whom (Gumilyov) had studied at the *gimnazia* in Tsarskoe Selo while Annensky was its director.

After the Concert
[После концерта]

The sky has cast its blackness down onto the path,
Tonight my heart cannot shake off its weariness . . .
The lights that have gone out, the voices gone silent,—
Can this be all that's left: the remnants of a dream?

How full of sadness was the satin of her gown,
How ghastly white that space between her black silk straps!
How piteous the sight of her unmoving eyes,
Her snowy kid-skin hands, how prayerfully submissive.

And how much of her soul was squandered in that place
Among the tearless, restless, dissipated ones.
Like sounds that spill out from the calm that nurtures them,
The sounds of stars, sounds lilac and caressing!

So like a string of beads we seize and snap in anguish:
The amethysts roll down onto the dewy grass,
They catch the fiery, tender rays of the full moon
And die without a trace.

TRANSLATED BY *Martha Kelly*

Bow and Strings
[Смычок и струны]

What heavy, dark delirium!
What unfocused, what lunar heights!
To touch the violin for years, although
Never to see her strings by light!

Who needs us now? Who has ignited
Two yellow faces, gloomy faces...
And suddenly the bow has noted:
Someone's lifted them and joined them.

"How long it's been! But in this darkness
Tell me one thing: are you the same, still?"
And the strings moved to caress him,
They rang, but as they moved they trembled.

"Surely this is all we need,
We'll never again be separated?"
The instrument responded *yes*,
But the violin's heart was aching.

The bow perceived it all, was muted,
While the echo possessed the violin...
And what people perceived as music
For the bow and violin was pain.

But the man did not extinguish
The lights till dawn... And the strings sang...
Only sunrise found them exhausted
On the black velvet of the bed.

TRANSLATED BY *Sibelan Forrester*

The Daughter of Jairus
[Дочь Иаира]

The grass is soft, the pavement white
And trumpets ring victoriously:
"We've broken the blue floes of ice,
And now they must be burned away!"

As if the sun is spinning, has
Forgot its long captivity;
The Paschal hymn holds calls of death
Inaudible to all but me.

For a heart *beat* beneath the snows,
And there a thread of life held fast:
That diamond-faceted frozenness
Needed to come awake at last.

For what, why is the snowy shroud
Rudely torn off from the tender
Outlines of immaculate beauty,
Why must her flowers all be burned?

For what, why is the flame so blue,
Why the white heat so very pale,
And why, in ringing, has the sound
Of bells commingled with the bells?

He who lifted this world's sins,
Who dried the world's rivers of tears,
Did Christ, once in another time,
Thus raise the daughter of Jairus?

The flaming lamp-wick did not flicker,
And no wind moved to stir the cloth . . .
The savior came close to the sleeper
And softly said to her, "Arise."

TRANSLATED BY **Sibelan Forrester**

To the Poet
[Поэту]

In the separate trace of rays
And in hazy blurring visions
The power of things hangs over us:
We can't escape the three dimensions.

You might expand the bounds of being
Or think up endless novel forms,
But in your 'I' you never will
Escape the eyes of 'Not-I.'

That power, made of god and rot,
She is a beacon, calling us,
And all the things we've made grow pale
And drop their guard before her face.

No, you will not escape their power
By conjuring vaporous clouds;
Verse draws us in not by its depth,
But merely by its arcane tricks.

The Pierides drew Orpheus in
With open faces, beauty's look.
And you think doll-like Isis' veils
You weave are worthy of him, too?

Love distinctness, love light's rays
For their innate, inborn aroma.
Fashion bright cups, craft them so
They capture integral perceptions.

TRANSLATED BY *Martha Kelly and Sibelan Forrester*

Translations:
In Chandler/Mashinski/Dralyuk; Markov/Sparks; Muchnik/Shafarenko; Obolensky; Yarmolinsky/Deutsch; Yevtushenko.

Bibliography:
Tucker, Janet G. *Innokentij Annenskii and the Acmeist Doctrine*. Columbus, OH: Slavica Publishers, 1986.

Nikolai Aseev

Nikolai Nikolaevich Aseev (ah-SAY-yeff, né Shtal'baum, 1889-1963) was born in the Kursk region; his father was an insurance agent. His mother died early, and he grew up with his maternal grandfather, a lover of songs and folktales. This grandfather had been a serf and told him stories from that era. Aseev studied in Moscow; his first publication was in Kharkov in 1913. This was followed by a decade of poetic "seeking," during which he (along with Pasternak, who remained a good friend) joined the Centrifuge group, which was close to the Futurists. Aseev was influenced by Khlebnikov—who appealed to his own interest in folklore and word-formation—and also by his friendship with Mayakovsky. Aseev later became a successful Soviet poet; in the 1920s he participated in several groups (a Futurist circle in Vladivostok; the LEF group) and later also wrote literary theory. He co-authored the screenplay for Eisenstein's film *The Battleship Potemkin*. Under Stalin he became a powerful literary bureaucrat, but in the Thaw period he actively supported young poets; he died in 1963 in Moscow.

The Volga
[Волга]

1

Here the waves have set out loiterously,
the foam's begun to whiten.
The mountain wind scatters white lily
of the valley above the wave.

The Volga's begun to thunder,
it's started to seethe, to play,
surrounding the lacework of ecstasy
with the dampity of a swell.

There are no higher waves in the world
than on these whitecap ridges,
and I'm allowed to sit on them
by the foamleader Breadman.*

And on them, asail like a stormcloud,
to the Muscovite clangor,
Mayakovsky teaches me
to seize the sky in steel claws.

And Burlyuk the barge-hauler drags
a load of vernal shoutings,
and, like an eagle's, the feathers
of wild freedom stand on end.

And behind those the currents smelt
the adzes of stringèd news,
which, intoxicated with song,
these friends rehearse together!

---

* SF: "Khlebnik," a reference to Khlebnikov.

2

A deep-blue crevice
in the black earth
is smoothed and crushed
by the tread of years.

Beaten out by gangs
of noisy bands,
it fluttered as seagulls
to loot the sky.

Is the song to boil
within these rags?
With dawn's wind I sew
these daysprings' bronze!

3

That bully Zhiguli,
bullets started humming,
coolies on a spree
in the midst of streets.

The columns went dancing,
the roofs all flew away:
you can't hear anything
with this iron revelry!

You'll just scare off drowsing,
you'll just scatter sleep—
Stepan Timofeich Razin†
flaps a scarlet flame!

---

† *SF*: Stepan (Sten'ka) Razin, leader of a seventeenth-century peasant rebellion in Russia.

They wave up, they wave down
the sparks' many glances...
lean over, lean over
acrossing these mountains!

River, overflood
through the whole white world!
Wash out the shoal,
foaming this very song!

1921

TRANSLATED BY Sibelan Forrester

Translations:

In Markov/Sparks; Obolensky; Yarmolinsky/Deutsch; Yevtushenko.

Konstantin Balmont

Konstantin Dmitrievich Balmont (kun-stahn-TEEN bal'-MONT, 1867-1942) was born in a noble family in a village in the Vladimir region. His last name comes from an old Scottish surname; his mother's family was Tatar. He began writing poetry at nine; his first publication was a collection of poems published in Yaroslavl in 1890. He was expelled from high school for joining a revolutionary circle and finished high school in the regional capital, Vladimir. In 1886 he entered the law faculty of Moscow University, and in 1887 was arrested during student disturbances, expelled and exiled to Shuya. At 22 he tried to commit suicide by jumping out a window. He traveled a great deal, left for Paris after the 1905 Revolution, and published a collection of revolutionary poems there; after that he could not return to Russia until an amnesty in 1913. Balmont was one of the founders of Symbolism, and one of the first Symbolists to become widely popular, with poems published in prestigious "thick" journals such as *Niva* (The Meadow), and a lengthy bibliography of publications. He married twice and had four children. In the early years of the twentieth century he was famous for his love affairs (see the first pages of Khodasevich's "The End of Renata," included in this volume); one notable passion was for the poet Mirra Lokhvitskaya, after whom he named a daughter. His reputation began to decline even in the 1910s as critics became more demanding; his poetry was described as a magnificent translation from an unknown original, though always praised for its musicality. He himself translated poetry from numerous languages; authors he rendered from English included Blake, Poe, Shelley, Whitman, and Wilde. Balmont emigrated to France in 1922 and lived there in poverty, as did most émigré poets; he suffered a gradual mental decline that limited his ability to write and died in 1942.

Verblessness
[Безглагольность]

In the nature of Russia there's some weary tenderness,
The unspeaking pain of a deep-buried sorrow,
Ineluctable grief, voicelessness, endlessness,
A high frozen sky, and horizons unfolding.

Come out here at dawn to the slope of the hillside—
A chill smoking over the shivering river,
The massive pine forest stands darkly, unmoving,
And the heart feels such pain, and the heart is not gladdened.

There the motionless reeds. There the sedge doesn't tremble.
Deep silence. This verblessness lying at rest.
The meadows are running away, far away.
There's exhaustion in everything—all mute and deaf.

Come at sunset, like moving into chilly billows,
To the cool overgrowth of a deep village garden—
The trees are so twilit and strangely unspeaking,
And the heart feels such sadness, the heart is not gladdened.

As if the soul's pleading for something it longs for,
And someone has caused it this undeserved misery.
And the heart keeps on pleading, but the heart begins aching,
And weeps, and it weeps, and it weeps without ceasing.

1900

TRANSLATED BY **Sibelan Forrester**

[Будем как Солнце!]

Let's be like the Sun! Let's forget about who
Is leading us over the roadway of gold,
Let's only remember that we're brightly striving
To reach for the different, the new and the strong,
And to reach for the evil, in our dreams of gold.
Let's always address our prayers to the unearthly
In all of our earthly desiring!
Let us, like the Sun who's eternally young,
Touch the flowers of fire with tender caresses,
The transparent air, and everything golden.
Are you happy? Then may you be happy twice over,
May you be incarnated as quick-risen dream!
Only don't tarry in motionless stillness,
Farther and on, to the line that is hidden,
Farther, we're drawn by the fateful equation
To Eternity, where new blooms flower and flare.
Let us be like the Sun, for the Sun is youthful,
And that is the bidding of beauty!

1902

TRANSLATED BY **Sibelan Forrester**

[Я в этот мир пришел, чтоб видеть Солнце]

I came into this world to see the Sun
And the deep-blue horizon.
I came into this world to see the Sun
And mountain summits.

I came into this world to view the Ocean
And the splendid valley flowers.
I've caught the world up in a single gaze,
For I'm in power.

I've vanquished cold forgetfulness,
With my new-created dream.
I'm every moment filled with revelation,
I always sing.

They awoke my dream of suffering,
But for that I'm loved.
Who's equal to me in my powers of singing?
No one at all, none.

I came into this world to see the Sun,
And if day has fled,
Still I will sing . . . I'll sing about the Sun
The hour before death!

1902

TRANSLATED BY *Sibelan Forrester*

[Я—изысканность русской медлительной речи]

I am the refinement of Russian sluggish utterance,
Other poets before me all warn of my coming,
It was I first uncovered this speech's declivities,
Polyphonally, wrathfully, tenderly tolling.

I'm a sudden fracture,
I'm the playful thunder,
I'm a translucent creek,
I'm for all and I'm no one's.

A multifoamed intersplash, torn-up-continuous,
Stones semi-precious of earth aboriginal,
Sylvan roll-calls in the green month of May—
I'll grasp it all, take it all, steal from the others.

Ever young as a dream,
Mighty, for I'm in love
With myself and with them,
I am—refined verse.

1902

TRANSLATED BY **Sibelan Forrester**

Autumn
[Осень]

Autumn. Dead space. Deepening sorrowful distances.
The ultimate murmur of winds that rustle the leaves.
Why are you not with me, friend, in these nights, in their sorrow?
So many stars shine in them, harbingers of winter snows.

I sit by the window. Restless shutters slightly tremble.
And endlessly, endlessly—somebody's plea in the stovepipe.
On my face rests a kiss—oh, yesterday's, it's still so recent.
Through the woods and the fields, the path of fate stretches away.

Far, far along on the path that was long ago beaten,
The little bell sings, overflowing, and the troika races.
The old house is emptied. Someone pale stands on the threshold.
That man weeping—who is he? Ah, and a yellowed leaf rustles.

This leaf, this leaf . . . It's torn loose, and it flies, it is falling . . .
Twigs beat at the window. Night again. Day again. Night.
I can't bear it. Who is it I hear out there, sobbing so madly?
Please hush. Oh, I beg of you! I cannot, I cannot help you.

Is it you yourself speaking? To yourself—and rejecting yourself?
Little bell, please come back. I'm frightened to stay here with phantoms.
Oh deepest night! Oh, cold autumn! Unspeaking autumn!
This inscrutable fate: to be parted, to suffer and love.

1908

TRANSLATED BY Sibelan Forrester

Translations:
In Markov/Sparks; Obolensky; Yarmolinsky/Deutsch.

Andrei Bely

Andrei Bely ("Andrew White"), pseudonym of Boris Nikolaevich Bugaev (boo-GAH-yiff, 1880-1934), was born in Moscow, where his father was a professor of mathematics at Moscow University. He attended the private Polivanov *Gimnazia*, and he graduated from Moscow University. He was strongly influenced by Vladimir Solovyov, whom he often saw at a neighbor's home in his childhood. Bely published and spoke under his pseudonym but was always addressed as Boris Nikolaevich. From early childhood he loved poetry and music, and he later added interests in philosophy (Nietzsche, Solovyov) and natural science. Among the Symbolists, he was most influenced by Blok, Bryusov, and Gippius, and by Merezhkovsky's "circle of ideas." Later he became a prominent leader of the Symbolists and various other aesthetic and theoretical movements. Bely had a complicated love life, including a triangle with Blok and his wife Lyubov Mendeleeva that left deep traces in the culture of the time, before he married Asya Turgeneva. In 1912-16 he mostly lived abroad, becoming deeply involved with Anthroposophy. Once he returned to Russia, he grew close to Ivanov-Razumnik (pseudonym of Razumnik Ivanov), took part in the "Scythian" literary group, and was active in the Petrograd "Free Philosophical Association" and then the Moscow Proletcult (1918-19), the Narkompros "Teo" group, and the Moscow

"Palace of the Arts." In 1921-1923 he lived in Berlin, and it looked for a time as if he might remain in emigration; this period of his life appears in Tsvetaeva's 1934 "A Captive Spirit." Bely died in January 1934, in Moscow. He wrote significant works in multiple genres and is now probably better known for his novels, *The Silver Dove* (1909) and *Petersburg* (1913-14), his autobiographical *Kotik Letaev* (1914-15), and his many theoretical and scholarly works, more than for his poetry.

Timothy Langen

Vladimir Solovyov
[Владимир Соловьев]
Dedicated to M. S. Solovyov

We choked on everyday vulgarity.
But you called us out into space.
It seemed to them that your unusual voice
sounded as if insane.

And then, when you burned out, tattered
with the great deed you had done,
various and senseless castes
claimed to count you as their own.

Fighting with routine you spent your strength,
without vanquishing oppression . . .
Let the blizzard tear the garland
from your grave with a lengthy moan.

The blizzard's done. Resentment falls silent.
The gloom of night is quiet.
Above the grave the blizzard has swept
the white drifts with delight.

They didn't understand you . . . Through swaying twilight
a scarlet light, tremorous.
Your icon lamp's flame will illuminate
twilight for me. Peacefully rest.

TRANSLATED BY *Sibelan Forrester*

The Sun
[Солнце]

To the author of "Let's Be like the Sun"

The heart's ignited by the sun.
The sun's for eternal striving.
The sun's an eternal window
into a golden blinding.

A rose is in its gold of curls.
The rose tenderly sways.
It pours out in a red heat,
In roses, the gold of rays.

In the poor heart a great deal
of evil is burnt and powdered.
Our souls are the mirrors
that reflect the gold.

1903

TRANSLATED BY **Sibelan Forrester**

Ash
Russia
Despair
[Пепел. Россия. Отчаяние]

to Z. N. Gippius

That's enough: don't wait, don't expect—
My poor people, scatter!
Fall into space and shatter
For year after tortured year!

Ages of want and unfreedom.
Let me in, oh mother-motherland,
To the raw, the deserted openness,
To sob through your openness:

There, on the hunchbacked plain—
Where the green oaks' flock
Is stirred in a rampant multitude
Into the clouds' shaggy lead,

Where Confusion rifles through the field,
Stood up like a dry-armed bush,
And whistles sharply into the wind
With its branchy shred of cloth,

Where they look from the night right into my soul.
Lifted over a net of hummocks,
The severe, the yellow eyes
Of your unreasoning taverns—

Over there—where the untamed track
Of deaths and diseases has passed—
Vanish into space, vanish,
Russia, oh my Russia!

TRANSLATED BY Sibelan Forrester

Hymn to the Sun
[Гимн Солнцу]

Let blind men say our lyres have fallen silent,
Let blind men say death threatens all of us.
That society's idols are subject to it,
That the old ideal's spat on and shattered.
That amid a desert, tormenting inferno
The ray of light we crave won't shine for us,
That we'll perish unredeemed in idleness,
That our path's cloaked in gloom, the light long gone . . .
...
Again the day will come, and it's not far,
When we will touch the iridescent heights.
When with sobs and tears as sweet as honey
The people, seeing the light ahead by night
Will run in ecstasy after these daydreams,
Rush forward, heading for the radiant east.

And a wondrous sun will glance from a distance,
Groans of joy go flying toward the west,
And the toppled cross will solemnly rise again,
And hymns to heaven's thunder start for the east,
And cherubim come flying down toward us.
Before the millions who have bent their knees
Christ will appear from the ignited stormclouds.

TRANSLATED BY **Sibelan Forrester**

Translations:

The Dramatic Symphony and the Forms of Art. Translated by Roger Keys, Angela Keys, and John Wilsworth. New York: Grove Press, 1989.

Petersburg. Translated by John Cournos. New York: Grove Press, 1959; Translated by John E. Malmstad and Robert A. Maguire. Bloomington: Indiana UP, 1978; Translated by David McDuff. London: Penguin, 1995; Translated by John Elsworth. London Pushkin Press, 2009.

Selected Essays of Andrei Bely. Translated by Steven Cassedy. Berkeley: University of California Press, 1985.

In Markov/Sparks; Obolensky; West; Yarmolinky/Deutsch; Yevtushenko.

Biography and Bibliography:

Alexandrov, Vladimir. *Andrei Bely, The Major Symbolist Fiction*. Cambridge, MA: Harvard University Press, 1985.

Cioran, Samuel D. *The Apocalyptic Realism of Andrej Belyj*. The Hague: Mouton, 1973.

Ellsworth, John D. *Andrey Bely, A Critical Study of the Novels*. Cambridge, UK and New York: Cambridge University Press, 1983.

Janacek, Gerald, ed. *Andrei Bely: A Critical Review*. Lexington, KY: University of Kentucky Press, 1978.

Langen, Timothy. *The Stony Dance: Unity and Gesture in Andrey Bely's Petersburg*. Evanston, IL: Northwestern University Press, 2005.

Malmsted, John. *Andrey Bely: Spirit of Symbolism*. Ithaca, NY: Cornell University Press, 1987.

Maslennikov, Oleg. *The Frenzied Poets: Andrey Biely and the Russian Symbolists*. Berkeley: University of California Press, 1952.

Steinberg, Ada. *Word and Music in the Novels of Andrey Bely*. Cambridge, UK and New York: Cambridge University Press, 1982.

Tsvetaeva, Marina. "A Captive Spirit." In *A Captive Spirit: Selected Prose*, translated by J. Marin King, 52-94. Ann Arbor: Ardis Publishers, 1980.

ALEXANDER BLOK

Alexander (Aleksandr) Aleksandrovich Blok (1880-1921) was born in an aristocratic family in St. Petersburg, son of a professor of government law at Warsaw University. One ancestor on his father's side was a physician from Mecklenburg who had attended Tsar Alexei Mikhailovich; Blok's maternal grandfather was the famous botanist Andrei N. Beketov. Blok inherited literary gifts from both parents (his mother and grandmother were outstanding translators, and his aunt was a poet); he began writing at five, then more seriously at eighteen. His first publications were poems written in 1902. Blok was educated in St. Petersburg, at Vvedenskaia *Gimnazia* and Petersburg University, first two years in law, then at the Philological Faculty, graduating in 1906. In 1903 he married Lyubov Mendeleeva, daughter of the famous chemist; she played a significant role in Symbolism as the presumptive incarnation of the Beautiful Lady. Due to Blok's sexual peculiarities (not wanting to besmirch his ideal woman), this marriage was not consummated for two years. Blok, handsome as a poster boy, became the most famous Symbolist poet; new aspiring poets sought Blok out to present him their poetry. He wrote copious verse, successful plays (*The Fair Booth, The Rose and the Cross*), reviews, and *publitsistika*, taking his role as a public intellectual quite seriously. An important example for Blok was the poet Nikolai Nekrasov (1821-1877), whose poetry concentrated on civic topics with attention to urban life, but whose lyrics also treated sexual passion. Blok died in Petrograd in August 1921, partly of starvation, and partly of depression exacerbated by syphilis. If you had to pick one poet to represent the Symbolists, Blok would be the one; many poets of the age measured themselves against him and were devastated by his early death.

Servus—Reginae

Don't send for me. No need to call,
   I'll come inside.
Onto my knees, I'll quickly fall
   Down by your side.

I'll tamely wait for your commands
   And hear them through,
And treasure every single chance
   Of meeting you.

Your servant, and your love, at times.
   Your passion's wave
Has conquered me. And always, I'm—
   Your humble slave.

October 14, 1899

TRANSLATED BY *Andrey Kneller*

[Ты горишь над высокой горою]

You burn bright above a high mountain,
In Your tower unapproachable.
Enrapt, I will hasten to you
To embrace my dream at evening tide.

You will hear me from afar
And will stoke your fire at sundown.
I, Destiny's faithful servant, will come
To grasp the fiery game.

And when shafts of sparks amidst the gloom
Begin to swirl in the smoke—
I will whirl away with the spiraling flames
And will reach You in your tower.

August 18, 1901

TRANSLATED BY *Martha Kelly*

[Девушка пела в церковном хоре]

A young girl sang in a cathedral choir
About all those tired souls in an alien land,
About all the ships that had left for the sea,
About all those who'd forgotten their very own joy.

So sang her voice, floating up to the dome,
And a ray of sun shone on her white shoulder,
And out of the gloom, everyone gazed and everyone listened
As the white gown sang in the ray of sun.

And everyone thought that there would be joy,
That all the ships in the silent bays,
That the tired souls in a faraway land
Had found for themselves a luminous life.

And the voice was sweet, and the ray of sun, soft,
And only above, at the Sacred Gates,
A child, sharing in the secret, sobbed
That no one would ever again return.

August 1905

TRANSLATED BY *Ellen Chances*

Stranger
[Незнакомка]

Above the restaurants, at night,
The deaf and wild air abounds,
The putrid springtime soul presides
Over the drunkards' screams and shouts.

Beyond the dusty countryside
And dachas, out of boredom, sleeping,
The baker's golden pretzel shines
And one can hear a child weeping.

Each night, beyond the lifting gates,
With bowler hats worn to the side,
The wise-guys stroll with pretty dates
Along the ditches, through the night.

Some woman's loud squeal resounds,
The rowlocks screech above the lake,
While in the sky, amidst the clouds,
The pointless crescent glows opaque.

And in my glass, as evening sinks,
My one and only friend's reflected
And with the strange, astringent drink,
Like me, he's humbled and dejected.

The restless lackeys, out of habit,
Sit at the tables, next to us,
The drunkards, with the eyes of rabbits,
Proclaim: "In vino veritas!"

And at a certain hour, nightly,
(Or am I dreaming, in a daze?)
A woman's figure walks by lightly,
Outside the window, through the haze.

Among the drunks, all on her own,
She slowly crosses through the room,
And by the window sits, alone,
Exuding mist and sweet perfume.

An air of something old and grand
Surrounds her presence in the room,
The bracelets on her skinny hand,
Her hat adorned with mourning plumes.

I can't resist it any more,
Entranced, my feelings now prevail,
I see a long, enchanted shore
And spreading valleys through her veil.

Deep secrets are revealed and told,
And someone's sun is in my hands,
And all the corners of my soul,
Are pierced with wine that never ends.

The ostrich tail feathers rise,
And madly sway inside my head,
And someone's blue, unending eyes
Are blooming in a distant land.

A treasure's buried deep inside
My soul, and now, the key is mine!
Hey, drunken creatures, you were right!
I know: the truth is in the wine.

April 24, 1906

TRANSLATED BY **Andrey Kneller**

Second Christening
[Второе крещение]

The blizzards opened wide my door,
My room has now grown cold.
In this new font of snow I'm christened
With a second christening.

I walk into this new world knowing
That there are people, deeds to do.
That the road to heaven may well welcome
All who walk the ways of evil.

I'm tired of my friend's caresses
On this earth that grows so cold.
And the whirlwind's precious gem
Flashes on my brow like ice.

And the pride of my new christening
Has turned my heart to solid ice.
Do you promise me a moment more?
Do you prophesy that spring will come?

But look how glad it makes the heart!
The firmament's blocked out by snow.
There'll be no spring: we don't need one,
For the third christening will be—Death.

January 3, 1907

TRANSLATED BY Martha Kelly

[Дым от костра струею сизой]

The fire is flowing away in smoke,
flowing away in the dusk of day,
while scarlet velvet, a scarlet cloak,
hoods me with sunset in all the grey.

All's false, a greyhair mist flown loose,
all creeps morose with the grief of place,
and like a purple cross the spruce
traces its cross of air on the haze . . .

Friend, at this feasting of evening, let
me keep you with me a moment's breadth,
Forget the old world of dread, forget
the anguish, breathe this ethereal depth.

Look on with sad delight—the length
of sunset is all encroached with smoke.
I'll circle you round with a fence of strength,
with the ring of my arms, with a ring of oak.

With encircling hands I'll fence you close,
in a living circle, a closing ring,
and we shall flow, like the smoke flown loose,
Like greyhair mist—in a scarlet ring.

August 1909

TRANSLATED BY *Angela Livingstone*

[Холодный ветер от лагуны]

A cold wind blows from the lagoon.
The silent tombs of gondolas.
Tonight I lie, young and sick,
Prostrate before a lion's pillar.

In the tower, with cast-iron song,
Giants beat the midnight hour.
Mark drowned in the moonlit lagoon
His patterned iconostasis.

In shadows of a palace arcade
That the moon has barely lit,
Salome passes, melts away,
and with her, too, my bloody head.

All sleeps—palaces, people, canals;
Just sliding steps of phantom feet,
Just a head on a black platter
Gazing out into the gloom.

August–October 1909

TRANSLATED BY Martha Kelly

[Ночь, улица, фонарь, аптека]

Night. A street light, a drugstore,
A street. A vacuous shadowy light.
Live five, ten, fifteen years more—
Nothing will change. There's no way out.

Die, you only start over
And it's all the same as before:
Night, ice in the dark gutter,
The street, the street light, the store.

October 10, 1912

TRANSLATED BY Paul Schmidt

[Красота страшна, вам скажут]
> *To Anna Akhmatova*

"Beauty is frightening," they will tell you—
And you will lazily toss
That Spanish shawl over your shoulder,
A red rose in your hair.

"Beauty is simple," they will tell you—
And you will clumsily cover
Your child with that gaudy shawl,
The red rose on the floor.

But listening distractedly
To all the words that echo 'round you,
You'll ponder sadly
And then decide:

"I'm not frightening, and I'm not simple.
I'm not so frightening you'd want me dead;
I'm not so simple that I don't know
Just how frightening life is."

December 16, 1913

TRANSLATED BY Martha Kelly

The Twelve (an excerpt)
[Двенадцать]

    I.

Black night.
White snow.
Windy outside!
A man can't withstand the blow.
Windy outside—
On God's earth, world-wide!

The wind weaves
White snow.
There's ice—below.
Slippery, startling,
Anywhere you go—
You'll slip—poor darling!

Throughout the city,
They've stretched a line.
On the line—a sign:
"All power to the Constituent Committee!"
An old woman slips, weeping,
Can't comprehend the meaning,
Who needs this charade,
Such large signs and flags?
How many shawls could be made
For the kids wearing rags . . .

Like a hen, the old one, reckless,
Steps through the snow-bank, brave.
"Oh, Mother of God—Our Protectress!"
"Those Bolsheviks will be my grave!"

The chill bites to the very bone!
And the winds holler!
The bourgeois on the corner, alone,
Tucks his nose in the collar.

And who's this?—A long haired mister
Speaking in half a whisper:
   "Russia has died now!"
   "Traitors!"
Must be a writer—
   Orator...

   And wearing a cassock, another
   Sidesteps, disappears in the trees...
   I see that you're in a pother,
   Eh, comrade priest?

   Remember, not long ago,
   How your belly stuck out
   Casting a blinding glow
   With its cross on the crowd?

   A lady wrapped in fur, in stride,
   With another conversed:
   "We cried and we cried..."
   She barely slipped, at first,
   and then—bang—head first!

      Oh my! Oh my!
      "Pull me up!" She cried.

      The mad wind gloats
      And doesn't decline.

      It twists the hems of the coats
      Mowing the passersby.
      It mangles, and rips from the sky
      The large placard sign:

"All power to the Constituent Committee!"
         And echoes of words fly by:

"... We too had a meeting...
 "... Right here, in this building..."
 "... We discussed and agreed—
 "To this decree:
"Ten rubles an hour, twenty-five for the night...
 "... Any less won't slide."
 "... Let's sleep." "All right."

 It's getting late now.
 The streets are clear.
 A vagrant stray
 Just stoops in fear,
 And winds grow greater...

 Oh, poor thing, hey!
 I'll kiss you—
 Here...

 Bread!
 What's there?
 Move along! Ahead!

A pitch-black sky hangs overhead.

A pitch-black, grievous spite
  Inside, begins to seethe...
A pitch-black, heavenly spite...

 Comrade! Keep
 Your eyes wide!

January 1918

TRANSLATED BY **Andrey Kneller**

Translations:

Alexander Blok's Trilogy of Lyric Dramas. Translated and edited by Timothy Westfalen. London, New York: Routledge, 2003.

The Stranger: Selected Poetry by Alexander Blok. Translated by Andrey Kneller. CreateSpace Individual Publishing Platform, 2011.

See also Lucy Vogel, below.

In Chandler/Mashinski/Dralyuk; Glad/Weissbort; Mager; Markov/Sparks; Muchnik/Shafarenko; Nabokov; Obolensky; Schmidt/Ciepiela; West; Yarmolinsky/Deutsch; Yevtushenko.

Biography:

Berberova, Nina. *Alexander Blok: A Life.* Translated by Robyn Marsack. New York: George Brazillier, 1996.

Pyman, Avril. *The Life of Alexander Blok.* Oxford, UK and New York: Oxford University Press, 1978.

Bibliography:

Goldberg, Stuart. *Mandelstam, Blok, and the Boundaries of Mythopoetic Symbolism.* Columbus, OH: The Ohio State University Press, 2011.

Forsyth, James. *Listening to the Wind: An Introduction to Alexander Blok.* Oxford, UK: W. A. Meeuws, 1977.

Presto, Jenifer. *Beyond the Flesh: Alexander Blok, Zinaida Gippius, and the Symbolist Sublimation of Sex.* Madison, WI: University of Wisconsin Press, 2008.

Sloane, David A. *Alexander Blok and the Dynamics of the Lyric Cycle.* Columbus, OH: Slavica Publshers, 1988.

Vogel, Lucy E. *Alexander Blok: The Journey to Italy, with English Translations of the Poems and Prose Sketches on Italy.* Ithaca: Cornell University Press, 1973.

VALERY BRYUSOV

Valery Yakovlevich Bryusov (vah-LAY-ree YAH-kuv-lee-vich BRYOO-suff, LoC Valerii Briusov, 1873-1924) was born in Moscow in a merchant family. His father's father had been a serf, while his mother's family were townspeople, almost middle class, and fond of literature. Bryusov received a good education, including science and economics as well as literature. He graduated from Moscow University, traveled a great deal in Russia and abroad. Bryusov started writing as a child, first novels à la Jules Verne and "scientific" articles, then poems "in the spirit of Nekrasov." His first serious publication was a series of poems in the collection "Russian Symbolists" in 1894. Bryusov's ambition as a young man was to start a literary movement, and he indeed became a leader of the Symbolist school, especially its Decadent strand. He was active in the Skorpion publishing house, in the journals *Libra* and *Russian Thought*, and also in the work of the Literary-Artistic Circle. He wrote poetry, prose, criticism, and translations. His novel *The Fiery Angel* (1908; see Khodasevich's "The End of Renata" later in this volume) made a great splash. After the October 1917 Revolution, Bryusov (an opportunist, or always a bit of a leftist, or both) joined the Communist Party and became a founding Soviet literary bureaucrat and censor. He died in Moscow in 1924. Bryusov was also important as a translator, and he rediscovered and reprinted important earlier poets such as Karolina Pavlova; the man was busy all the time. His poetry is still read, though mostly as an example of certain trends in Symbolism and less for its own sake; he is considered less important now as a poet, though still recognized as an important literary figure.

[Как царство белого снега]

Like a kingdom of whitest snow
My soul is cold and still.
What strange and wondrous bliss
In a world of cold, still dream!
Like a kingdom of whitest snow
My soul is cold and still.

Pale shadows pass us by,
They look like wizards' charms,
Here oaths and penalties resound,
And words of love and of victory...
Pale shadows pass us by,
They look like wizards' charms.

While I, unchanging, forever
Say prayers to unearthly beauty;
I have yielded to that cold dream,
And the world's woes cannot touch me.
I have yielded to that dream—forever
I say prayers to unearthly beauty.

March 23, 1896

TRANSLATED BY *Martha Kelly*

To Z. N. Gippius
[Неколебимой истине]

I have long disbelieved in
Truth that will not give way;
All oceans and all heavens
I love, I love the same.

I wish for my free vessel
To set sail everywhere,
And both God and the Devil
I glorify in my prayer.

When, all in white enshrouded,
I pass to sleep, let me
Dream, one after another,
Every abyss and bay.

December 1901

TRANSLATED BY **Sibelan Forrester**

Dagger
[Кинжал]

> *Else never at voice of vengeance*
> *Will you tear your wedge from golden knives . . .*
> M. Lermontov

Torn from among the knives, it flashes in your eyes,
Just as in bygone days, sharp and finely honed.
A poet is with the people whenever thunder sounds,
A song is always sister to the storm.

When I could see no sign of bravery or strength,
When you still bowed your head, wordless, beneath the yoke,
I made out for that country of silence and of graves
In ages now mysteriously bygone.

How much I loathed the cast of all this earthly life,
Its shameful, petty order, its ugliness, injustice;
Yet at the call of battle, I merely laughed at times,
No faith had I in those meek cries.

But at the faintest sound of that awaited trumpet,
At the quickest glimpse of fiery banners unfurling,
I will yell in answer, I, the song of battle,
I will echo the horizon's thunder.

Dagger of poetry! A bloody streak of lightning
Has coursed as once before along your faithful steel.
Once more I'm with the people because I am a poet,
Because the lightning flashed anew.

1903

TRANSLATED BY Martha Kelly

To the Poet
[Поэту]

You must be as proud as any banner,
You must be whetted as a sword.
Your cheeks must be singed, like Dante's,
By the tongues of an underground fire.

Be a frigid observer of everything,
Directing your gaze at it all.
And may your constant virtue be
Readiness to mount the pyre.

Perhaps all of life's just a pretext
For dazzlingly musical verse,
And starting in untroubled childhood
You must seek combinations of words.

In moments of amorous clutching,
Make yourself stay dispassionate,
And in the hour of cruel crucifixions,
Hymn your frenzied ecstasies.

In morning dreams and the depths of evening
Hunt for what Fate whispers to you,
And keep in mind that for all eternity
The poet's sacred crown has been of thorns.

1907

TRANSLATED BY **Sibelan Forrester**
(WITH THANKS **to Boris Dralyuk**)

Translations:

The Republic of the Southern Cross, and Other Stories. Translator unknown. Westport, CT: Hyperion Press, 1918, 1977.

In Chandler/Mashinski/Dralyuk; Markov/Sparks; Obolensky; Yarmolinsky/Deutsch; Yevtushenko.

Biography and Bibliography:

The Diary of Valery Bryusov. Edited and translated by Joan Delaney Grossman. Berkeley: University of California Press, 1980.

Sergei Esenin

Sergei Aleksandrovich Esenin (yee-SAY-neen, 1895-1925) was born in a village in the Ryazan region, in a poor peasant family. He was raised by a grandfather who was better off than his parents were. Esenin was a good student, graduating from the local school at sixteen; they expected him to enter the pedagogical institute in Moscow and become a teacher. He started writing poems at nine, growing more serious in his late teens. In 1912 he moved to Moscow, where he worked as a shop assistant, and in 1915 to Petersburg, where he became friendly with Klyuev. Esenin began publishing in 1914 and soon enjoyed success, learning a great deal from Blok and Klyuev and eventually meeting the royal family. During the war he traveled extensively, and despite his leftist tendencies (not surprising given his work experience and life as a penniless beginning poet) he adopted the persona of a "hooligan," drunk and problematic during the first years of Soviet power. Esenin was married briefly to Isadora Duncan (he was twenty-six, she was forty-four), but this too failed to turn his life around. His suicide in Leningrad in late December 1925 provoked a rash of copycat suicides; Mayakovsky wrote a famous poem addressing Esenin, intended to dissuade others. Esenin is buried in Moscow at Vagankovo Cemetery. His musical and generally unpretentious verse is still widely beloved by Russian readers, especially those who share his village background or are less drawn to more intellectual poetry.

[Нивы сжаты, рощи голы]

The fields are cut, the groves are bare,
Fog and damp from the water.
Like a wheel the quiet sun's
Rolled down behind the blue of hills.

The ploughed-up road is fast asleep.
Today it had a dream
That hardly any time remains
'Til grey-haired winter comes.

Ah, I, too, in the sonorous woods
Saw in yesterday's fog:
Like a colt with rusty coat
The moon was harnessed to our sleigh.

1917

TRANSLATED BY Martha Kelly

[Я последний поэт деревни]
To Mariengof

I am the last country poet,
A plank bridge of modest songs.
I stand up for the farewell service,
When birches swing censers of leaves.
The candle will burn up with golden flame
Fueled by its body of wax,
And the wooden clock of the moon
Will screech out my twelfth hour.
Soon an iron guest will come out
On the path of the pale blue field;
Sunset will spill onto grains of oat,
His black cupped hand will gather them up.
You other hands, not living hands,
May these songs not live in your presence!
But the ears of grain, like horses,
Will mourn for their old master.
The wind will suck at their neighing
As it turns in a requiem dance.
Soon, soon the wooden clock
Will screech out my twelfth hour!

1920

TRANSLATED BY Martha Kelly

Translations:

Confessions of a Hooligan: Fifty Poems by Sergei Esenin. Translated by Geoffrey Thurley. Cheadle Hulme, UK: Carcanet Press, 1973.

In Chandler/Mashinski/Dralyuk; Glad/Weissbort; Mager; Markov/Sparks; Muchnik/Shafarenko; Obolensky; Schmidt/Ciepiela; Yarmolinsky/Deutsch; Yevtushenko.

Biography and Bibliography:

Mariengof, Anatoly. *A Novel without Lies.* Moscow: GLAS New Russian Writing, 2000.

McVay, Gordon. *Esenin: A Life.* Ann Arbor: Ardis Publishers, 1976.

Zinaida Gippius

Zinaida Nikolaevna Gippius (also spelled Hippius; Zee-nah-EE-duh GEE-pee-oos, 1869-1945) was a major Russian Symbolist poet, playwright, and fiction writer; she also wrote criticism using the male pseudonyms Anton Krainii (Anthony "The Extreme") and Tovarishch German (Comrade Herman), among others. She was a regular contributor to leading literary journals of the period, as well as to *Mir Iskusstva* (World of Art), and she played a crucial role in the Religious-Philosophical Meetings, which helped foster a religious renaissance in Russia at the beginning of the twentieth century. Together with her husband, writer Dmitri Merezhkovsky, she ran an influential literary salon in St. Petersburg and later in Paris, where they were in exile following the 1917 Revolution, living in an apartment they had bought earlier. Although Gippius worked in a number of genres, she is best known for her poetry, which is characterized by innovative metrical schemes, a metaphysical longing for "that not of this world," and a preference for an unmarked, masculine voice. Of her eschewal of femininity in her writing, she reported that she desired to write "like a human being, and not just like a woman." While Gippius's masking of her sex in her writing and her stylization as a female dandy in the salon reflect the fascination with androgyny in fin-de-siècle Russian literary and artistic circles, many of her critics and contemporaries intimated that it was rooted in her unique physiology. The notion that Gippius may have been a hermaphrodite gained currency in her day and continues to be seriously discussed. In recent years, much scholarship on the poet in both Russia and the West has focused on her unconventional gender practices and on her idiosyncratic form of Symbolist self-creation or *zhiznetvorchestvo*.

JENIFER PRESTO

Delight
[Отрада]

My friend, I am not tormented by doubt.
Long have I felt how close death is to me.
I know that when they lay me in the tomb
It will be damp and suffocating, dark.

Not in the ground, though—I'll be here with you,
I'll be in the wind's breath, in the sun's rays,
And I'll be in the sea, as a pale wave,
And as a cloudy shadow in the heavens.

Earth's sweetness will be alien to me then,
Even earth's sadness, so dear to my heart,
As strange as joy and gladness to the stars . . .
Yet knowing this occasions no regret,

I long for peace . . . My soul has grown so weary . . .
Mother-nature calls me to herself . . .
How easy, how the weight of life has vanished . . .

1889

TRANSLATED BY Martha Kelly

Snow
[Снег]

Once more it falls, so marvelously silent,
   It gently hesitates and then sinks down...
Ah, what delight the heart finds in its happy flight!
   No form or substance, yet it is reborn.

Here it all is again, its provenance unknown,
   In it temptation's chill, in it oblivion...
I wait for it always as I await God's wonders,
   I find in it a solitude most strange.

Once more it leaves, and yet I do not fear its loss.
   Its enigmatic parting gives me joy.
I will eternally await its reticent return,
   Oh you, my tender one, oh you my only.

How silently it falls, both powerful and slow...
   Its victory my source of endless gladness...
Oh splendid snow, of all earth's wonders it is you
   I love... Why I love you, I do not know.

1897

TRANSLATED BY Martha Kelly

Curse
[Заклинание]

Gouge yourselves out, disobedient spirits,
Come apart, intractable bonds,
Come asunder, you stifling dungeons,
Lie down, whirlwinds, insatiable and black.

The secret is forbidden and formidable.
There are vows one never must undo.
Human blood is sacrosanct:
One never must reveal blood to the sun.

May it split open whole in imprecation!
Fly apart, you clouds of agitation!

Beat, oh heart, each one separately,
Resurrect, oh liberated spirit!

1905

TRANSLATED BY Martha Kelly

She
[Она]

In her unscrupulous and wretched nastiness,
She's gray as dust motes, as the grit of being.
And I am dying from her too-close ghastliness,
Her stubborn clinginess.... her bond with me.

She's scabrous, scratchy—and she's pointy, prickly—
She's cold and clammy—she's a slinky snake.
I'm sorely wounded by her jagged-slippery,
Repulsive-scorching, scaly-sly physique.

O, how I long to feel her stinger stabbing me!
But she is clumsy, she is blunted, soft.
She hangs so heavily, she droops so flaccidly,
And there's no access to her—she is deaf.

Caressing, twining round me, sweetly obstinate,
She strangulates me with her oozing coils.
And this dead creature, yes this black monstrosity,
This gruesome fantasy is called—my soul.

1905

TRANSLATED BY Alyssa Dinega Gillespie

Translations:

Between Paris and St. Petersburg: Selected Diaries of Zinaida Hippius. Edited and translated by Temira Pachmuss. Urbana: University of Illinois Press, 1975.
Selected Works of Zinaida Hippius. Edited and translated by Temira Pachmuss. Urbana: University of Illinois Press, 1972.
In Chandler/Mashinski/Dralyuk; Kelly; Markov/Sparks; Obolensky; Pachmuss 1978; Tomei; Yevtushenko.

Biography and Bibliography:

Matich, Olga. *The Religious Poetry of Zinaida Gippius*. Munich: Fink, 1972.

Pachmuss, Temira. *Zinaida Hippius: An Intellectual Profile*. Carbondale: Southern Illinois University Press, 1971.

Presto, Jenifer. *Beyond the Flesh: Alexander Blok, Zinaida Gippius, and the Symbolist Sublimation of Sex*. Madison, WI: University of Wisconsin Press, 2008.

Zlobin, Vladimir. *A Difficult Soul: Zinaida Gippius*. Berkeley: University of California Press, 1980.

NIKOLAI GUMILYOV

Nikolai Stepanovich Gumilyov (goo-mee-LYOFF, 1886-1921; LoC Gumilëv) was born in Kronstadt, near St. Petersburg, the son of a naval doctor. He graduated from the *gimnazia* in Tsarskoe Selo in 1906 while Annensky was principal there. Gumilyov attended the Sorbonne in Paris, then the Philological Faculty of St. Petersburg University, taking classes until 1914, when he volunteered for the army. He married Anna Akhmatova in 1910 after courting her for several years; the couple had one son, who was raised by Gumilyov's mother. Gumilyov began writing poetry as a child; his first book was *Path of the Conquistadores*, published in 1905, while he was still at the *gimnazia*. He was active in Symbolist circles before becoming a founder of the Poets' Guild or Acmeists in 1911, in part as a way to move beyond the poetic and philosophical concerns of the Symbolists. He traveled to exotic places, which supplied material for his poetry. He remarried after his separation from Akhmatova. Gumilyov became a very influential critic as well as a poet and translator; later readers and scholars have tended to agree with his judgments on the authors and the literary scene of his time. His reputation as a poet has been somewhat overshadowed by his fellow Acmeists, Akhmatova and Mandelstam, but also by the circumstances of his death in August 1921, when he was shot for supposed participation in a monarchist plot (see Irina Odoevtseva's memoir of him in the prose section). Though this seems more plausible than many of the official reasons given for the state's killing or repressing poets in the USSR, it kept his writing largely out of public discourse in Russia until the Thaw period, and not much of his work was republished in Russia until the late 1980s.

Giraffe
[Жираф]

Today I can see that your gaze is especially sad;
Your hands are especially slender, encircling your knees.
But listen to this: far away, far away, near Lake Chad
A giraffe paces elegantly.

A figure of grace and a lifetime of bliss are his boon,
And a magical pattern adorns his magnificent hide,
Which no one would dare to compare with, except for the moon
As it glitters and sways on the lakes that are misty and wide.

From afar he might look like a ship's billowed sails painted bright,
And his gait is as smooth as the jubilant winging of birds.
I know the earth witnesses many a marvelous sight,
When at sunset he hides in the grotto of marble unheard.

I know the gay tales of mysterious realms, and the songs
Of an African maiden, of a young baron's passion and pain;
But you have been breathing this slumberous fog much too long,
You will not believe, not in anything, save for the rain.

So how can I tell you my tales of that tropical land,
The slim, bending palm trees, the scent of unthinkable green? . . .
—You weep? Well, then listen to this . . . far away, near Lake Chad
A giraffe paces elegantly.

1907

TRANSLATED BY *Alyssa Dinega Gillespie*

Adam
[Адам]

Adam, humiliated Adam,
Your face is pale, your gaze possessed.
Are you still grieving for those fruits
You plucked when you were sinless yet?

Are you still grieving for that time
When, still a maiden, still a child,
At fragrant noontime on a hill
Eve danced before you, innocent?

But now you know laborious work
And how the scent of death wafts in;
You know the fury of each minute
That brings to mind the words, "Too late."

And fiercest pain, and awful shame,
Unquenchable and passionless,
That torments you exquisitely,
Voluptuously tortures you.

In paradise you were a tsar,
And honor was your guarantee.
The haughty pay threefold in pain
For happiness of bygone days.

Because you were not like a corpse,
You burned, you searched, you were deceived.
In heaven high the trumpet choirs
Will never cease to groan your name.

Be steady in your lot severe,
Be sullen, pale, and bow your head,
But grieve no longer for those fruits
Contemptible and unredeemed.

1910

TRANSLATED BY *Martha Kelly*

Animal Tamer
[Укротитель зверей]

> ... How beautiful my red umbrella
> Scoured with the grit of shoes.
> Anna Akhmatova

Once more I tread a path I know by heart,
Boldly approaching the threshold of promise;
Just past the doors, beasts are waiting for me,
Motley beasts behind strong bars.

They'll roar, and my whip will scare them,
They'll be more treacherous than ever today.
Or more submissive... what do I care?
I'm young, and my blood is hot.

Yet... I am seeing more and more often
(I see and know it's delirium)
A wonderful beast who is not really there,
He is golden, six-winged, ever silent.

Long he observes me with vigilant eye,
Watches each movement I make,
He never plays with the other beasts there,
He never comes out for his food.

If I am to die the death of a tamer
In the arena, I know that this beast—
A beast that the audience never will see—
Will be the first one to attack me.

Fanny, the flower you gave me has faded,
You're as happy as ever up there on your cable;
My beast, who lies dozing right by your bed,
Looks into your eyes like a faithful dog.

1911

TRANSLATED BY Martha Kelly

The Word
[Слово]

God had bowed his face one day to look
On his new world, when, like a lightning flash,
The sun came to a halt, stopped by a word,
And by a word the cities were destroyed.

Eagles ceased the beating of their wings,
Stars huddled near the moon in terror
If they sensed the word come sailing past,
A rosy flame in flight across the heavens.

Baser life relied on sums and figures,
Like docile cattle underneath the yoke;
And we know that clever sums and figures
Best convey all subtleties of meaning.

The graying patriarch who had subdued
Good and evil underneath his hand
Feared the power of sound and drew instead
Figures in the sand with his own cane.

We forgot, though, that the word alone
Shines amidst the troubles of the world,
And that in the Gospel of St. John
It is said the Word is God himself.

We have used reality's scant bounds
To set around the Word our meager limits.
And, like bees in an abandoned hive,
Dead words waft a rank scent of decay.

1919

TRANSLATED BY Martha Kelly

Translations:

Swan Songs: Akhmatova and Gumilev. Edited and translated by Frances Laird. Bloomington, IN: First Books, 2002.

In Chandler/Mashinski/Dralyuk; Glad/Weissbort; Markov/Sparks; Muchnik/Shafarenko; Natchez; Obolensky; Yarmolinsky/Deutsch; Yevtushenko.

Biography and Bibliography:

Strakhovsky, Leonid I. *Craftsmen of the Word: Three Poets of Modern Russia: Gumilyov, Akhmatova, Mandelstam.* Westport, CT: Greenwood Press, 1949, 1969.

Vyacheslav Ivanov

Vyacheslav Ivanovich Ivanov (ee-VAH-nuff, 1866-1949) was born in Moscow, the son of a surveyor who died early. He started writing poetry and novels in school. He was always the top pupil in the *gimnazia* and particularly loved classical Greek and Latin. At the Philological Faculty of Moscow University he won a prize for his work in ancient languages and graduated in only two years. He traveled to France, Germany, and Italy and became an admirer of Nietzsche. In 1895, after divorcing his first wife, he began a relationship with the writer Lidia Zinovieva-Annibal, whom Ivanov credited with his flowering as a poet. In 1899 they were married (against church prescriptions for the divorced), and he completed his doctoral dissertation in history. In 1905 he and the family moved to St. Petersburg, and Ivanov at once became a central figure among the Symbolists. He wrote some of the seminal theoretical works of Symbolism, and as both a scholar and a writer had particular influence on their perceptions of classical culture. He shaped the syncretic religious aesthetic of the Silver Age through his own writings and ritual experiments, and he was an important poetic mentor to younger poets (see for example Mandelstam's letters to Ivanov in the prose section), with deep erudition and exquisite manners. His Petersburg residence, known as "the Tower," became one of the most important and well-known salons of the Russian twentieth century, attracting actors, musicians, philosophers, scholars, and writers of all kinds. For quite a while Kuzmin lived in the ménage, and Ivanov and Zinovieva-Annibal experimented with the shape of their marriage as well. After her death in 1907, Ivanov married Zinovieva-Annibal's daughter Vera Shvarsalon, his stepdaughter, who was then fifteen years old. After the 1917 Revolution he worked in Moscow in cultural institutions, then taught at Baku University, but eventually emigrated to Western Europe and died in Rome in 1949.

The Alpine Horn
[Альпийский рог]

In mountains far away I met a shepherd
Who blew into a long alpine horn.
His song flowed pleasingly; yet this loud horn
Was but an instrument meant to wake
A captivating echo in the mountains.

And every time the shepherd made small sounds
And waited for the echo in response,
It carried through the passes with the most
Unutterably sweet accord.

It seemed an unseen choir of spirits was
Translating on unearthly instruments
In heaven's speech the language of the earth.

And so I thought, "Oh, genius! how this horn
Must sing the song of earth to rouse in hearts
Another song. Blessed is he who hears."
And from the hills another voice called out,
"Nature's a symbol, like this horn. It calls
For a response, and that response is God.
Blessed, who hears the song and the response."

1902

TRANSLATED BY Martha Kelly

Translations:

Freedom and the Tragic Life: A Study in Dostoevsky. Translated by Norman Cameron, S. Konovalov, and Cecil Maurice Bowra. New York: Noonday Press, 1952.

Selected Essays. Translated and edited by Robert Bird and Michael Wachtel. Evanston, IL: Northwestern University Press, 2001.

In Glad/Weissbort; Markov/Sparks; Obolensky; Yarmolinsky/Deutsch; Yevtushenko.

Biography and Bibliography:

Bird, Robert. *The Russian Prospero: The Creative Universe of Vyacheslav Ivanov.* Madison: University of Wisconsin Press, 2006.

Davidson, Pamela. *The Poetic Imagination of Vyacheslav Ivanov: A Russian Symbolist's Perception of Dante.* Cambridge, UK and New York: Cambridge University Press, 1989.

Jackson, Robert Louis, and Lowry Nelson. *Vyacheslav Ivanov: Poet, Critic, Philosopher.* New Haven, CT and Columbus, OH: Yale Center for International and Area Studies, 1986.

Wachtel, Michael. *Russian Symbolism and Literary Tradition: Goethe, Novalis, and the Poetics of Vyacheslav Ivanov.* Madison, WI: University of Wisconsin Press, 1994.

West, James D. *Russian Symbolism: A Study of Vyacheslav Ivanov and the Russian Symbolist Aesthetic.* London: Methuen, 1970.

VELIMIR KHLEBNIKOV

Velimir (sometimes Velemir; born Viktor Vladimirovich) Khlebnikov (KHLYEB-nee-kuff, 1885-1922) was born in the Kalmyk steppe, near Saratov. As a small child he moved to a prince's estate in Volhynia, then to a village in the Simbirsk region. He studied at the *gimnazia* in Kazan and was always a good student, especially in mathematics. He began university in Kazan but became interested in politics in 1905 and moved to St. Petersburg, then dropped out of the university there and got involved in literature. Khlebnikov began writing in 1903 and became one of the founders of Russian Futurism. His first publications were the plays *The Marquise Dedes* and *The Iron Horse* in the collection *A Trap for Judges*, 1908-09. After living in St. Petersburg from 1905 to 1910, he moved to Moscow (1912-15). Khlebnikov was a quiet and gentle person, but he could be aroused when he sensed injustice; he climbed on stage to protest and had to be forcibly removed from the hall when Filippo Marinetti (visiting Russia) claimed to have invented Futurism. Khlebnikov was a master of linguistic invention, and his poetic works have attracted a great deal of scholarly attention in the West as well as in Russia. Unlike most Futurists, he mined archaic language material, pagan folk traditions, and neologisms based on recognizable word roots, more than urban scenes and new technology. After the 1917 Revolution he traveled more, living precariously; see Mayakovsky's obituary of him in this volume. In 1922 he returned from Persia almost a beggar and died of blood poisoning in a village outside Novgorod. Khlebnikov left a mass of unpublished manuscripts—about a thousand poems and perhaps a hundred long narrative poems, tales, and plays. Some of this material was eventually published by his friends. Khlebnikov also worked on a theory of poetic language and created an idiosyncratic system using mathematical laws to study universal history. During his life most of his work was published not in books but in various collections, almanacs, and journals, and much was lost. Although the basis in nature (with plants, birds, insects, and animals) and sometimes ecstatic, shamanic tone of Khlebnikov's verse can make his poetry seem timeless or transcendental, he also wrote political criticism and pointed antiwar poetry.

[Мы чураемся и чаруемся]

We chant and enchant,
oh charming enchantment!
No raving, no ranting,
no canting enchantment!
This ranting enchantress
has cast her enchantment—
we see what her chant meant!
Here rant! There cant!
You charming enchanter,
cast out her enchantment,
uncast it, uncant it,
discount it, discant it,
descant: Decant! Recant!
He can't. She can't.
Why can't she recant?
Why can't he uncant?
Ranting chanting,
no recanting.
Discant, descant.

1908

TRANSLATED BY **Paul Schmidt**

Velimir Khlebnikov

[Бо-бэ-о-би пелись губы]

Bo-beh-óh-bee is the lipsong
Veh-eh-óh-me is the eyesong
Pee-eh-éh-oh is the eyebrowsong
Lee-eh-éh-ay is the looksong
Gzee-gzee-gzéh-oh is the chainsong
On the canvas of such correspondences
somewhere beyond all dimensions
the face has a life of its own

1908-1909

TRANSLATED BY *Paul Schmidt*

Grasshopper
[Кузнечик]

Glitter-letter wing-winker
gossamer grasshopper
packs his belly-basket
with credo-meadow grass.
Zin! Zin! Zin! sings
the raucous racket-bird!
Swan-white wonder!
Brighter, brighter, bright!

1908-1909

TRANSLATED BY *Paul Schmidt*

Incantation by Laughter
[Заклятие смехом]

Hlaha! Uthlofan, lauflings!
Hlaha! Uflofan, lauflings!
Who laughen with lafe, who hlaehen lewchly,
Hlaha! Uflofan hlouly!
Hlaha! Hloufish lauflings lafe, hlohan utlaufly!
Lawfen, lawfen,
Hloh, hlouh, hlou! Luifekin, luifekin,
hlofeningumm, hlofeningum.
Hlaha! Utlofan, lauflings!
Hlaha! Uflofan, lauflings!

1908-1909

TRANSLATED BY **Paul Schmidt**

To Vladimir Vladimirovich Mayakovsky
[Владимиру Владимировичу Маяковскому]

Three V's, three M's, three words—
Your name towers over your father's!
Tall as a teamster
You chew up the steel of silence!
Cracking away with a whip of words,
you stampede nations in nervous tandems!

TRANSLATED BY **Paul Schmidt**

[Зеленый леший — бух лесиный]

A goblin grabbles in the greeny forest—
Wood-willy, slurping his mouth-organ—
where a clump of aspens quivers
and benefolent spruces cascade.

A smear of pungent forest honey
licky on the tongue-tip of daylight;
Oh! His grasping arms were icy:
I was completely taken in.

I couldn't stand his eyes' unblinking
point-blank confrontation—
his look, full of pleading promises,
the icicle anguish in his eyes.

Lawn-rake fingers crabbing at me
from a shaky clump of catkins;
he had dark blue sighters
and a body all mush-flesh and flow.

I had missed a turn or two, tearing
along in a juveny frenzy. Slying,
the wood-wart winked and jostled
me: "Which way where? And why?"

1912?

TRANSLATED BY Paul Schmidt

[Где волк воскликнул кровью (part 7 of "Война в мышеловке")]

"Hey!" the wolf cries out in blood,
"I eat the meat of strong young men!"
And a mother says, "My sons are gone."
But we are your elders! *We* decide!

Anyway, young men are cheaper nowadays,
no? Dirt-cheap slop-cheap, coal-chute-cheap!
Pale apparition, scything our man-crop,
sinews all sunburst, be proud of your work!

"Come get your young men, your dead men,"
the city wails along its streets,
wails like the barrow-boy hawking his birds—
new feathers for all your caps!

A man who once wrote "Last Deer Songs"
now hangs beside a silver rabbit pelt,
trussed up by the knees, in the larder
next to the meat and eggs and cream!

Consolidated's up and Petroleum is down
but the young man is gone, the dark-eyed king
of our talk after dinner is gone,
and we loved him and needed him, understand?

1915

TRANSLATED BY *Paul Schmidt*

[Татлин, тайновидец лопастей]

Tatlin!* Poet of propellers,
austere oracle of airflow!
One of the Sun-catchers!
His unmoving hand twists spider-
rigging into a horseshoe curve!
Giant forceps of imagination!
Dumb-struck blind men stare
at what he shows us.
Inaugural, unheard-of,
these tracings of metalwork miracles!

1916

TRANSLATED BY Paul Schmidt

---

* Refers to the artist Vladimir Tatlin (1885-1953).

[Сегодня строгою боярыней Бориса Годунова]

Unbending as Boris Godunov's boyarina,
you sailed on past today, swan on a lake,
And I'd been expecting as much, I suppose.
I hadn't read daybreak's letter over.

But remember, once you were really divine,
the goddess of this place, all-knowing and passionate,
your braids like evening doves descending
to perch on your suntanned shoulders.

It really was you! You hid in the rye field,
rusalka-like, playing the lyre-strings of your braids.
It really was you! To make yourself beautiful
you oiled your body with honey, enchanting the bees...

Their golden beads
you wore like jewels,
on face and eyes and hair.
You taught your voice to punctuate
with the commas of bee-bites,
unwilling to quarrel with joy.

Here Our Lady walks the rye field,
moves at night through fields of rye;
here I grew to feel as I feel
and became no longer I.

Here had no "yes," will have no "but"—
what was is forgotten; what will be, who knows?
Here the dove descends at teatime
and Our Lady lays her washing out in rows.

1916, 1922

TRANSLATED BY **Paul Schmidt**

Excerpt from ZANGEZI
[Зангези]

They are the bright blue stilland,
The sky full of bright blue eye-fall.
Never-never fleeing things
Whispering on irrelevant wings.
Ledglings in flight, seeking their selfland,
Flocking through darkness to vanishment.
A swelling of heavenly everings,
A swirling of wing-welling overings.
They have flown, faded and groaning,
Forgetting their getting, their names,
Unwillingly lulled in their own unwantings.
Cryers and callers, all whirled into wasteland,
Earth's own backyard, the everlasting everlost of heaven,
Into the goneness of here and the notness of now,
Hovering haveless through star-frost and sea-spray
Toward elsewhere. Wayfarers on the evening air,
Thistening like thought-secrets, heaven's harriers,
These nestlings of nowhere, a lattering flutter
Of wings in flight to some elsewhere
Of ledglings in flights, seeking their selfland!
Hover-home, breeder of streaming light,
Of strange unattainable flutter and fluxion!
Wing-wavers white as drifting down,
Weary wizards of downward drift,
Wavering dowsers of dawn,
River of blue skystead
Weary wings of the dreamstead
Broad harmonies of the downstead
Barefooted in star clusters
There you died.
Heaven hovers in their hair
Heaven hovers in their voices
Streaking the eastern stream of everland
They fly away into their neverland

With the nevering eyes of earthlings
Like notnesses of earth-law.
Fleet flight to the blue of heaven,
Flight fleet into blue, hovering,
Shrouded in all-knowing sorrow,
They fly to the source of pre-knowledge,
Wingings of no-where, mouths of now-here!
Singings of not-here, mouths of no-there!
Heaven hovers in their faces:
They are the dwellers in the blue places,
High heaven's harriers, a flood of flame,
The heavenly fire-rover over us all.
Their untamed eyes all vanishing vision,
Their untamed mouths saying: not here.

1920-1922

TRANSLATED BY Paul Schmidt

Translations:

Collected Works of Velemir Khlebnikov. Edited and translated by Charlotte Douglas. Cambridge, MA: Harvard University Press, 1987.

Collected Works of Velimir Khlebnikov 3: Selected Poems. Translated by Paul Schmidt. Edited by Ronald Vroon. Cambridge, MA: Harvard University Press, 1997.

The King of Time: Selected Writings of the Russian Futurian. Translated by Charlotte Douglas. Cambridge, MA: Harvard University Press, 1985.

Snake Train: Poetry and Prose. Translated by Gary Kern. Ann Arbor: Ardis, 1976.

In Chandler/Mashinski/Dralyuk; Glad/Weissbort; Markov/Sparks; Obolensky; Schmidt/Ciepiela; Yarmolinsky/Deutsch; Yevtushenko.

Biography and Bibliography:

Cooke, Raymond. *Velimir Khlebnikov: A Critical Study.* Cambridge, UK and New York: Cambridge University Press, 1987.

Markov, Vladimir. *The Longer Poems of Velimir Khlebnikov.* Berkeley: University of California Press, 1962.

Weststeijn, Willem G., editor. *Velimir Chlebnikov, 1885-1922: Myth and Reality: Amsterdam Symposium on the Centenary of Velimir Chlebnikov.* Amsterdam: Rodopi, 1986.

Vroon, Ronald. *Velimir Xlebnikov's Shorter Poems: A Key to the Coinages.* Ann Arbor: Department of Slavic Languages and Literatures, University of Michigan, 1983.

VLADISLAV KHODASEVICH

Vladislav Felitsianovich Khodasevich (khuh-dah-SAY-veech, 1886-1939) was born in Moscow, son of a Polish nobleman from Lithuania who moved to Russia and became a photographer. His mother was the daughter of a well-known Jewish writer who had converted to Catholicism. Khodasevich began writing in childhood and was a part of the Moscow literary scene, interacting with Symbolists though not officially part of the school. He studied law and then history at Moscow University but never graduated. By 1914, when his second book of poems appeared, he was a professional literary figure and author of reviews; persistent tuberculosis kept him from army service. He was married twice before the Revolution; after 1917 he was active for a time in the new Soviet literary institutions but emigrated in 1922, accompanied by the much younger Nina Berberova, whose own important writing took place after she left Russia. They lived first in Berlin, then with Maxim Gorky in Sorrento, and then in Paris. After 1927 Khodasevich almost stopped writing poetry, though his verse had grown sharper and more distinctive in emigration. He made his living largely as a literary critic and memoirist—not much of a living, particularly by the 1930s. Vladimir Nabokov considered him the greatest Russian poet of the twentieth century and based the admirable character of the poet and critic Koncheyev (in his novel *The Gift*) in part on Khodasevich. Khodasevich died in 1939 in Paris. His letters and literary biographies are as valuable as his poetry, and perhaps even more influential. Since the late 1980s he has gradually returned to readers in Russia as an important and respected author.

[Люблю говорить слова]

I love to utter words
That aren't entirely suitable.
Tangle me up, blueness,
With threads that all but ring!

Out of all chains and unfreedoms
They wrest lines that are unfaithful,
Where each word is a password
To enter the secrets of evening.

Your words are tormenting,
As if nailed to the cross.
In the evening the grass whispers
Caressingly sleepy speeches to me.

Monotonous rhymes wash me clean
From all kind of passwords.
The worn-out pain falls quiet
To sadly-passionless refrains.

The blueness sings at liberty
Songs that ring unclearly.
Words give birth to a secret—
Not entirely appropriate.

April 30-May 22, 1907, Lidino

TRANSLATED BY *Sibelan Forrester*

The Monkey
[Обезьяна]

There was a heatwave. The woods were burning. Time
Dragged tediously by. At the neighbors' dacha
The rooster crowed. I went outside the gate.
There on a bench, leaning against the fence,
A wandering Serb was dozing, skinny and dark.
A heavy silver cross was hanging
On his half-naked chest. Drops of sweat
Were rolling down it. Higher, on the fence,
There sat a monkey dressed in a red skirt
And greedily chewing on the leaves
Of dusty lilac. A leather dog-collar,
Pulled back by a heavy chain,
Squeezed her throat. The Serb heard me,
Woke up, wiped the sweet and asked me to give him
Water. But after he tasted one sip—
Was it too cold?—he put the bowl down
On the bench, and at once the monkey,
Dipping her fingers in the water, seized
The bowl in both her hands.
She drank, standing on all fours,
Leaning with her elbows on the bench.
Her chin almost touched the bench's wood,
Her back bent high above
Her balding head. Thus, it must be,
Darius once stood, bending low
To a puddle beside the road, the day he fled
The powerful phalanges of Alexander.
The monkey drank all the water and knocked
The dish off the bench, then half rose
And—will I ever forget that moment?—
Stretched out her black, callused hand,
Still cool from the moisture, toward me...
I've shaken the hands of beauties, poets,

Leaders of the people—no other hand
Had in it such a nobility
Of lines! Not a single other hand
Touched mine in such a brotherly way!
And, God's my witness, no one ever looked
Into my eyes so wisely and so deeply,
In truth—down to the bottom of my soul.
That begging beast awakened in my heart
The sweetest legends of profound antiquity,
And in that moment my life seemed complete,
And it seemed a choir of suns and ocean waves,
Of winds and the spheres broke into my ears
As organ music thundered, as before,
In other, not so memorable days.

And the Serb went off, beating on his drum.
The monkey took a seat on his left shoulder,
And rocked in the same rhythm,
Like an Indian maharajah on an elephant.
An enormous raspberry sun,
Deprived of its rays,
Hung in the opalescent smoke.
The Thunderless Saint poured heat on the wilted wheat.
That was the day war was declared.

June 7, 1918; February 20, 1919

TRANSLATED BY **Sibelan Forrester**

My Soul
[Душа]

My soul's like a full moon:
It's cold and clear.

In the heights it burns away, it burns—
And won't dry my tears;

And it doesn't feel pain from my misfortune,
And my passions' moan is inaudible to it;

Meanwhile how much longer I must suffer here—
It's not worth the shining soul's knowing.

January 4, 1921

TRANSLATED BY **Sibelan Forrester**

Ballad
[Баллада; Сижу, освещаемый сверху]

I sit, illuminated from above,
In my round room.
I look at the plastered sky
At the thirty-watt sun.

All around—likewise illuminated
Are chairs, and table, and bed.
I sit—and in confusion I don't know,
Where to put my hands.

The frosty white palm trees
On the windows bloom silently.
The watch with a metallic sound
Ticks in my vest pocket.

Oh, sluggish, impoverished squalor
Of my life with its dead-end!
Who can I confide in, tell how sorry
I am for myself and all these things?

And I begin to sway,
Embracing my knees,
And suddenly, in forgetfulness,
I start talking to myself in verse.

Disconnected, passionate speeches!
I understand nothing in them,
But the sounds are more honest than meaning
And the word most powerful of all.

And music, music, music
Entwines into my singing,
And a narrow, narrow, narrow
Blade pierces into me.

I myself grow taller than I am,
I stand up over dead existence,
With my feet in underground flames,
My brow in the flowing stars.

And I see with giant eyes—
With the eyes, it may be, of a serpent—
How my unfortunate objects
Pay heed to the wild singing.

And in a flowing, circular dance
The whole room measuredly moves,
And someone uses the wind to put
A heavy lyre into my hands.

And there is no plaster sky
And no thirty-watt sun to see:
On the smooth black cliffs
Orpheus places his feet.

December 9-22, 1921

TRANSLATED BY **Sibelan Forrester**

Translations:

Derzhavin, a Biography. Translated by Angela Brintlinger. Madison, WI: University of Wisconsin Press, 2007.

Vladislav Khodasevich: Selected Poems. Translated by Peter Daniels. London: Angel Classics, 2013.

In Chandler/Mashinski/Dralyuk; Glad/Weissbort; Markov/Sparks; Muchnik/Shafarenko; Nabokov; Obolensky/Yarmolinsky/Deutsch; Yevtushenko.

Biography and Bibliography:

Bethea, David. *Khodasevich, His Life and Art*. Princeton, NJ: Princeton University Press, 1983.

NIKOLAI KLYUEV

Nikolai Alekseevich Klyuev (KLYOO-yiff, 1887-1937) was born in the north of Russia; his mother taught him to read. He always presented himself as a peasant poet, which he was, though some acquaintances felt he overdid the performance. His work is marked by the vocabulary of village, field, and forest (with frequent inventive improvisations), and by his interest in Old Believers and minority religious sects, such as the Khlysts (flagellants) and Skoptsy (castrates). His first poetic success was furthered by the Symbolists, many of whom were eager to make connections between educated, upper-class Russians and peasants (see, among others, Gumilyov's review of Klyuev in this volume). Klyuev originally welcomed the 1917 Revolution with enthusiasm (see his "Youth," below), but the horrors of collectivization and other Bolshevik policies persuaded him, given his concern with the people who lived on the land, that the Soviet Union was coming to no good. His writing on this topic, combined with his homoerotic verse and identity as a gay man, made him *persona non grata* under Stalin. He was arrested and exiled in 1933, then arrested again and killed in 1937 in Tomsk; some of his manuscripts survived only in secret police archives. Although he was "posthumously rehabilitated," his poetry was not reprinted until the 1970s, and he has yet to attract due attention in the West. Since 1991 a sort of cult has arisen around Klyuev in Russia: some readers claim that his incantatory poems can be used for purposes of spiritual and physical healing.

[Любви начало было летом]

The start of love was the summer,
The end—an autumnal September.
You came up to me with a greeting
In a maiden's simple garments.

You handed me a red egg
As a symbol of blood and love:
Don't make haste to the north, little bird,
Wait for spring in the south!

The copses are smoky dark blue,
On the alert and silent,
Beyond the little curtain's pattern
Thawing winter isn't visible.

But the heart senses: there are mists,
A confused movement of the forests,
The unavoidable deceptions
Of lilac-dove-grey evenings.

Oh, don't fly to the mists as a birdie!
The years will leave in grey-haired gloom—
You'll be standing as a beggar nun
On the church porch, in the corner.

And, perhaps, I'll come walking by,
Just as skinny and impoverished . . .
Oh, give me the wings of a cherub
To fly after you invisibly!

I can't leave you out in my greeting,
Without repenting afterwards . . .
The start of love was the summer,
The end—autumnal September.

1908

TRANSLATED BY *Sibelan Forrester*

[О, ризы вечера, багряно-золотые]

Oh, raiment of evening, scarlet-golden,
You'll get me drunk like raging wine!
More joy to the soul are grey-haired ruins
Of mists—heralding the fire of dawn.

Burn more gloomily, sunset curtains!
The Ambassador of Powers walks to rout twilight;
Let night demons gloat in pits of darkness,
As ransom, retell them the angry bronze weapons.

Axes sing more ringingly just before dawn,
From the headsman's block a black shadow—before dawn . . .
Evening's garments intoxicate with scarlet color,
But morning shrouds calm with their whiteness.

1912

TRANSLATED BY *Sibelan Forrester*

[Галка-староверка ходит в черной ряске]

Old Believer jackdaw goes round in a black cassock,
In decorated bast shoes, in a dove-grey kirtle.
Dove in a button accordion, sparrow in a short caftan,
Hen in a woman's coat—holes pecked through.
Goose in a padded coat and duck in the backyard
Were granted a swagger in granddad's worn-out shoes.

In the jackdaw's twilight, loading up on thin poles,
New-laying hens sleep, tipping up their gizzards.
Only the cock-sorcerer, wrapped in a cerement,
Counts the starry pearls, scents grassy incense.

In the country churchyard rotten stumps flow like candles.
The forest-spirit's almost woven a bast shoe on the verge.
A fussy little wee 'un glimmers in the sedge . . .
The cock waits for the crack of dawn to dress up in a garland.

Dawn has thrice-nine lovely outfits stashed away . . .
The hens dream sweetly in the night's wee hours:
The jackdaw-nun is sleeping, the pea-gardening sparrow . . .
But the moment dawning's headdress glimmers—

The winged star-counter blows into a magic horn:
"Awake, ye birds, the hour of praise has struck,
And flour for the winged ones, on the knoll, on the river shore,
The sun is scattering millet of gold!"

1914 or 1915

TRANSLATED BY *Sibelan Forrester*

Youth
[Юность]

My red tie is first rate;
I look like a carnation in it.
A carnation is a merry flower for
Him, to whom old age seems far,
And for her, on whose youthful neck,
Rosier than apple trees in spring,
There glows a raspberry shawl.
The carnation's a furious flower!

My exuberant tie is a flock of birds,
Crimson-winged finches, blackbirds
Sing in concert with the spring,
The blizzard's sail sinking
In the fog of the creaking launch,
So the blue of celestial satin
Won't be rent by fangs of lightning.
My beaming tie, a flock of birds.

Let the raven croak by night,
Grumble keys of the ravine,
And the wolf comes out to the edge
Like goatlings into their shed.
I've driven in the songs and rays . . .
Let owls hoot in the gloom!

Beloved world, severe oak,
And a coniferous fir coat,
Hundred-tonne flocks of bison
Live in the light of my pupils;
As my blush beneath the mountain,
Wild rose blooms young,
And the firm-breasted cliff
Took perseverance from my muscles.

My red tie, akin to finches,
Flush from the dusts of apple trees,
From October's red-glowing leaves,
And from you, my glistening dawn,
Who lift high the golden hammer
Above the beloved country!

1927

TRANSLATED BY Pola Lem

Translations:

In Glad/Weissbort; Markov/Sparks; Obolensky; Yarmolinsky/Deutsch; Yevtushenko.

Biography and Bibliography:

Makin, Michael. *Nikolai Klyuev: Time and Text, Place and Poet*. Evanston, IL: Northwestern University Press, 2009.

ALEXEI KRUCHONYKH

Alexei Eliseevich Kruchonykh (kroo-CHO-nykh, 1886-1968) was born in Ukraine. He was a playful Futurist and verbal artist, a well-known practitioner of "zaum" or trans-sense language, creating new wordlike verbal units for his avant-garde poetry. Unlike Khlebnikov, whose neologisms deployed known roots and could usually be interpreted, Kruchonykh often worked with resonant nonsense syllables, as in his famous "Dyr bul shchyl," which additionally violates Russian spelling rules in a way that must make any educated person squirm (perhaps with delight). He wrote the libretto for the famous Futurist opera, *Victory Over the Sun* (1912); in 1912 he married the avant-garde artist Olga Rozanova (1886-1918), with whom he collaborated in creating new kinds of Futurist art books. As he aged, Kruchonykh became a well-known book collector and an object of pilgrimage for admirers of the Russian Futurists whom he had outlived. He died in Moscow in 1968, after almost every other poet from this era.

[Взорваль]
sadness
      of fire
horse
   roubles
of willows
      in the hair
of wonders
      exploded

1913

TRANSLATED BY *Martha Kelly*

[3 стихотворения]

3 poems
written in
my own tongue
differs from others:
its words don't have
a particular meaning

Holl roll shil
runoffinch
mack
you with ro
r l ez

Frot fron it
won't argue I'm in love
black tongue
wild tribes had it too

That sa may
ha ra bau
Saem this oak
oakbow saytar
al

1913

TRANSLATED BY *Martha Kelly*

Translations:
In Chandler/Mashinski/Dralyuk; Markov/Sparks; Yevtushenko.

Mikhail Kuzmin

Mikhail Alekseevich Kuzmin (kooz-MEEN, 1872-1936) was born in Yaroslavl, in a family from the minor nobility. He studied composition under Rimsky-Korsakov at the Conservatory in St. Petersburg, and his poetic work ran alongside songwriting; he would often perform his songs at literary gatherings for eager listeners. Kuzmin began publishing in 1905 and wrote actively for the journals *Libra, Apollon,* and *Golden Fleece;* he was a friend and collaborator of both Acmeists and Symbolists. Besides poetry and prose, he published a series of operettas, novels, and "musical illustrations" to plays by Blok, Alexei Remizov, and others. His writing is strongly marked by homoerotic and religious elements, as well as by music. His article "On Beautiful Clarity" proved crucial to the theoretical and aesthetic formation of the Acmeist movement, though in fact the article addresses prose rather than poetry. Kuzmin never signed on with a single artistic movement. His novel *Wings* (1907) was the first openly homosexual novel published in Russia, and reputedly one of the first works banned by the new Bolshevik censorship in 1917. It includes scenes set in an Old Believer community on the Volga, as well as more typical urban or foreign scenes depicting the formation of a young man's sexuality. Kuzmin has attracted attention in the West as a gay writer, which has sometimes caused this important element to overshadow his other aesthetic and philosophical concerns. Throughout his career he considers the ways the sensuous and fleeting connect us to the eternal. He is a poet of spiritual journey, taking art as a vehicle for the spirit; the novel *Wings* also makes aesthetic appreciation central to what we now call gay culture and its shaping (education and refinement) of new members. Kuzmin lived in great poverty after the 1917 Revolution, though he was writing some of his best poetry. He died in 1936 in Leningrad.

(from "Alexandrian Songs")
[Александрийские песни; Не напрасно мы читали богословов]

Not for nothing did we read the theologians
and studied the rhetoricians not in vain,
for every word we have a definition
and can interpret all things seven different ways.
In your body I can locate the four virtues,
and, needless to say, the seven sins;
nor am I backward in tasting these delights;
but of all words one is changeless:
when, gazing deep into your gray eyes,
I say, "I love you"—the cleverest rhetorician
will understand only, "I love you"—nothing more.

1906

TRANSLATED BY Neil Granoien and Michael Green

(from "Alexandrian Songs")
[Сегодня праздник]

Today's a holiday:
the bushes are all in bloom,
the currants have ripened
and the lotus floats like a beehive on the pond!
If you like,
we'll race each other
along the path bordered with yellow roses
to the lake where the goldfish swim.
If you like,
we'll go to the summer-house,
and sweet drinks will be brought to us,
pies and nuts;
a boy will wave a fan over us
and we'll gaze at the distant fields of corn.
If you like,
I'll sing a Grecian song to the harp—
but on one condition:
you're not to fall asleep,
and you have to praise both singer and accompanist.
If you like,
I'll dance the "wasp"
all by myself on the green lawn,
for you alone.
If you like,
I'll give you currants—but not with hands:
you'll take the red berries
with your lips from mine,
and with them
kisses.
If you like, if you like,
we'll count the stars,
and whoever loses count will pay a forfeit.
Today's a holiday,

the garden's all in bloom—
come, dearest love,
and make this holiday a holiday for me!

1906

TRANSLATED BY Neil Granoien and Michael Green

[Где слог найду, чтоб описать прогулку]

Where shall I find the style to describe a stroll,
Chablis on ice, French bread that's just been toasted
And the sweet agate of ripe cherries?
The sunset is far off, and the sea echoes
With splashing bodies glad for the wet coolness.

Your tender gaze, sly and alluring,
Is like the sweet nonsense of a tinkling comedy
Or the capricious pen of Marivaux.
Your Pierrot nose and the intoxicating slant of your lips
Whirls my mind like the Marriage of Figaro.

Spirit of small things, delightful and airy,
Of the love of nights tender or stifling,
Of the gay lightness of thoughtless living!
Ah, faithful am I, far from obedient wonders,
To your flowers, gay earth.

1906

TRANSLATED BY Martha Kelly

[Ах, уста, целованные столькими]

Oh, lips, kissed by so many,
So many other lips,
You pierce with bitter arrows,
Bitter arrows, hundreds.

You'll bloom in animated smiles
Like radiant springtime bushes,
Like a caress by gentle fingers,
Gentle, dear, sweet fingers.

A pilgrim or a daring thief—
Each kiss will find its way to you.
Antinous or vile Thersites—
Each will find his happiness.

As it touches you, the kiss
Lies down like a strong seal.
Who communes with a lover's lips
Is linked with all past lovers.

The gaze of prayer left on the icon
Will lie there like strong chains:
The ancient countenance, by prayers made glorious,
With that same chain binds those who pray.

And so you walk in slippery places,
In slippery, sacred places.—
Oh, lips, kissed by so many,
So many other lips.

1906

TRANSLATED BY Martha Kelly

[Стекла стынут от холода]

The cold has frozen windowpanes,
    But the heart knows
    The ice is melting—
    It will be young like spring.

The rooms smell of incense,
    Languor melts
    When it finds out
    How soon joy will be given us.

Gold flashes on icon casings,
    Candles are lit for
    A longed-desired meeting—
    What once was split in two, now whole.

The buildings gleam with snow.
    Foreseeing our meeting,
    I warm the candles—
    I await a wise encounter.

When I believed in that sweet shrine,
    Was I not waiting for you?
    Now angels have heeded
    Passionate wishes.

In the narrow, light-filled room
    In the twilight of May
    A wondrous guest has appeared,
    He keeps his armor on.

Who will catch his whisper
    In the singing of this place?
    How the heart loves and breathes
    With vernal breezes.

Perhaps my thoughts have frozen,
    My memory gone dumb,
    Remember, didn't you appear
    In the twilight of May?

Puncture the rock with a spear,
    Call forth water
    So it flows, golden
    Once more to freedom!

1912

TRANSLATED BY **Martha Kelly**

[Мудры старики да дети]

Children and old folk are wise,
Adults have no wisdom to speak of:
Some still dwell in the light,
Others see the light already.
But if you're in the dismal wilds,
Take comfort: through captivity's pangs
You'll see—we are children of God,
By those warm, familiar knees.

1915

TRANSLATED BY **Martha Kelly**

Kind Feelings Conquer Time and Space (from "Panorama with Panels")
[Добрые чувства побеждают время и пространство...]

I have something I cherish,
A gift from friends of mine;
And if you see it in a dream
You'll never lose your mind.

It came into my life
One cloudless little day.
By log paths and by hillocks
It's led me since that time.

If I should tire or doze off
Along uneven paths—
My unseen friends already
Stretch out their arms to me.

If ever we fall captive
To craven dreams and grief—
This comforter attentive,
Like Mozart, will sing out.

It's not a crutch, however,
Or flute or clarinet,
Though on it slanting eyes
Have left their special mark.

Friendship and art together,
A low and narrow hall,
Those covenanted feelings
And friends who remain true.

They may now be in Paris
Or Berlin, any place—
On earth, though, they could never
Be closer or more loved.

And still I will not tell you
The name of this dear thing—
For if I do, the pythoness
Will surely split in two.

1926

TRANSLATED BY Martha Kelly

The Third Thrust
(from "The Trout Breaks the Ice")
[Как недобитое крыло]

Like a wing, a wing shot through,
Hangs the ship: a model sloop.
The radiance of a hothouse
Lurks in the glazing of such libraries.

Yesterday's journey and the knife,
The oaths in frenzy taken
Held seeds of falsity for me,
A parody of fearsome crime...

I felt like asking... What a shame...
But this manly kind of ease
Hinted strongly that this spot
Was not intended for such talk.

You have just gone out, Shakespeare
Lies open, cigarette smoke drifts...
"The Sonnets!" How simple the world is
To the March lilt of a question.

As embroidery of snowflakes
Melts at vernal ray's assault,
In such a way a young man's life
May follow a capricious path.

1927

TRANSLATED BY *Michael Green and Stanislav Shvabrin*

Translations:

The Kuzmin Collection. Edited and translated by John Barnstead. Dalhousie University Electronic Text Centre. Last modified January 14, 1999. http://dalspace.library.dal.ca/bitstream/handle/10222/21661/safe.html?sequence=27.

Selected Prose and Poetry of Mikhail Kuzmin. Edited and translated by Michael Green. Ann Arbor: Ardis, 1980.

Selected Writings. Edited and translated by Michael Green and Stanislav Shvabrin. Lewisburg: Bucknell University Press, 2005.

Wings. Translated by Hugh Aplin. London: Hesperus, 2007.

Wings. Prose and Poetry. Edited and translated by Neil Granoien and Michael Green. Ann Arbor, MI: Ardis Publishing, 1979.

In Chandler/Mashinski/Dralyuk; Markov/Sparks; Obolensky; Yarmolinsky/Deutsch; Yevtushenko.

Biography and Bibliography:

Malmsted, John. *Mikhail Kuzmin: A Life in Art*. Cambridge, MA: Harvard University Press, 1999.

Malmstad, John, ed. *Studies in the Life and Works of Mixail Kuzmin*. Vienna: Wiener Slawistischer Almanach 24, 1989.

Panova, Lada, and Sarah Pratt, eds. *The Many Facets of Mikhail Kuzmin: A Miscellany*. Bloomington, IN: Slavica, 2011.

Tsvetaeva, Marina. "An Otherworldly Evening." Translated by Marian Schwartz and Richard Sylvester. In *A Captive Spirit*, edited by J. Marin King, 95-105. Ann Arbor: Ardis Publishers, 1980.

Mirra Lokhvitskaya

Mirra Lokhvitskaya (LOKH-veets-kuh-yuh, née Maria Aleksandrovna; married surname Zhiber, LoC Lokhvitskaia, 1869-1905) was born in St. Petersburg, where her father was a criminologist and lawyer. She studied at the Moscow Aleksandrovsky Institute, where her poetic gifts began to attract attention. Her younger sister Nadezhda, also a gifted writer, used the pseudonym Tèffi so they would not both be publishing as Lokhvitskaya (see "The Demonic Woman" in this volume). In 1888 several of Lokhvitskaya's poems were published as a separate book. In 1897 she received a prestigious Pushkin Prize for her first volume of poems, and in 1905 she received a joint (posthumous) Pushkin Prize for the fifth volume. Her writing addresses typical Symbolist concerns with beauty, music, love, and the mysteries of perception; her later work becomes darker in tone, no doubt in part because she knew she was dying of tuberculosis. She died in St. Petersburg in 1905, before her role in the poetry of the time was completely clear or had its full impact, though her works remained in print and popular until after the 1917 Revolution. (The Futurist Elena Guro, 1877-1913, has similarly been underestimated due to her early death.) Some later scholars consider Lokhvitskaya a crucial precursor of poets such as Akhmatova and Tsvetaeva, who were surely reading her poetry as they began to write, along with that of Romantic women poets such as Evdokia Rostopchina (1811-1858) and the more widely recognized Karolina Pavlova (1807-1893).

[Не знаю, зачем упрекают меня]

I don't know why they're reproaching me
That there's too much fire in my creations,
That I strive towards a living ray
And want to ignore the slanders of depression.
That I gleam, a *tsaritsa* in sumptuous verses,
With a diadem on my luxuriant hair,
That I weave myself a necklace of rhymes,
That I sing love, that I sing beauty.
No, I won't buy deathlessness with my own death,
And for songs what I love are ringing songs.
And my burning, my feminine verse won't betray
The madness of my insignificant daydreamings.

1898

TRANSLATED BY Sibelan Forrester

[В моем незнанье — так много веры]

In my unknowing there's so much faith
In the flowering of spring days to come;
My hopes, my chimeras,
Shine the brighter in darkening gloom.

In my silence there's so much torment,
The suffering of proud, invisible tears,
Of sleepless nights, eons of separation,
Of unshared, incinerated daydreams.

In my madness there's so much happiness,
Of greedy ecstasies, powerful forces,
That the heart hates the peace of passionlessness,
Like the dead cold of mute graves.

But my shield is firm—in my unknowing
From the fear of death and being.
In my silence is my vocation,
My madness—is my love.

1898-1900

TRANSLATED BY **Sibelan Forrester**

Incantation
[Заклинание]

You fly, my dream, you fly,
Touch the wild rose on the way,
Weigh down the curly hops,
Ruffle the fir and the reed.
And, flinging off flowering herbs
Into globeflowers' white chalices,
Splash with a caressing wave
Onto the watery pitcherleaf.
You fly off into mute heights,
Touch the horns of the moon,
Barely breathing the cool currents,
Puff on the clear stars.
And, sinking to the pleasant gloom,
Down to the pacified earth,
Do not rustle with a soft sigh
In the enchanted silence.
Don't you hide in the rippling fields,
Be obedient, be braver
And, leaving the rye berries,
Close your imperious eyes.
And in the thrill of sweet fantasies,
Purer than lilies, brighter than roses,
Bring my kiss back to life,
Seduce and enchant!

1899

TRANSLATED BY **Sibelan Forrester**

[Избрав свой путь, я шествую спокойно]

With my path chosen, I walk on calmly.
        You want some of my tears?
My verse resounds, confident and harmonious—
        You shall not see them here.

No room for dreams, no space for joyful hope
        In my distempered soul.
I do not trust, do not trust as once I did
        In the dawn of days to come.

I'm just the same; but, chosen forever,
        My earthly path is thorny.
Thorny my path, straying in the wilderness—
        You shall not follow me.

It's dark all round. I see the distant glimmer
        Of straying fires.
And I'll perish, and perish—alone,
        But not as your slave.

1896-1898

TRANSLATED BY **Sibelan Forrester**

Things
[Вещи]

The daytime nightmare of unceasing boredom,
That every day consumes my life,
Crushes my mind and tires out my hands,
That I vainly burn up and give away,
Oh you boxes, plumes, threads, folders,
Trimmings of lace, ribbons, scraps
Little hooks, vials, buckles, beads, rags
The daytime nightmare of melancholy and longing!
Where from? What point? What are you for?
Will that unknown hero ever come
Who won't look to see whether you're old or new,
But will throw all this rubbish on the floor!

TRANSLATED BY Sibelan Forrester

Translations:

In Pachmuss; Tomei.

OSIP MANDELSTAM

Osip Emil'evich Mandelstam (mun-deel'-SHTAHM, 1891-1938) was born in Warsaw (then part of the Russian Empire) in a Jewish merchant family. His family moved to St. Petersburg in 1897; he had an excellent education and later studied at Petrograd University. He was a critic, translator, theorist, essayist, and one of the major poets of the era. Gippius encouraged his early poems (though some other Symbolists would make comments about her "little Yid"), and he was soon visiting Ivanov's "Tower," studying versification and corresponding with Ivanov. Mandelstam converted to Finnish Lutheranism in 1911, partly to avoid the residence quotas on Jews in the Russian empire; nevertheless, both Judaism and Russian Orthodoxy were always important in his poetry. His first book *Stone* appeared in 1913. He met Akhmatova in 1911 and soon became a central member of the Acmeist Poets' Guild; in 1915 and 1916 he was close to Tsvetaeva and wrote some poems to her. His second book, *Tristia*, came out in 1922, the same year he married Nadezhda Khazina. After some years of poetic silence, he made a trip to Armenia and returned to writing. Mandelstam had an odd relationship to the Soviet state, combining wise cynicism about his fate with attempts to conform and even occasional enthusiasm about the new state and its system. Nikolai

Bukharin was Mandelstam's protector, as long as he had the power to protect anyone. Mandelstam was famously undone by an epigram he wrote about Stalin: he read it aloud to a number of friends, and one reported him. He survived his first arrest and exile to Voronezh, where he wrote a great deal of poetry that remained unpublished until many years later. After a second arrest, he died in a transit camp in 1938. His wife survived, preserving his archive, and much of what we know of his biography is from her detailed, partisan, irreverent memoirs (cleverly translated, at her suggestion, as *Hope against Hope* and *Hope Abandoned*; "nadezhda" means *hope* in Russian). Mandelstam's later writings could have been lost forever in many ways, suggesting that other wonderful poets may simply have disappeared, body and oeuvre, under Stalin. Mandelstam has been translated by such great poets as Paul Celan and has inspired critics such as Hélène Cixous. His work has also attracted the attention of gifted scholars, and many books about Mandelstam are not only informative but also deeply enjoyable.

Silentium

She has yet to be born:
she is music and word,
and she eternally bonds
all life in this world.

The sea breathes gently;
the day glitters wildly.
A bowl of dazed azure
sways pale foam-lilac.

May I too reach back
to that ancient silence,
like a note of crystal
pure from its source.

Stay, Aphrodite, as foam.
Return, word, to music.
Heart, be shy of heart,
fused with life's root.

1910

TRANSLATED BY *Robert Chandler and Boris Dralyuk*

Hagia Sophia
[Айя-София]

Hagia Sophia: it was at this place
The Lord ordained that peoples and Caesars halt.
Your dome is, in a witness's phrase,
As if hung by a chain from heaven's vault.

And when Ephesian Diana allowed the looting
Of a hundred and seven green marble columns
For alien gods, it proved for ages yet to come
A monument to Justinian.

But what was it your generous builder meant
When he laid down apses and exhedrae,
As great his spirit as his intent,
Indicating to them east and west?

And bathing in the world, the shrine inspires awe,
Its forty windows are a celebration of light;
On the dome's supporting vaults, the four
Archangels cause the most delight.

And the wisdom of his hemispherical dome
Shall outlive peoples, outlast the ages still to come,
While the full-voiced sobbing of the Seraphim
Shall not let its darkened gilding dim.

1912

TRANSLATED BY **Bernard Meares**

[Есть иволги в лесах, и гласных долгота]

There are orioles in the forests and the only real measure
In tonic verse is the quantity of vowels.
But once a year Nature is bathed in length,
Which is the source of Homer's metric strength.

Like a caesura that day yawns wide,
From dawn there's repose and drowsy lengths of life;
The oxen are at pasture and at noon's golden tide
It would cost too much effort to draw a note from a fife.

1912 (?)

TRANSLATED BY Bernard Meares

[В полоборота, о печаль]

Half-turned, o sorrow,
She glanced at indifferent ones.
Slipping from shoulders,
A faux-classical shawl turned to stone.
The ominous voice, bitter hops—
Unchains a soul's deepest depths:
Thus, an indignant Phaedra,
Rachel once stood.

1914

TRANSLATED BY Margo Rosen

[Бессонница. Гомер. Тугие паруса]

Insomnia. Homer. The tight-rigged sails.
I've read the list of ships—halfway, at least:
that long parade, that crane-flotilla once
that rose and sailed beyond the land of Greece.

A cry of cranes to pierce an alien shore,
you kings all crowned with heavenly foam—
where are you sailing? What would Troy mean,
Achaeans, if Helen had stayed home?

Homer, the sea . . . and love, that moves us all.
What's left to hear. Homer is silent, fled—
And the wine-dark sea recites and roars,
thunders hard and wild against my bed.

1915

TRANSLATED BY **Paul Schmidt**

Solominka
[Соломинка]

When you lie there, Salome, in your vast
room, when you can't sleep, when you lie and wait
for the tall ceiling to descend, to brush
your delicate eyelids with its grave weight;

When you can't sleep, things seem to gain in weight
or else are lost—the silence is so full;
white pillows glimmer palely in the glass;
the bed is mirrored in a round pool;

And pale blue ice is streaming through the air.
Salome, broken straw, you sipped at death,
drank all of death, and only grew more sweet.
December now streams out her solemn breath.

Twelve moons are singing of the hour of death,
the room is gone, the Neva takes its place,
Ligeia, winter herself, flows through my blood,
and I have learned to hear you, words of grace.

*

Lenore, Solominka, Ligeia, Seraphita.
The heavy Neva fills the spacious room.
Salome, my beloved straw, Solominka,
poisoned by pity, slowly sips her doom.

And pale blue blood runs streaming from the stone.
From all I see only a river will remain.
Twelve moons are singing of the hour of death.
And Salome will never dance this dance again.

December 1916

TRANSLATED BY **Robert Chandler**

Tristia

1

I've studied well the art of separation
In nighttime tears, in wild-haired wails of grief.
The oxen chew their cud, and expectation
Drags on; the vigil's final hour beats.
And I revere the rooster-night observance,
When, having donned the traveler's sorrow-load,
Tear-reddened eyes would gaze into the distance
And maiden's cry and muse's song would meld.

2

Who fathoms, at a word like *separation*,
What kind of parting waits for each of us;
What augurs in the rooster's exclamation,
When fire burns bright in the Acropolis;
And at some sort of new life's mystic dawning,
When in the courtyard lazy oxen chaw,
Wherefore the rooster, herald of that dawning,
Flaps with his wings upon the city wall?

3

I love the loom, its measured, soothing rhythms:
The shuttle zigzags and the spindle hums.
Behold now, like a bit of swan's down risen,
Already toward us barefoot Delia runs.
O, meager warp on which we weave our being,
How destitute the glossary of bliss!
All that once was is once again repeating;
The flash of memory startles like a kiss.

4

May it be so: a half-translucent figure
Upon a clean ceramic platter curls,
As if a squirrel's splayed-out hide transfigured,
And bent above the wax—a gazing girl.
It's not for us to prophesy of Hades;
Wax is to women as cold bronze to men.
Our destined lot falls out in battle plainly,
Prophetic death is granted but to them.

1918

TRANSLATED BY Alyssa Dinega Gillespie

The Twilight of Freedom (An Anthem)
[Сумерки свободы]

Brothers, let us celebrate liberty's twilight,
The great and gloomy year.
Into the seething waters of the night
The cumbersome frame of nets is cast.
You're rising to times of oblivion,
O sun, O justice, O people!

Let us prise the fateful load
That the people's leader assumes in tears.
And praise the twilight burden power bears,
Its insupportable goad.
He who has a heart must hear, O time,
Your ship as it sinks to the ocean floor.

We've pressed the swallows into battle legions,
And now the sun's concealed;
All the elements twitter and stir alive;
Through the nets, while the dusk lies thick,
The sun can't be seen and the earth's adrift.

So we might as well try setting sail:
Huge and clumsy creaks the turning wheel:
The earth's at sea. Men, be brave.
Like a plough it furrows the ocean wave,
And we'll still recall in Lethe's cold
That earth cost us a dozen heavens.

Early May, 1918, Moscow

TRANSLATED BY Bernard Meares

[Вот дароносица, как золотое солнце]

There: the Eucharist, a gold sun,
hung in the air—an instant of splendor.
Here nothing should be heard but the Greek syllables—
the whole world held in the hands like a plain apple.

The solemn height of the holy office; the light
of July in the rotunda under the cupola;
so that we may sigh from full hearts, outside time,
for that little meadow where time does not flow.

And the Eucharist spreads like an eternal noon;
all partake of it, everyone plays and sings,
and in each one's eyes the sacred vessel
brims over with inexhaustible joy.

1920

TRANSLATED BY Clarence Brown and W. S. Merwin

[Сестры — тяжесть и нежность — одинаковы ваши приметы]

Heaviness, tenderness—sisters—your marks are the same.
The wasps and the honey bees suck at the heavy rose.
Man dies, heat drains from the once warm sand,
and on a black bier they carry off yesterday's sun.

Oh, you tender nets and you heavy honeycombs,
Easier to lift a stone than to speak your name!
Only one care is left to me in the world:
a care that is golden, to shed the burden of time.

I drink the mutinous air like some dark water.
Time is turned up by the plow, and the rose was earth.
Slowly they eddy, the heavy, the tender roses,
roses of heaviness, tenderness, twofold wreath.

Koktebel', March 1920

TRANSLATED BY Peter France

[В Петербурге мы сойдемся снова]

In Petersburg we'll meet again
As though it was where we'd laid the sun to rest
And there we'll utter one first time
The word that's senseless but blessed.
In the black velvet of the Soviet night,
In the velvet of the universal void,
The beloved eyes of blesséd women still sing
And immortal flowers still bloom.

The wildcat capital arches its back,
On the bridge a sentinel stands watch.
Only a cuckoo car horn blares,
Through the dark its angry engine roars.
I don't need a permit for the night:
Sentinels don't frighten me;
For the senseless and blesséd word
I shall pray in the Soviet night.

I hear the theater's gentle rustle,
And the young girls' surprise;
A huge bouquet of immortal roses
Is held up by Aphrodite's arms.
We warm ourselves from boredom round a brazier fire,
Maybe after centuries have passed,
The beloved hands of blesséd women
Will gather our frail ashes at last.

Somewhere scarlet flowerbeds of stalls,
Sumptuous chests of drawers, the boxes round the walls,
And an officer like a clockwork doll;
Not for the vile and unctuous or the lowly soul....
So, you might as well snuff out our lights
In the black velvet of the universal void;
The blesséd women's sloping shoulders still sing
But the nocturnal sun won't be seen by you.

November 25, 1920

TRANSLATED BY Bernard Meares

Leningrad
[Ленинград]

I have come back to my city, so known my very being weeps:
Old illness, old comforts, gauzy dreams, swollen sleeps.

Now, now, child, little one, take your medicine, drink it down:
A little sip of fish oil from the streetlamps that light this dark town.

Look alive: it's December, remember how near you are
To night: already the yolk of light marred with toxic tar.

Petersburg! I don't want to die.
I watch my telephone with a watched eye.

Petersburg! I know every floor, every door the dead
Do not answer: one by one they open in my head.

I have come back to my city, quietly, so quietly,
But the doorbell's wired to my nerves, rooted in the meat of me,

And all night I itch untouchable, as with a paraplegic's pains,
Waiting for the door to rattle in its chains.

December 1930

TRANSLATED BY Christian Wiman

[Мы живем, под собою не чуя страны]

We live without feeling beneath us firm ground,
At ten feet away you can't hear the sound

Of any words but "the wild man in the Kremlin,
Slayer of peasants and soul-strangling gremlin."

Each thick finger of his is as fat as a worm,
To his ten-ton words we all have to listen,

His cockroach whiskers flicker and squirm
And his shining thigh-boots shimmer and glisten.

Surrounding himself by scrawny-necked lords,
He plays on his servile half-human hordes

Some mewl, some grizzle, some moan,
Prodded by him, scourging us till we groan.

Like horseshoes he hammers out law after law
Slamming some in the gut and some in the eye,
And some in the balls and some in the jaw;

At each execution, he belches his best
This Caucasian hero with his broad tribesman's chest.

October (?), 1933

TRANSLATED BY *Bernard Meares*

Flat*
[Квартира]
> Now that you've got a flat you can write poetry.
> —Boris Pasternak

The flat is quiet as paper,
Stripped of keepsakes and of schemes;
Walls so thin you hear your neighbor gargle,
And some, their neighbor's dreams.

All our affairs are in order.
The phone squats like a watched frog.
All our traveling rags and tatters
Travel still in stillness, like fog.

Even the radiator gives a start,
Though there's nowhere left to run,
And dissembling is my highest art,
Virtuoso of the comb and clucking tongue.

Ruder than a Komsomol cell,
Cruder than the students' chanted plan,
I teach an executioner how to kill
By teaching birdsongs to a man.

Ration books are all I read,
Loudspeaker speeches all I hear.
Listen: even a lullaby can bleed.
Learn, little kulak child, to fear.

Some realist neo-ruralist hack,
Some sheep-shit worm of a collective farm,
Some ink-bleeding, praise-needing party flack—
Deserves just this kind of calm.

Soon enough, when the last purge has boiled
All but salt from the public pot,

---

* *Eds.* Flat = (American) apartment.

Some family man, some salt-of-the-earth old soul,
Will see this moth of me, and swat.

Oh, the malice of mildness, these thumbscrew thank-yous,
The devil's poetry of politesse:
As though right through these flimsy walls and windows
Dead Nekrasov himself still hammered us.

Believe me, it won't be sweet Hippocrene
That roars through these walls in the end,
Though it will be ancient, and sudden,
And will completely possess us, my friend.

November 1933

TRANSLATED BY **Christian Wiman**

Black Earth
[Чернозем]

Too black, too much indulged, living in clover,
all little withers, all air, all loving care,
all crumbling and all massing in a choir—
damp clods of soil, my freedom and my earth...

With early plowing it is black to blueness,
and unarmed labor here is glorified—
a thousand hills plowed open wide to say it—
circumference is not all circumscribed.

And yet the earth is blunder and obtuseness—
no swaying it, even on bended knee:
its rotting flute gives sharpness to the hearing,
its morning clarinet harrows the ear.

How sweet the fat earth's pressure on the plow,
how the spring turns the steppe to its advantage...
my greetings then, black earth: be strong, look out—
black eloquence of wordlessness in labor.

April 1935

TRANSLATED BY Peter France

[Вооруженный зреньем узких ос]

Armed with the eyesight of thin-waisted wasps
that suck at the earth's axis, the earth's axis,
I sense it all, all that I ever saw,
and vainly, word for word, try to recall it…

I make no pictures, neither do I sing
nor draw the black-voiced bow across the string:
I only suck on life, and love to envy
the wasps, so potent and so sly.

Oh if I too could one day be impelled
by summer's heat and by the air's sharp practice
to feel, as I avoided sleep and death,
earth's axis, yes, to penetrate earth's axis…

February 8, 1937

TRANSLATED BY Peter France

[Я скажу это начерно, шепотом]

I'll say it in draft in a whisper
Since we cannot speak openly yet:
The game of irrational heaven
Is attained via experience and sweat.

Beneath the temporary sky of purgatory
We frequently fail to recall
That this happy heaven-roofed depository
Is a flexible lifetime home.

March 9, 1937, Voronezh

TRANSLATED BY Bernard Meares

Rough Draft[†]

Provisionally, then, and secretive,
I speak a truth whose time is not:

It lives in love and the pain of love,
In sweat, and the sky's playful vacancy.

A whisper, then, a purgatorial prayer,
A testament of one man, in one place:

Our bright abyss is also—and simply—happiness,
And this expanding, life-demanding space
A lifetime home for us.

March 9, 1937

TRANSLATED BY Christian Wiman

Translations:

50 Poems. Translated by Bernard Meares, introductory essay by Joseph Brodsky. New York: Persea Books, 1977.

Modernist Archaist: Selected Poems by Osip Mandelstam. Translated by Charles Bernstein and Kevin Platt. Santa Monica, CA: Whale and Star, 2008.

Poems of Osip Mandelstam. Translated by Peter France. New York: New Directions, 2014.

Selected Poems by Osip Mandelstam. Translated by Clarence Brown and W. S. Merwin. New York: Atheneum, 1974.

Selected Poems. Translated by David McDuff. Farrar, Straus and Giroux: New York, 1975.

Stolen Air: The Selected Poems of Osip Mandelstam. Translated by Christian Wiman and Ilya Kaminsky. New York: Ecco, 2012.

Tristia. Translated by Bruce McClelland. Barrytown, NY and New York: Station Hill, 1987.

---

† Eds. This poem is a translation of "Я скажу это начерно, шепотом . . .," Bernard Meares's translation of which appears immediately above. The title "Rough Draft" is given by the translator, Christian Wiman.

The Voronezh Notebooks. Translated by Richard McKane and Elizabeth McKane. Newcastle upon Tyne, UK: Bloodaxe, 1996.

In Chandler/Mashinski/Dralyuk; Glad/Weissbort; Mager; Markov/Sparks; Muchnik/Shafarenko; Nabokov; Natchez; Obolensky; Schmidt/Ciepiela; Yarmolinsky/Deutsch; Yevtushenko.

Biography and Bibliography:

Brown, Clarence. *Mandelstam*. Cambridge, UK: Cambridge University Press, 1973.

Cavanagh, Clare. *Osip Mandelstam and the Modernist Creation of Tradition*. Princeton, NJ: Princeton University Press, 1995.

Corrigan, Elena Glazov. *Mandel'stam's Poetics: A Challenge to Postmodernism*. Toronto: University of Toronto Press, 2000.

Freidin, Gregory. *A Coat of Many Colors: Osip Mandelstam and His Mythologies of Self-Presentation*. Berkeley: University of California Press, 1986.

Goldberg, Stuart. *Mandelstam, Blok, and the Boundaries of Mythopoetic Symbolism*. Columbus, OH: The Ohio State University Press, 2011.

Harris, Jane Gary. *Osip Mandelstam*. Boston: Twayne, 1988.

Isenberg, Charles. *Substantial Proofs of Being: Osip Mandelstam's Literary Prose*. Columbus, OH: Slavica Publishers, 1987.

Mandelshtam, Nadezhda. *Hope Against Hope: A Memoir*. London: Collins, Harvill Press, 1971.

Taranovski, Kiril. *Essays on Mandel'štam*. Cambridge, MA: Harvard University Press, 1976.

Vinokur, Val. *The Trace of Judaism: Dostoevsky, Babel, Mandelstam, Levinas*. Evanston, IL: Northwestern University Press, 2008.

VLADIMIR MAYAKOVSKY

Vladimir Vladimirovich Mayakovsky (vlah-DEE-meer muh-yah-KOFF-skee, LoC Maiakovskii, 1894-1930) was born in the village of Bagdady in Georgia, then part of the Russian Empire. In 1906 his father (a forester) died of blood poisoning after cutting his finger on a wire, leaving Mayakovsky with a lifelong phobia of germs. The family moved to Moscow, where he entered *gimnazia*. Impressed by some of the young men renting rooms from his mother, he was most interested in Marxism and not a good student. In 1908 (at fourteen!) he joined the Bolshevik wing of the Russian Communist Party and worked as a propagandist; he was arrested twice and spent eleven months in prison, intensively reading new Russian literature from the prison library. After this he stopped party work (indeed, he never rejoined the Party) and set about getting an education. He eventually entered the School of Painting, Sculpture, and Architecture, where he met David Burlyuk, the "splendid friend" and "true teacher" who he said made him a poet. Before long he and Burlyuk were expelled from the institute; he traveled around Russia with a group of Cubo-Futurists, writing and painting and eventually lecturing and performing. The Futurists typically had to publish their own work: though crowds flocked to their scandalous performances, publishers would not accept their texts. In 1915 Mayakovsky was drafted; at this point he was beginning to enjoy some poetic success and did not want to go to the front, although some of his war poetry is jingoistic in a way that prefigures his formulaic pro-Soviet agitational poetry of the 1920s. Around this time he began the intense relationship with actress Lily Brik that would last the rest of his life (see "Lilichka!" included in this collection). He participated with great enthusiasm in the February and October 1917 Revolutions. In 1919 he began working in "ROSTA," the Russian Federal Telegraph Agency, for which (he claimed) he made three thousand posters. He acted in some movies (largely playing his own persona, as he had in early Futurist plays) and wrote advertising copy for new Soviet products or institutions, as well as his own long and short poems and plays. He traveled frequently to Western Europe and in 1925 made a trip to Mexico and the United States, where he saw Burlyuk again and admired the Brooklyn Bridge. Mayakovsky took trouble to present poetic work as serious labor that made a significant contribution to the new Soviet state; he also enjoyed the special privileges he received as a prominent supporter of the regime. As literary politics developed, his projects were stymied, and aggressive members of "literary" organizations expected him to toe the line. Mayakovsky shot himself in 1930; it is not clear whether he meant to commit suicide or (as a man fond of gambling) was playing a kind of Russian roulette by himself. Mayakovsky's poetry became an obligatory part of Soviet school curriculum; this ruined it for many Russians who were required to read his least interesting poems. In the West, he has attracted many translators, who respond to the technical challenges of his avant-garde poetics and the undying energy of his provocative, self-centered, larger-than-life persona.

What About You?
[А вы?]

I splintered the landscape of midday
by splashing colors from a tumbler.
I charted on a tray of aspic
the slanting cheekbones of Atlantis.
Upon the scales of an iron turbot,
I found ladies' lips, aloof.
And you,
         could you have played a nocturne
using a drainpipe for a flute?

1913

TRANSLATED BY Maria Enzensberger

To Shop Signs
[Вывескам]

Read those iron books!
To the flute of the gilded letter
will sprout glamorous beetroot
and smoked sardines and salmon.

And once you turn joyous and pranky
among the constellations of 'Maggi',
a formidable undertaker
will sternly parade his sarcophagi.

And when, sullen and dismal,
the street has extinguished its lamp-posts,
fall in love in the starlight of taverns
with glittering poppies on teapots!

1913

TRANSLATED BY Maria Enzensberger

ME
[Я]

1.

All along the sidewalks

        of my stepped-on soul

The crazies beat the patter
of a run of rowdy words.
And it makes

     me

      cry.

The city is a meatrack of hanged men
Skyscrapers dangling

       in nooses of clouds.

And it makes

     me

      cry.

On street corner crossings
they crucify cops
And it makes

     me

      cry.

2.
A Few Words About My Wife

I have married the moon and she combs the water,
the beaches of uncharted seas.
She's my lunar lady, she has long red hair
and she drives a herd of horses
through a screaming streak of stars!
She gets married every evening in a greasy garage
and she kisses all the pictures
on the newspaper stands.
Her pretty boy winks, he wraps
the Milky Way around her,

he gets glitter on his fingers
and stars all over his hands.
And what about me?
The yoke of your eyebrows brings buckets of water
from the cool cool wells of your eyes,
it douses my desire and the lake-silk shimmers
on the singing amber cello of your thighs.
I sink into boulevards! I drown
in desire for deserts of sand.
Don't you recognize your baby?
It's my poor little poem, she wears fishnet stockings
and she drinks in a bar
as empty as this barren land.

    3.
    A Few Words About My Momma

My momma's on the wallpaper, cornflower blue.
But I run around in peacock clothes
stomping down the mop-top daisies
                                  with my long long stride.
Evening's rusty music starts playing.
                     Oboes,
and I head for the windows
knowing I'll see what I always do:
squatting on top
            of the house,
                        that great big cloud.
Now my momma's sick,
she's got a crowd of people running
back and forth between
                    the empty corner
                                  and her bed.
Momma always knows, she can recognize
the muddle of a mad idea when it crawls
from under the roof of the liquor factory shed.
And when fire breaks out in the window,

and there's blood all over my face
and my fine felt hat, oh my.
I break the back
                of the storm
                                  with my big bass voice
And I cry:

"Momma,
if I start feeling sorry
for your bottles of pain,
pounded to pieces by heels in the dancing clouds,
who's gonna kiss the golden hands
hanging apart
                and helpless
                            in Avanzo's ads?"

    4.
    A Few Words About Me

I love to watch children dying.
Have you seen my obscene
                yearning
                                protruding,
and behind the surf of laughter
the dark shadow of a tidal wave?
And what about me?
How many nights have I spent in the streets
reading the waiting list for the grave?
Midnight gropes me with soaking fingers
behind a broken fence, and a downpour beats
on the slick round dome of that crazy cathedral.
I've seen Christ
                climb
                      down from his cross
and run screaming, while the slush of the street
kissed the hem of his garments.
I cry to the concrete and jam my words

in the soft underbelly
of the swollen sky.
     Sun!
       Father!
Won't you please have mercy,
won't you please take it easy
on me?
For this is my blood and you spill it
and it runs down the disappearing street.
And this is my soul and you tear it to pieces,
tie it to a steeple in a burnt-out sky.
Time, you crippled icon painter,
paint me on your wall.
Make me look
    like the freak
       of the century!
I am more alone
than the one good eye
of a man
going steadily blind.

1913

TRANSLATED BY **Paul Schmidt**

Take It!
[Hate!]

In another hour, out of the foyer,
all your sizzling dripping will flow, man by man.
And I have revealed such hoards of verse before you,
I—squanderer and prodigal of priceless words.

Sir, I say, there's cabbage in your beard
left over from yesterday's meals.
Madam, hey, your make-up is smeared;
you stare like an oyster from the shells of things.

All of you, filthy, in galoshes or without,
will clamber onto the butterfly of the poet's heart;
the crowd'll go wild, get roused,
it will throw up its legs, the hundred-headed louse.

And what if today, I, coarse Vandal,
refuse to entertain you, still worse—
burst out laughing and spit into your faces,
I—squanderer and prodigal of priceless words.

1913

TRANSLATED BY Maria Enzensberger

And Yet...
[А все-таки]

The street's sunk like the nose of a syphilitic.
The river is lust, trickling away with saliva.
Having cast off its underwear down to the last twig,
the garden is shamelessly basking in the summer.

I came out into a square.
                         A scorched house
I put onto my head like a ginger wig.
People are afraid—out of my mouth,
an unuttered cry is wriggling its feet.

But they won't blame me, won't bellow.
Living my road with flowers, they'll honor me like a prophet.
Those, with sunken noses, know
I am their poet.

I fear your last judgment no more than a throng.
Me alone, through blazing cities roaming,
prostitutes, like an idol, will carry along
and show to God as their atonement.

And God will start crying over my book:
these are not words—convulsions compressed into lumps.
He'll run through the sky, my poems in his hands,
and, spluttering, show them to his friends.

1914

TRANSLATED BY *Maria Enzensberger*

You!
[Вы!]

You, wallowing in orgy after orgy,
owning a bathroom and a warm loo,
how do you feel learning about the awards of St Georgy
from the papers in your morning room?

Do you know, insentient nonentities,
thinking only of how to fill your maw,
that this moment, the legs of Petrov the lieutenant
were ripped off by a bomb?

And what if he, brought for slaughter,
suddenly saw, unrepining,
how you, with your mouths oily,
lasciviously hum Severyanin?

To give my life for the sake of you—
lips driveling with lust?
I'd sooner serve pineapple booze
to the whores in Moscow bars.

1915

TRANSLATED BY Maria Enzensberger

Lilichka!
(in place of a letter)
[Лиличка! (вместо письма)]

Tobacco smoke's etched out the air.
The room's
a chapter in a Kruchonykhish hell.
Remember—
in ecstasy
outside that window
I stroked, for the first time, your hands.
Today you sit there,
hard heart in armor.
One more day
and you'll drive me out,
maybe with a good scolding.
For a long time, in the dull entryway,
my trembling arm won't go into my sleeve.
I'll run out,
fling my body into the street.
A wild man,
I'll lose my reason,
hollowed out with despair.
That's not right,
darling,
good girl,
let's say our goodbye now.
No matter what
my love's
a heavy weight, after all—
it hangs from you
no matter where you run.
Let me bawl out in a summary shout
my bitter offended complaints.
If they wear out a bull with labor—
he'll leave,
go lie him down in cold waters.

Besides your love,
for me
there's no sea
and you can't beg a break from your love even by lamenting.
If a weary elephant wants a bit of peace—
he'll lie down, like a tsar, in the bonfired sand.
Besides your love,
there's no sun
for me,
and I don't even know where you are and who's your friend.
If you tormented a poet that way
he'd
trade his beloved for money and fame,
but for me
no chime is cheering
besides the chime of your darling name.
And I won't throw myself down a flight,
and I won't gulp down poison,
and I won't be able to pull the trigger.
No knife's blade,
besides your glance,
has power over me.
Tomorrow you'll forget
that I'm the one who crowned you,
that love burned out a flowering soul,
and futile days in a ploughed-up carnival
will tatter my booklets' pages . . .
The dry leaves of my words,
shall they make you stop,
greedily breathing?

At least
let me spread a last tenderness
beneath your departing step.

1916

TRANSLATED BY Sibelan Forrester

Order to the Arts Army
[Приказ по армии искусств]

They fiddle, the oldies' brigades,
the same old-fashioned parts.
Comrades!
Man the barricades!
barricades of souls and hearts.
All genuine communists
have burnt the boats of retreat.
Don't just walk, you futurists—
into the future—leap!
What good is just building an engine
that goes off in a whirl of wheels?
If your song doesn't deafen the station,
why have AC and DC?
Sing and whistle, pile sound on sound,
and forward
march.
There are still good letters around.
R
Sha
Shcha.
What good is just forming ranks
with gold piping on your breeches?
Politicians can't move men or tanks
without the musicians' marches.
Haul plans out to street corners,
at your windows beat with an oar
on the drum.
Split open the pianos.
But let there be thunder,
let it roar.
Why disguise your face in soot
and sweat on the factory floor,
then off duty
stare like a fool

at the rich life they live next door?
Enough of your twopenny truths.
Clean your heart of all its old wares.
The streets are the brushes we'll use,
our palettes the city squares.
Revolution is still a blank sheet
in the thousand-page book of time.
Futurists, out on to the street—
drummers and makers of rhyme!

1918

TRANSLATED BY Peter France

Our March
[Наш марш]

Beat the squares with rebellion's tread.
Raise your heads still higher with pride.
We shall wash clean with a second Flood
towns and cities universe-wide.

The bull of days is pied.
Slow the years' ox-cart.
Our god is speed,
A drum is our heart.

Is there gold diviner than ours?
Shall we fall to the bullet-wasps?
Our weapon is the song in our mouths,
Our gold our echoing voice.

Meadows lie green
beneath days outspread.
Rainbow's arc, rein in
the years' swift steeds.

How dull for the starry sky
when without it we make our song!
Hey, Great Bear, take us alive
up to heaven where we belong!

Sing songs, drink joy!
In our veins spring has come.
Heart, beat for war
on the breast's brass drum!

1918

TRANSLATED BY Peter France

"Proletarianess, Proletarian,
Stop into the Planetarium"*
[«Пролетарка, пролетарий, заходите в планетарий»]

You walk in
        and you hear
                the learned din
in the lecture hall.
The viewers have taken their seats
                and wait
to have the sky shown to them.
The sky's chief director
                has arrived,
in heavenly
        affairs
                he's an expert.
He has arrived,
        pressed a button,
                and set to turning
all the
        million
                of heavenly bodies.
A daughter says to her papa:
"Ask them
        to arrange night.
We very much
        would like to know,
starry Bear,
how you
        go about
                in the night,
how you
        ride about in the night!"
The sky-director
                guiding with his finger,

---

*   KR: Written to celebrate the opening of the first planetarium in the Soviet Union, November 5, 1929.

points out
        the star-bear.
In the fall
        the stars
                are scant.
But here
        the cupola's strewn with stars.
Not just anything,
                not just anyhow,
but night as it should be
                      and the Milky Way.
Both here,
      and there,
              and everywhere:
the heavenly firmament
                studded with stars.
Like a Primus stove
                they'll set about twinkling,
burning
      amorous hearts.
The sky-director
              was politely asked,
"What stars are there
              over Brazil?"
The sky-director
          fired up
                the Southern Cross,
not at all visible
        from our part of the world.
They glow
      like little dears,
the heavenly
        lamps.
Any old housemaid
              can organize

a lunar eclipse
        or even
                a solar one.
Perish, priestly desecration!
Having been
        in the celestial spheres,
we know—
        there is no God,
and there is no
        sense
              in faiths.
Every proletarian
        should
have a look
        at the planetarium.
1929

TRANSLATED BY **Kevin Reese**

Translations:

See Michael Almereyda, ed., *Night Wraps the Sky*, below.

For the Voice. Facsimile edition with images and layout by El Lissitzky. Translated by Peter France. Cambridge, MA: The MIT Press, 2000.

Listen! Early Poems. Translated by Maria Enzensberger. San Francisco: City Lights Books, 1991.

Mayakovsky: Plays. Edited and translated by Guy Daniels and Robert Payne. Evanston, IL: Northwestern University Press, 1968, 1995.

Vladimir Mayakovsky: Selected Poems. Translated by James H. McGavran III. Evanston, IL: Northwestern UP, 2013.

In Chandler/Mashinski/Dralyuk; Glad/Weissbort; Mager; Markov/Sparks; Muchnik/Shafarenko; Obolensky; Schmidt/Ciepiela; Yarmolinsky/Deutsch; Yevtusehenko.

Biography and Bibliography:

Almereyda, Michael, ed. *Night Wraps the Sky: Writings by and About Mayakovsky.* New York: Farrar, Straus and Giroux, 2008.

Brown, Edward J. *Mayakovsky: A Poet in the Revolution*. Princeton, NJ: Princeton University Press, 1973.

Humesky, Assya. *Mayakovsky and His Neologisms*. New York: Rausen Publishers, 1964.

Shklovsky, Viktor. *Mayakovsky and His Circle*. Edited and translated by Lily Feiler. New York: Dodd, Mead, 1972.

Stepanian, Juliette. *Mayakovsky's Cubo-Futurist Vision*. Houston, TX: Rice University Press, 1986.

Terras, Victor. *Vladimir Mayakovsky*. Boston: Twayne, 1983.

Woroszylski, Wiktor. *The Life of Mayakovsky*. New York: Orion Press, 1970.

Dmitri Merezhkovsky

Dmitri Sergeevich Merezhkovsky (mi-reesh-KOFF-skee, 1865-1941) was born in St. Petersburg in a noble family; his father worked in the palace administration. He began writing poetry at thirteen, publishing his first poem in 1881. He studied at the Third Classical *Gimnazia* in St. Petersburg and in 1884 entered the Historical-Philological Faculty at the university there. In the early 1890s he became interested in Symbolism. After graduation he left for the Caucasus and married the poet Zinaida Gippius in Tiflis. Around that time he underwent a "religious overturn" and became a mystic. Merezhkovsky had an important long-term relationship with Dmitri Filosofov that most scholars agree was sexual as well as familial; Filosofov often lived with the couple at their home. In these years Merezhkovsky traveled often to Europe, translated Classical Greek tragedies, and began the novelistic trilogy *Christ and Antichrist*. He and Gippius were among the organizers of religious-philosophical gatherings in St. Petersburg and of the journal *The New Path*, which published transcriptions of these meetings as well as poetry, prose, and criticism. Blok published his first poems in this journal. Merezhkovsky was a mentor to several key Silver Age writers, including Blok and Bely from the "younger generation" of Symbolists. After a dramatic escape from the country following the October 1917 Revolution, he and Gippius lived as émigrés, mostly in

Paris in an apartment they owned. Merezhkovsky was known internationally as a novelist, much translated and even re-translated, rather than as a poet or philosopher; he (like Maxim Gorky) was a candidate for the Nobel Prize in Literature in 1933, when it was awarded to Ivan Bunin. Perhaps seeking a possible counterweight to communism, Merezhkovsky turned towards fascism in the late 1930s, especially to Mussolini; for some later readers this tarnished his reputation. He died in 1941 in Paris.

Morituri

We're endlessly alone,
Priests of abandoned gods.
Come, you new prophets!
Come, prophetic singers,
Still unknown to the world!
And we'll hand over our lyre
To you, the God-sent poet...
We'll be first to answer your hunger,
With the first smile greet your dawn,
Oh, Sun of the future, we'll meet you,
And in your matinal brilliance,
Greeting you, we shall die!

"*Salutant, Caesar Imperator,
Te morituri.*" All our people,
Like gladiators in the arena,
Await death before the new era.
We die in sacrifice to redemption,
Different generations will arrive.
But on that day, before their judgment,
Let them not place a curse upon us:
You must merely recall the way,
How much we suffered, brethren!
New world of the coming faith,
Greetings from those who perish!

1891

TRANSLATED BY Sibelan Forrester

Exiles
[Изгнанники]

There's joy in the fact that people hated,
    Considered good as evil,
And walked past, not seeing your tears,
    Counting you as an enemy.

There's joy in eternally being an exile,
    And like a wave of the seas,
Like a stormcloud in the sky, a lonely wanderer,
    And in being friendless.

Only unseen sacrifice is splendid:
    I want to pass like a shadow,
And may the burden of the cross be sweet
    To me on my earthly path.

1893

TRANSLATED BY **Sibelan Forrester**

Dark Angel
[Темный ангел]

Oh, dark angel of loneliness,
    You waft anew,
And whisper anew your prophecies:
    "Don't believe in love.

Did you recognize my mysterious voice?
    Oh, my dear one,
I'm the angel of childhood, your only friend,
    Always—with you.

My gaze is deep, though not joyful,
    But grieve not at this:
It will be chill and ambrosial,
    My kiss.

It spreads a scent of lasting separation—
    And in the quiet
I will rock you, as your mother did.
    Come here to me!"

And the prophecies come to pass:
    It's dark all around.
Oh, fearful angel of loneliness,
    My final friend,

Full of funereal unrebelliousness
    Are your steps.
The ones I love with deathless tenderness,
    They too—are foes!

1895

TRANSLATED BY Sibelan Forrester

Translations:

Akhnaton, King of Egypt. Translated by Natalie Duddington. New York: E. P. Dutton, 1927.

Calvin. Translated by Constantin Andronikoff. Paris: Gallimard, 1942.

The Death of the Gods. Translated by Herbert Trench. New York: G. P. Putnam's Sons, 1901; as *Julian the Apostate: The Death of the Gods*. New York: The Modern Library, 1929.

The Menace of the Mob. Translated by Bernard G. Guerney. New York: N. L. Brown, 1921.

Peter and Alexis: The Romance of Peter the Great. New York, London: G. P. Putnam's Sons, 1906; as *Peter and Alexis*. Translated by Bernard G. Guerney. New York: The Modern Library, 1931.

The Romance of Leonardo da Vinci. Translated by Herbert Trench. New York: G. P. Putnam's Sons, 1924; translated by Bernard G. Guerney. New York: Random House, 1928; New York: The Modern Library, 1928; New York: Heritage Reprints, 1938.

The Secret of the West. Translated by John Cournos. New York: Brewer, Warren & Putnam, 1931; reprint as *Atlantis/Europe: The Secret of the West*. Blauvelt, NY: Garber Communications, 1989.

In Yevtushenko.

Biography and Bibliography:

Bedford, Charles H. *The Seeker: D. S. Merezhkovsky*. Lawrence, KS: University Press of Kansas, 1975.

Pachmuss, Temira. *D. S. Merezhkovsky in Exile: The Master of the Genre of Biographie Romancée*. New York: Peter Lang, 1990.

Rosenthal, Bernice Glatzer. *Dmitri Sergeevich Merezhkovsky and the Silver Age: The Development of a Revolutionary Mentality*. The Hague: Martinus Nijhoff, 1975.

SOFIA PARNOK

Sofia Yakovlevna Parnok (par-NOK, 1885-1933) was born in Taganrog on the Black Sea, the daughter of a respected pharmacist. She began to write at the age of seven and received a secondary education, part of it at the St. Petersburg Conservatory. Her first poetic publication was in 1906. Parnok converted from Judaism to Russian Orthodoxy and listed her ethnicity as Russian, though her literary connections included many fin-de-siècle Jewish writers and publishers. Parnok was a poet, translator, librettist, and literary critic; she wrote criticism under the pseudonym Andrei Polyanin ("Andrew Fields"), creating a persona that was both male and ethnically Russian. Her brother was the poet Valentin Parnakh (immortalized for readers as "Parnok" in Mandelstam's "Egyptian Stamp"). Parnok is important, among other things, as a lesbian poet in an era when homoerotic writing by women in Russia tended to cloak the speakers' gender with masculine or ambiguous grammatical forms. Her earlier writing often treated Classical themes, with references to Sappho in the style of the time, perhaps as a less problematic way of raising the topic; her view of Classical Greece was influenced by Ivanov, though unlike Ivanov she took on the personae of Sappho herself or one of her students. Parnok is known in part for a love affair with Marina Tsvetaeva (1914-16) that left traces in both their poetry; Parnok's serious reading of earlier women writers such as Karolina Pavlova influenced Tsvetaeva as well. After the 1917 Revolution, Parnok wrote movingly about the privations of Soviet life, aging and failing health, and love. She died in 1933 in Moscow.

Sapphic Strophes
[Сафические строфы]

I will remember everything.

If I catch the song of the Aeolian lyre,
I burst into flame, I don't walk—I dance,
my voice imitates, my hand is nimble—
in my veins, music.

I'm not trying the pen, I'm tuning strings,
occupied with an inspired concern:
to release into freedom, pour from my heart
the stringèd sounds.

I've not, as you see, in this life forgotten
the unforgettable joys of unforgettable songs,
which of old my girlfriends sang
in Sappho's classroom.

1915

TRANSLATED BY **Sibelan Forrester**

[Так на других берегах, у другого певучего моря]

So on other shores, by another singing sea,
millennia later, in just such a youthful spring,
vaguely recalling her ancient Aeolian childhood,
a thoughtful maiden runs her fingers over the strings.

Hellas's breath flows to her as a wind from the sea;
the wind, unsensed by others, moves her heart:
the maiden feels she will complete your dreams, Sappho,
she'll sing the songs that have not fully sounded to us.

1922

TRANSLATED BY Sibelan Forrester

The Church Organ
[Орган]

I remember a solemn voice,
An alien service and temple.
I'm a teenager. In the sun my hair
Shines like fire; my tread is stubborn.

Grown tired of the prayerful glances,
Of the foreign, too-pious shrines,
I was almost gone when the choir-loft
Thundered a whole new Latin . . .

Who are you, light or wrathful angels?
I hadn't known paradise cried.
Is it from bliss they sing like that,
Or from an enormous longing?

And what flash has pierced through this
Thunderpounding dark?
I close my eyes. —This is how Isaac
Waited, patiently, to be slain.

And that's when a seed of fire fell
Onto my soul. That's when, seized
By the ultimate madness, all
The organ's voices exploded.

And it wasn't me who cried out—
This terror of bliss, this intolerable
Wholeness, for the first time
Unlocked the lips of a poet!

1922

TRANSLATED BY Sibelan Forrester and Irina Mashinski

In the Crowd
[В толпе]

You came in as thousands would come in,
But a fire breathed from the doors,
And I knew: the very same
Telling sign is carved on your palm.

Yes, I know—the girdle of Venus
Marks your hand as well.
Your gait is way too measured,
The fire of your glance too dull.

You've powdered the traces of crying,
And blood tinges your lips, like rouge—
Yes, sister, yes, that's just the way
It bruises us with kisses—love!

1922

TRANSLATED BY Sibelan Forrester and Irina Mashinski

Translations:
In Chandler/Mashinski/Dralyuk; Kelly; Markov/Sparks; Tomei. See also Burgin, below.

Biography and Bibliography:
Burgin, Diana L. *Sophia Parnok: The Life and Work of Russia's Sappho.* New York: New York University Press, 1994.

BORIS PASTERNAK

B oris Leonidovich Pasternak (1890-1960) was born in Moscow. His father, Leonid Osipovich Pasternak, was a prominent artist and member of the Russian Academy of the Arts, and his mother Rosa (née Kaufman) a gifted pianist who in a different era would have been a famous performer. Important cultural figures visited their house, including Leo Tolstoy, and as a child Pasternak met Rainer Maria Rilke. Raised in a secularized Jewish family, Pasternak considered himself a Christian. No records of his conversion exist but during his lifetime the poet grew more and more engaged in Orthodox Christian practice, especially in the second half of his life. At first he hoped to become a composer, and family connections meant that he could show his compositions to Alexander Scriabin, but he was discouraged that he did not have perfect pitch, as his mother did. He studied at the Fifth Classical *Gimnazia* in Moscow and, after shifting his interests, graduated from Moscow University in 1913 with a philosophy degree. He pursued graduate study of philosophy in Germany, but before completing his dissertation decided he wanted to be a writer. Both music and philosophy left notable traces in his writing, even after a vow in the 1930s to become simpler and more accessible in his style and ideas. He was a member of various para-Futurist groups and had published two books before his first significant success, *My Sister—Life* (1922). Pasternak married twice and tended to be artistically inspired by love affairs. Like many poets who remained in the Soviet Union, he had a tormented relationship with political power, especially Stalin, though most memoirs show him behaving with consistent dignity and honesty—no mean trick, in those days. He was able to help a number of important writers (Akhmatova, Tsvetaeva, Varlam Shalamov), or their surviving children. Pasternak gained fame in the West for his novel *Doctor Zhivago* and for the scandal around the 1958 Nobel Prize in Literature: he was not allowed to leave the country to receive it, and at home faced anti-Semitic unpleasantness that had a suspiciously government-sponsored look. Pasternak died at his dacha in Peredelkino outside Moscow in 1960. He remains one of the best-known and most-translated poets of the era not only because of his writing, which bristles with ideas and phonetic complexity, but also for the moral force of his personality.

[Февраль. Достать чернил и плакать!]

It's February. Grab the ink and weep!
Sob and write of February
As you watch the thunderous muck
Burn black with spring.

Stop a droshky. For six grivnas
Catch a ride through toll of bells,
Through call of wheels to where the shower's
Louder still than ink and tears.

Where rooks by thousands plunge from trees
Like carbonized pears that explode
Into the puddles, hurling down
Dry grief into the depths of eyes.

Beneath her, patches thaw to black,
And stormy cries uproot the wind:
The more the verses fall by chance,
The truer, sobbing, they're composed.

1912

TRANSLATED BY Martha Kelly

Spring
[Весна; Что почек, то клейких заплывших огарков]

How many sticky buds, how many candle-ends
Are glued to the branches now! April
Is lit. The wind from the park reeks of puberty
And the woods are more blatant still.

A tight loop of feathered throats holds the wood's windpipe
Lassoed like a steer, and it groans
In nets as the gladiatorial organ
Steel-throated sonatas intones.

Now, Poetry, be a Greek sponge with suckers
And let the green succulence drench
You, under the trees on the sodden wood
Of a green-mottled garden bench.

Grow sumptuous flounces and furbelows,
Suck clouds and gullies in hour by hour,
And, Poetry, tonight I'll squeeze you out
To make the thirsty paper flower.

1916

TRANSLATED BY *Jon Stallworthy and Peter France*

[Сестра моя—жизнь и сегодня в разливе]

My sister, Life, is today overflowing
And smashing herself in spring rain on our coats,
But people with monocles are not amused
And bite, quite politely, like snakes in the oats.

The older ones have their own reasons for this.
But yours is a comical reason, no doubt:
That under the storm, eyes and lawns appear lilac
And mignonette sweetens the wind from the south.

That when, on your journey in May, you're consulting
The timetable on the Kamyshin line,
The Bible itself is not more exalting.
Your eyes, mesmerized, are to all else blind.

That, setting, the sun has only to highlight
Girls crowding the railway track, as the train slows,
For me to discover it is not my station,
The sun to extend its regrets as it goes.

And splashing a third time, the bell swims behind,
Its "Sorry, not here" sounding near, further, far.
The burning night filters in under the blind
And the steppe plunges on from the steps to the star;

Winking and blinking, but sweetly somewhere,
My love, like a mirage, and others all sleep
While, splashing along carriage footboards, the heart
Scatters bright windows across the dark steppe.

1917

TRANSLATED BY *Jon Stallworthy and Peter France*

Thunderstorm for a Moment Forever
[Гроза моментальная навек]

Then afterwards summertime waved goodbye
To the railroad crossing. That night hatless
Thunder took a hundred blinding snapshots
In order to have something to remember.

A branch of lilac darkened. Then thunder
Snatched a sheaf of lightning from the fields
And in a single moment blazed a monument
Of light upon the dazzled county courthouse.

And when the gutters of the courthouse overflowed
With waves of some perverse delight
And the cloudburst descended like streaks
Of charcoal across the face of a drawing,

Collapsing consciousness began to blink:
Illumination! Illumination! Even
For those corners of the mind
That now seem full of light as noon.

1917

TRANSLATED BY Paul Schmidt

To Anna Akhmatova
[Анне Ахматовой; Мне кажется, я подберу слова]

I think I can summon up words
As pristine as those in your song.
But if I don't, I won't give a damn.
I don't care if I'm wrong.

I hear the murmur of wet roofs,
Faint eclogues of pavement and curb.
A certain city, from the opening lines,
Resounds in every noun and verb.

Spring is all round, but one can't leave town.
The customer's deadline must be met.
Dawn glows and sews by the light of a lamp,
Her back unbending, her eyes wet.

Inhaling the calm of distant Ladoga,
She walks to the water with trembling legs.
Such strolls afford her no relief.
The dark canals smell of musty bags.

The wind bobs about like a walnut shell,
A hot wind flutters the glancing gleam
Of branches and stars, landmarks and lamps,
And the seamstress gazing upstream.

In different ways, the eyes can be sharp,
And images precise in different ways.
But a solution of terrible strength
Is out there under the white night's gaze.

And so I see your face and your glance.
The pillar of salt does not bring it to mind,
The one with which five years ago
You transfixed your fear of looking behind.

But from your first books, where the grains
Of keen prose crystallized, to the last,
Your eye, like the spark that makes the wire tremble,
Has forced events to vibrate with the past.

1928

TRANSLATED BY *Jon Stallworthy and Peter France*

[О, знал бы я, что так бывает]

If I had known that this is what happens,
When I at first stood up and read;
That poetry is murderous,
Will strangle you and leave you dead;

I would have decided not
To play games with reality.
It all began so far away,
So long ago, so timidly.

But from an actor, age like Rome
Demands no cabaret routine—
Instead of a performance,
Irrevocable ruin.

When feeling dictates your lines,
You step out, like a slave, to pace
The stage, and here art stops,
And earth and fate breathe in your face.

1931

translated by Jon Stallworthy *and* Peter France

from *In Memory of Marina Tsvetaeva*
[Памяти Марины Цветаевой]

It's as hard to imagine
you don't exist
as to imagine you a miser-millionaire
among starving sisters.

What can I do for you? Say.
There's a quiet reproach
in the way
you've gone your way.

Losses are riddles. In vain
I try to find
an answer.
Death has no outline.

Half-words, tongue-slips, delusion—
and only
faith in resurrection
by way of direction.

Winter makes a splendid memorial:
a glimpse of twilight,
add currants, pour on wine
—and there's your remembrance meal!

An apple tree in a drift, the town
wrapped in snow,
seemed all year long
to be your grave, your headstone.

Facing God, you reach out
towards him, from earth,
just as before
your days had reached their final count.

25-26 December, 1943

TRANSLATED BY Robert Chandler

Fresco Come to Life
[Ожившая фреска]

Again the shells were falling.
As on board ship, the cloud
And night sky over Stalingrad
Rocked in a plaster shroud.

Earth droned, as if in prayer
To ward off the shrieking shell,
And with its censer threw up smoke
And rubble where it fell.

Whenever, between fighting, he
Went round his company under fire,
A sense of strange familiarity
Haunted him like desire.

These hedgehog buildings, where could he
Have seen their bottomless holes before?
The evidence of past bombardments
Seemed fabulous and familiar.

What did it mean, the four-armed sign,
Enclosed in the pitch-black frame?
Of whom did they remind him,
The smashed floors and the flame?

And suddenly he saw his childhood,
His childhood, and the monastery; heard
The penitents, and in the garden
The nightingale and mocking-bird.

He gripped his mother with a son's hand,
And devils, fearing the archangel's spear,
Leaped from the chapel's somber frescos,
Into just such pits as here.

And the boy saw himself in armor.
Defending his mother in shining mail,
And fell upon the evil one
With its swastika-tipped tail.

And nearby in a mounted duel
Saint George shone down on the dragon,
And water-lilies studded the pond
And birds sang crazily on and on.

The fatherland, like the forest's voice,
A call in the wood and the wood's echo,
Beckoned with an alluring music
And smelt of budding birch and willow.

How he remembers those clearings
Now, when in pursuit he impales
And tramples enemy tanks
For all their fearful dragon scales.

He has crossed the frontiers of the world,
And the future, like the firmament,
Already rages, not a dream,
Approaching, and magnificent.

1944

TRANSLATED BY *Jon Stallworthy and Peter France*

Hamlet*
[Гамлет]

The hum dies down; alone on stage,
my back against the wall, I try
to sense within a distant echo
the twists and turns of destiny.

A thousand glinting opera glasses
focus the dark into my eyes.
O Father, should it be possible—
allow this cup to pass me by.

I like your stubborn, bold design,
and I've agreed to play this part.
But other forces are at play now—
this once, please count me out . . .

The acts cannot be rearranged
and there's no turning from the road.
Alone, a sea of cant all round me:
Life is not a walk across a field.

1946

TRANSLATED BY *Robert Chandler*

---

*   RC: Pasternak first published his translation of *Hamlet* in 1941. It is the best known of his translations—and the most popular Russian version of Shakespeare's play. It has been staged many times, and Grigory Kozintsev used it for his 1964 film. The poem is included in his novel *Doctor Zhivago*.

[Во всем мне хочется дойти]

In everything I want to reach
The very essence:
In work, in seeking a way,
In passion's turbulence.

The essence of past days
And where they start,
Foundations, roots,
The very heart.

Always catching the thread
Of actions, histories,
To live, to think, to feel, to love,
To make discoveries.

If only I could do it
After a fashion,
I should compose eight lines
On the properties of passion,

On lawlessnesses, sins,
Pursuits, alarms,
On unexpectednesses,
Elbows, palms.

I should deduce its principles,
Its laws proclaim,
Repeating the initials
Of name after name.

I should plant out my stanzas
And flowering limes,
Their veins astir with sap,
Would bloom in lines.

I should have mint and roses
Breathing there—
Sedge, meadows, haymaking,
And thunderous air.

So Chopin once enclosed
The plenitude
Of farmsteads, parks, groves, graves
In his *Etudes*.

The torment and delight
Of triumph so
Achieved tightens the bowstring
Bending the bow.

1956

TRANSLATED BY Jon Stallworthy and Peter France

Translations:

Doctor Zhivago. Translated by Richard Pevear and Larissa Volokhonsky. New York: Vintage Classics, 2011; Translated by Manya Harari and Max Hayward. New York: Knopf, 1958 and multiple editions.

I Remember: Sketch for an Autobiography. Edited by David Magarshak. Translated by Manya Harari. Cambridge, MA: Harvard University Press, 1959, 1983.

Letters, Summer 1926: Correspondence between Pasternak, Tsvetayeva, Rilke. Translated by Margaret Wettlin and Walter Arndt. San Diego, CA: Harcourt, Brace, Jovanovich, 1985.

My Sister—Life and *A Sublime Malady*. Translated by Mark Rudman and Bohdan Boichuk. Ann Arbor: Ardis, 1983.

My Sister—Life and the Zhivago Poems. Translated by James E. Falen. Evanston, IL: Northwestern University Press, 2012.

Safe Conduct: An Autobiography and Other Writings. Introduction by Babette Deutsch. Translated by C. M. Bowra, Babette Deutsch, Robert Payne, and Beatrice Scott. New York: New Directions, 1958.

Selected Poems. Translated by J. M. Cohen. London: Drummond, 1946.

Selected Poems. Translated by Jon Stallworthy and Peter France. London: Allen Lane, 1983.

The Voice of Prose. Edited and translated by Chris Barnes. New York: Grove Press, 1986; Edinburgh: Polygon, 1986.

In Chandler/Mashinski/Dralyuk; Glad/Weissbort; Markov/Sparks; Muchnik/Shafarenko; Obolensky; Schmidt/Ciepiela; Yarmolinsky/Deutsch; Yevtushenko.

Biography and Bibliography:

Barnes, Christopher J. *Boris Pasternak: A Literary Biography*. Cambridge, UK and New York: Cambridge UP, 1989.

Ciepiela, Catherine. *The Same Solitude: Boris Pasternak and Marina Tsvetaeva*. Ithaca: Cornell UP, 2006.

Clowes, Edith. *Doctor Zhivago: A Critical Companion*. Evanston, IL: Northwestern UP, 1995.

Corrigan, Elena. *Art After Philosophy: Boris Pasternak's Early Prose*. Columbus, OH: The Ohio State UP, 2013.

Evans-Romaine, Karen. *Boris Pasternak and the Tradition of German Romanticism*. Munich: Verlag Otto Sagner, 1997.

Fleishman, Lazar. *Boris Pasternak: The Poet and His Politics*. Cambridge, MA: Harvard University Press, 1990.

Gifford, Henry. *Pasternak, A Critical Study*. New York: Cambridge UP, 1977.

Hingley, Ronald. *Pasternak, A Biography*. London: Weidenfeld and Nicolson, 1983.

Hughes, Olga R. *The Poetic World of Boris Pasternak*. Princeton, NJ: Princeton UP, 1974.

Livingstone, Angela. *Boris Pasternak: Doctor Zhivago*. New York: Cambridge University Press, 1989.

de Mallac, Guy. *Boris Pasternak, His Life and Art*. Norman, OK: University of Oklahoma Press, 1981.

O'Connor, Katherine T. *Boris Pasternak's My Sister—Life and the Illusion of Narrative*. Ann Arbor: University of Michigan Press, 1988.

Pasternak, Evgenii B. *Boris Pasternak: The Tragic Years 1930-60*. London: Harvill, 1990.

Plank, Dale. *Pasternak's Lyric: A Study of Sound and Imagery*. The Hague: Mouton, 1966.

Rudova, Larissa. *Understanding Boris Pasternak*. Columbia, SC: University of South Carolina Press, 1997.

Igor Severyanin

Igor Vasilyevich Severyanin (né Lotaryov, si-vir-YAH-neen, LoC Severianin, 1887-1941) was born in St. Petersburg. His father was a retired staff captain; his mother a member of the noble Shenshin family (and thus related to the nineteenth-century Russian poet Afanasy Fet). Severyanin finished high school in Cherepovets. His first publication was a poem in 1905. Severyanin was the founder of Ego-Futurism, a subgroup of Futurism in which he was clearly the most active and talented member. He produced a great many collections of poems with fanciful titles, some published abroad, and his name became a by-word for a certain over-the-top poetic and presentational style. He emigrated shortly after the October 1917 Revolution. Severyanin strove to be provocative, playing up the "ego" element of his literary movement and referring to his poems as "poèsy" or *poesies*. Later in life he wrote amusing parodies of well-known Russian poets, sometimes disappointing émigré audiences who came to readings hoping to see some of his old-style antics. He died in 1941 in Tartu, Estonia.

Igor Severyanin

[Я, гений Игорь-Северянин]

I, the genius Igor-Severyanin,
am drunken with my victory:
I'm being screened throughout the cities!
I'm ensconced omni-cordially!

From Bayazet unto Port Arthur
I have traced a stubborn line.
I have mastered all of literature!
I've eagled, thundering, to the throne!

One year ago, I said "I shall be!"
The year flashed by, and here I am!
Among my friends I glimpsed a Judas;
I rejected revenge—not him.

"I'm solitary in my task!"
I publicized insightfully.
They came to me, those who had vision,
And lent me not strength, but ecstasy.

Soon we were four, but all the power
Was mine, the only one, and growing.
It didn't go begging for support
And didn't grow manly from numbers.

Autocratic and filled with pride,
It grew in its uniqueness—
And, in enraptured suicide,
A horde staggered into my tent.

From a snowcliffed hypnotism
A few ran into the rot of fens;
Each one had a thorn in his shoulder—
For ailing is their flight who fled.

I welcomed them: I have the gift
Of all-welcome—by God, Hello!
Fly bravely, my dove, to the serpent!
Snake, twine the eagle in response!

(from the cycle "Epilogue," 1913[?])

TRANSLATED BY **Sibelan Forrester**

Translations:
In Mager; Markov/Sparks; Yevtushenko.

Biography and Bibliography:
Laauwers, Lenie. *Igor'-Severjanin: His Life and Work—The Formal Aspects of His Poetry*. Leuven: Uitgeverij Peeters en Departement Oriëntalistiek, 1993.

Maria Shkapskaya

Maria Mikhailovna Shkapskaya (SHKAHP-skuh-yuh, née Andreevskaya, LoC Shkapskaia, 1891-1952) was born in St. Petersburg, the daughter of a Russian official and a German mother. She finished her education in France; unlike some poets who later claimed to have been leftists all along, Shkapskaya had problems because of her politics and moved to Western Europe before the 1917 Revolution. She began writing poems in childhood and first published some in newspapers in 1910-12. Her early poems are competent and interesting, but it was after returning to Russia that she began to write in a strikingly different way, largely abandoning stanza form (though not rhyme and meter) to present her poetry in paragraph shape, and turning to "women's" topics such as stillbirth, abortion, and various aspects of sexuality. Her poems of this period were praised by Maxim Gorky, a powerful figure at the time. In the late 1920s, however, she stopped writing poetry and turned to journalism; despite this switch to less problematic genres, her son was arrested and spent time in the camps. Shkapskaya's reputation was at its height in the mid-1920s, but later she was largely forgotten as a poet. She died in 1952 in Moscow. Her poetry has since been rediscovered by scholars and general readers, though it is not yet as well-known as it should be.

[Было тело мое без входа]

My body was lacking an entrance, and singed by a black smoke. The black enemy of the human race avidly bent over it.
And, forgetting my great pride, I gave up every trace of my blood to him for one single hope: of a son with dear features of face.

1921

TRANSLATED BY **Sibelan Forrester**

[Да, говорят, что это нужно было]

Yes, they say that it was necessary . . . . And there was dreadful feed for the greedy harpies, and my body slowly lost its powers, and the calming chloroform rocked me to sleep.
And my blood flowed without drying—not joyfully, like the time before, and afterward we looked in confusion and were not gladdened by the empty cradle.
Once again, in pagan manner, we bring human sacrifices for our children's lives. And Thou, o Lord, Thou dost not arise from the dead at that crunch of infants' bones!

1921

TRANSLATED BY **Sibelan Forrester**

[Не снись мне так часто, крохотка]

Don't come into my dreams so often, tiny one, don't judge your mother. After all, your little bit of milk remained in my breast untouched. For in life—as I learned long ago—there are very few free places; your little place stands in my heart like a cross.
Why does your little hand touch my breast at night? It seems that a guilty mother isn't fated to fall asleep!

1921

TRANSLATED BY **Sibelan Forrester**

[О, эта женская Голгофа]

Oh, this female Golgotha!—Drain all your firm strength for the babe, carry it in yourself, feed it with yourself—you get no rest, no pause for a sigh.
Until, dried out, you collapse on your path—the ones who want to come keep gnawing at you from inside. The laws of the earth are simple and strict: birth 'em, and then you die.

1922

TRANSLATED BY **Sibelan Forrester**

[Людовику XVII. Фрагмент]

To Louis XVII
(A Fragment)

The people's fury once again
Must be calmed by a horrible game.
Alexis the Second has become
Your brother, Louis the Seventeenth.

He too was made the ancient ransom
For people of burning fires,
To redeem that every year
Millions of village kids died.

For their fathers' tavern binges
And the mineshaft splashed with blood,
For the crunch of bones in common graves
In Manchurian fields and others.

For the thin backs of their mothers,
For grey hair's early bitter gleam,
For the son of Gesya Gelfman, taken
By force at the hour he was born.

For all the exiled brothers,
For all the unmarked graves,
Rus' has written in the memory book
Over these three hundred years.

For the hot south, for the deadly north
Fulfilled over you and him,
We carry it out untouchably,
The law of implacable bibles.

But I recall sadly and clearly—
I'm a mother, and we have a simple law:
In this blood we are not accomplices,
As we weren't in that other blood.

1922

TRANSLATED BY **Sibelan Forrester**

[Расчет случаен и неверен]

The reckoning's chancy and slipshod—what did my forefather know of me
when, almost like a beast, he covered my foremother in a Neolithic cave?
And I myself, what do I know further of the one who will grow anew, in turn,
from my innermost parts like a seed in a ploughed field up into the millennia?

1925

TRANSLATED BY Sibelan Forrester

Translations:

In Kelly; Markov/Sparks; Tomei; Yevtushenko.

Biography and Bibliography:

Heldt, Barbara. "Motherhood in a Cold Climate: The Poetry and Career of Mariia Shkapskaia." *Russian Review* 5, no. 2 (April 1992): 160-71.

Fyodor Sologub

Fyodor Kuz'mich Sologub (suh-lah-GOOB, né Teternikov, 1863-1927) was born in St. Petersburg in a proletarian family: his father was a tailor, his mother a peasant. His father died early, and his mother worked as a servant while raising her children. Sologub got an education and had access to literature of all kinds in the cultured house where she worked, and he began writing poetry at twelve, publishing his first poem in 1884. His mother was not gentle with him and was still using a whip to punish him when he grew up. He studied at the Petersburg Teachers' Institute. When he graduated (1882) he found work as a teacher and spent several years in various provincial cities, gathering material along the way for his prose fiction, especially the remarkable novel *The Petty Demon* (1905). In 1892 he moved to St. Petersburg and grew close to the group around Gippius and Merezhkovsky, writing a lot while still teaching. He soon became prominent in the Symbolist movement, usually considered one of the decadents, and in 1905 he began to write for broader publication. In 1907, after twenty-five years of teaching, he retired with a pension and turned entirely to literature, writing poetry, plays, criticism, and prose fiction. He married the translator and critic Anastasia Chebotarevskaya in 1908; she helped advance his career and take his weekly literary salons to a new level. He was bereft after her suicide in 1921. Sologub was opposed to the Bolsheviks but did not emigrate; after the 1917 Revolution he published more in Germany and elsewhere abroad than in the USSR, as long as that was possible. He died in Leningrad in 1927.

[Мы—плененные звери]

We are beasts in a cage,
We give voice as we can.
The doors are locked tight,
We don't dare open them.

If the heart's true to tradition,
We howl, consoled by howling.
We don't know, we've long forgotten,
That the bestiary smells foully.

The heart's accustomed to repetitions—
On and on we cuckoo dully.
Everything in the zoo is faceless.
We've long stopped longing for free will.

We are beasts in a cage,
We give voice as we can.
The doors are locked tight,
We don't dare open them.

1908

TRANSLATED BY Sibelan Forrester

[Я был один в моем раю]

I was alone in my paradise,
And someone was calling me "Adam."
The flowers praised my flesh
With incense from the origin.

And the first-created bestiary
Crowding around me, gazed
At my body, still innocent,
With a love untamed.

At my feet a stream rustled,
Rushing to kiss my naked soles,
And the reflections of eyes
Looked at me with kindly smiles.

When the steps of mountain slabs
Were scattered with the evening dew,
The enchantress Lilith would come
To me on her path of azure.

And she was all entirely weightless,
Like a soft dream—sinless as sleep,
And her speech was consoling as laughter,
And as tender Laughter—sweet.

And I wouldn't have wished for another!
But under the evil tree's shade
I fell asleep . . . I woke—and before me
Eve was standing and laughing . . .

When the azure day went dim,
As the glow over the seas sank lower,
My Lilith passed by like a shadow,
Passed by—she hid away forever.

1908?

TRANSLATED BY **Sibelan Forrester**

[Насытив очи наготою]

After sating my eyes with the nudity
Of ethereal, passionless bodies,
I wanted to become incarnate
Through passionate earthly beauty.

Then they gave me the name of Phryne,
And in the charm of tender powers
I enraptured my Athens
And dipped my body in the waves.

Innocence made hymns to me,
Vice was ashamed of nakedness,
And it filled its sting with poison
In the dust of creeping slander.

A harsh punishment threatened me,
I was slandered by rumor,
But the living power of divinity
Transformed spite into victory.

When my terrible enemy
Aimed a poisoned word at me,
The Areopagus suddenly perceived
My unshrouded beauty.

Cruel persecution was eclipsed,
Slander twisted up and died,
And there was—an obeisance of old men,
A passionless rapture and praise.

1908

TRANSLATED BY *Sibelan Forrester*

[Сквозь туман едва заметный]

Through a barely visible mist
Quietly shimmers Kostroma,
Just like Kitezh, sacred city—
Churches, towers, palaces.

Kostroma is memories,
Dreams out of history,
Legendary sagas,
The voice of ancient Russian times,

A corner of gray-haired daily life,
And of new factories and merchants.
Where there was hidden so much
Pure power and prophetic dreaming.

In the cathedrals' golden crowns,
Kostroma, so bright, so white,
In days of agreement and of conflict
Has lived a storied Russian life.

But what has it kept from this glorious,
storied life in preservation?
Like Yaroslavna in Putivl'
Is she a faithful wife, waiting?

1920

TRANSLATED BY **Lisa Woodson**

Translations:

The Kiss of the Unborn, and Other Stories. Translated by Murl G. Barker. Knoxville: University of Tennessee Press, 1977.

The Little Demon. Translated by Richard Aldington and John Cournos. New York: A. A. Knopf, 1916.

The Little Demon. Translated by Ronald Wilks and Pamela Davisdon. London: Penguin Classics, 2013.

The Old House and Other Tales. Translated by John Cournos. London: Secker, 1915.

The Petty Demon. Translated by Andrew Field and Ernest J. Simmons. New York: Random House, 1962.

The Petty Demon. Translated by Samuel D. Cioran and Murl Barker. Ann Arbor: Ardis, 1983.

The Sweet-Scented Name: and Other Fairy Tales, Fables and Stories. Translated by Stephen Graham. New York: G. P. Putnam's Sons, 1915; reprint Westport, CT: Hyperion Press, 1977.

In Chandler/Mashinski/Dralyuk; Markov/Sparks; Obolensky; Yarmolinsky/Deutsch; Yevtushenko.

Biography and Bibliography:

Greene, Diana. *Insidious Intent: An Interpretation of Fedor Sologub's The Petty Demon*. Columbus, OH: Slavica Publishers, 1986.

Rabinowitz, Stanley J. *Sologub's Literary Children: Keys to a Symbolist's Prose*. Columbus, OH: Slavica Publishers, 1980.

Vladimir Solovyov

Vladimir Sergeevich Solovyov (LoC Solov'ev, 1853-1900). No other nineteenth-century Russian figure influenced the poets of the Silver Age more than the philosopher, poet, and essayist, Vladimir Solovyov. Solovyov grew up amid the intellectual elite of late-Imperial Russia and, like many in his generation, was initially drawn to the positivist philosophies entering Russia from the West. Ultimately he turned instead toward an Orthodox-based religious philosophy, and in his master's and doctoral work penned some of the strongest arguments *against* Western rational philosophy in any language. Solovyov gradually moved from Slavophilism to a liberal view of human dignity, although elements of this humanist strain were present from the beginning. The biggest change came in 1881, when he called for leniency toward the assassins of Tsar Alexander II (incidentally ruining his career prospects). Famous for his twelve public *Lectures on Godmanhood*, which attracted Dostovesky in the late 1870s, and for his late *poema, Three Encounters* (1898), describing three visions of the Divine Sophia, he also published dozens of works on Russian national identity, on the "Universal Church," on Jews and Judaism, on Plato, aesthetics, literature, and love, and a moral treatise, *Justification of the Good*—not to mention hundreds of poems, plays, and stories. Solovyov never married, living with friends and family in Moscow, St. Petersburg, and abroad. He spent many summers on the estate of a niece of Alexei Tolstoy, one of the creators of the satiric poet Koz'ma Prutkov. Humor played an important role throughout Solovyov's life, and he was known among contemporaries for his raucous laugh and sometimes bawdy poetry. Despite his earthy sense of humor, however, Solovyov's legacy permeates the serious, ethereal writing of the Silver Age. Blok, Bely, and Ivanov seized on the poet-philosopher's mystical visions of Sophia, transforming her into a "beautiful lady" and Solovyov himself into a "knightly monk," the title of a short reminiscence by Blok. Along with Sophia, the Symbolists were drawn to Solovyov's lyrics about Lake Saima in Finland and to many of his later works, including the philosophical "The Meaning of Love" and a pseudo-Platonic dialogue, *Three Conversations*, in which they focused on the apocalyptic "Short Story of the Antichrist." For the Silver Age Symbolists, Solovyov's ethics, his political and social philosophy, and even his literary criticism tended to fade from view.

Judith Deutsch Kornblatt

[Вся в лазури сегодня явилась]

My tsaritsa appeared to me
Today, wrapped all in azure—
My heart beat with a sweet delight,
And in the rays of approaching day
My soul shone with a quiet light.
While smoldering in the distance
Rose the fierce flame of earthly fire.

Cairo, 1875

TRANSLATED BY Judith Deutsch Kornblatt

Song of the Ophites
[Песня офитов]

    We make a bouquet of red roses,
Red roses with lilies, lilies of white.
    Prophetic, mysterious dreams
Reveal to us truth, reveal truth eternal.

    Speak now a prophetic word!
Hurry up, throw your pearl into the goblet!
    Tie up our dear little dove
With new rings brought forth from the ancient snake.

    The heart once free feels no pain . . .
Why should it fear the fire of Prometheus?
    The innocent dove is at liberty
In the fiery rings of the powerful snake.

    Sing through the furious thunder,
In the furious thunder we'll yet attain peace . . .
    We make a bouquet of red roses,
Red roses with lilies, lilies of white.

1876

TRANSLATED BY Martha Kelly

Ex Oriente Lux

"Light and strength come from the East!"
And through the Pass of Thermopylae
Iran's fierce tsar drove on his slaves
Towards the great might of the Goths.

But not in vain did Prometheus give
His heavenly gift to Hellas.
Mobs of slaves run pale and scared
Before a few heroic men.

Who was it walked the glorious path
From the Indus to the Ganges?
A Macedonian phalange,
Or Rome's imperial eagle.

And by the force of thought and right—
The ground of all that's human—
The West reared up its mighty head,
And Rome brought union to the world.

So what is it that we still lack?
Why is the world once more at war?—
The universal soul has longed
For the spirit of faith and love!

And the prophetic word lies not,
A light from the East has yet blazed forth,
And all that was impossible,
It yet has promised and announced.

And spreading out both wide and far,
Full of portents and of force,
That light that has come from the East
Has reconciled the East and West.

O, Rus'! in this most lofty vision
You're occupied in arrogant thoughts;
What kind of East would you, then, be:
The East of Xerxes or of Christ?

1890

TRANSLATED BY Martha Kelly

Translations:

Freedom, Faith and Dogma: Essays by V. S. Soloviev on Christianity and Judaism. Translated by Victor Wozniuk. Albany, NY: State University of New York Press, 2008.

God, Man and the Church: The Spiritual Foundations of Life. Translated by Donald Attwater. Milwaukee, WI: The Bruce Publishing Company, 1939.

The Heart of Reality: Essay on Beauty, Love, and Ethics by V. S. Soloviev. Edited and translated by Vladimir Wozniuk. Notre Dame, IN: University of Notre Dame Press, 2003.

Lectures on Godmanhood. Translated by Peter P. Zouboff. London: D. Dobson, 1948.

The Meaning of Love. Translated by Thomas R. Beyer. Hudson, NY: Lindisfarne Press, 1985.

Politics, Law and Morality. Translated by Vladimir Wozniuk. Introduction by Gary Saul Morson. New Haven: Yale University Press, 2000.

A Solovyov Anthology. Translated by S. L. Frank and Natalie Duddington. New York: Scribner, 1950

War, Progress and the End of History: Three Conversations, Including a Short History of the Antichrist. Hudson, NY: Lindisfarne Press, 1990.

In Yevtushenko.

Biography and Bibliography:

Cioran, Samuel D. *Vladimir Solov'ev and the Knighthood of the Divine Sophia.* Waterloo, Ontario: Wilfrid Laurier University Press, 1977.

Hellerman, Wendy F. *Solovyov's Sophia as a Nineteenth-Century Russian Appropriation of Dante's Beatrice.* Lewiston, NY: Edwin Mellen Press, 2011.

Kornblatt, Judith Deutsch. *Divine Sophia: The Wisdom Writings of Vadimir Solovyov.* Ithaca, NY: Cornell University Press, 2009.

Munzer, Egbert. *Solovyov: Prophet of Russian-Western Unity.* New York: Philosophical Library, 1956.

Smith, Oliver. *Vladimir Soloviev and the Spiritualization of Matter.* Boston, MA: Academic Studies Press, 2011.

Solovyov, Sergei M. *Vladimir Solovyov: His Life and Creative Evolution,* 2 volumes. Translated by Aleksey Gibson. Fairfax, VA: Eastern Christian Publications, 1999.

Sutton, Jonathan. *The Religious Philosophy of Vladimir Solovyov: Towards a Reassessment.* New York: St Martin's Press, 1988.

Zouboff, Peter P. *Godmanhood as the Main Idea of the Philosophy of Vladimir Solovyev.* Poughkeepsie, NY: Harmon Printing House, 1944.

Marina Tsvetaeva

Marina Ivanovna Tsvetaeva (tsvi-TAH-ye-vuh, 1892-1941) was born in Moscow. Her mother was a gifted pianist with an aristocratic background (via Polish and Baltic German ancestors). Her father was the son of a village priest; he attended university, became a professor, and eventually founded the Alexander III Museum of Fine Arts, now the Pushkin Museum, in Moscow. Tsvetaeva grew up speaking German and French as well as Russian; for a few years as a child she lived (sometimes at boarding schools) in Italy, Switzerland, and Germany, while her mother was being treated for tuberculosis. After her mother died in 1906, she and her younger sister had the run of their house and formed more adult acquaintances, some of them with minor Moscow Symbolist poets. Tsvetaeva published her first book of poetry at her own expense when she was eighteen; it received surprisingly positive reviews for an unknown author, including one by Maximilian Voloshin that led to a lasting friendship. She met her husband at Voloshin's summer house in Koktebel', where they continued to visit yearly until the 1917 Revolution. Her first child was born in 1912. She had a poetically important affair with Sofia Parnok in 1914-16 and a brief but generative fling with her friend Osip Mandelstam in 1916. At the same time she was writing cycles to the best-known poets of the day, Akhmatova and Blok. Tsvetaeva's husband joined the army during WWI and then the White Army, was evacuated through Constantinople, and wound up in Czechoslovakia. After difficult years in Moscow under War Communism (during which her second child died of starvation in 1920), Tsvetaeva left Russia in 1922. For months in Berlin and years in Prague she wrote prolifically, including long poems that in some ways recalled Futurist innovations. The family moved to Paris in 1925 and lived there in worsening poverty, moving from one cheap rental to another. Partly to make ends meet, Tsvetaeva began writing more theoretical and critical essays as well as autobiographical prose and memoirs (with pieces about Bely, Bryusov, Pasternak, Mayakovsky, Pushkin, Voloshin, and Kuzmin); she wrote less poetry as time passed. Her husband and daughter returned to the USSR in 1937; Tsvetaeva and her son Georgy followed in spring of 1939. She made a poor living doing literary translation; her sister was already in a camp, and her husband and daughter were soon arrested. After being evacuated eastward shortly after WWII reached the Soviet Union in June 1941, she committed suicide in a village in Tatarstan. Tsvetaeva's biography is so rich in significant incident that it can overshadow discussion of her writing. She is one of the best-known poets of the Russian Silver Age, and her work in other genres (including drama) is increasingly an object of study.

[Под лаской плюшевого пледа]

Beneath the plush plaid's sweet caresses,
I piece together last night's dream.
Who's been defeated?—Who's successful?—
What has it been?

Rethinking everything once more,
I'm tortured and the pain persists.
In this, for which I know no word,
Did love exist?

Who was the hunter?—And—the prey?
The roles reversed, and all was blurred!
What did the cat perceive today
Just as it purred?

When our two wills clashed in this battle,
Who in whose hands was but a ball?
Whose heart had burst into a gallop?
Do you recall?

And after all—what has it been?
What makes me miss it so and need it?
I still don't know: so did I win?
Was I defeated?

October 23, 1914

TRANSLATED BY **Andrey Kneller**

[Гибель от женщины. Вот знак]

Woman will be your downfall. There's—the mark,
In the palm of your hand, stripling!
Eyes to the ground! Pray! Be on your guard! The dark
Enemy lurks at midnight.

Neither your songs, gift of heaven,
Will save you, nor the haughtiest purse of your lips.
You are favored for this,
That you are of heaven.

Ah, just look at your head thrown back,
Hiding—eh?—half-closed eyes.
Ah, but your head will be thrown back—
Otherwise.

With bare hands they'll take you—stubborn! grim!—
The land will ring all night with your shrieking!
They'll scatter your wings unto all four winds,
Seraph!—Young eaglet!—

March 17, 1916

TRANSLATED BY **Robin Kemball**

[Канун Благовещенья]

Eve of the Annunciation.
The Cathedral of the Annunciation
Is shining beautifully.
Above the grand cupola,
Under the sickly moon,
A star—that reminds me of
Constantinople.

Round the grey parvis,
A group of old women
Beg for almsgiving
In strident voices.
Like large pearls, gleaming
Lamps are burning
Round the Holy Virgin.

Aglow with black insomnia
The saints' faces shine,
Inside the back cupola
Ice covers the window cases.
Like a golden bush, like a family
Tree, it dangles there,
The huge chandelier.
—Blessèd is the fruit of Thy womb,
Merciful
Virgin!

It has journeyed
From hand to hand—the flame,
It has journeyed
From mouth to mouth—the name:
—Holy Virgin.

Radiant with heat,
The candle is lit.

Lost in the shadows there,
I, too, turn to the Sun Mother,
Offer her, joyfully, my prayer:
Mother—of mothers,
Preserve and guide
My blue-eyed
Daughter!
Instruct her
In enlightened wisdom,
Conduct her
Upon the lost path—
Of blessedness.
Grant her health,
At her pillow head
Install—the Angel
Since fled
From me.
Keep her from—pompous wordiness,
Lest she become, like me—a predatoress,
A sorceress.

The service is over.
The sky is cloudless.
Crossing themselves with fervor,
The people go on their way.
Some—to their homes,
And those with—nowhere,
Go—God knows where,
All—God knows where!

A group of peasant
Women, gray and old,
Linger by the entrance—
Crossing themselves severalfold,
Before that limpid blaze,
Before the candles' rays.

As for me, I merrily—
As through unsteady waves,
Thrust my way through the crowd,
I run down to the river Moskva
To watch the ice flow there.

March 24-25, 1916

TRANSLATED BY Robin Kemball

[Да с этой львиною]

But with that leonine
Golden fair head of his,
And with that sash of his,
And with that whistling—
How not go chasing then
The wide world after him—
After that sash of his,
After that whistling!

Down the street, as I stride—
People all turn aside:
As from some brigand or
Someone but lately died.
They all know long ago
Which saints I pray unto—
In chapels, teeny ones,
In apple greeny ones.

I am the guilty one,
I, friends, and I alone.
Blue linen's not to be:
Weave no fine shroud for me.
So, in eternity,
Since I slept not alone,
'neath the wild apple tree
I shall lie, incense-free.

Palm Sunday, 2 April 1916

TRANSLATED BY Robin Kemball

from the cycle "Insomnia," 1
["Бессонница"; Обвела мне глаза кольцом]

It's enveloped my eyes with
A shadowy ring—insomnia.
It's woven about my eyes, insomnia
A shadowy crown.

What did I tell you. Do not pray
Of nights—to idols!
Your secret I have betrayed,
Idolatress.

Little enough—for you—the day,
The sun's fierce flame!

A pair of rings,
Wear them, pale-faced one.
I called for—and conjured
The shadowy crown.

So little—for me—you cried?
So little—slept—by my side?

Your face will be light when you lie.
People will bow in homage.
I'll be your reader, I,
Insomnia:

—Sleep, my placated one,
Sleep, venerated one,
Sleep, consecrated
Woman.

That you—may sleep—quieter,
I'll be—your—chorister:

—Sleep, dearest heart of mine,
Restless and fretful one,
Sleep, precious pearl of mine,
Sleep, ever-wakeful one.

Whom didn't we write letters to.
Whom didn't we give pledges to . . .

Lo, they are separated,
The inseparable ones.
Lo, and set free from my hands
Your fair hands.

Now you've ceased martyrizing
Yourself. Dear martyress.

Sleep—is divine.
Asleep—everyone.
Torn off—the crown.

8 April 1916

TRANSLATED BY **Robin Kemball**

from the cycle "Insomnia," 3
["Бессонница"; В огромном городе моем—ночь]

My enormous city is full of night.
I leave my sleeping house to go—out.
These people think of me as daughter, wife,
But I can think of one thing only—night.

Mid-July. A breeze sweeps down the road.
Music from a window, barely heard.
From now till dawn the breeze bows hard
Between my fragile ribs into my heart.

Light in a window. A chime from a tower.
A plane-tree shadow. In my hand a flower.
These are my footsteps, which no one can hear.
This is my shadow, and I am not here.

Street lights are strings of golden beads.
In my mouth the taste of nighttime leaves.
Free me, all of you, from the day's claims
And understand. I am in your dreams.

June 17, 1916

TRANSLATED BY **Paul Schmidt**

from the cycle *Poems about Moscow*, IV
[Настанет день — печальный, говорят!]

The day will come—a sad one, people say!
There will have reigned, have cried, have shined, have shamed,
—Cured by your pair of double-headed eagles—
My eyes critical, like flame, and eager.
And—as a twin discovering its twin—
An aery mask will surface through the mien.

Oh, finally at last I'll be endowed
With you, serenity's enchanting shroud!

And pilgrims (see You there among the guests?)
Will, crossing inconsolably their chests,
Stretch, from afar, along a beaten track to
My hand that won't be bashfully retracted,
My hand, whose guardianship was dismissed,
My hand, that does not any more exist.

Your—oh, alive ones—kissing lips' persistence
For once—will not be met with my resistance.
For I have been enveloped heel to head
In you, serenity's enchanting plaid.
No cause will prompt a blush of mine to blossom;
This is my Holy Easter, saint apostles!

Along the streets of Moscow left behind
We will begin: you—treading; riding—I,
And more than one shall wearily walk off, and
First clods of dirt will fall onto the coffin—
And finally, at last there will be blessed
That egotistic, solitary rest.

And nothing will be needed ever in it
By Her Serenity lamented late Marina.

April 11, 1916
the 1st day of Easter

TRANSLATED BY *Alexander Givental and Élysée Wilson-Egolf*

[Руки люблю]

Hands that I so love
To kiss and I so love
Attributing names,
Yes, and opening
Doors!
—Gaping—into dark night!

Clasping my head,
Hark, how a heavy tread
Somewhere is fading,
How the wind cradles
The sleepy, unsleeping
Wood.

Ah, night!
Somewhere streams are in flow,
I'm gently drowsing.
I'm sleeping—not quite.
Somewhere in the night
A person is drowning.

May 27, 1916

TRANSLATED BY *Robin Kemball*

[Я тебя отвоюю у всех земель, у всех небес]

I'll conquer you from any land and from any sky,
For the forest is my cradle and it's where I'll die,
Because, here, on this earth, I stand—only on one foot,
And because I'll sing for you—as no other could.

I'll conquer you from any epoch, from any night,
From any golden banner, any sword in a fight,
I'll chase the dogs off the porch, toss away the key
For in this night, no dog's so loyal as me,

I'll conquer you from all others and from that one too,
I'll be no one's wife—you'll be no one's groom.
I'll win the last battle—hush!—and pull you aside
From the one with whom Jacob fought all night.

Before I cross your arms on your chest—I'm cursed!—
And until that day, you will remain—just yours,
This is why your wings aim for the upper sky—
For the world's your cradle and the world's where you'll die!

August 15, 1916

TRANSLATED BY *Andrey Kneller*

[Каждый стих дитя любви]

Every poem is a love-child,
A penniless first-born
Bastard, set by the roadside
To beg from the winds.

Heart's poison, heart's adoration,
Heart's paradise, heart's grief.
His father may have been an emperor—
May have been a thief.

1918

TRANSLATED BY *Paul Schmidt*

Psyche
[Психея]

I'm neither an imposter nor a guest!
I'm not the maid! I am your seventh
Day, your longed-for Sunday's rest,
Your passion and your seventh heaven!

On earth, they wouldn't offer me a dime,
Hung millstones on my neck to spite me.
My love! Do you not recognize me? I'm
Your little bird, your swallow—Psyche!

April 1918

TRANSLATED BY *Andrey Kneller*

[Восхищённой и восхищённой]

Held captured and enraptured deeply,
I saw my dreams during the day—
All saw me sleeping where I lay,
Nobody saw me tired and sleepy.

And all because throughout the day,
The dreams were floating in my sight.
I can't sleep now, and here I stay
And like a lonesome shadow sway
Over my sleeping friends at night.

May 19, 1920

TRANSLATED BY Andrey Kneller

To Mayakovsky
[Маяковскому]

High above cross and trumpet
baptized in smoke and fire
my clumsy-footed angel—
Hello there, Vladimir!

Carter and horse at once
justice and whim together.
He used to spit on his palms—
Hold on, carthorse of glory!

Singer of gutter miracles,
grubby, arrogant friend—
Hullo there, you who prefer
topaz to diamond!

Now yawn, play your trump card
my thunderbolt of cobbles,
and rake this horse's shaft
once more with your angel wing.

1921

TRANSLATED BY *Elaine Feinstein*

from the cycle "Parting," 3
[Разлука; Всё круче, всё круче]

Harder and harder
Start wringing my hands!
Between us not earthly
Vyorsts—but divisive
Celestial rivers, azure nations,
Where my friend is forever already—
Inalienable.

The high road races
In silvery harness.
I don't wring my hands!
I only extend them
—In silence!—
Like a tree-(waving)-rowan
To parting,
The wake of a crane-wedge flying.

The crane train is racing,
Racing, no backward glances.
I'll not desert haughtiness!
In death—I'll abide
Elegant—to your gold-fledged quickness
The very last buttress
To the losses of space!

June 1921

TRANSLATED BY *Sibelan Forrester*

(from Earthly Signs)
[Земные приметы; Руки — и в круг]

Hands up—and jump
Into the circle of breaching and bleeding!
Just so the lips,
Just so the hands don't confuse or mislead me!

Piles of care,
Trifles that pilfer my sleep, make me restless.
Hands in the air,
Friend, I invoke my own remembrance!

So that in poems
(Vast garbage heaps of my past Beloveds!)
You won't corrode,
You won't decay in the manner of others.

So in my breast
(Million-hilled domicile of my common
Grave!)—chilly rains,
Passing millennia won't wash you spotless . . .

One corpse of lots,
—You, who for me were a two-star shambles . . . !—
So you won't rot
Under the caption: nameless.

July 9, 1922

TRANSLATED BY Alyssa Dinega Gillespie

[Неподражаемо лжет жизнь]

Flawlessly, matchlessly life lies:
Beyond any likeness, beyond fibs . . .
But by the thrill of my whole fiber
I can espy: life!

As in a field of rye: hum, blue . . .
(So what if the field's a lie!)—heat, hill.
Murmur—of lilac flesh—all through . . .
Celebrate! He called!

And do not scold me, friend; it seems
The souls of us bodies are spell-prone
So that already I lunge—dream.
For, why else had you sung?

Into your silences' scroll, white,
Into your yes-sayings' clay, wild,
Meekly I cup my brow's steep rise:
For, in my palm's—life.

July 8, 1922

TRANSLATED BY Alyssa Dinega Gillespie

Dawn on the Rails
[Рассвет на рельсах]

Before the new day's rise—
Its deeply chiseled passion—
From dampness and from ties
I reassemble Russia.

From dampness—and from piles,
From dampness—and from grayness—
Before the new day's rise,
The switchman's interference.

The mist has mercy yet,
Still wrapped in canvas sacking
The mighty granite rests,
The checkered fields sleep blackly...

From dampness—and from flocks...
Still winged with prankish tidings
The burnished steel distorts—
Still Moscow's past the sidings!

And so, my stubborn gaze—
My most unfleshly aptitude—
Calls forth a Russia splayed
Profusely through the atmosphere!

Unfurled now triple-wide:
A car—a railway phantom—
With burned-out folks inside,
I launch into the dampness:

They're lost for good and all
To God and to humanity!
(A sign hangs: "Forty souls,
Eight horses—max. capacity.")

Thus, on the rails, where sky
Lifts like a gate and beckons,
From dampness and from ties,
From dampness—and bereftness,

Before the new day's rise—
Its deeply chiseled passion—
Along the whole horizon
I reassemble Russia!

No baseness, and no lies:
Deep sky, two rails of blue ...
Hey, there she is!—Hold tight!
Chug-chugging, coming true ...

October 12, 1922

TRANSLATED BY *Alyssa Dinega Gillespie*

Appointment
[На назначенное свидание]

I'll be late for the meeting
we arranged. When I arrive, my hair
will be grey. Yes, I suppose I grabbed
at Spring. And you set your hopes much too high.

I shall walk with this bitterness for years
across mountains or town squares equally,
(Ophelia didn't flinch at rue!) I'll walk
on souls and on hands without shuddering.

Living on. As the earth continues.
With blood in every thicket, every creek.
Even though Ophelia's face is waiting
between the grasses bordering every stream.

She gulped at love, and filled her mouth
with silt. A shaft of light on metal!
I set my love on you. Much too high.
In the sky   arrange my burial.

1923

TRANSLATED BY **Elaine Feinstein**

To Sneak Through
[Прокрасться]

It may be that a better way
to conquer time and world
is to pass and not to leave a trace—
to pass, and not to leave a shadow

on the walls... To be, but by denial:
to break both mirror and reflection.
To ride the Caucasus like Lermontov
and not to wake the rocks.

It may be that the better art
is with the hand of Bach
to leave the organ undisturbed—
to vanish, not to leave a cinder

for the urn... To be, but by deceit:
to strike yourself from latitudes.
To slip through time as through the sea
and not to break the waves.

1923

TRANSLATED BY *Paul Schmidt*

Rails
[Рельсы]

The bed of a railway cutting
    has tidy sheets. The steel-blue
parallel tracks ruled out
    as neatly as staves of music.

And over them people are driven
    like possessed creatures from Pushkin
whose piteous song   has been silenced.
    Look, they're departing, deserting.

And yet lag behind and linger,
    the note of pain always rising
higher than love, as the poles freeze
    to the bank, like Lot's wife, forever.

Despair has appointed an hour for me
    (as someone arranges a marriage): then
Sappho with her voice gone
    I shall weep like a simple seamstress

with a cry of passive lament—
    a marsh heron! The moving train
will hoot its way over the sleepers
    and slice through them like scissors.

Colors blur in my eye,
    their glow a meaningless red.
All your women at times
    are tempted—by such a bed!

1923

TRANSLATED BY *Elaine Feinstein*

[Рас-стояние: вёрсты, мили...]
To B. Pasternak

Dis-tances: miles, vyorsts...
They dispelled us till we dis-persed,
So we would do as we were told
In two corners of the world.

Dis-tances: vyorsts, spaces...
They dislocated us, they displaced us,
They disjoined us, crucified on display,
And observed to their dismay,

How our sinews fused and ideas broadened...
Without discord—just in disorder.
Distorted...
    Disconnected by wall and dike.
They disbanded us just like

Eagle-conspirators: vyorsts, spaces...
Not disunited—they disarrayed us.
Across the slums of the globe's range
As if orphans, we're disarranged.

For how many Marches have our hearts
Been cut, like a deck of cards?!

March 24, 1925

TRANSLATED BY *Andrey Kneller*

Translations:

After Russia. Translated by Michael Naydan and Slava Yastermski. Ann Arbor: Ardis, 1992.

Art in the Light of Conscience: Eight Essays on Poetry. Translated by Angela Livingstone. Cambridge, MA: Harvard University Press, 1992.

A Captive Spirit: Selected Prose. Translated by J. Marin King. Ann Arbor: Ardis Publishers, 1980.

Dark Elderberry Branch. Translated by Ilya Kaminsky and Jean Valentine. Farmington, ME: Alice James Books, 2012.

The Demesne of the Swans. Translated by Robin Kemball. Ann Arbor: Ardis, 1980.

Earthly Signs: Moscow Diaries, 1917-1922. Translated by Jamey Gambrell. New Haven: Yale University Press, 2002.

Letters, Summer 1926: Correspondence between Pasternak, Tsvetayeva, Rilke. Translated by Margaret Wettlin and Walter Arndt. San Diego, CA: Harcourt, Brace, Jovanovich, 1985.

Milestones. Translated by Robin Kemball. Evanston, IL: Northwestern University Press, 2003.

Phaedra: with New Year's Letter and Other Long Poems. Translated by Angela Livingstone. London: Angel Books, 2012.

The Ratcatcher. Translated by Angela Livingstone. Evanston, IL: Northwestern University Press, 1999.

Selected Poems of Marina Tsvetayeva. Translated by Elaine Feinstein. New York: E. P. Dutton, 1986.

Three Russian Women Poets: Anna Akhmatova, Marina Tsvetaeva, Bella Akhmadulina. Translated by Mary Maddock. Trumansburg, NY: Crossing Press, 1983.

Also in: Chandler/Mashinski/Dralyuk; Glad/Weissbort; Kazakova; Kelly; Mager; Markov/Sparks; Obolensky; Rzhevsky; Schmidt/Ciepiela; Tomei; Yarmolinsky/Deutsch; Yevtushenko.

Biography:

Feiler, Lily. *Marina Tsvetaeva: The Double Beat of Heaven and Hell.* Durham: Duke University Press, 1994.

Karlinsky, Simon. *Marina Cvetaeva: Her Life and Art.* Berkeley: University of California Press, 1966.

Karlinsky, Simon. *Marina Tsvetaeva: The Woman, Her World, and Her Poetry.* Cambridge, UK and New York: Cambridge University Press, 1986.

Razumovskaya, Maria. *Marina Tsvetayeva: A Critical Biography.* Translated by Alexey Gibson. Newcastle upon Tyne: Bloodaxe Books, 1994.

Schweitzer, Victoria. *Tsvetaeva.* Translated by Robert Chandler and H. T. Willetts. New York: Farrar, Straus and Giroux, 1993.

Bibliography:

Ciepiela, Catherine. *The Same Solitude: Boris Pasternak and Marina Tsvetaeva.* Ithaca: Cornell University Press, 2006.

Dinega [Gillespie], Alyssa. *A Russian Psyche: The Poetic Mind of Marina Tsvetaeva.* Madison, WI: University of Wisconsin Press, 2001.

Hasty, Olga Peters. *Tsvetaeva's Orphic Journeys in the Worlds of the Word.* Evanston, IL: Northwestern University Press, 1996.

Makin, Michael. *Marina Tsvetaeva: Poetics of Appropriation.* Oxford, New York: Clarendon Press, Oxford University Press, 1993.

Stock, Ute. *The Ethics of the Poet: Marina Tsvetaeva's Art in the Light of Conscience.* Leeds, UK: Maney Publishing for the Modern Humanities Research Association, 2005.

MAXIMILIAN VOLOSHIN

Maximilian Aleksandrovich Voloshin (né Kirienko-Voloshin, 1877-1932) was born in Kiev; his ancestry included Zaporozh'e Cossacks. He grew up in the south, then moved to Moscow, where he began to study law but was expelled and exiled to Tashkent for participating in student "disorders." He began writing poetry at eleven and published his first poem in 1895, eventually publishing nine books of poems and countless articles. From 1901 to 1915 he lived partly in Paris, partly in Koktebel', where he had a house on the shore of the Black Sea. Voloshin was a poet, critic, theorist, and practitioner of creative mystifications, as active in painting as in literature: he exhibited his paintings with the World of Art and wrote that he considered visual art "the greatest pleasure." He married Margarita Sabashnikova in 1906 but the relationship with his wife, also an artist, became complicated when she was drawn into the ménage of Vyacheslav Ivanov and Lidia Zinovieva-Annibal. After 1907 he spent much more time in Koktebel', where every summer he welcomed guests like Mandelstam, Parnok, and Tsvetaeva to an unofficial artists' colony. Between 1917 and 1924 he stayed in Koktebel' and almost starved as the battle lines of the Civil War moved back and forth across Crimea. Voloshin's poetry was strongly influenced by French literature; his artistic character in person was quite different, humorous and effectively bohemian. He remarried in 1927 and died in 1932 in Koktebel'; his widow Marya Zabolotskaya (from his second marriage) managed to preserve his house as an artists' colony after his death.

To Baltrushaitis
[Балтрушайтису]

I'm drawn to your lines not by novelty,
Not by the bright flash of lights:
I seem to see in them the glum severity
Of brows knit tight.

I seem to see in them grey-haired indifference,
The steely waters' drowse,
The gloomy grandeur of raw earth
And a bitterly pursed mouth.

1903, Moscow

TRANSLATED BY **Sibelan Forrester**

[Обманите меня... но совсем, навсегда...]

Fool me... but fully, forever...
So I won't wonder why, so I won't recall—
                              when...
So I'll believe the lie freely, without pondering,
To follow someone in the dark at random...
And not know who's come, who tied on my blindfold,
Who leads me through a maze of unknown halls,
Whose breathing sometimes burns on my cheek,
Who presses my hand so firmly in their hand...
And on coming to, to see but night and brume...
Fool me, and you too believe the deception.

1911

TRANSLATED BY **Sibelan Forrester**

Translations:
In Chandler/Mashinski/Dralyuk; Glad/Weissbort; Markov/Sparks; Obolensky; Yarmolinsky/Deutsch; Yevtushenko.

Biography and Bibliography:
Tsvetaeva, Marina. "A Living Word about a Living Man." In *A Captive Spirit: Selected Prose*, translated by J. Marin King, 3-51. Ann Arbor: Ardis, 1980.

Walker, Barbara. *Maximilian Voloshin and the Russian Literary Circle: Culture and Survival in Revolutionary Times*. Bloomington, IN: Indiana University Press, 2005.

COLLECTIONS OF POETRY TRANSLATIONS REFERENCED ABOVE:

Chandler, Robert, Irina Mashinski, and Boris Dralyuk, eds. *The Penguin Anthology of Russian Poetry from Pushkin to Brodsky*. London: Penguin Classics, 2015.

Glad, John, and Daniel Weissbort, eds. *Russian Poetry: The Modern Period*. Iowa City, IA: University of Iowa Press, 1974.

Kazakova, Rimma, ed. *The Tender Muse*. Moscow: Progress Publishers, 1976. A few poems by Akhmatova and Tsvetaeva are included along with a wide range of female poets, often little-known, from various Soviet republics.

Kelly, Catriona. *An Anthology of Russian Women's Writing, 1777-1992*. Translated by Catriona Kelly, Sibelan Forrester, Diana Greene, Elizabeth Neatrour, Brian Thomas Oles, Marian Schwartz, and Mary Zirin. Oxford: Oxford University Press, 1994. The translations of women's writing in Russian include several lesser-known Silver Age writers.

Mager, Don, ed. and trans. *Us Four Plus Four: Eight Russian Poets Conversing*. New Orleans, LA: UNO Press, no date. A bilingual edition with uneven but interesting translations.

Markov, Vladimir, and Merrill Sparks, eds. *Modern Russian Poetry*. Indianapolis and New York: Bobbs-Merrill Company, Inc., 1967.

Muchnik, Slava, ed. *Salt Crystals on an Axe/Как соль на топоре. Twentieth-Century Russian Poetry in Congruent Translation. A Bilingual Mini-Anthology*. Translated by Alex Shafarenko. Godalming, Surrey: Ancient Purple, 2009. "Congruent" translations preserve the rhyme and meter of the originals, sometimes at the expense of tone. Most poets in the anthology are more recent, but some from the Silver Age are included.

Nabokov, Vladimir, trans. *Verses and Versions: Three Centuries of Russian Poetry*. Edited by Brian Boyd and Stanislav Shvabrin. Orlando: Harcourt, Inc., 2008.

Natchez, Meryl, trans., with Boris Wolfson and Polina Barskova. *Poems from the Stray Dog Café: Akhmatova, Mandelstam, Gumilev*. Hit & Run Press, 2013. Well-introduced translations focusing on the Acmeist poets.

Obolensky, Dimitri, ed. *The Heritage of Russian Verse*. Bloomington & Indianapolis: Indiana University Press, 1976. Formerly *The Penguin Book of Russian Verse*; poems in Russian and plain prose translations. The brief introductions to each poet are valuable as well.

Pachmuss, Temira. *Women Writers in Russian Modernism: An Anthology*. Urbana: University of Illinois Press, 1978. Includes poems by Gippius, Lokhvitskaya, Cherubina de Gabriak (described in the "horoscope" by Maximilian Voloshin in this volume), and a number of less well-known women, mostly aligned with the Symbolists.

Schmidt, Paul, trans. *The Stray Dog Cabaret: A Book of Russian Poems*. New York: NYRB Classics, 2006. Quirky, effective versions of the big names of Russian Modernism (even some who never visited the Stray Dog).

Tomei, Christine, ed. *Russian Women Writers*. New York: Garland Publishing, 1998. Includes a substantial biographical/critical article of each writer represented, as well as translations of her work and bibliographical information.

Yarmolinsky, Avrahm, ed. *Two Centuries of Russian Verse: An Anthology, from Lomonosov to Voznesensky*. Translated by Babette Deutsch. New York: Random House, 1966. Rhyming, scanning translations by Deutsch in the context of longer Russian poetic history.

Yevtushenko, Yevgeny, ed. Albert G. Todd and Max Hayward (with Daniel Weissbort). *20th Century Russian Poetry: Silver and Steel*. New York: Doubleday, 1993. This thick anthology includes work by many valuable lesser-known poets, as well as all the big names.

SECTION II: BEYOND POETRY

Most of these works were written by the poets included in Section I, but some are by other authors. For the reader's convenience, the texts are listed in alphabetical order by author within each section (English alphabetical order, again, rather than Russian), though the Futurist manifestos come under "F" for Futurist, since they had so many authors and signatories.

For the authors not represented in Section I:

Kornei Chukovsky (1882-1969): Born Nikolai Vasil'evich Korneichukov in St. Petersburg, he grew up in Odessa. Chukovsky became a largely self-educated literary critic, children's poet, diarist, editor, translator, publicist, and scholar. Despite his success as a critic before the 1917 Revolution and his sympathy for the Revolution, Chukovsky gave up his career as a critic when that became too risky. Lenin spoke highly of his edition of the poetry of Nikolai Nekrasov (the first uncensored edition published in Russia), and that probably saved him several times later from official unpleasantness. He is best known today for his book *A High Art* on literary translation, and for his beloved children's poems.

Benedict Livshitz (1886-1938): A poet and translator, born in Odessa, he was a member of the Futurist group "Hyleia," though he also worked for the

Acmeist journal *Apollon*. His memoir *The One and a Half-Eyed Archer* (1933, whose title alone, requiring creative translation into any foreign language, hints at the avant-garde riches within) is a crucial source for information on the formation and activities of the Cubo-Futurists. He was arrested in 1937 and executed in 1938.

Irina Vladimirovna Odoevtseva (pesudonym of Iraida Gustavovna Geinike, 1895 or 1901(?)-1990): Author of two volumes of memoirs (*On the Banks of the Neva* and *On the Banks of the Seine*), one of cultural life in Petrograd immediately after the 1917 Revolution, and one of cultural life in emigration. She was a junior member of the Poets' Guild and reputedly Nikolai Gumilyov's favorite student. Her husband, Georgy Adamovich, was a minor Acmeist poet who became an important figure in Paris, especially as a literary critic. They emigrated in 1922. She returned to the Soviet Union in 1987 and lived to see publication of her memoirs there in the glasnost years.

Vasily Rozanov (1856-1919): A Russian religious philosopher, translator, admirer of Dostoevsky, author of *publitsistika* as well as all kinds of essays and philosophical works. His take on "the Jewish question" is provocative and problematic. *The Apocalypse of our Times* was one of his last works; he died largely of starvation in 1919.

Viktor Shklovsky (1893-1984): An important literary and film critic, cultural critic, and scholar with roots in the "Formal School," Shklovsky was one of the first (then very young) scholars to take note of the Futurists and attend their readings.

Nadezhda Tèffi (pseudonym of Nadezhda Alexandrovna Lokhvitskaya, married name Buchinskaya, 1872-1952): Mirra Lokhvitskaya's younger sister; Tèffi began writing as a poet (and has some very good poetry), but became one of Russia's outstanding humorist authors. Her writing has undoubtedly been neglected because she emigrated in 1919, eventually settling in Paris, and avoided the unpleasantness encountered by her younger, male, and Soviet colleague in humorous writing, Mikhail Zoshchenko. "The Demonic Woman" is one of her best-known stories and gave its title to a recent Russian edition of her work.

ESSAYS

KONSTANTIN BALMONT

From Poetry as Enchantment (1915)

Translated by Sibelan Forrester

Feeling ecstasy over the music of forms in its depth, the Sea, from above, booms with its waves and throws all kinds of shells onto the shore—a man will hang one of them on his chest as a talisman, to be rich and free like the Sea, while he will pile others up into mounds and trample them, and make graded roads covered with that gravel, and he will string yet a third kind of shells, small light-colored ones with patterns, into a necklace, while the fourth kind, twisted like screws, resembling bent horns, which clearly hold in themselves the threatening voice of the Sea, he will put to his lips, to his greedy lips, and that will be the first battle trumpet, he will play his battle song on it, when, seeking refreshment, he goes out to kill.

Heeding the music of all Nature's voices, the primitive mind lulls them within itself. Gradually attaining a patterned multiplicity, it forms them into an internal music and expresses that externally with a melodious word, a folktale, enchantment, an incantation.

Poetry is internal Music, expressed externally with measured speech.

[. . . .]

The nineteenth century's most brilliant poet, Edgar [Allen] Poe, who wielded like no one else the sorcery of the word (moreover strangely coinciding at times with the prophetic utterances of ancient peoples, the Egyptians, the Chinese, the Hindus), wrote marvelous lines about the creative magic of the word in the philosophical tale "The Power of Words." Agathos and Oinos are conversing. As spirits, they fly through among the stars. "The true philosophy has long taught us that thought is the source of any kind of movement, and God is the source of any kind of thought. I have been speaking with you, Oinos, as with a child of the beautiful Earth, and while I was speaking, didn't any thought of the PHYSICAL POWER OF WORDS flash into your mind? Is not every word a motive that influences the air?" "But why are you crying, Agathos? And why, oh why do your wings weaken as we soar over that beautiful star, the greenest and the strangest of all that we have met in our flight? Its shining colors are like a fairy dream, but its harsh volcanoes resemble the passions of a rebellious heart." "It is SO, it is SO! They are exactly what you see in reality. This mad star—it was three centuries ago that I, clenching my fists, and with eyes full of tears, at the feet of my beloved—told her—in a few passionate words—gave her birth. Her shining colors VERILY are the most secret of all the dreams that have not taken flesh, and her roiling volcanoes VERILY ARE the passions of the most stormy and most wounded of all hearts."

[....]

If all Earthly life is an ineffable wonder that arose by the power of the creative word from non-being, our human word, with which we measure the Universe and rule over the elements, is the most miraculous wonder of all that is precious in our human life. It is hard for us to remember, with our imperfect memories, how it tore for the first time out of our human throats, but verily that joy must have been great, or a great pain, or a minute when bliss was inseparably mixed with pain, and muteness had to be overcome, and we had to speak. And since all the parts that make up the Wonder are magical, all this makes it precisely a wonder. It is indubitable that every letter of our alphabet, every sound of our human speech, be it Russian or Hellenic, Chinese or Peruvian, is a small magic-making elf and gnome, every letter is sorcery. That has its separate charm, and we express it in separate words, and we choose it in their particular combinations, it's just easier for us to feel, to sense the reality of the verbal wonder than to define it exactly and verify with reason what precisely inheres in our lettered and verbal divination, and by way of the interweaving of syllables and words, a spiritual divination, when our comprehending heart suddenly forces us to sing out a prophetic song, which will rush like the wind through the whole country. Or to say one word that will be so true that it will be passed on from people to people, and will be sent down from century to century.

Andrei Bely

Symbolism and Contemporary Russian Art (1908)

Translated by Ronald E. Peterson

What is Symbolism? What does contemporary Russian literature represent?

Symbolism is confused with modernism. Modernism implies a multitude of literary schools that have nothing in common. *Sanin*'s bestialism, and neo-realism, and the revolutionary-erotic exercises of Sergeev-Tsensky, and preaching the freedom of art, and L. Andreev, and the elegant trifles of O. Dymov, and Merezhkovsky's preaching, and the Pushkinianism of Bryusov's school, etc.—we call this whole discordant chorus of voices in literature either modernism or Symbolism, forgetting that, if Bryusov is connected with anyone, then it is Baratynsky and Pushkin, in no way with Merezhkovsky; Merezhkovsky is related to Dostoevsky and Nietzsche and not to Blok; Blok is closer to the early Romantics and not to G. Chulkov. But people say: "Merezhkovsky, Bryusov, Blok—these are modernists," and oppose them to other people and other things. Thus, if we define modernism, we are not defining a school. What are we defining? A professed literary credo?

Or is Russian modernism perhaps a school in which the irreconcilable literary currents of yesterday and the reconcilable currents of today mingle harmoniously in the same channel? In this case, modernism's uniformity is not found at all in the external features of literary works, but in the means of evaluating them. But then, for modernism, Bryusov is as new as Pushkin or Derzhavin, as is all of Russian literature. Then why is modernism—modernism?

Beginning with *Mir Iskusstva* [*The World of Art*] and ending with *Vesy* [*Libra*], the journals of Russian modernism have been conducting a battle on two fronts: on the one hand they support young talents, on the other—they resurrect the forgotten past. They arouse interest in the exceptional examples of Russian painting in the eighteenth century, they renew the cult of the German Romantics, Goethe, Dante and the Latin poets, they bring Pushkin and Baratynsky to us in a new light, they write outstanding essays about Gogol, Tolstoy, Dostoevsky; they foster new interest in Sophocles, they are engaged in new productions of Euripides on the stage, and they renew ancient theater.

And so: modernism is not a school. Do we have here, perhaps, an external unity of various literary devices? The mingling of literary schools gives rise to a multitude of modernistic insipidities: impressionism is coarsened in Muyzhel's stories, populism is also coarsened: it's neither fish nor fowl, it's a little bit of everything.

But perhaps modernism is characterized by a deepening of the methods of any school, no matter which one: the method, taking on more depth, turns out to be something different than it first seemed. This transformation of a method is found, for example, in Chekhov. Chekhov departs from naïve realism, but by deepening realism, he begins to come in contact with Maeterlinck and Hamsun. And he completely departs from the literary devices not only of Pisemsky and Sleptsov, for examples, but also of Tolstoy. But do we call Chekhov a modernist? Bryusov, in contrast to this trend, passes from the Romantic side of Symbolism to even more real images: finally in *The Fiery Angel* he paints life in ancient Cologne. But the public and the critics stubbornly rank Bryusov among the modernists. No—the true essence of modernism is neither in the mingling of literary devices nor even in deepening the method of working.

Is it, perhaps, refining the tools of the trade, or sharpening artistic vision in the bounds of this or that literary school, broadening the sphere of perceptions? The Symbolist and the Realist and the Romantic and the Classicistic author can deal with the phenomena of colored sound, the refinement of memory, the splitting of one's personality and so forth. The Symbolist and the Realist and the Romantic and the Classicistic author will each concern himself with these phenomena in his own way. But artistic images of the past—don't they display a remarkable refinement at times? And the Romantic Novalis is indeed more refined than Muyzhel, and Goethe's lyrics are indeed finer than those of Sergei Gorodetsky.

And so, does the character of the convictions we express remain the criterion for modernism? But L. Andreev preaches about life's chaos, Bryusov—the philosophy of the moment, Artsybashev—the satisfaction of sexual need, Merezhkovsky—a new religious consciousness, V. Ivanov—mystical anarchism.

Again modernism is broken down into a multitude of ideological currents.

The whole order and system of notions about reality has changed under the influence of the evolution that is taking place in science and the theory of knowledge. The order and system of thinking in regard to moral values has changed, thanks to the sociological treatises of the second half of the ninteenth century; the antimony between the individual and society has deepened; the dogmatic solutions to basic contradictions in life have again become problems and only problems. Together with the change in understanding yesterday's dogmas, the question about the creative attitude toward life has been put forth with special vigor; before, an individual's creative growth was connected with this or that religious attitude toward life. But the very form for expressing this growth—religion—has lost its ability to get in touch with life; it has retreated into the area of scholasticism; science and philosophy negate scholasticism.

And the essence of a religious perception of life has passed into the area of artistic creation; when the question of a free, creative individual has been put forth, the significance of the application of art has grown. A reevaluation of the basic ideas about the existing forms of art was needed; we recognized more clearly the connection between the product of creativity (a work of art) and the very process of creativity that transforms an individual. We began to derive the classification of literary works more and more often from the processes of creativity; this type of classification collided with the old classification of views of art that were established on the basis of studying the works of art, and not on the basis of studying the very processes. Studying the processes of cognition shows us that the very cognitive act bears the character of creative affirmation, that creation precedes cognition; the former predetermines the latter.

Consequently, the definition of creation by a system of views, not tested by the criticism of cognitive abilities, cannot be at the base of judgments about elegance, and all that metaphysical, positivistic, and sociological aesthetics unconsciously gives us is a narrowly preconceived elucidation of these questions. Dogmas with these views are dependent on the tools of analysis, but these tools are often not tested by critical methods. We now consider the judgments of literary schools about literature as possible methods of relating to it, but not as commonly obligatory dogmas of literary creeds. True judgments should flow from studies of the processes of creation, free from the dogmatics of any school. We should find, at the base of future aesthetics, the laws of creative processes, combined with the laws for embodying these processes in a form, i.e., with the laws of literary technique. The study of the laws of the techniques, styles, rhythms, forms of depiction lies within the area of experiment. The future aesthetics is simultaneous and free (i.e., it recognizes the regularity of cognitive processes as goals in themselves, not as the application of these processes for the utilitarian goals of dogmatics). But it is exact in so much as it puts experiment at the base of literary technique. Thus it offers its own method, not a method drawn from disciplines that have no direct relation to creation.

People will object: symbolism of a certain type is peculiar to any literary school; what have contemporary Symbolists contributed that is special? Of course they have contributed nothing more valuable than Gogol, Pushkin, Goethe and others did in terms of images. But they realized that art is entirely symbolic, "to the limit," not just "to a certain degree," and that aesthetics relies on symbolism alone and takes all its conclusions from it. Everything else is not essential. This "everything else," meanwhile, has been considered the true criteria for evaluating literary works.

The principles of classification of literary works can be either a division made by schools or a division according to the strength of talent. It is important to know what kind of credo a writer has and how much talent he possesses. If a limited credo weakens a powerful talent, we struggle with his credo for him. This is the essence of the discord between us and the talented representatives of realism and mystical anarchism. We fight with Gorky and Blok because we value them; we accept *The Confession* and pass by Chulkov.

If I name Gorky, Andreev, Kuprin, Zaytsev, Muyzhel, Artsybashev, Kamensky, Dymov, Chirikov, Merezhkovsky, Sologub, Remizov, Gippius,

Auslander, Kuzmin, the poets Bryusov, Blok, Balmont, Bunin, V. Ivanov and others who approach them, and among the philosophers I name L. Shestov, Minsky, Volynsky, Rozanov, and the publicists Filosofov, Berdyaev, Anichkov, Lunacharsky, and other critics, then everyone will agree with me that I touch on contemporary Russian literature (I make no reference to those modern belletrists, among whom there are a few talented authors, but even so there are talented readers like Kozhevnikov).

These names fall into several groups. The first group of writers is from *Znanie* [*Knowledge*]. Their center is Gorky. Their ideologues are a group of critics who at one time came out with the *Essays of a Realistic World View*. Artsybashev and Kamensky stand apart from this group because they have taken on certain features of cheap Nietzscheanism.

The former and the latter groups adhere to realism.

Then follows the group united around *Shipovnik* [*Sweetbriar*]. This group has two flanks; on the one hand there are writers here who form the transitional link from realism to Symbolism, i.e., impressionism; the left flank consists of writers who form the transition from Symbolism to impressionism; there are attempts to create schools of symbolic realism and mystical anarchism from this transition. The group of neo-realists has no ideologues of its own; they partially merge with realism (Zaytsev is one example), partially with Symbolism (like Blok). Mystical anarchists, on the other hand, have their own ideologues: first of all, A. Meyer, the only theoretician of mystical anarchism that we can halfway understand. Then there is V. Ivanov, who stands apart from the *Shipovnik* group but influences them from afar, and like the two-faced Janus, he is also turned toward *Vesy*. The latter group is the most complex, the most varied group of modernists. Their ideology is a mixture of Bakunin, Marx, Solovyov, Maeterlinck, Nietzsche and even... Christ, Buddha, and Mohammed. The following group consists of Merezhkovsky, Gippius, and the publicistcritics—Filosofov and Berdyaev; then begins a group of authors who work problems of religion: Volzhsky, S. Bulgakov, Florensky, Sventitsky, Ern. Here we encounter religious sermons, of a more or less revolutionary hue. The remarkable L. Shestov, V. V. Rozanov, and Minsky's slightly boring philosophy of *meonism* stand entirely apart. I will not deal with them here.

There remains, finally, the last group of actual Symbolists, whose central figure is Valery Bryusov; it is united around *Vesy*. This group rejects all hasty slogans about overcoming or explaining Symbolism. It realizes the tremendous responsibility that lies on the shoulders of Symbolism's theoreticians. It acknowledges that the theory of Symbolism is the result of the varied work of all of culture and that every theory of Symbolism that appears now is in the best case only a sketch of a plan, a blueprint, according to which we must construct a building. Consciousness of the construction of a theory of Symbolism, the freedom of symbolization—this is the slogan of this group.

What is the relationship of these literary groups to Symbolism?

What ideology does the group of realist writers bring us? 1) Faithfulness to reality; 2) an exact depiction of how people live; 3) serving social interests and, from this, 4) an assortment of common features of society that makes contemporary Russia appear before us, with its various social groups and their relationships (Gorky's tramps, Kuprin's "Duel," and Yushkevich's *Jews*); this or that tendency shows through everywhere, whether it's populistic, or social-democratic, or anarchical.

Well, what then?

Are all these features rejected by Symbolism? Not in the slightest; we accept Nekrasov, greatly value Tolstoy's realism, recognize the social significance of *The Inspector General* and *Dead Souls*, Verhaeren's socialism, and so on. And where Gorky is an artist, we value Gorky. We only want to protest against the idea that the task of literature is to photograph the way people live; we do not agree that art expresses class contradictions; statistics' figures and special treatises speak to us eloquently about social injustice, and we trust Mehring's *History of Social Democracy* more than Minsky's poem, "Workers of the World Unite." Reducing literature's purpose to illustrating social treatises is naive; for a person with a vital social temperament the figures are more eloquent. Reducing literature to number (the essence of the sociological method) is the "non-sense" of art. Both Gogol and Boborykin are equally reducible to numbers; then why is Gogol—Gogol, and Boborykin—Boborykin? And the sociological critics' conclusions are often devoid of sense: when mysticism, pessimism, Symbolism, and impressionism are derived from the contemporary conditions of capital and labor, we fail to understand why we meet mystics, pessimists, and Symbolists in a pre-capitalist culture. The sociologist is correct when he approaches everything with his own method, but the aesthetician is also correct when he subjects sociology's method to the criticism of the theory of knowledge at that moment when the sociologist relegates aesthetic values to numbers and clothes his ciphers in the cloaks, regal mantles, and overcoats of literary heroes. And so the indication that the *Znanie* writers express a defined social tendency cannot be accepted as an indication of their pre-eminence.

No, if anything unites the *Znanie* writers, it is the dogma of naive realism (in the spirit of Moleschott, not at all in the spirit of Avenarius); in accordance with this dogma, reality is the reality of visible objects and experience. But then where do we put the reality of experience? To reduce experience to physics and mechanics now, when all of contemporary psychology and philosophy tends to examine groups of external experiences as parts of internal experience, is impossible. It is unthinkable to fail to see the subjective limits of the external world: we need only recall our experiences with a specter, with a siren, and so on. But if the boundaries of an objectively given appearance are unstable, then we are doomed to subjectivism. Where then are the limits of subjectivity in the area of talent? In this way the certainty of naive realism disappears; realism crosses over into impressionism; Andreev changes from a realist more and more into an impressionist. Certain pages of Gorky's *Confession* are thoroughly impressionistic. Consequently, it is impossible to remain a realist in art; everything in art is *more or less real*, you cannot build the principles of a school on "more or less"; "more or less" is not aesthetics at all. Realism is only an aspect of impressionism.

But impressionism, i.e., a view of life through the prism of experience, is already a creative view of life. My experience transforms the world; by going deeper into experience, I delve more deeply into creativity; creativity is, at the same time, the creativity of experiences and the creativity of images. The laws of creativity are the only aesthetics of impressionism. But these are the aesthetics of Symbolism. Impressionism is superficial Symbolism; the theory of impressionism could use some presuppositions borrowed from the theory of Symbolism.

The theoreticians of realism should understand their own duty as a private duty; our common duty, and theirs too, is the construction of Symbolist theory; until they realize the inescapability of such a duty, we will label them narrow-minded dogmatists who are trying to fit art into a framework. A great artist who blindly submits to the dogmas of this school reminds us of a giant in Lilliputian clothes; Gorky sometimes appears in such a costume. Fortunately his tight costume of naive realism sometimes tears and before us stands an artist in the real, not the dogmatic sense.

These are the artistic precepts of the dogmatists of realism and impressionism.

Semi-impressionism, semi-realism, semi-aesthetism, semi-tendentiousness all characterize the right flank of writers grouped around *Shipovnik*. The person on the extreme left of this wing is of course L. Andreev. The left flank is comprised of open and often talented writers, even typical Symbolists. But the ideological credo of this left group is mystical anarchism.

What is mystical anarchism?

We have before us two theoreticians: G. Chulkov and V. Ivanov. I feel uncomfortable speaking about the substance of G. Chulkov's theoretical views; I'd have to say a lot of bitter things; I will only remark that Chulkov's principal slogan, "non-acceptance of the world," is indeterminate; definitions of the concepts of "non-acceptance" and "world" are lacking and prevent us from understanding this slogan. I don't know what the world is, in the sense that Chulkov uses it. I don't know how to understand "nonacceptance"; I know only that if one understands them in the broadest sense, then there is no one theory that would totally accept the world. All the further conclusions from Chulkov's "hundred-mouthed" declarations have either a hundred senses or none. What we get are snippets of at least a hundred world views, each of which has a great founder—that I don't doubt; I also do not doubt that, for Chulkov, Christ, Buddha, Goethe, Dante, Shakespeare, Newton, Copernicus, etc., are mystical anarchists. I also do not doubt that he numbers himself among his famous family of friends and chases enemies from it. I absolutely cannot say anything more about G. Chulkov's theory.

Another mystical anarchist—Meyer—has hardly expressed himself; there is cause for hope that we will finally be able to assess Chulkov's incomprehensible philosophical experiences in Meyer's transpositions.

The most interesting and serious ideologue of this movement is V. Ivanov. If mystical anarchism were not compromised by Chulkov's unfortunate dithyrambs, we would reckon more seriously with V. Ivanov's words; but G. Chulkov has discovered hidden imperfections in V. Ivanov's views.

Both Chulkov and Ivanov start out with the slogan about the freedom of creativity; both understand and value the techniques of writing; both declare that they have outlived individualism; both value Nietzsche highly; consequently, both gather ideological baggage from Symbolists at the starting point of their development. V. Ivanov brings, in his opinion, substantial improvement on the objectives stated by the older Symbolists.

What is this improvement?

V. Ivanov seeks that focus in art where the rays of artistic creativity, so to say, cross; he finds that focus in drama. Drama includes the basis for broadening art to the point where artistic creativity comes closer to life's creativity. Wilde recognized just such a role for art; only the form of Wilde's creed is different; he called the creativity of life a lie. It is not without justification that he is called the singer of falsehood. But if Wilde himself believed that the creation of an image is not a falsehood at all, that a series of images, united by unanimity, is predetermined by some law of internal creativity, he would recognize the religious essence of art; V. Ivanov is entirely correct when he affirms that there is a religious sense behind art. But by dating the moment of the transition from art to religion from the moment of the reform of the theater and the transformation of drama, he falls into error. Artistic visions are internally real for Ivanov; the connection of these visions forms a myth; the myth grows out of a symbol. Drama deals primarily with myth; consequently, the origins that will transform the forms of art are concentrated in it. He turns his attention to the classification of art forms; he compels them to follow one after the other in the direction of an ever-increasing embrace of life. Meanwhile, the forms of art, under modern conditions, are parallel; they gain profundity in parallel. Each has in it a peculiar feature that religiously deepens the given form; the theater is only one of art's forms, not at all the basic one.

According to Ivanov, contemporary Symbolism does not adequately see the religious essence of art; therefore, it is unable to inspire the masses; the Symbolism of the future will co-mingle with the people's religious element.

And so: 1) the religious essence of art is affirmed behind myth; 2) the origin of myth from symbol is affirmed; 3) the dawn of a new mythocreation is perceived in contemporary drama; 4) a new symbolic realism is affirmed; 5) a new populism is affirmed.

But after all, every deepening and transformation of experience that comprises the true essence of its aesthetic choice presupposes the basis of that choice; i.e., the norm of creativity. Let the artist ignore this norm; it will come out in the ever-deepening stream of creativity; and the artist who experiences freedom (and is, so to say, outside the criteria of good and evil) only submits more totally to the higher order of the *same* duty. The objective of Symbolist theory consists of the establishment of certain norms; how it relates to the norms is a different matter. As a theoretician, I can only state the norms; as a practitioner, I realize that these norms are aesthetic or religious realities. In the first case, God's name is hidden from me; in the second I name that name. Theoreticians of Symbolism in art can study the processes of religious creativity as one of the forms of aesthetic creativity, if they want to remain in the area of knowledge that deals with refinement. Thus, as practitioners, they can experience the established norm either as a vital, super-individual connection (God), or as a broadened artistic symbol. The theory of artistic Symbolism neither rejects nor establishes religion; it studies it. This is a condition of the seriousness of the movement, not its drawback. And so Ivanov's attacks on the theory of Symbolism would be justified from his point of view if he fell upon the aesthetes as a candid preacher of a defined religion. He would then have to admit that art is godless, but that the freedom of investigating the processes of creation demands limitations, constrictions by determined religious requirements. But he neither abandons the ground of art, nor appears before us as a definitely religious preacher, nor does he shy away from theories of art; for us, his call for religious realism remains lifeless as preaching and dogmatic as a theory. It is impossible to demand religious practice theoretically and only theorize practically; that is not candid, not irreproachably honest. Ivanov's religious realism seems to us, as Symbolists, an attempt to cast the area of theoretical investigations into the area of dreams, or even worse, to create new dogmatics of art from dreams, even more narrowly than the dogmatists of realism and Marxism do. Believing that mystical anarchism is a religion, we fool ourselves and find no God in it; believing that mystical anarchism is a theory, we fall into dogmatic sectarianism.

As for the origin of myth from symbol, who among us will deny it or relinquish the right to experience mythical creativity religiously? We only feel that to affirm this on the basis of the theory of Symbolism is premature, for now the theory of Symbolism is entirely in the future. It is impossible to crown the foundation of a temple directly with a steeple; what do we do with the temple's walls?

There is a movement toward mystery plays in contemporary drama; but it is impossible to build a mystery play on indeterminate artistic mysticism; a mystery play is a divine service; which god will be served in the theater: Apollo or Dionysus? God have mercy, what a joke! *Apollo, Dionysus*—these are only artistic symbols; but if these symbols are religious, then give us a candid name that symbolizes God. Who is Dionysus? Christ, Mohammed, Buddha? Or Satan himself? To unite people who are connected to various divinities with a Dionysian experience means to arrange a wax museum of gods or (what's even worse) to turn religion into a spiritual seance. Fashionable ladies and gentlemen of all modes will say, "interesting, piquant," and accept mystical anarchism without reservation.

But can we Symbolists, for whom the method of answering a question of this or that direction is a question of life, we—among whom there are people who confess to the name of only one God, and not all gods together—can we relate to a theory that throws us into the embrace of surprise without feeling extreme pain and irritation? Here they accuse us of polemicizing, of vehemence; but if we were to exhibit a smiling breeziness in regard to all the questions raised, we would be "decorated coffins," without God, without duty.

V. Ivanov affirms a new Symbolist realism, forgetting that the artist for whom the artistic image is internally unreal is not an artist; only charlatans can call themselves illusionists in the literal sense of the word. For illusionists of Edgar Allen Poe's type, illusionism is a form of confession of faith. Symbolist realism is raising something to one squared; if Ivanov is able to divide true artists into realists and illusionists, then he is busying himself in vain; the square of one is one. A futile occupation!

We know that here and there a defined social program is connected with the slogan of populism; Symbolism walked the narrow line between the artist's political conviction and his creativity so that art would not cloud the area of economic struggle for us, but this latter feature would not kill the artist in the artist. When they taunt us with the multi-faceted slogan of uniting with the people in artistic creativity, it still seems to us that they just want to make us utopians in the areas of politics and aesthetic theory.

Utopianism, either here or there, is dangerous.

Symbolists know by experience all the harm that dogmatism and groundless utopianism in the sphere of artistic theory can cause. They want a sober theory; they know that only a concerted series of investigations will lead to a firm foundation for aesthetics. And if they raise a question about the theories of various artistic schools, only because these theories are predetermined by a method that does not lie within the essence of aesthetics, then of course they do not hesitate to pull the weeds of vague guessing about art that grow around them. This is the basis of their disagreement with mystical anarchism; all of its positive aspects in these theories are contained in Symbolism; everything specific is weeds, which they should pull.

They will dispute the straightforward requirement concerning the submission of Symbolist theory to religious dogmatism, but they are able to respect only those people who exhibit such a requirement in the name of a defined religion; where the confession of religious convictions is not directed against art, then we disunite and unite with that confession, depending on whether we are religious or not, depending on which religion we confess. "*Confession*" is our "*Privat-Sache*,"[1] while we are theoreticians of art. It is obvious from these words what position we occupy in relation to the religious movement which has appeared in Russian literature, beginning with Solovyov and ending with Merezhkovsky. I personally depart from Solovyov in many areas and unite with Merezhkovsky in many ways; some of my artistic brothers-in-arms do not. This is a divergence that lies beyond the bounds of that area where we defend Symbolism.

---

1 *Eds.* German, meaning "private matter."

A Wreath or a Crown (1910)

Translated by Ronald E. Peterson

Let the poet create not
his books, but his own life.

Grief awaits the person who
exchanges a crown for a wreath.

Valery Bryusov

The exchange of opinions about the destinies and purposes of Symbolism which has taken place on the pages of *Apollon* prompts me to say a few words.

Radically disagreeing with V. Ia. Bryusov's article "About Servile Speech, in Defense of Poetry," I unwillingly quote V. Ia. Bryusov's words from his article "A Holy Sacrifice" (*Vesy*, No. 1, 1905).[2] Here are these words:

> We demand from a poet that he tirelessly bring his "holy sacrifices" not only with his verses, but with every hour of his life, with every feeling—his love, his hate, accomplishments, and failures.

And I subscribe to every word ... In his beautiful, deeply felt article, A. Blok says essentially this: he sort of asks himself and us if we will bring our "holy sacrifices" with every feeling, every hour of our lives. On the other hand, V. Ivanov definitely expressed the thought that Symbolism is not only a school of art. It seems that Bryusov, who spoke several years ago on behalf of Russian Symbolist poetry with his credo, would only rejoice at the coincidence of V. Ivanov's declaration with his own.

"Symbolism neither wanted to be, nor could it be, 'only art,'" V. Ivanov confesses.

"We demand from a poet that he tirelessly bring his 'holy sacrifices,' not only with his verses," V. Ia. Bryusov confessed in 1905.

Both slogans openly declare that Symbolism is something greater than a literary school; in the current type, formed in France as a literary school and in Germany as a new world view (even Nietzsche numbered himself among

---

2   *Eds.* Included in this volume, below.

the Symbolists), something greater than arguing about coining verse should and must be present. French Symbolism, it's true, was created as a literary school, but German Symbolism was formed not only within the bounds of the history of literature. And what is important for us is not how Symbolism was formed historically, but what is important is—What is Symbolism, reflected here as a school, and there as the propagation of a new attitude. The declaration of two of the most important representatives of Russian Symbolism that Symbolism is not only a literary school does not at all indicate a betrayal of the precepts of Symbolist art, but points out the character of Russian Symbolism as it was originally expressed.

Bryusov, who in 1905 gave the same definition of the artist's task as Ivanov and Blok in 1910, takes exception to Ivanov and Blok with the following humorous, but entirely unconvincing words:

> A hammer is used for driving nails, not for painting pictures. It's better to shoot with a gun than to drink liqueur from it . . . Grandpa Krylov warns us against those singers whose chief merit is that they "never touch spirits."
>
> (*Apollon,* No. 9, p. 3)

It doesn't follow, from the notion that a hammer is used for driving nails, that if I were attacked by robbers and had no weapon other than the hammer, that I would let myself be killed and not defend myself with the hammer simply because it is used for driving nails. It is true that people don't drink liqueur from a rifle, but in an army a rifle fulfills two essentially divergent purposes: 1) people shoot with it, 2) a bayonet is attached to it and people use it as cold steel. Of course the beauty of a singer is not that he doesn't touch alcohol; but this doesn't mean at all that a singer shouldn't dare worry about his sobriety; as we know, wine weakens creativity. What does V. Ia. Bryusov want? Does he want people not to defend themselves with a hammer, even when there is no other weapon; and soldiers who have used all their bullets and see the enemy attacking the fortress, is it better for them to throw down their rifles and be taken prisoner than to fix their bayonets? Or doesn't he want poets to fight against alcoholism? Of course V. Ia. Bryusov would deny such a clear application of Tolstoy's principle of non-resistance to evil in relation to his beloved art, but it comes out in this case that such non-resistance is what he is preaching.

Art has been symbolic from time immemorial; no one can argue against the symbolism of any kind of art; this symbolism comes nearer to us when we ascend to the snowy heights of the creative Olympus. The symbolism of Goethe, Dante, and Shakespeare is aristocratic not only in the figurative sense, but also in the literary, and genuine science and genuine philosophy are aristocratic as well.

Since the middle of the nineteenth century, the democraticization of knowledge and philosophy has grown; whole strata which had nothing to do with art until now are more and more the legislators of its fate; in our present epoch the circles of aesthetically educated people are not the active participants in the life of art; the democratic masses have been actively concerned with art, the line of art's development has been displaced; art is in jeopardy.

The development of the Symbolist school in art, as well as Ibsen's and Nietzsche's propagation of Symbolism, appeared as an answer to the spreading vulgarization of art; the aristocratic depths of eternal Symbolism appeared before the masses in its clear propagatory form: the Symbolist school in poetry summed up individual slogans of artists (confessed as a *Privat-Sache*[3]), with the proclamation of these slogans as paragraphs of an artistic platform; the propagation of Symbolism began in democratic taverns, not on the heights of academic Olympianism. The first Symbolists stepped forth both as theoreticians and as artists: they threw the "elusive" aspect of every symbol over the surface of an image. In the Symbolism of the French school, the "secret" of each image, outwardly distinct, became "evident," a mist—an image. Goethe is outwardly clear; and only under the clarity of form, somewhere in the depths, the endless corridors of the "elusive" meet us; Verlaine is outwardly hazy; but under the hazy cover a simple and clear thought often shows through in his works. The former is an aristocrat, the latter a democrat.

If the question about the origin of the mystical smoke of what lies beyond the limit that is based on art does not arise with persistence in the classically finished forms of Goethe's symbolism, then in the exaggeratedly clamorous stressing of this smoke among the latest Symbolists this question does arise; together with it the question about the aim, about the sense of Artistic

---

3   *Eds.* German for "private matter."

Creativity, about its place in the hierarchy of knowledge and creativity (for example, of something religious) arises anew. This question now agitates not only the theoretician, it agitates the artist as well; to understand the purposes and aims of art, independent of its historically established forms, this is now a question of conscience for an artist, especially a Symbolist artist, who by the strength of his position emphasizes much of what had been previously kept silent, and clearly displays before us, like a slogan, the individual announcements of the artists of the past. The *laurel wreath* that shamefully covered the *priestly crown* has been torn off by the Symbolists in the persons of Ibsen and Nietzsche; the religious searching of Baudelaire, Verlaine, Wilde, Huysmans, Strindberg, V. Ivanov, and Blok is not stifled by the questionnaires about free verse; in the torments of conscience, in the struggle for the distant horizons of life, not only a love for art has been manifested among contemporary Symbolist poets; "Only a priest's knife, cutting our breasts, gives us the right to be called a poet," Bryusov himself wrote. The wreath was exchanged for a crown. Bryusov exchanged his own wreath for a crown, the one who had stated quite clearly:

> Grief awaits the person who
> Exchanges a crown for a wreath.

But in his article in *Apollon*, No. 9, he precisely trades his crown for a wreath: one doesn't want to reply to him with his own words: Grief...

We perceive the introduction of the aim dictated for art in the propagatory note that appeared in the works of the greatest Symbolists of our time, Ibsen and Nietzsche, in the fact that they recognize the creator of life in the artist: a new life and the salvation of humanity proceed from art. This is the bayonet that the artist-conqueror fixes to his rifle; the religious creativity of life itself, which defines cognition itself, is in art; the development of the major courses of contemporary psychology and the theory of knowledge answers as follows: the bayonet is given to the artist by the philosopher; the bayonet is necessary; but Bryusov at the critical moment ridicules the use of a bayonet with his lame comparison of a bayonet with liqueur. Acting thus, he chops off the branch he's sitting on, he renounces his own words: "We throw ourselves on the altar of our divinity."

V. Ivanov and Blok, as literary figures, throw their activities on the altar of their divinity, believing in the magical power of creativity, as the origin of the transformation of life; they live up to Bryusov's precepts; we believe that because of this the flame of their artistic creativity only flares up even more: V. Ivanov will give us even more accomplished sonnets, Blok—dramas. But Bryusov laughs at their worshipful attitude towards art.

I will not answer him with his words: Grief...

I fashioned this reply to Bryusov on the continuation and development of his joke about the rifle and liqueur. Apart from this joke V. Ia. Bryusov refutes Ivanov's reference to the fact that Symbolism is a definite historical phenomenon; Bryusov proposes that we remain contemporary Symbolists on that theoretical ground that the French Symbolists had beneath them. But we confess: they had no theoretical ground to stand on; the very interest in verse, the very discussions about form are only good when we know what art, form, and verses are; Symbolists' slogans demand philosophical justification and exposure, it is impossible to remain on the grounds of history, to regret that contemporary Russian Symbolists went beyond the circle of interests of the French Symbolists means the same as regretting that mankind went beyond the primitive state. And, moreover, to ascribe Symbolism to France is too narrow; after all, Nietzsche definitely declared himself a Symbolist, and the circles of his themes cannot be compared with those worked out in France. Symbolism is a phenomenon of worldwide, historical significance; it is still entirely in the future, to hammer it into France and measure it by a decade is cruel; nothing of Symbolism will remain. "Ask Verhaeren and Vielé-Griffin," Bryusov exclaims, "and I'm certain that they will all say, unanimously, that they wanted one thing..." It would be offensive for Symbolism if its fate were to be decided by the personal opinions of Verhaeren and Vielé-Griffin. I hope that Symbolism is something greater than Vielé-Griffin...

The Symbolist's aspiration is not to destroy millennia of art in the past, but to illuminate and deepen these millennia with the light of the future. This belief in the future moves all of us, and we declare openly that the fate of Russian Symbolism does not depend on the definitions taught in schools. Otherwise Bryusov would have to agree with the fierce criticism of French Symbolists printed in the same issue of *Apollon*, in the article "Parisian Dialogue." This is what the author of the dialogue writes: "Consistent Symbolists will not leave behind any creations or will leave what in a hundred years will be read only for the sake of curiosity." Symbolism, understood as the method of a literary school, is doomed to perish; that's clear. Does Bryusov really want to see the demise of Symbolism? But there are two Bryusovs.

"Let the poet create not his books, but his own life," he writes in 1905. "Symbolism wanted to be and always was only art," he writes in 1910.

> Grief awaits the one who
> Exchanges a crown for a wreath.
> *Val. Bryusov.*

A wreath or a crown?

Valery Bryusov

Keys to the Mysteries (1904)

Translated by Ronald E. Peterson

I

When unsophisticated people are confronted with the question "What is art?" they do not try to comprehend where it came from, what place it holds in the universe, but accept it as a fact, and only want to find some application for it to their lives. Thus arise the theories of useful art, the most primitive stage in the relationship between man's thought and art. It seems natural to people that art, if it exists, should be suitable for their dearest small needs and necessities. They forget there are many things in the world that are completely useless in terms of human life, like beauty, for example, and that they themselves constantly commit acts that are totally useless—they love and they dream.

It seems ridiculous to us now, of course, when Tasso assures us that poetic inventions are similar to the "sweets" that are used to coat the edge of a dish with bitter medicine; we read, with a smile, Derzhavin's poems to Catherine the Great, in which he compares poetry to sweet lemonade. But did not Pushkin partially under the influence of echoes of Schelling's philosophy and partially arriving at the same opinions independently, reproach the dark masses for seeking "usefulness" and say that they were worth less than a "cooking pot," and didn't his tongue slip in "Monument" when he wrote these verses:

> And I will long be the favorite of the people,
> Because I aroused good feelings with my lyre.

And didn't Zhukovsky, adapting Pushkin's poems for print, furnish the following line in a more direct way: "That I was useful because of the vital charm of my verses...," which gave Pisarev cause for rejoicing.

In the greater public, the public that knows art in terms of serialized novels, operatic productions, symphonic concerts, and exhibits of paintings, the conviction that art's function is to provide noble diversion prevails, indivisibly, to this day. Dancing at balls, skating, playing cards—these are also diversions, but less noble ones; and people who belong to the intelligentsia, meanwhile, read Korolenko, or even Maeterlinck, listen to Chaliapin, go to the Peredvizhnaya, and to decadents' exhibits. A novel helps to pass the time in a train or in bed, before falling asleep, you meet acquaintances at the opera, and find diversion at art exhibits. And these people attain their goals, they really relax, laugh, are entertained and fall asleep.

None other than Ruskin, an "apostle of beauty," speaks out in his books as a defender of "utilitarian art." He advised his pupils to draw olive leaves and rose petals, in order to discover for themselves and to give others more information than we have had up to now about Grecian olives and England's wild roses. He advised them to reproduce cliffs, mountains and individual rocks, in order to obtain a more complete understanding of the characteristics of mountainous structure. He advised them rather to depict ancient, disappearing ruins, so that their images could be preserved, at least on canvas, for the curiosity of future ages. "Art," says Ruskin, "gives Form to knowledge, and Grace to utility; that is to say, it makes permanently visible to us things which otherwise could neither be described by our science, nor retained by our memory." And more: "the entire vitality of art depends upon its being either full of truth or full of use. Great masters could permit themselves awkwardness, but they will never permit themselves uselessness or unveracity."

A very widespread, if not prevailing, school of literary historians treats poetry in the same way that Ruskin does the plastic arts. They see in poetry only the exact reproduction of life, from which it is possible to learn the customs and mores of that time and country where the poetic work was created. They carefully study descriptions of the poet, the psychology of the characters he has created, his own psychology, passing on then to the psychologies of his contemporaries and the characteristics of his times. They are totally convinced that the whole sense of literature is to help in the study of life in this or that century, and that readers and poets themselves fail to realize this, as uneducated people, and simply remain in error.

Thus the theory of "useful art" has rather eminent supporters, even in our time. It is more than obvious, however, that it is impossible to stretch this theory to cover all the manifestations of art, that it is ridiculously small for it, as a dwarf's caftan would be for the Spirit of the Earth. It is impossible to limit all art to Suderman and Bourget, just to please the good bourgeois, who want "noble diversions" from art. Much in art does not come under the concept of "pleasure," if one considers this word only in its natural sense, and does not put the term "aesthetic pleasure" under it because it does not say anything and itself demands an explanation. Art terrifies, it shakes us, it makes us cry. In art there is an Aeschylus, an Edgar Allen Poe, a Dostoevsky. Just recently L. Tolstoy, with his customary accuracy of expression, compared those who seek only pleasures in art to people who would try to convince us that the only goal of eating is the pleasure of taste.

It is also just as impossible to please science and knowledge by seeing only reflections of life in art. Although the most divine Leonardo wrote essays about *come lo specchio è maestro de' pittori*,[1] and although until recently in literature and the plastic arts, "realism" seemed to be the final word (that is what is written in today's textbooks)—art has never reproduced but has always changed reality: even in da Vinci's pictures, even among the most ardent realist authors, like Balzac, our Gogol, and Zola. There is no art that can repeat reality. In the external world, nothing exists that corresponds to architecture and music. Neither the Cologne cathedral nor Beethoven's symphonies can reproduce what surrounds us. In sculpture there is only a form without any paint, in a painting there are only colors without form, but in life, however, the one and the other are inseparable. Sculpture and painting give immobile moments, but in life everything flows in time. Sculpture and painting repeat only the exterior of objects: neither marble nor bronze is able

---

1   *Eds.* Italian, "how the mirror is the painters' master."

to render the texture of skin; a statue has no heart, lungs, or internal organs; there are no hidden minerals in a drawing of a mountain ridge. Poetry is deprived of any embodiment in space; it snatches up only separate moments and scenes from countless feelings, from the uninterrupted flow of events. Drama unites the means of painting and sculpture with the means of poetry, but beyond the decoration of the room there are no other parts of the apartment, no streets, no city; the actor who goes off into the wings stops being Prince Hamlet; what in actuality lasted twenty years can be seen on the stage in two hours.

Art never deceives people, with the exception of anecdotal cases, like the foolish birds pecking at fruits painted by Zeuxis. No one believes a picture is a view through an open window, no one greets the bust of his acquaintance, and not one author has been sentenced to prison for an imaginary crime in a story. Besides, we refuse to call artistic precisely those works which reproduce reality with a singular resemblance. We recognize neither panoramas nor wax statues as art. And what has been accomplished if art succeeds in mimicking nature? Of what use can the doubling of reality be? "The advantage of a painted tree over a real one," says August Schlegel, "is only that there won't be any caterpillars on it." Botanists will never study a plant according to drawings. The most expertly depicted marina will never replace a view of the ocean for the traveler, if only because a salty breeze will not blow in his face and the sounds of waves crashing against the beach rocks will not be heard. We will leave the reproduction of reality to photography and the phonograph-technicians' inventions. "Art belongs to reality as wine does to grapes," Grillparzer said.

The defenders of "utilitarian art" have, it's true, one refuge. Art does not serve the goals of science. But it can serve society, the social order. The use of art could be that it unites separate personalities, transfusing one person's feelings into another, so that it welds the classes of society into one whole and helps their historic struggle among themselves. Art from this point of view is only one means of communication for people among a number of different means, which are, first of all, the word, then writing, the press, the telegraph, the telephone. The common word and prose speech render thoughts, art renders feelings ... Guyau defended such a sphere of thought with force and wit. Here in Russia, L. Tolstoy has recently preached the same ideas, in a slightly altered form.

But does this theory really explain why artists create and why audiences, readers, and viewers seek artistic impressions? When sculptors knead clay, when painters cover canvases with paints, when poets seek the right word in order to express what they have to—not one of them sets his mind on transmitting his feelings to others. We know of artists who have scorned humanity, who have created only for themselves, without a goal, without the intention of making their works public. Is there really no self-satisfaction in creation? Did no Pushkin say to the artist: "Your work is your reward?" And why don't the readers cut this telegraph line between themselves and the soul of the artist? What is there for them in the feelings of someone they don't know, who may have lived many years ago, in another country? The task of scholarship about art is to solve the riddle of what consolidates the artist's dark cravings and the corresponding cravings of his listeners and viewers. And there is no solution in the scholastic answer: "art is useful because it facilitates the intercourse of feelings; and we want intercourse by feelings because we have a special instinct for communication."

The stubbornness of the advocates of "utilitarian art" despite all attacks on them by European thinkers of the last century, has not weakened yet and will probably not run dry as long as arguments about art continue to exist. There is always the possibility of pointing to its usefulness in one way or another. But how easy it is to use this object, that force! Archeologists learn about ancient life from the remains of buildings, but we don't build houses so that their ruins can help archeologists in the twenty-fifth century. Graphologists affirm that it is possible to learn about the character of a person from his handwriting. But the Phoenicians (according to the myth) invented writing for an entirely different purpose. The peasants in Krylov's fable condemned the ax to cut chips. The ax noted with justification that it was not guilty of being dull. In Mark Twain's book about the prince and the pauper, poor Tom once he is in the palace, uses the state seal to crack nuts. Perhaps Tom cracked nuts very successfully, but the state seal was meant to be used for other things.

II

People who think differently, who put aside the question of what art is needed for, what use it is, have asked themselves another metaphysical question: What is art? Separating art from life they examine its creations as something self-important, self-contained. Thus arose the theories of "pure art"—the second stage in the relationship between man's thought and art. Carried away by the struggle with the defenders of applied, utilitarian art, these people have gone to the other extreme and have affirmed that art need never have any kind of utility, that art is diametrically opposed to all profit, all purpose: art is purposeless. Our Turgenev has expressed these thoughts with merciless frankness: "Art has no purpose other than art itself. And in a letter to Fet he is even more explicit. "It's not that useless art is rubbish; useless-ness is precisely the diamond in its crown." When the supporters of these views asked: what unites into one class the creations that people recognize as artistic, the pictures of Raphael, and Byron's verses, and Mozart's melodies—why is all of this art?—what do they have in common? They answered—Beauty!

This word, first uttered in the same sense in antiquity, then seized upon and repeated thousands of times by German aestheticians, has become an incantation *sui generis*. They have satiated themselves, made themselves drunk with it, not even wanting to fathom its sense.

> A genius should admire
> Only youth and beauty...

said Pushkin. Maykov repeated his precept almost word for word when he said that art:

> Is like revelations
> From the heights above the stars,
> From the kingdom of eternal youth
> And eternal beauty.

Baudelaire, who it would seem would be foreign to them, created a stunning image of Beauty, destructive and attractive:

> *Je suis belle, ô mortels! comme un rêve de pierre,*
> *Et mon sein, où chacun s'est meurtri tour à tour,*

Est fait pour inspirer au poète un amour
Eternel et muet ainsi que la matière
....
Et jamais je ne pleure et jamai je ne ris.[2]

When the theory of pure art had just been created, it was possible to understand that beauty meant exactly what it means in the language. It was possible to apply the word "beautiful" to almost every work of ancient art and to the art of the time of pseudo-classicism. The nude bodies of statues, the images of gods and heroes were beautiful; tragedies' myths were sublimely beautiful. There were, however, hanged slaves, incest, and a Thersites in Greek sculpture and poetry—which did not fit too well with the concept of beauty. Aristotle and his later imitator Boileau had to advise artists to depict ugliness in such a way that it seemed, nevertheless, attractive. But the Romantics and their successors, the realists, rejected this embellishment of reality. All the world's ugliness invaded artistic works. Deformed faces, rags, the pitiful conditions of reality stepped out into pictures; novels and poems changed their place of action from regal castles to dank cellars and smoky attics. Poetry took on the hustle and bustle of everyday life, with the vices, horrors, and vanity of the petty, commonplace, little people of today. When the talk turned to Plyushkin, there was not any possibility of referring even to spiritual beauty. Beauty, like the virgin Astrae of mythology, the *ultima coelestum*,[3] evidently abandoned art once and for all, and after Gogol, after Dickens, after Balzac, one was able to praise revelations only with an eye completely blind to the surroundings:

> From the heights above the stars,
> From the kingdom of eternal youth
> And eternal beauty.

In addition, even the very concept of beauty is not immutable. There is no special, universal measure of beauty. Beauty is no more than an abstraction, a

---

2 *Eds.* I'm beautiful, o mortals! like a dream of stone, / And my breast, where each man is murdered one by one, / Is made to inspire a love in the poet / Eternal and mute just like matter / . . . / And never do I cry and never do I laugh.

3 *Eds.* Latin, "last of the heavenly ones." A quote from Book One of Ovid's *Metamorphosis*.

common notion, similar to the notions of truth, good, and many other widespread generalizations of human thought. Beauty varies with the centuries. Beauty is different for different centuries. What was beautiful to the Assyrians seems ugly to us; fashionable clothes, which captivated Pushkin by their beauty, arouse laughter in us; what the Chinese now consider beautiful is foreign to us. But in the meantime, works of art from all ages and all nations conquer us equally. History was recently a witness to how Japanese art subjugated all of Europe, even though beauty in these two worlds is completely different. There is inalterability and immortality in art, which beauty doesn't have. And the marble statues of the Pergamon altar are eternal not because they are beautiful, but because art has inspired its own life in them, independent of beauty.

In order to reconcile the theory of "pure art" with the facts somewhat, its defenders have had to violate the notion of beauty in every possible way. Since ancient times, when speaking about art, they began to give the concept of "beauty" different, often rather unexpected meanings. Beauty was identified with perfection, with unity in diversity, it was sought in undulating lines, in softness, in moderateness of dimensions. "The unfortunate notion of beauty," says a German critic, "has been stretched in all directions, as if it were made of rubber... they say that, in relation to art, the word 'beauty' should be understood in a broader sense, but it would be better to say too broad a sense. To affirm that Ugolino is beautiful in a broader sense is the same as avowing that evil is good in a broader sense and that a slave is a master in a broader sense."

The substitution of the word "typicality" for "beauty" has enjoyed particular success. People have assured us that works of art are beautiful because they represent types. But if you lay these two concepts one on top of the other, they are far from congruent. Beauty is not always typical, and not everything typical is beautiful. *Le beau c'est rare,*[4] says one whole school of art. Emerald green eyes seemed beautiful to many people, although they are rarely encountered. Winged human figures in Eastern pictures are striking because of their beauty, but they are the fruit of fantasy and themselves create their own types. On the other hand, are there not animals that are ugly by their very distinguishing marks, which are impossible to depict typically in any other way than ugly? Such as cuttle-fish, skates, spiders, and caterpillars? And the types of all inner ugliness, all vices, all that is base in a man, or stupid, or trite—how

---

4   *Eds.* French, "The beautiful is the rare."

could they become beauty? And isn't the new art, more and more boldly entering into the world of individual, personal feelings, sensations of the moment and of just this moment, breaking absolutely and forever with the specter of typicality?

In one place Pushkin speaks about the "Science of love," about "love for love," and notes:

> this important amusement,
> Praised in our forefathers' time,
> Is worthy of old apes.

These same words can be repeated about "art for art's sake." It separates art from life, i.e., from the only soil on which something can grow into humanity. Beauty (with a capital letter) is dead art. No matter how irreproachable the sonnet's form, no matter how beautiful the marble fact of a bust, if there is nothing beyond these sounds, beyond the marble, what will attract me to it? Man's spirit cannot be reconciled with peace. "*Je hais le mouvement qui déplace les lignes*"—I hate any movement that displaces lines," says Baudelaire's Beauty. But art is always seeking, always an outburst, and Baudelaire himself poured not deathly immobility, but whirlpools of grief, despair, and damnation into his chiseled sonnets. The same state seal that Tom used to crack nuts in the palace probably sparkled very prettily in the sun. But even its beautiful shine was not its purpose. It was created for something greater.

III

People of science have approached art in completely different ways. Science has no pretensions about penetrating the essence of things. Science knows only the relations of phenomena, knows only how to compare and contrast them. Science cannot examine anything without knowing its relation to another things. Science's conclusions are observations about correlations between objects and phenomena.

Science, approaching works of art with its special methods, first of all has refused to consider them by themselves. It understands that works of art without any relation to man—to the artist/creator and the person who is perceiving someone else's creation—give no more than a painted canvas, chiseled stone, words and sounds connected into periods. It is impossible to find anything in common between Egyptian pyramids and Keats' poems if you forget about the designs of the builder and the poet, and about the impressions of the viewers and readers. It is possible to identify one with the other only in the human spirit. Art exists in man and nowhere else. The honor of recognizing this truth belongs to the philosophers of the English school. "Beauty," wrote Brown, "is not anything that exists in objects independently of the mind which perceives them, and permanent therefore, as the objects in which it is falsely supposed to exist. It is an emotion of the mind, varying, therefore, like all our other emotions, with the varying tendencies of the mind, in different circumstances."

Relying on this truth, science has naturally discovered two ways of studying art: studying the emotional excitement that seizes the viewer, reader, or listener when he surrenders to artistic impressions, and studying the emotional excitement that prompts an artist to create. Science started out on these two paths, but almost from the first step it lost its way.

We must recognize as hopelessly unsuccessful the attempt to connect the study of aesthetic excitement, those impressions that works of art give us, with physiology. The connection between psychological and physiological facts poses a riddle for science even in the most elementary phenomena. It still cannot explain the transition between the prick of a pin to the sensation of pain. The desire to reduce immeasurably complex artistic emotions to something like the pleasant or unpleasant movement of the eyeball cannot provide us with anything but a subject for ridicule. Every physiological explanation of aesthetic phenomena goes no further than dubious analyses. We could achieve the same measure of success looking for answers to the questions of higher mathematics in physiology (at its present stage of development).

Psychology could do no more here. But even this science, which Maeterlinck said had "usurped the beautiful name of Psyche," is also still far from maturity. Up to now it has investigated only the simplest phenomena of our spiritual life, although with a flippancy characteristic of children, it hastens to affirm that it already knows everything, that there is nothing else in the human spirit, and if there is, it is carried out according to the same models. Finding itself confronted by one of the most mysterious phenomena of human spiritual existence, the sphinx-like riddle of art, psychology began to solve this complex mathematical problem, which demands the most refined methods of advanced analysis, using only the four principles of arithmetic. The problem remained unresolved, of course, the answer obtained was most arbitrary. But psychology announced that the work had been done. And if the facts themselves did not fit the pattern, so much the worse for the facts!

Psychological aesthetics gathered a number of phenomena, which it recognized as "direct producers of aesthetic sensation," such as, for example, in the area of vision: combinations of chiaroscuros, harmonies of colors and their unification with luster, the beauty of complex movements and forms, the proportions of parts, the firm and soft support of weight—or in the area of sound: special combinations of tones called melody and harmony, tempo, emphasis, cadence. It added various pleasant sensations, procured by means of association, to these "producers." And psychological aesthetics now intends to solve the question of art with addition and subtraction, without even using "multiplication and division." They seriously think that every artistic creation can be divided, in its crudest sense, into these basic elements: brilliance, curvature, and melody, and that after this division there is no remainder.

Without even saying that the simplicity of many of these quasi-elements is extremely dubious, the whole matter comes down to the fact that only in art do these impressions evoke "aesthetic excitement." We all know the brilliance of the sun, it is often pretty, pleasant, one can find pleasure in it; but there is none of that unique thrill in it that works of art pour into everyone who truly knows how to cling to it. But in a poem, where the same sun is depicted, although it is made of verses and "does not enlighten" (Lotze's expression)—it shines for us with an entirely special brilliance, the brilliance of a work of art. And it is like this everywhere. If we break down Klinger's bust of Beethoven into its pieces, to the varicolored marble, the dull and lustrous metals, and even add the "associative" feelings about the creator of the Ninth Symphony, the rapture that grips us when we confront the creation of a new Phidias will not be there! And the non-artificial beauty of nature, the nicest, most elegant and triumphant landscapes that enchant and captivate us, will never give us just that which is called "aesthetic excitement." Only special divine emissaries are destined to evoke this sensation—the ones who have been given the significant name of creator—*poietes*.

Another path has led science to study the emotional excitement that causes man to sculpt statues, to paint pictures, to compose poems. Science has begun to try to find out what kind of desires attract the artist, compel him to work—sometimes to exhaustion—and find self-satisfaction in his work. And that spirit that wafted over science in the century just past, which in its time removed things and phenomena from their places, even though they seemed immobile to the philosophical eighteenth century, turned them into an uncontrollable stream of the eternally changing, eternally evolving world, the spirit of evolutionism—this spirit fixed the researchers' attention on the origin of art. As in many other cases, science substituted the word to "become" for the word to "be" and began to investigate not "What is art" but "Where did art come from," thinking that it was answering one and the same question. And so detailed research appeared about the origin of art among aboriginal people and savages, about the crude powerless rudiments of ornament, sculpture, music, poetry ... Science thought it would solve the mystery of art by analyzing its genealogical tree. In its own way, the theory of heredity was applied here, with the assurance that a child's soul depends entirely on the combination of his ancestors' spiritual characteristics.

The investigation of art's ancestors led to the theory that was first expressed by Schiller with complete definiteness. Spencer picked up and developed this theory in passing, but with overwhelming scientific detail. The forefather of art was recognized as the game. Lower animals do not play games at all. Those who, thanks to better nutrition, have a surplus of nervous energy, feel the need to expend it—and they spend it on games. Mankind spends it on art. A rat that gnaws on things that are not good for it, a cat that plays with a ball of yarn, and especially children playing are already indulging in artistic activity. It seemed to Schiller that he was not debasing the significance of art at all with this theory. "Man," he says, "plays only when he is a person in the full sense of the word, and he is only a person when he plays." This theory adjoins, of course, the theories of useless art, which Spencer realizes: "To seek an end, which would serve life, i.e., good and utility," he writes, "inevitably means to lose sight of its aesthetic character."

Similar to the other scientific solution to the enigma of art, this theory is also too broad to define art accurately, as the theories of "utilitarian" and "pure" art were too narrow. In its search for the simplest elements that make up aesthetic excitement, science has offered elements that are often not art and which completely fail to explain the idiosyncratic, unique influence of art. In its search for what causes us to be attracted to a creation, it has also named things that often do not lead to art at all. If all art is a game, then why is not every game art? How can we draw a boundary between them? Are not children playing with a ball more like adults playing cards than Michelangelo creating David? And why was this Michelangelo an artist when he sculpted his statues and was not an artist when he played knucklebones? And why do we recognize aesthetic excitement when we listen to the flight of the Valkyries but are only amused when we watch kittens playing? How, finally, do we explain that admiration which artists of all ages arouse in mankind: we see them as prophets, as life's leaders, as teachers. Are Ibsen and L. Tolstoy only organizers of the great, universal games of our days?

Present-day science has until now turned out to be powerless in grappling with the enigma of art. The theories it has posited cannot stand because they conceal contradictions in themselves. But if we could even allow that the science of the future will luckily avoid all the submerged rocks and carefully, checking every step, feeling every inch of soil with the staff of its methods, come to all the conclusions that it can attain—will it give us the answer to what is art? But such a question cannot even exist for science, since it nonetheless asks about the essence of something. Science only answers about the position that aesthetic excitement occupies in the series of other emotional excitements that man has, and exactly what causes brought man, in the past millenia of his existence, to artistic creation. Will this satisfy our intentions? Will we be calmed by these sober answers of exact science?

Of course not. Returning to the example that has already served us twice, we can say that science will only break down in a crucible the state seal that poor Tom took possession of. Science will tell him only how much gold and how much ligature are in it, will only explain how its brilliance influences human eyes and how heavy it is to carry. But as before, poor Tom will know nothing about the purpose of this thing. Who will solve the mystery of what art is, this state seal in the great state of the universe?

IV

The most striking thing is that all these theories posited have irrefutable facts behind them. Art gives us pleasure—who's going to argue! Art teaches—we know this from thousands of examples. But together with this there are often no easily attainable goals, no use in art—only fanatics can deny this. Finally, art unites people, opens the heart, makes everyone communicants of the artist's creation. What is art? How can it be both useful and useless? serve Beauty and often be ugly? be a means of communication and seclude the artist?

The only method that can hope to answer these questions is intuition, inspired guessing—the method that philosophers and thinkers, who have sought the solution to the mystery of existence, have used in all ages. And I will point to one solution to the enigma of art that belongs precisely to a philosopher, which—it seems to me—gives an explanation to all those contradictions. This is the answer of Schopenhauer. The philosopher's own aesthetics are too closely tied to his metaphysics. But, tearing his guessing loose from the restricting chains of his thought, freeing his teachings about art from his accidentally entangled teachings about "ideas," the intermediaries between the worlds of noumena and phenomena—we arrive at a simple and clear truth: art is the comprehension of the world by other, non-rational ways. Art is what in other areas we call revelation. Works of art are doors half-opened to Eternity.

The world's phenomena, as they open up to us in the universe—extended in space and flowing in time, subject to the law of causality—must be studied by the methods of science, by rationality. But this study, based on the indications of our higher senses, gives us only approximate knowledge. Our eyes deceive us, attributing characteristics of a sunny ray to a flower that we are looking at. Our ears deceive us, reckoning vibrations of air as characteristics of a ringing bell. All our consciousness deceives us, transferring its characteristics, the conditions of its activity, to external objects. We live in the midst of an eternal, primordial lie. A thought, and consequently science, are powerless to expose this lie. The most that they could do is to point it out, to explain its inevitability. Science only brings order to the chaos of false concepts and arranges them according to rank, making it possible, making it easier to learn about them, but not to have cognition of them.

But we are not hopelessly locked in this "blue prison," using Fet's image. Signs are those moments of ecstasy, of supersensible intuition, that offer different comprehensions of worldly phenomena, that penetrate more deeply under their external covering, into their core. The primordial task of art consists of fixing forever these moments of insight, of inspiration. Art begins at the instant when the artist tries to make his dark mysterious sensations clear to himself. Where there is none of this clarification, there is no artistic creation. Where there is no mystery in a feeling, there is no art. A person for whom everything in the world is simple, clear, attainable, cannot become an artist. Art is only where there is audacity beyond the edge, breaking through the boundaries of the cognizable with the craving to scoop up at least a drop of

An alien element, from the beyond.

"The gates of Beauty lead to cognition," said the same Schiller. In all the centuries of their existence, unconsciously, but unchangingly artists have carried out their mission: to explain the mysteries revealed to them, and at the same time they have sought other, more perfect means of attaining cognizance of the universe. When the savage drew zigzags on his shield and affirmed that it was a "Serpent," he had already performed an act of cognition. In the same way the ancient marble statues, the images of Goethe's *Faust*, Tyutchev's poems—all of these are precisely renderings, in a visible, tangible form, of those insights that the artist had. True cognitions of things in them was revealed to the degree of completeness that imperfect materials of art (marble, paints, sounds, words...) allowed.

But in the course of long centuries, art has not given a clear and definite account of its purpose. Various aesthetic theories knocked artists off the path. And they raised idols, instead of praying to the true god. The history of the new art is primarily a history of its liberation. Romanticism, Realism, and Symbolism are three stages in the struggle of artists for freedom. They have finally thrown off the chains of enslavement to different random goals. Now art is finally free.

Now it is consciously devoted to its highest and singular purpose: to be the world's cognition beyond rational forms, beyond thinking about causality. Don't hinder this new art in its task, which at another time might seem useless and alien to present-day needs. You measure its use and modernity with standards that are too short. Our personal benefit is tied to the benefit of mankind. All of us live in eternity. Those questions of existence that art can answer will never stop being topics. Art is perhaps the greatest power that mankind possesses. At the same time when all the crowbars of science, all the axes of public life, are not able to break down the walls and doors that enclose us—art conceals within itself awesome dynamite, which can shatter those walls, and moreover it is the *sesame* that makes doors open by themselves. Let contemporary artists consciously form their works in the shape of keys to the mysteries, in the shape of mystical keys that will unlock for mankind the doors of its "blue prison" to eternal freedom.

VALERY BRYUSOV

A Holy Sacrifice (1905)

Translated by Ronald E. Peterson

>   Until Apollo calls for a
>   *Holy sacrifice* from a poet,
>   He is faintheartedly absorbed
>   By the bustle of a vain world.
>   His sacred lyre is silent,
>   His soul partakes of cold sleep,
>   And among the world's
>   Insignificant children, perhaps,
>   He is the least significant.
>
>   *Pushkin*

When Pushkin read Derzhavin's poem, "Let me be gnawed for my words, for my deeds the satirist will honor me," he said: "Derzhavin is not quite right. The words of a poet are his deeds." This was retold by Gogol, who added: "Pushkin is right." In Derzhavin's time, a poet's words, his works, seemed to be the *celebration* of deeds, something that accompanied life, that decorated it. "You are the glory, I will live by your echo," Derzhavin says to Felitsa. Pushkin placed the words of a poet not only on the same level as deeds, but even higher: a poet should reverentially bring his "holy sacrifice," but at other times he can be the "least significant," without demeaning his high calling. From this avowal it is just a short step to the recognition of art as something more important and more real than life, to the theory formulated with crude directness by Théophile Gautier:

> *Tout passe.— L'Art robuste*
> *Seul à l'éternité*

[Everything passes. Only powerful art is eternal.]

In Pushkin's poems the cry of one of Count Alexei Tolstoy's letters before his death is already heard: "there is more worth living for than art!"

Pushkin has few works which are so foreign, so strange to us, as these verses about a poet, even with his keen hearing and ability to foresee the future quivering in our souls today!

Glorifying the poet's "words," as Derzhavin belittled them, Pushkin agrees with him in the certainty that these two areas are separate. Art is not life but something else. A poet is a dual being, an amphibian. That "among the world's insignificant children," he "rules vanity's affairs"—plays faro like an "eternally idle rake" (Pushkin), whether he serves as a minister, as a confidant of tsars (Derzhavin)—suddenly, by divine command, he is transformed, his soul takes wing, "like an eagle awakening," and he stands like a priest before the altar. In Pushkin's life this separateness was earned to the external differentiation of ways of living. Having "understood the rhymes," he "fled into the country" (Pushkin's own expression in a letter), literally on the "banks of wasteland's waves, in the broad, noisy oak groves." And all of Pushkin's school looked, with the same eyes, at poetic creation as something different from life. The duality was even carried to convictions, to a worldview. It seemed completely natural that a poet would have one set of views of the world in his poems, and a different set in his life. It was possible to state with certainty that Lermontov, who wrote a poem about a demon, didn't believe in the actual existence of demons: a demon was for him a fairy tale, a symbol, an image. Only a very few poets of the time were able to retain the unity of their personalities in life and art. Such a person was Tyutchev: the world view which others professed only for creativity was in fact his belief. Such a person was Baratynsky: he was able to transfer his everyday understand of the world into his poetry.

The road along which the artist who separated creativity from life travels leads straight to the barren heights of "Parnasse." "Parnassians" are those who bravely proclaimed the extreme conclusions of the Pushkinian poet, who agreed to be "least significant" until Apollo's command "called him," a conclusion which of course would have horrified Pushkin. The same Théophile Gautier who came up with the formula about the immortality of art, the last Romantic in France and the first Parnassian, left his own definition of a poet. "A poet," he writes, "is first of all a worker. The effort to put him on an ideal pedestal is utterly senseless."

He must have precisely the same amount of intelligence as any worker, and is obliged to know his work. Otherwise, he's a poor day-laborer. The poet's work is polishing words and placing them in settings of verses, as a jeweler does—the processing of precious stones. And true to this precept, the Parnassians worked on their verses like mathematicians on their problems, perhaps, not without inspiration ("inspiration is needed as much in geometry as it is in poetry"—Pushkin's words), but most of all with attention, and in any case without excitement. The young Verlaine, who had certainly been previously under the influence of Parnassianism, with his characteristic lack of restraint, noted straightforwardly: "we, who chisel words like bowls and very coldly write passionate verses. Poor people! Art is not for squandering one's soul. Is the Venus de Milo made of marble or not?"

> ... *nous, qui ciselons les mots comme des coupes*
> *Et qui faisons des vers émus très froidement* ...
>
> *Pauvres gens! l'Art n'est pas d'éparpiller son âme:*
> *Est-elle en marbre, ou non, la Venus de Milo?*[1]

But contemporary art, which is called "Symbolism" and "Decadence," did not pass along that deserted road. Two blossoms opened on the stem of

---

1 *Eds.* The translation for these lines immediately precedes them in Bryusov's essay.

Romanticism: Realism together with Parnassianism. The latter, although it perhaps "burns with eternal gold in chants," now has indisputably "dried up and collapsed," and the former gave seed to fresh sprouts. And everything that is new, that arose in Europe in the last quarter of the nineteenth century, grew out of those seeds. Baudelaire and Rops, who are still foreign to us in form, but familiar in their outbursts and experiences, the true predecessors of the "new art," appeared precisely in the epoch when Realism was the leading school: they would have been impossible without Balzac and Gavarni. They began within the ranks of the Parnassians, but they took only their understanding of form and its significance. Having left the Parnassians to collect their own *Trophées* the "decadents" left them, in all the violence, all the grandeur and baseness of life, departed from dreams about the luxurious India of the rajahs and the eternally beautiful Hellas of Pericles, for the fires and hammers of factories, for the rumble of trains (Verhaeren, Arno Holz), for the customary arrangements of contemporary rooms (Rodenbach, Rimbaud) for all the torturous contradictions of the contemporary soul (Hoffmannsthal, Maeterlinck), for that contemporaneity that Realists hoped to realize. It's not accidental that the City of our time, which first entered art in the Realists' novels, found its best singers precisely among the decadents.

Romanticism tore away the ropes which Pseudoclassicism had used to bind the poet's soul, but it did not completely free it. The Romantic artist was still convinced that art should depict only the noble and the beautiful, that there are many things which do not belong to art, about which it must remain silent ("A genius should be an admirer of only youth and beauty," Pushkin wrote). Only Realism returned the whole world to art, in all its manifestations, great and small, beautiful and ugly. The liberation of art from its closed, prescribed limits was accomplished in Realism. After this it was sufficient for the thought that *the whole world is in me* to penetrate deeply into consciousness—and then our contemporary understanding of art arose. Like the realists, we accept life as the only subject for realization in art, but while they sought it outside themselves, we turn our gaze inwards. Each person can say of himself, with the same right by which all methodological conventions are affirmed: "Only I exist." To express one's experiences, which is the only reality accessible to our consciousness—this has become the artist's task. And this task has consequently defined the peculiarities of form—so characteristic of the "new art." When artists believed that their aim was to reproduce the external, they tried to imitate external, visible images, to repeat them. Realizing that an object of art is in the depths of feeling, in the spirit, called for a change in the method of creation. This is the path that led to the symbol. New, symbolic creativity was the natural consequence of the Realistic school, a new, further, inevitable step in the development of art.

Zola collected "human documents." He turned the writing of a novel into a complex system of study, simplified the work of an investigative attorney. Much earlier, our Gogol zealously filled his notebooks with materials for his future works, he wrote down conversations, bons mots, and sketched types he had seen. But the artist can only offer as a fateful image that which is in him. A poet can only reproduce his own soul; it's all the same whether it's in the form of a lyrical, frank confession, or if it fills the universe, like Shakespeare, with masses of eternally vital visions that he has created. The artist must fill up his own soul, not notebooks. Instead of making piles of notes and clippings, he must throw himself into life, into all its whirlwinds. The abyss between the artist's "words" and "deeds" disappeared for us when it turned out that creation is merely a reflection of life and nothing more. Paul Verlaine, standing on the threshold of the new art, already personified the type of person who did not know where life ends and art begins. This repentant drunkard, who had fashioned hymns to the flesh in taverns, and to the Virgin Mary in hospitals, did not renounce himself, bringing his "holy sacrifice," and did not scorn himself, his past, when he heard the "divine word." Whoever accepts Verlaine's verses must accept his life; whoever rejects him as a person, let him reject his poetry: it is inseparable from his person.

Pushkin, of course, was only taking refuge in the formula "until a poet is called" to a significant degree . . . It was necessary for him, as an answer for his enemies, who spitefully whispered in each other's ears about his "debauchery," about his passion for cards. Despite Pushkin's own confession that he was "least significant," his image seems much more lofty to us in life than does Yazykov's, who posited the totally opposite ideal for a poet ("Be majestic and holy in the world"). But it cannot be argued that as a Romantic (in the broad sense of the term), Pushkin gave us access to only certain sides of his soul in his works. At certain moments in his life *he* did not consider himself worthy to stand before the altar of his divinity for a "holy sacrifice." Like Baratynsky,

Pushkin divided his experiences into "revelations of Purgatory" and "heavenly dreams." Only in those creations, so accidental for Pushkin, like "Hymn in Honor of the Plague," "Egyptian Nights," and "I remember school at the beginning of my life...," are hints about the dark side of his soul preserved for us. The storms of passion that he experienced in Odessa or during the days that led to his tragic duel—Pushkin hid them from people, not only because of his personal pride, because he didn't want to exhibit his suffering for "the simple-minded to gape at," but also with the modesty of an artist, who separated life from art. What revelations perished in this enforced silence! It seemed to Pushkin that these confessions would debase his work, although they did not debase his life. By force, he tore himself, as a poet, away from himself, as a person, compelled himself to write "Angel" and all the while dreamed about fleeing "to a pure refuge of works and peaceful delights," thinking that there he would find a second Boldino. There was no "refuge of delights and works," but days of painful separation from his bride, nightmares of his "criminal youth" that arose in solitude, and the threat of death drawing near!

We, for whom Edgar Allen Poe revealed the whole temptation of his "imp of the perverse," we, for whom Nietzsche reappraised old values, cannot follow Pushkin on this path of silence. We know only one precept for an artist: sincerity, extreme and ultimate. There are no special moments when a poet becomes a poet: he is either always a poet or never one. And the soul does not have to wait for the divine word in order to take wing like an "awakened eagle." This eagle must look at the world with eternally sleepless eyes. If the time has not come for bliss in this insight—we are ready to compel him to be watchful at any rate, at the price of suffering. We demand from a poet that he tirelessly bring his "holy sacrifices," not only with his verses, but with every hour of his life, with every feeling—his love, his hate, accomplishment and failures. Let the poet create, not his books, but his own life. Let him keep the altar fire burning, like Vesta's fire, let him kindle a great bonfire, unafraid of burning himself and his life in it. We throw ourselves on the altar of our divinity. Only a priest's knife, cutting our breasts, gives us the right to be called a poet.

Nikolai Gumilyov

Symbolism's Legacy and Acmeism (1913)
(first published in *Apollo*, No. 1)

Translated by Robert T. Whittaker, Jr.

To the attentive reader it is clear that Symbolism has completed its cycle of development and is now declining. And it is clear that Symbolist works scarcely ever appear anymore, and if they do appear, they are extremely weak even from the point of view of Symbolism; and that there have appeared Futurists, Ego-futurists, and other hyenas which always follow the lion.[1] Taking Symbolism's place is a new movement, however it may be called—whether Acmeism (from the word *acme*, the highest degree of any thing, the flower, florescence) or Adamism (a manfully firm and clear view of life)—in any case it is a movement which demands a greater balance of forces and a more precise knowledge of the relationships between subject and object than was the case with Symbolism. However, in order for this trend to establish itself completely and become a worthy successor to that which precedes it, it must accept the legacy of its predecessor and reply to all the problems previously posed. The fame of one's forefathers entails obligations, and Symbolism has been a worthy father.

French Symbolism, the wellspring of all Symbolism as a school, brought to the fore purely literary problems, free verse, a more unique and protean style,

---

[1] *Author's note:* The reader should not think that with this phrase I have dispensed with all the extreme aspirations of contemporary art. A special article in one of the next issues of *Apollo* will be devoted to an analysis and evaluation of them.

metaphor elevated above all else, and the notorious "theory of correspondences." The latter completely divulges its non-Romanic and consequently non-national, superficial basis. The Romanic spirit loves far too much that element of light which distinguishes objects, which sharply outlines; this very Symbolist melding of all forms and things, this inconstancy of their images could have been born only in the murky gloom of Germanic forests. A mystic might say that Symbolism in France was a direct consequence of Sedan. But at the same time this disclosed in French literature an aristocratic thirsting for the uncommon and the difficult to attain, and in this way saved it from an ominous, vulgar naturalism.

As Russians we cannot avoid coming to terms with French Symbolism, even if only because the new trend of which I was speaking above yields a decisive preference to the Romanic spirit over the Germanic. In like manner as the French sought a new, freer verse, the Acmeists strive to smash the bonds of meter by the omission of syllables, by a transposition of stress freer than ever before, and there are already poems written according to the newly conceived syllabic system of versification. The dizzying quality of Symbolist metaphors has conditioned Acmeists to audacious turns of thought; the instability of those words to which they lent an attentive ear motivated them to search in our living national speech for new words with more stable content; and bright irony, which does not undermine the roots of our faith (an irony which could not help but emerge, however infrequently, in Romanic writers), has taken the place of that hopeless German seriousness which our Symbolists have so assiduously courted. Finally, while highly esteeming the Symbolists for having shown us the significance of the symbol in art, we do not concur in offering up in sacrifice to it all other manners of poetic effect, but seek their complete coordination. Thus we answer the question of the comparative "sublime difficulty" of the two trends: it is more difficult to be an Acmeist than a Symbolist, as it is more difficult to build a cathedral than a tower. And it is one of the principles of the new movement always to travel the line of greatest resistance.

Germanic Symbolism in the person of its originators Nietzsche and Ibsen brought forward the question of the role of man in the universe, of the individual in society, and resolved it by locating some kind of objective goal or dogma which was to be served. This betrayed the fact that Germanic Symbolism has no feeling for each phenomenon's independent value, which needs no external justification. For us, hierarchy in the world of phenomena is only the specific gravity of each of them, whereby the weight of the most insignificant is nonetheless immeasurably greater than the absence of weight, than nonexistence, and therefore upon confrontation with nonexistence all phenomena are brothers.

We would never take it upon ourselves to force an atom to bow to God if this were not in its nature. But sensing ourselves to be phenomena among phenomena, we become involved in a world rhythm, we accept all influences upon us and in turn exert an influence ourselves. Our duty, our will, our happiness, and our tragedy is to guess hourly what the next hour shall be for us, for our cause, for the whole world, and to hasten its approach. And yet, not holding our attention even an instant, as the highest reward there appears to us an image of the final hour, which will never come. To revolt in the name of some existential conditions here, where there is death, is just as strange as for a prisoner to break down a wall when there is an open door before him. Here ethics becomes aesthetics, expanding itself to encompass the area of the latter. Here individualism in its greatest intensity creates society. Here God becomes the Living God, because man has felt himself worthy of such a God. Here death is a curtain separating us, the actors, from the audience, and in the inspiration of our acting we despise any cowardly peeking to see what will happen next. As Adamists we are somewhat animals of the forest, and in any case we will not give up any of that which is animalistic in us in exchange for neurasthenia. But this is the time to speak to Russian Symbolism.

Russian Symbolism dispatched its main forces into the area of the unknown. Alternately it fraternized with mysticism, with theosophy, and with occultism. Certain of its quests in this direction almost approached the creation of myth. And it has a right to ask of that trend coming up to take its place whether it can boast only of animalistic virtues, and what its relationship is to the unknowable. The first answer that Acmeism can give to such an interrogation will be to point out that what is unknowable, according to the very meaning of this word, cannot be comprehended. The second is that all efforts in this direction are immodest. The entire beauty, the entire sacred significance of stars rests in the fact that they are infinitely far from the earth and through no successes of aviation will they become closer. He demonstrates a poverty of imagination who imagines the evolution of the individual always in terms of time and space. How are we able to recall our former existences (if this is not clearly a literary device), when we were in an abyss where there were myriads of other existential possibilities, about which we know nothing except that they exist? After all, each of them is negated by our existence and in turn negates ours. Child-like, but wise, and sweet to the point of pain is the sensation of one's own lack of knowledge: this is what the unknown gives us. Francois Villon, upon asking where the most beautiful ladies of antiquity are now, answers himself with the mournful exclamation:

Mais où sont les neiges d'antan![2]

And this gives us a more powerful sensation of the otherworldly than whole volumes of discussions concerning which side of the moon the souls of the departed are found on ... Always keep in mind the unknowable, but do not offend the thought of it with more or less probable speculations—this is Acmeism's principle. This does not mean that it relinquishes its right to depict the soul in those moments when it trembles in approaching another; but at that point it should only shudder. Of course, the comprehension of God, the beautiful lady Theology, shall remain on her throne. But Acmeists wish neither to lower her to the level of literature, nor to elevate literature to her diamond-like frigidity. As concerns angels, demons, elemental and other spirits, these are part of the artist's material and should not outweigh by greater earthly gravity the other images taken up by him.

Every new movement experiences a love for one or another artist or epoch. Fond graves bind people more than anything. In those circles close to Acmeism the names of Shakespeare, Rabelais, Villon, and Théophile Gautier are heard most often. Each of them represents a cornerstone for the building of Acmeism, an extreme intensity of one or another of its elements. Shakespeare showed us the inner world of man; Rabelais—the body and its joys, a wise physiologism; Villon told us about life, without in the least doubting in himself and while knowing everything—God, vice, death, and immortality; Théophile Gautier found in art the worthy raiments of irreproachable forms for this life. To combine in itself these four moments—this is the dream which now unifies those people who so boldly have called themselves Acmeists.

---

2   *Eds.* From Francois Villon's *Testament* (*Le Testament*): "But where are the snows of yesteryear!"

Vyacheslav Ivanov

Nietzsche and Dionysus (1904)

Translated by Robert Bird

I

There is an ancient myth: when the Hellenic warriors were dividing the spoils and booty of Troy, the dark lot fell to Eurypylus, the marshal of the Thessalian troops. From the threshold of the royal treasuries, which was engulfed in flames, furious Cassandra hurled to the feet of the victors the renowned ark, fashioned by Hephaestus, which had always been kept locked. Zeus himself had given it to old Dardanus, the builder of Troy, as a sign of divine patrimony. The foresight of the secret god had bestowed the hallowed relic on the Thessalian as battle tribute. Eurypylus's fellow leaders tried in vain to persuade him to beware of the snares of the frenzied prophetess: it would be better, they assured him, to cast his gift to the depths of the Skamander. But Eurypylus was eager to test his mysterious lot, and he carried the ark off; opening it, he saw by the reflected light of the burning city not a bearded man in a coffin, crowned with sprawling branches, but a fig-wood idol of King Dionysus in an ancient sarcophagus. Hardly had the hero glanced at the image of the god when he went mad.

Thus appears before us the holy tale as sketched by Pausanius. Our imagination is tempted to follow Eurypylus along the burning paths of his Dionysian madness. But the myth, which went unnoticed by ancient poets, is silent. We hear only that at times the king regained his senses, and in these intervals of healthy understanding, he set sail from the shores of ruined Ilium heading not for his native Thessaly, but for Cyrrha, the Delphic harbor, in order to seek healing at Apollo's tripod. Pythia promised him redemption and a new homeland on the shores where he would encounter foreign sacrifice and set up an ark. The wind carried the seafarers to the coast of Achaia. In the borderlands of Patrae, Eurypylus stepped onto dry land and saw a youth and a maiden being led to be sacrificed at the altar of Artemis Triclaria. Thus, he recognized the final resting place that had been foretold him; and the inhabitants of that country, for their part, recognized in him the promised savior who would free them of the obligation to offer human sacrifice, the one whom the oracle had taught them to expect in person of a foreign king bearing an ark with a god unknown to them who would cease the bloody worship of the wild goddess. Eurypylus was healed of his holy ailment; he replaced the cruel sacrifices with merciful ones in the name of the god he proclaimed. Having instituted the veneration of Dionysus, he died and became the guardian hero of the liberated nation.

This ancient patronal legend seems to me a mythical reflection of the fate of Friedrich Nietzsche. Thus also, together with other people strong of spirit, did he attempt to conquer Beauty, the Helen of the Hellenes, by burning ancient strongholds; thus did he win the destined sacred object. Thus did he go mad as a result of his mysterious acquisition and insight. Thus also did he proselytize Dionysus and seek protection from Dionysus in Apollo's power. Thus did he with new divine knowledge abolish human sacrifice to the old idols of a narrowly understood and externally imposed duty, removing the yoke of despondency and despair that hung over people's hearts. Like this hero he was mad in life, and from out of the depths of the earth, he became the benefactor of the human race he liberated, a true hero of the new world.

Nietzsche returned Dionysus to the world: this was his mission and his prophetic madness. Dionysus's name sounded in his mouth like the falling of "many waters." The charm of Dionysus gave him an immense influence on our epoch and made him the forger of our future. The hollow magic of a stifling illusion, the bewitched captivity of dim souls, was shaken. Meadows became verdant under the vernal breath of the god; hearts began to bum bright; the muscles of sublime will became taut. Each fleeting moment became significant and vatic; every breath became lighter and fuller; every heartbeat became stronger. Life glanced into people's souls more brightly, more deeply, more fully, and more penetratingly. The universe shuddered with echoes, as if the sighs of an unseen organ were echoing through the Gothic pillars made of pipes bundled like barrels and plaited into a sheer, arrowlike form. We felt ourselves, our earth, and our sun taken up in the eddy of a universal dance ("the Earth dancing around the Sun," as Shelley sang).[1] We have tasted of the universal divine wine and become dreamers. Our dormant potential for human divinity made us sigh over the tragic image of the Superman, over the resurrected Dionysus that was made incarnate in us.

There glistened in our souls the fulfillment of the covenant:

> Whoever breathes you, o god, He is a wing!
> He is not burdened
> By the mountainous masses,
> Nor by the blue glass of moisture
> Resting in the solemn noon!
> Whoever breathes by you, o god,—
> In the many-winged altar of creation
> He is a wing!
> In the storm of fraternal powers
> Around the suns
> He hurries the burning sacrifice
> Of the suffering earth ....[2]

There are geniuses of pathos, just as there are geniuses of the good. Without revealing anything essentially new, they force us to sense the world in a new way. Such was Nietzsche. He turned the funereal yearning of pessimism into the flame of a heroic funeral repast, into the phoenix fire of universal tragedy. He gave life back its tragic god ... *Incipit Tragoedia!*[3]

---

1   RB: A paraphrase (cited in English) of lines from Percy Bysshe Shelley's 1820 poem "The Cloud": "from my wings are shaken the dews that waken / The sweet buds every one, / When rocked to rest on their mother's breast, / As she dances about the Sun."
2   RB: From Antistrophe 3 of Ivanov's "Rebirth" ("Vozrozhdenie"), first published in *Pilot Stars*; Also quoted in *Hellenic Religion* [Eds.: *Ellinskaia religiia stradaiushchego boga*].
3   RB: Ivanov probably borrows this Latin phrase meaning "the tragedy begins" from Nietzsche's *Gay Science*, sec. 342, 382 [...].

II

In order to equip Nietzsche for the labor of his life, two Moirae with differing images bestowed contrasting gifts on him at birth. This fateful dichotomy can be defined as the antithesis of spiritual Sight and spiritual hearing.

Nietzsche had to possess sharp vision to distinguish the pale forms of primeval writing on the palimpsest of hidden traditions, which was covered over by a later hand. His small and elegant ears, an object of vanity for him, had to be vatic ears filled with "noise and sound," like the hearing of Pushkin's Prophet, sensitive to the inner music of the world soul.[4]

Nietzsche was a philologist, as Vladimir Solovyov defined him. In order to discover Dionysus, Nietzsche had to wander through the Elysium of pagan shadows and converse with the Hellenes in their own language, as he obviously could since many of his pages seem translations from Plato (who knew, the ancients said, the speech of the gods). Following the mountaineers of scholarship, he was to ascend to the point where we now find the study of the Greek world. It was necessary that Hermann reveal to us the language, Otfried Müller the spirit, August Boeckh the life, and Welcker the soul of the Dionysian nation. It was necessary that the future author of *The Birth of Tragedy* have Ritschl as an instructor and that he critically anatomize Diogenes Laertius or the poem about the contest between Homer and Hesiod.

Nietzsche was an orgiast of musical raptures: this was his second soul. Not long before his death, Socrates dreamed that a divine voice was exhorting him to take up music: the philosopher Nietzsche fulfilled this wondrous testament. He was to become a participant in the Wagnerian throng dedicated to the worship of the Muses and Dionysus. He was to assimilate musically what Wagner had perceived in the legacy of Beethoven: his prophetic mantle and his Promethean, fire-bearing, hollow thyrsus—in other words, his heroic and tragic pathos. It was necessary that Dionysus be revealed in music (the mute art of deaf Beethoven, the greatest proclaimer of the orgiastic mysteries of the spirit) before he could be revealed in the word or in the "ecstasy and frenzy"[5] of Dostoevsky, that great mystagogue of the future Zarathustra.

---

4 RB: Cf. Pushkin's "The Prophet" (1826); the imagery of "The Prophet" is drawn largely from Is[aiah] 6:5-10.

5 RB: The words of Zosima from Dostoevsky's *Brothers Karamazov* (pt. 2, bk. 6, chap. 3, sec. g: "On prayer, love, and the touching of other worlds").

And it was also necessary that the state of minds in the epoch during which Nietzsche appeared correspond to his dichotomous nature: that his critical lucidity and visual striving for classical clarity and plastic precision be tempered in the positive frigidity of his epoch's scientific spirit; that his orgiastic egress beyond the bounds of the self encounter ancient Indian philosophy (which Schopenhauer's pessimism had grafted onto contemporary thought) together with its faith in the illusoriness of individual division and its anguish at the separation that is caused by the haze of appearances. To the student of the spirit of tragedy, this philosophy revealed the essence of Dionysus as a principle that destroys the charms of "individuation."

Nietzsche's genius needed the Apollonian (formative, cohesive, and centripetal) elements of personal predispositions and external influences as limits within which to circumscribe the boundlessness of the musical, dissolving, and centrifugal Dionysian element. But the dichotomy of his gifts or, as he himself would say, of his "virtues," inevitably led them into mutual conflict and conditioned his fatal inner discord.

Only on the condition of a certain inner antinomy is it possible to play at self-bifurcation, a game of which Nietzsche often speaks—to play at seeking oneself, catching oneself, eluding oneself; to have a vital sense of wandering within oneself and encountering oneself, an almost palpable vision of the interminable passages and inscrutable recesses of one's emotional labyrinth.

III

Dionysus is the divine all-unity of "What Is" in its sacrificial separation and suffering transubstantiation into the many-faced nothing (mè ón) of the world, which flutters spectrally between appearance and disappearance. The eternal sacrifice and eternal resurrection of the suffering god—this is the religious idea of Dionysian orgiasm.

The "son of God," the inheritor of the father's throne, mutilated by the Titans in the cradle of the ages; the same god in the image of a "hero," i.e., a godman, born in time from an earthly mother; the "new Dionysus," whose mysterious appearance was the only possible hope of a consoling divine descent for the Hellene, who knew not Hope: this is the god of ancient philosophical and theological doctrines who is so close to our religious understanding of the world. In the universal, naturalistically tinged belief, he is the god of the martyr's death, of hidden life in the pregnant depths of death, and of an exultant return from the shadow of death, of "rebirth" and "palingenesis."

The mysticism of the religious veneration of Dionysus, which is the same in both its esoteric and popular forms, is immediately accessible and universally close to us. It combines Dionysus the sacrifice, Dionysus the resurrected, and Dionysus the comforter into a single integral experience; each instant of true ecstasy reflects the entire mystery of eternity in the living mirror of an inner, suprapersonal event of the frenzied soul. Here Dionysus is the eternal miracle of the world heart in the human heart, and the world heart is irrepressible in its fiery beating, in the tremors of penetrating pain and unexpected joy, in the fading of mortal anguish and in the renewed ecstasies of ultimate fulfillment.

The Dionysian principle, antinomial by its nature, can be variously described and formally defined, but it is fully revealed only in experience, and one would seek in vain to comprehend it by studying *what* forms its living composition. Dionysus accepts and simultaneously rejects any predicate; in his conception "a" is "not-a"; in his cult, the sacrificial victim and priest are united as an identity. Only the Dionysian *how* presents to inner experience its essence, which is not reducible to verbal interpretation, just like the essence of beauty or poetry. This pathos of universal reconciliation within the divine resolves the polarities of living forces in liberating storms. Here that which is spills over the edge of the phenomenon. Here the god, playing in the womb of divided being, breaks the limits of this womb by growing within it.

Universal life as a whole and the life of nature are definitely Dionysian:

> Orgiastic madness in wine,
> It rocks the whole world in laughter;
> But in sobriety and peaceful quiet
> That same madness sometimes breathes.
> It's silent in the hanging branches
> And it guards the greedy cave.
> (F. Sologub)[6]

---

6 RB: The first half of an untitled poem by Fyodor Sologub (1902) from a cycle "Hymns of the Suffering Dionysus," printed immediately after the first installment of Ivanov's study "The Hellenic Religion of the Suffering God" in the first issue of *The New Path* for 1904; quoted by Ivanov with a minor inaccuracy.

Equally Dionysian are the dances of satyrs in oak groves and the motionless silence of a maenad lost in the inner contemplation and sensation of the god. But the human soul can reach such a state only on the condition of its egress, its ecstatic transport beyond the limits of the empirical "I," on the condition that it partake of the unity of the universal "I" in its willing and suffering, fullness and schism, breathing and lamentation. Within this holy intoxication and orgiastic oblivion, one should distinguish the state of tortuously blessed oversaturation, the sense of miraculous power and a surfeit of strength, the consciousness of an impersonal and will-less elemental force, and the terror and ecstasy of the loss of the self in chaos and of the new discovery of the self in God. Even this, however, does not exhaust the innumerable rainbows that embrace and inflame the soul as a result of the refraction of the Dionysian element within it.

Nietzsche's musical soul knew this *how*. But from this sea, where, in Leopardi's words, "shipwreck is sweet,"[7] his other soul sought to summon forth a clear vision, a certain visual *what*, and then to retain it, captivate it, give it logical definition and lasting stability; to petrify it, so to speak.

The psychology of Dionysian ecstasy is so rich in content that he who gathers even a drop of the "moisture that encompasses worlds"[8] remains sated. Nietzsche sailed in the seas of this living moisture but did not want a "sweet shipwreck." He wished to land on a firm shore and look from this shore at the agitation of the purple depths. He experienced the divine intoxication of the element and the loss of his personal "I" in this intoxication, and this experience was sufficient for him. He did not go down into the deep caves—to meet his god in the gloom. He recoiled before the religious mystery of his purely aesthetic raptures.

It is telling that in the heroic god of Tragedy Nietzsche almost failed to notice the god who experiences suffering (*Dionúsou páthē*).[9] He knew the ecstasies of orgiasm, but he knew nothing of the mourning and moaning of passionate worship that allowed the grieving women to summon from the

---

7   RB: From the last line of Giacomo Leopardi's poem "L'infinito" ("Endlessness," c. 1820), which Ivanov translated in 1887 (published in 1904 in *Transparency*): "And shipwreck is sweet for me in this sea." [....]
8   RB: Cf. Tyutchev's "Just as the ocean surrounds the earthly sphere" ("Kak okean ob"emlet shar zemnoi," 1830).
9   RB: The sufferings (passion) of Dionysus.

depths of the earth the son of Zeus after his suffering and death. The Hellenes, according to Nietzsche, were "pessimists" due to the fullness of their vitality; their love for the tragic, *amor fati*,[10] was their overflowing strength; self-destruction was their way out of the blessed torment of overabundance. Dionysus is the symbol of this abundance and excess, this ecstasy caused by a sudden influx of vital energies. Thus runs Nietzsche's narrow conception. There can be no doubt that Dionysus is the god of excessive wealth, that he makes his abundance the rapture of death. But historically and philosophically, an abundance of life and dying comprises the *prius* of his religious idea and is subject to dispute. Tragedy arose from the orgies of the god who was mutilated by his frenzied worshipers. But what is the origin of this frenzy? It is closely tied to the cult of the souls and the primitive funeral repasts. The celebration of the funeral repast, this sacrificial worship of the dead, was accompanied by the unleashing of sexual passions. Was it death or life that tipped the overloaded and teetering scales? But, in the eyes of those ancient people, Dionysus was, after all, not the god of wild weddings and sexual intercourse, but the god of the dead and of the mortal shade; surrendering himself to be mutilated and carrying off into the night countless victims, he introduced death into the exultation of the living. And in death he smiled with the smile of exultant return, this divine witness of the indestructible generative force. He was the good news of joyful death, which concealed in itself promises of another life there, below, and of renewed raptures of life here, on earth. The suffering god, the exultant god: these two images were from the very beginning visible in him undivided and unconfused.

It is terrifying to see that it was only after the onset of his emotional disorder that Nietzsche intuited in Dionysus the suffering god, as if unconsciously and at the same time prophetically; at any event, he intuited this outside and in spite of the dogma he had completed and propagated. In one letter, he calls himself "the crucified Dionysus." This belated and unanticipated admission of the kinship between Dionysianism and Christianity, which he had so severely rejected up to then, shocks the soul like the clear

---

10   *RB*: "Love of fate" [...]

voice of Tyutchev's lark, unexpected and horrifying, like the laughter of madness, at an inclement and dark hour of nightfall . . . .[11]

[. . . .]

VI

"This happens," says Faust, blinded by the sunrise, "when a longing hope, having achieved the goal of its highest striving, sees the gate of fulfillment wide open: the flaming abundance bursts from the eternal depths, and we stand in shock. . . . We wished to ignite the enlivening torch and we ourselves are engulfed in a sea of flame! Is it love or hatred that embraces us with its burning, equally monstrous in its periods of pain and joy? So that we again lower our eyes to the earth, seeking to conceal ourselves under its veil of infancy." Nietzsche saw Dionysus—and reeled away from Dionysus, as Faust recoils from the luminous orb in order to admire its reflections in the rainbows of the waterfall.

Nietzsche's tragic guilt lies in his not having believed in the god whom he himself revealed to the world.

He understood the Dionysian principle as an aesthetic principle, and life as an "aesthetic phenomenon." But it is first and foremost a religious principle, and the rainbows of life's waterfall, toward which Nietzsche turns his face, are refractions of the divine Sun. If the Dionysian intoxication of life is only an aesthetic phenomenon, humanity is a throng of "Dionysus's craftsmen," as actors were called in antiquity. It was with good reason that the psychological mystery of playacting always fascinated the Dionysian philosopher. And, of course, life is divinely inspired and transparent, and the deep spirit is true to its eternal "I," if we keep alive the consciousness that we only wear our temporary masks for play, having clothed ourselves in the incidental forms of our individuation (*upadhi* in Hindu doctrine). Originally, however, "Dionysus's craftsmen" were his clergy and priests; moreover, they were his hypostases and "Bacchae"; and a truly Dionysian understanding of the world requires that in our consciousness our mask be the countenance of the

---

11   RB: The lark usually sings in the morning, which explains why Tyutchev's lyrical hero is terrified by its evening song ("Dark and inclement evening, / Hark, is that the voice of a lark?" ["Vecher mglistyi i nenastnyi," 1836]).

many-faced god himself and that our playacting at his cosmic altar be a holy rite and sacrificial worship.

Like Eurypylus the Thessalian, Nietzsche wanted to see the god with his own eyes, and having accepted him as a visual perception of beauty, he fell into the snares deployed by providential powers. Eurypylus should have accepted the ark as a sanctuary, and he should have accepted the mission of a god-bearer as his fate; he should have begun with a prayer at the prophetic tripod and fulfilled what had been entrusted to him without tempting the secret god, and he would not have fallen into fatal madness. But he recklessly glanced at the mysterious idol, and a divine force made him the bearer of good news. His attitude toward Dionysus was the resistance of unbelief and not the obedience of faith. Nietzsche's fate was determined by the very same features of insight into the divine and resistance to it.

Like the mythical Lycurgus, "who raised his hand against the heaven-dwelling gods" (*Iliad* VI.131), and who was punished with madness and a martyr's death for persecuting "furious Dionysus," Nietzsche was both a theomachist and the victim of theomachy.

But the peculiar feature of Dionysian religion is that it identifies the sacrificial victim with the god and the priest with the god. Theomachist types in the cycle of Dionysian myths themselves take on Dionysus's image. Suffering, they mystically reproduce the sufferings of those who suffer at their hands. And, just as Jacob the theomachist elicited a blessing, so also did Nietzsche take on the suffering imprint of the suffering god, whom he both proclaimed and rejected. Prophet and foe of Dionysus in his passions and torments, in his guilt and his death, he displays the tragic features of the god whom the Hellenes believed to have himself experienced universal martyrdom repeatedly beneath the heroic masks of mortals.

Vyacheslav Ivanov

The Precepts of Symbolism (1910)

Translated by Ronald E. Peterson

I

Any thought that is uttered is a lie. With this paradox-confession Tyutchev, unintentionally revealing the Symbolic nature of his lyrics, bares the root of the new Symbolism: a contradiction painfully experienced by the contemporary soul—the need to "express oneself" and the impossibility of doing it.

Thus the commanding world of "secretly-magical" thoughts in Tyutchev's poetry is not made definitively *communicative* for its listeners, it only markedly *incorporates* them in its first secrets. Breaking the rule of "cloaked" language, because of a desire to disclose and reveal, is avenged by the distortion of what is revealed, by the disappearance of what has been disclosed, by the lie of the "uttered thought..."

> Breaking out, you muddy the springs,
> Live by them and be silent...

And this is no conceited zeal, no dreamy pride or pretense—but the realization of the common truth about the discrepancy that has arisen between an individual's spiritual growth and the external means of communication: the word is no longer equivalent to the contents of internal experience. The attempt to "utter" it—is to destroy it, and the listener does not receive life in his soul but the dead covers of a life that has flown away.

Because it is impossible to explain this discrepancy with examples of a purely psychological concept of "existence," for example—as expression and expressible. Independently of the gnoseological point of view of "existence," as one of the cognitive forms, it is hardly possible to negate the inequality of the internal experiences expressed by it. A notion of existence in one's consciousness can be presented in such a variety of ways that the person who feels that the "mystical" sense of life has been revealed to him will sense the verbal attribute of this sign to objects of contemplative conceivability in the everyday meaning of the common word—as an "uttered lie"—sensing, at the same time, the lie and its negation of what language has marked as a symbol of "existence." It is absurd—this contemplator will say—to affirm that the world exists and that God exists—if the word "exist" means the same thing in both cases.

What should we think about the attempts at a verbal construction not only of judgments but also syllogisms from such ambiguous terms? *Quaternio terminorum*[1] will unswervingly accompany the efforts logically to use the data of supersensible experience. And is the formal logic of word-concepts, after all, applicable to the material of concept-symbols?

Meanwhile our living language is a mirror of eternal empiric cognition, and its culture is expressed by the force of its logical element, at the expense of purely symbolic, or mythologic, energy, woven at one time from its most delicate natural fabrics—and now the only thing capable of restoring the truth of the "uttered thought."

II

Russian Symbolism is created first in Tyutchev's poetry as a consistently applicable method, and is internally defined as dual vision and thus—a demand for another poetic language.

The poet experiences a certain dualism—a splitting, or rather a doubling, of his spiritual person—equally in consciousness and in creativity.

---

1   *Eds.* The so-called "fallacy of four terms."

> O my prophetic soul!
> O heart filled with anxiety!
> How you beat on the threshold
> Of a dual existence!...
>
> So, you are the dwelling of two worlds.
> Your day is painful and passionate,
> Your dreams are prophetically vague,
> Like the revelation of spirits.

Such is self-consciousness. Creativity is also divided between the "external," "daily" world that "grips" us in the "full brilliance" of its "displays"—and the "unresolved, nighttime" world that frightens us but also attracts us because it is our own innermost essence and "family inheritance," the "incorporeal, audible, invisible" world, woven, perhaps, from "thoughts freed by dreams..."

This same dualism of day and night, of the world of perceptible "phenomena" and the world of supersensible revelations is found in Novalis. Tyutchev, like Novalis, breathes more freely in the nighttime world, which spontaneously joins a person to the "divine-universal life." But both worlds are not divided by the final difference; it is bestowed only in an earthly, personal, imperfect consciousness:

> Are they not inimical?
> Or is the sun not the same for them,
> And, dividing them by motionless means,
> Doesn't it unite them too?

They are together in poetry. Now we call them Apollo and Dionysus, we know their infusibility and inseparability, and we sense in every true creation of art their effective dual unity. But Dionysus is mightier than Apollo in Tyutchev's soul, and the poet must escape from his spells to the altar of Apollo:

> He tears away from a mortal breast
> And craves fusion with infinity.

In order to preserve his individuality a man *limits* his craving for fusion with "infinity," his aspiration for "self-oblivion," "destruction," "merging with the slumbering world," and the artist turns to the brightest forms of daytime existence, to the patterns of the "cover woven from gold," that was thrown over the "world of secret spirits, the nameless abyss," by the gods—i.e., the abyss that cannot find its name in the language of daytime consciousness and external experience ... And still the most valuable moment in our experience and the most prophetic in creativity is delving into that contemplative ecstasy, where "there is no barrier" between us and the "uncovered abyss," which opens into—Silence.

> There is a certain hour of universal silence,
> And at that hour of appearances and miracles
> The vital chariot of the universe
> Rolls openly in the sky's temple.

Then, with this noumenal openness, a creativity that we call Symbolic becomes possible: everything that remained in the consciousness of the phenomenal "is suppressed by the unconsciousness"—

> The gods agitate only the virgin soul
> Of the Muse in prophetic dreams.

Such is the nature of this true poetry—of a somnambulist, marching through the world of essences under the cover of night.

> Night falls, and the elements beat
> Against its beach with noisy waves.
> Then its voice: it compels us and begs us.
> A magic boat has come to life again in the harbor ...

In the midst of dark "immeasurability," dual vision is revealed in a poet. "Like deaf and dumb demons," the Macrocosm and the Microcosm wink at each other with their lights. "What is above is also below."

> The heavenly vault, burning with a starry glory,
> Glances secretly from the depths:
> And we swim, surrounded on all sides
> By a fiery abyss.

The same notion about poetry, as about the reflection of a dual secret of the world of phenomena and the world of essences, we find under the symbol of the "Swan":

> It fondles your all-seeing dream
> Between a dual abyss,
> And you are surrounded on all sides
> By a firmament full of starry glory.

And so poetry should provide the "all-seeing dream" and the "full glory" of the world, reflecting the "dual abyss" of its external, phenomenal and its internal, noumenal achievement. A poet would want another, special language to explain this last feature.

> How can the heart express itself?
> How can another understand you?
> Will he understand how you live?

But there is no such language; there are only hints, and even the charms of a harmony that can inculcate the listener with an experience similar to something that cannot be expressed with words.

> The game and sacrifice of a private life,
> Come and overthrow the deceit of senses
> And plunge, vigorous and autocratic,
> Into that life-giving ocean!
> Come and wash your martyred breast
> With its ethereal stream,
> And commune at least for a moment
> With divine universal life.

The word-symbol becomes a magical suggestion that *joins* the listener with the mysteries of poetry. So for Baratynsky "sacred poetry" is the "secret power of harmony," and a person's soul is its "communicant . . ." How far this view is from the views of the eighteenth century, which are still very much alive in Pushkin, about the adequacy of the word, about its sufficiency for *reason,* about the direct communicability of "beautiful clarity," which could be always transparent when it didn't prefer to dissemble!

III

Symbolism in the new poetry seems like the first, vague reminiscence about the sacred language of the priests and magi, who at one time gave the words of national language a special, secret significance, which could be revealed only to them because of the correspondences that only they knew between the world of the secret and the boundaries of popular experience. They knew the other names of the gods and demons, people and things, not the ones people normally use, and they based their power over nature on the knowledge of the true names. They taught the people to appease terrible forces with tender and flattering appeals, to call the left side the "best," the furies "sweet goddesses," subterranean rulers "bearers of riches and all sorts of abundance." But they kept for themselves the continuity of other names and verbal signs, and only they understood that a "mixing bowl" (a crater) means the soul, and a "lyre"—the world, and a "cave"—birth, and "Asteria"—the island of Delos, "Scamandrius"—the youth Astyanax, Hector's son, and long before the Eleatics and Heraclitus, of course, that "to die" means "to be born," and "to be born"—"to die," and that "to be" means "to truly be," that is, "to be, like the gods are," and that "you are" means "there is divinity in you," but the unabsolute "to be" of popular usage and world view (*doxa*) related to the illusion of real or potential existence (*meon*).

Rickert's teaching about the hidden presence in every logical judgment of a third normative element, in addition to the subject and predicate (a certain "yes" or "so be it"), with which the will affirms the truth as a moral value, helps us to understand the religious-psychological moment in the history of language, expressed, in the use of the concept of "existence" for establishing the connection between subject and predicate that has first brought the whole structure of a grammatical sentence to fruition (*pater est bonus*).[2] The words of primeval, natural speech are joined together, like cyclopic blocks; the emergence of their cementing copula seems like the beginning of the artificial elaboration of the word. And since the verb "to be" had, in ancient times, the sacred sense of divine existence, then it is permissible to suppose that the sages and theurgists of those days introduced this symbol into every judgment that was uttered in order to consecrate it with all future cognition and to nourish—or only to sow—the sense of truth as a religious and moral norm in people.

Thus the eternal "pastors of the people" controlled the speech that the Hellenes called the "language of the gods"; and the transfer of this notion and the definition as the poetic language marked the religious-symbolic character of the sung, "inspired" word. The new realization of poetry as "Symbolism" by the poets themselves was the recollection of the ancient "language of the gods." For at that time, when the poet, delayed (if we are to believe Schiller) in Olympian castles, saw, when he returned to earth, not only that the material world had been divided without him and that there was no allotment for a singer in the earthly part, but (and Schiller still doesn't know this) that all the words of his ancestral language had been usurped—it was now possessed by the landlords of life—and used every day for ordinary needs—nothing more remained for the poet than to recall the dialect that had been given to him to chat with the sky-dwellers—and through this be unintelligible to the masses, especially at first.

Symbolism seems like a premonition of that hypothetically conceivable, properly religious epoch of language, when it will embrace two different types of speech: discourse about empirical objects and relations, and discourse about things and relationships of another order, revealed in internal experience—the hieratic discourse of prophecy. The first discourse, now the only one that is customary for us, will be the discourse of logic—the one whose basic inner form is analytic judgment; the second, now accidentally mixed with the first, winding sacred mistletoe around the oaks of poetry that are friendly with it and deafening the nurseries of science with parasitical growth, rising in thick ears of native cereal grains in pastures of inspired contemplation and foreign weeds in the field plowed by exact thought—will be mythological speech, whose basic form will serve "myth," understood as a synthetic judgment, where the subject

---

2   *Eds.* Latin: the father is good.

is a conceptsymbol, and the predicate is a verb; for a myth is the dynamic mode (*modus*) of the symbol—the symbol, seen as movement and motive power, as action and active force.

IV

Symbolism seems like poetry's reminiscence about the original, primordial ends and means.

In the poem "The Poet and the Crowd," Pushkin depicts the Poet as an intermediary between the gods and the people:

> We are born for inspiration,
> For sweet sounds and prayers.

The gods "inspire" the messenger of their revelations to the people; the people also pass their prayers to the gods through him; "the sweet sounds"— the language of poetry—is the "language of the gods." The dispute is not between the worshipers of an abstract outside-of-life beauty and those people who recognize only the "useful" in life, but between the "priest" and the crowd that no longer understands the "language of the gods," now dead and thus useless. The crowd, demanding earthly language from the Poet, has wasted or forgotten religion, and is left with only a utilitarian moral. The Poet is always religious because he is always a poet; but now he only strums the precious strings with an "absent-minded hand," seeing that no one around him is paying any attention.

People have wrongly seen in this poem, which was written in the austerely restrained style of antiquity, for which the formula "art for art's sake" was unknown, the proclamation of the artist's right to creativity that has no purpose in life and that shuts him in his own detached world. Pushkin's poet remembers his calling—to be a religious organizer of life, an interpreter and consolidator of the divine connection of the existing, a theurgist. When Pushkin speaks about Greece, he perceives the world as the Hellenes did, not as the contemporary Hellenizing aesthetes do: the words about the divinity of the Belvedere marble are not an irresponsible literary affirmation of some "cult" of beauty in the godless world but a confession of faith in the vital engine of universe-building harmony, not a rhetorical metaphor—the expulsion of the "uninitiated."

The purpose of poetry was the conjuring magic of rhythmical speech, mediating between the world of divine beings and man. The melodic word forced the will of higher kings to kneel, secured for the clan and tribe the subterranean help of the hero promised by the poet, warned about the inevitable god-given laws of morality and legal organization, and, affirming worship of gods by people, affirmed the world order of vital forces. Truly, the stones in the city walls were formed by lyres' spells and, without any allegory, illnesses of the body and soul were cured by rhythms, victories were won, civil strife was quieted. Such were the direct duties of ancient poetry, elegiac, epic, and hymnal. The "language of the gods" served as the means, as the system of enchanting symbolism of the word with its musical and orchestral accompaniment, from whose elements the body of the original, "syncretic" ritualistic art was formed.

Symbolism's recollection about this historically almost immemorial but unforgettable, because of the elemental force of its native heritage, time of poetry is expressed in the following phenomena:

1) in the new discovery of the symbolic energy of the word, prompted by the new requirements of the individual, not subjugated through long centuries of service to external experience, thanks to religious tradition and people's conservatism;
2) in representations of poetry as the source of intuitive cognition, and of symbols as the means of realizing that cognition;
3) in the significant self-definition of a poet not only as an artist but also as an individual—a bearer of the inner word, an organ of the universal soul, a celebrant of the secret connection of the existing, a seer of secrets and secret creator of life.

It's no wonder that the cosmic themes became the chief contents of poetry, that fleeting and barely perceptible experiences acquired the echo of "Weltschmerz," that refinement of external susceptibility and internal sensibility, bequeathed by aestheticism, served the aims of experience in the search for new world-attainments, and illusionism itself was experienced as the universal tragedy of a solitary individual.

V

The evaluation of Russian "Symbolism" depends on the correctness of the notion about the international community of this literary phenomenon and about the nature of Western influence on the newest of our poets, who began their activities with an oath of allegiance to the poly-semantic, but multi-meaningful slogan heard in the West. Closer studies of our "Symbolist school" will later show how superficial this influence was, how immaturely thought out, and basically how little the borrowing and imitation produced, and how deeply the roots of everything genuine and viable in our poetry of the last one and a half decades go into the native soil.

The brief interval of pure aestheticism, nihilistic in its contemplation of the world eclectic in its tastes and psychologically ailing, separates the emergence of the so-called "school of Symbolists" from the epoch of great representatives of the religious reaction of our national genius against the wave of iconoclastic materialism. Not examining the works of Dostoevsky, which long determined the path of our spirit, because they are not germane to the sphere of the rhythmical word, we remind the reader of the dear names of Vladimir Solovyov and the singer of the *Evening Lights* [Afanasy Fet]—two lyric poets who are preceded in the suggestion of the Symbolist tradition of our poetry, according to mental designs and artistic method, by Tyutchev, the true father of our true Symbolism.

Tyutchev was not alone as the originator of the school, destined—we believe—to show in the future the precious sanctuary of our people's soul. He was surrounded, after Zhukovsky, on whose lyre the Russian Muse first found the airy harmony of mystical spirituality, by Pushkin, whose genius, like a diamond of the rarest purity and sparkle, could not help but refract, in his facets, where all of life was reflected, even the broken but blinding rays of inner experience; Baratynsky, whose pensive and hollowly triumphant melody seems like the voice of a dark memory about some knowledge long ago vital, which revealed once to the Poet's seeing gaze the secret book of the universal soul; Gogol, who knew the anxiety and rapture of second sight given to the "lyric poet," and condemned to being only a frightened spy on life, which in order to hide from his wise soul the last sense of his own symbolism, surrounded everything before him with a magical-swaying veil of freakish myth; finally the seraphic (as they said in the middle ages) and at the same time demonic (as Goethe loved to say) Lermontov, who was equally tormented by a "strange desire," in angry revolt and prayerful affection, by a longing for a secret meeting and other songs than the "boring songs of Earth," Lermontov, the first

Russian poet to be excited by the premonition of the symbol of symbols—the Eternal Feminine, the mystical flesh of the Word born in eternity.

But it would be incorrect to call these poets Symbolists, like Tyutchev, in the narrowest sense of the word, on the basis of the motifs of their lyrics observed above, inasmuch as the distinguishing features of pure Symbolist art are, in our view:

1) a parallelism, consciously expressed by the artist, of the phenomenal and noumenal; a harmonically-found consonance of what art depicts as external reality *(realia)* and what it sees in the external, as internal and higher reality *(realiora)*; a commemoration of the correspondences and interrelationships between appearance ("only a resemblance," "nur ein Gleichnis") and its essence, which can be comprehended by the mind or perceived mystically, which casts off its shadow of visible events;

2) a sign, properly peculiar to Symbolist art and in those cases of so-called "unconscious" creation, which does not comprehend the metaphysical connection of what is depicted—a special intuition and energy of the word, which is directly sensed by the poet as cryptography of the unspoken, that absorbs in its sound many echoes of native subterranean keys, which resound from unknown places and serve in this way, together with a boundary and an exit into the "beyond," as letters (commonly understood patterns) of external experience and hieroglyphs (hieratic transcription) of internal experience.

The historical purpose of the newest Symbolist school was to reveal the nature of the word as a symbol and the nature of poetry as the Symbolism of true realities. There can be no doubt that this school has in no way fulfilled its twofold purpose. But it would be unfair to negate certain of its first achievements, primarily in the bounds of the first part of the problem, and especially the significance of the Symbolist pathos in the universal shift, experienced by all of us, of the system of the spiritual values that make up culture as a world view.

VI

Within the bounds of the evolution of our newest Symbolism, generalizing study easily differentiates two successive moments, the characteristics of which allow us to mutually contrast them, like a thesis and antithesis, and postulate a third, synthetic moment, that can include the described period with certain definitive realizations in a series of the closest of selected goals.

The pathos of the first movement consisted of the cognition, suddenly revealed to the artist, that the world was not narrow, flat, or poor, not measured out or counted, that there is much in it that yesterday's wise men did not dream of, that there are passages and openings into its secret from the labyrinth of man's soul, if only—(it seemed to the first heralds, that everything was said by this)—man learned to dare to "be like the sun," forgetting the difference, suggested to him, between the permissible and the impermissible—that the world is magical and man is free. This optimistic moment of Symbolism is characterized by confidence in the world, as something given: harmonious correspondences (*correspondances*) were revealed in it, and others, even more enigmatic and captivating, awaited the new Argonauts of the spirit, for to know them meant to rule them—and the teaching of Vl. Solovyov about the theurgic sense and purpose of poetry, still not fully understood, already sounded in the poet's soul like an imperative appeal, like Faust's vow—"to aspire continually to the highest existence" ("zum höchsten Dasein immerfort zu streben"). The wordsymbol vowed to become the sacred revelation or the miracle-working "mantra" that would lift the spell from the Earth. Artists were faced with the task of wholly incarnating in their lives and in their works (and certainly in life's exploits as well as creative feats) the world view of mystical realism—or in Novalis' words—the world view of "magical realism"; but they must have earlier endured the religio-moral test of the "antithesis": and the discord, if not the disintegration, of the former phalanx in our time clearly shows how difficult this conquest was and how many losses it cost... The world of your glorious, suffering shadow, immortal Vrubel!

It follows from every line written above that Symbolism neither wanted to be nor could be "only art." If Symbolists were not able to experience, with Russia, the crisis of war and the liberation movement, they would be resounding brass and crashing cymbals. But to suffer the common ailment meant a lot to them; for the people's soul ached, and they had to turn the finest poisons of this ailment into their own vigilant and reckless soul. The world did not seem henceforth to be a Golconda of magical miracles, a sunny lyre, awaiting the fingers of the lyricistenchanter—but a mound of "ashes," watched by the Gorgon's petrifying gaze. In the works of Z. N. Gippius, Fyodor Sologub, Alexander Blok, Andrei Bely, cries of final desperation were heard. A free man, resembling the sun, turned out to be a worm, ruined by chaos's "given," weakly persisting in affirming the god denied by reality in himself. The Beautiful Lady seemed like a "cardboard bride" to her paladin. The image of the expected Woman began to double and be confused with the apparent image of a whore. In the name of a religious acceptance of the imperishable Earth beneath its decay, the religious non-acceptance of "this world" was proclaimed; and these "non-accepters" of the world, with all the pain of its decay, were angry because of what was called by name the most painful. People began to be jealous of suffering and, seized by panic, to fear pronouncing words that burned the soul in silence. Positive religious feeling persuaded them that the "uncompromising No" is the necessary path to the unmasking of the "blinding Yes," and recent artists, shaking the dust from their feet in testimony against the temptations of art, aspired to religious actions in a different field—like Alexander Dobrolyubov and D. S. Merezhkovsky.

What confronted those who remained artists? All delay in the "antithesis" was equal, for artistic creation, to the refusal of its theurgical ideal and the affirmation of its Romantic origin. Recollection of the former radiant visions had to be strengthened in the soul only as recollection, losing the vitality of a real presence—to soothe the aching soul with dreamy melodies about the distant and the unrealizable, the contradiction of daydream and reality—to cultivate Romantic humor. And it was even possible, following Leonid Andreev's example, to threaten someone and curse something; but it would no longer be art, and would soon lose all efficiency and consistency, even with Byronic forces.

It was easier and more feasible to leave the vicious circle of the "antithesis" by renouncing the practice of flights above the clouds and feelings outside the individual—by capitulating before the present "given" of things. This process of wing-clipping regularly leads more mature Romantics to Naturalism, which, while it is still on the border of Romanticism, is usually colored with genre-description humor, and in the area of "poetry" proper—leads to delicacies of polishers' and jewelers' skills, raising with love to a "pearl of creation" everything that is not "beautiful" in this, in all probability, most literary of worlds. This trade just mentioned promises a pleasant flowering among us; and at this time, such a vital study of the poetic canon will doubtlessly be a useful service . . .

"Parnassianism" would have had, however, full rights to existence if it had not distorted—too often—the natural qualities of poetry, especially the lyrical; it is too prone to forgetting that lyrical poetry by its nature is not at all fine art, like the plastic arts and painting, but, like music, is a motive art; not contemplative, but active, and in the final analysis, not icon-creating but life-creating.

VII

An appeal to the canon of form, generally productive—not under school-dogmatic conditions, but the genetic study of traditional forms—and harmful only with the tendency to lifeless-academic ideology and epigonism, has a special purpose in relation to the purposes of Symbolism: it exerts a purgative influence on art; it reveals the inelegance and internal falseness of unjustified innovations; it sweeps away everything casual, temporary, superficial; it cultivates a strict taste, an artistic severity, a sense of responsibility and a careful restraint in dealing with old and new: to put the poet-Symbolist face to face with his true and ultimate goals—finally, it develops in him an awareness of the vital succession and internal connection with past generations, makes him truly free, for the first time, in the hierarchical subordination of creative efforts, gives experience to his audacity and consciousness to his aspirations.

But the external canon is fruitless, as is any norm, if there are no vital forces, in the elemental agitation of which it bears the origin of order, and is feebly tyrannical, as is any norm, if its organizing principle does not enter into an organic union—if not even a marriage—with the element that seeks order, but forcibly coerces and subjugates the element. The further paths of Symbolism are conditioned—in our view—by the victory and rule of that origin in the artist's soul which we would call the "internal canon."

By "internal canon" we mean: in the experience of the artist—the free and entire recognition of a hierarchical order of real values that form, in their agreement, a divine unity of the final Realities, in creativity—a vital connection of the correspondingly subordinated symbols, from which the artist weaves a priceless cover for the Soul of the World, as if creating a second nature, more spiritual and transparent than the varicolored peplos[3] of nature. Only when forms are correctly united and subordinated does art immediately become vital and significant: it turns into a commemorative secret sight of innate (to the form) correlations with higher essences and into a sacred secret action

---

3   *Eds*. In ancient Greece, a robe worn by women.

of love, conquering the division of forms, into the theurgical, transfiguring "Fiat." Its mirror, turned toward the mirrors of smashed consciousness, restores the original truth of what is reflected, correcting the fault in the first reflection that distorted the truth. Art is made with the "speculum speculorum"—the "mirror of mirrors," everything—in its very mirroring—is one set of symbols of the one common existence, where every cell of live, fragrant tissue creates and praises its petal and every petal radiates and praises the shining center of the unconfessable flower—the symbol of symbols—the Word's Flesh.

Symbolism still contemplates symbols in the distinctions of accidentally manifested correlations, which seem to have been torn from the bond of the whole; it still has not perceived to the end and "sees passing people as trees." In the symbolic system of the final attainments, the way to which leads through the "internal canon," there are no longer any symbolic forms; there is only one form, one image, as a symbol, and the justification of all forms is in it. Fet, "looking straight from time into eternity," sang his swan song, which "floats and melts," about it, perceiving the "Sun of the world":

> And motionless on fiery roses
> The living altar of the universe smokes;
> In its smoke, as in creative dreams,
> All power trembles, and all eternity is dreamed.
>
> And everything that rushes along ether's abysses,
> And every ray, corporeal and incorporeal
> Is only your reflection, O Sun of the world,
> And only a dream—only a passing dream . . .

Only the person who has managed to be spun in the Dionysian whirlwind can mix Dionysianism with internal anarchisms and amorphism. When a maenad loses herself in her god, she stops with her hand outstretched, ready to take and carry whatever her god gives her—a torch or a thyrsus with the head of her son, a sword or a flower—totally and selflessly obedient to someone else's will. Her unuttered word: "Venial! Fiat!"—"And so you, my heart, greeting god-stand! stand, my heart! . . . At the final threshold, my heart, stand, my heart . . ."

The "internal canon" signifies the internal feat of *obedience* in the name of that to which the poet says "yes," to which he is betrothed with the golden ring of a symbol:

> A wedding band fell
> Onto the purple bottom:
> Stormy confusion, in the azure,
> O Face! Appear!

And whence has the Soul of the World come? from the bluing crystal of untold distances? from the light blue nimbus of unuttered proximity?—the poet answers:

> I wear a ring
> And my face is—
> The meek ray of
> The mysterious "Yes..."

The fate of the Symbolist poet depends on this uniting act of his totally surrendering will and the religious system of his entire being. That is how Symbolism obligates us.

Until now Symbolism has complicated life and complicated art. From now on, if it is destined to *be*—it will simplify. Before, symbols were isolated and scattered, like a shower of precious stones (and hence arose the preeminence of lyric poetry); from now on Symbolists' creations will resemble symbol-monoliths. Before there was "symbolization"; from now on there will be *Symbolism*. It will be revealed in the poet's whole world view, whole and unified. The poet will discover religion in himself, if he finds a *bond* in himself, and the "bond" is "duty."

In the terminology of aesthetics, the bond of subordination means: "high style." Generic, hereditary forms of the "high style" in poetry are epic poetry, tragedy, and mystery plays: three forms of the same tragic essence. If Symbolist tragedy turns out to be possible, it will mean that the "antithesis" has been overcome: epopee is the negative affirmation of the individual through the renouncement of the individual, and the positive affirmation of the common origin; tragedy is its coronation, and celebration by passing through the gates of death; mystery is victory over death, the positive affirmation of the individual, its resurrection. Tragedy is always realism, always a myth. Mystery is the abolition of the symbol as a likeness and of myth as reflected action; it is the restoration of the symbol as incarnated reality and of myth as the realized "fiat . . ."

In conclusion—some words to young poets. Everything in poetry that has poetic spirituality is good. It is not necessary to want to be a "Symbolist"; it is possible to discover the Symbolist in yourself by yourself—and then it is better to try to hide it from people. Symbolism binds. The old clichés have been erased. Nothing new can be purchased at any price other than by the inner deed of the individual. One should remember the precept about a symbol: "Do not accept it in vain." And even a person who does not accept a symbol in vain must work on it for six days, as if he were an artist who knows nothing about *"realiora"*—and create his things in these six days, so that he can reserve the seventh day of the week, in the more highly interpreted, solemn sense:

>   for inspiration,
> For sweet sounds and prayers.

Vyacheslav Ivanov

Thoughts on Symbolism (1912)

Translated by Robert Bird

Amidst the silent hills I met a shepherd
Who blew a long alpine horn.
His song flowed pleasant to the ear, but this
Rich horn was but an instrument to waken
A captivating echo in the mountains.
And every time, creating little sound,
The shepherd would await the mountain echo,
It flowed among the steep ravines in such
A harmony, so inexpressibly sweet,
It seemed: an invisible chorus of spirits
Upon otherworldly instruments translated
The language of the earth by speech of heaven.
And then I thought: "O genius! Like this horn
You must sing earthly songs, and in men's hearts
Awaken other songs. And blessed is he who hears."
Above the mountains then a voice gave answer:
"So nature is a symbol like this horn.

She sounds for echoes. The echo then is God.
Blessed is he who hears both song and echo."[1]

I

If, as a poet, I am able to *paint* in words ("poetry is like unto painting"; "*ut pictura poesis*," as classical poetics expressed this thought in the words of Horace, who was himself following ancient Simonides); to *paint* so that the listener's imagination reproduces what I depict as distinctly and as vividly as I see it, and so that the things I name are represented to his soul as palpably textured and vitally colorful, whether shaded or radiant, whether in motion or static, in accordance with the nature of their visual appearance.

If, as a poet, I am able to *sing* with magical force (for "it is not enough that poems be beautiful: let them also be sweet and capriciously attract the soul of the listener wherever they desire"—*non satis est pulchra esse poemata, dulcia sunto et quocumque volent animum auditoris agunto*—as classical poetics described this tender violence in the words of Horace); if I am able to sing so mellifluously and powerfully that the listener's soul becomes enamored of the sounds and follows my flutes obediently, yearning with my desire, is saddened with my sadness, ignited with my ecstasy, so that with the harmonious beating of his own heart he might answer each shudder of the musical wave that bears the melodious poem;

if, as poet and sage, I command the knowledge of things; if I instruct the listener's reason and educate his will, while giving pleasure to his heart;

—but if I am a poet crowned with this threefold crown of melodious power, yet, despite this threefold charm, am still unable to compel the very soul of the listener to sing together with me in a voice different than my own, not in the unison of its psychological surface but in the counterpoint of its innermost depths, to sing of what is deeper than the depths I show and higher than the heights I disclose, if my listener is but a mirror, but an echo, only accepting, only accommodating; if the ray of my *word* does not seal my *silence* and his silence with the *rainbow* of a secret *covenant*:

then I am not a *symbolic* poet ...

---

1   RB: This poem, under the title "The Alpine Horn," was published in Ivanov's first collection of verse, *Pilot Stars*. It is closely tied to Pushkin's "The Echo" ("Ekho," 1831). [*Eds*. See this poem, in a different translation, in the present volume.]

II

If art per se is one of the most powerful means of human union, then one could say of symbolic art that the principle of its efficacy is union par excellence, union in the immediate and profoundest meaning of the word. In truth, symbolic art not only unites but also connects. Two are connected by a third, higher element. The symbol, this third element, can be likened to a rainbow that flares up between the ray of the word and the moisture of the soul that reflects the ray . . . . And Jacob's ladder begins in each work of truly symbolic art.

Symbolism connects consciousnesses in such a way that they give birth together "in beauty." According to Plato, the goal of love is "to give birth in beauty." Plato's depiction of the paths of love is a definition of Symbolism. In its growth the soul ascends from a state of attraction to a beautiful body up to the love of God. When an aesthetic phenomenon is experienced erotically, the artistic creation becomes symbolic. The enjoyment of beauty, like an attraction to corporeal beauty, becomes the initial step in an erotic ascent. When a work of art is experienced in this way, its meaning is inexhaustible. The symbol is the creative principle of love, the guiding Eros. An ancient, naively profound Italian song speaks of what then occurs between the two lives—the one made incarnate in creation and the one that partakes of it creatively (*creatively*, for Symbolism is art that turns the perceiver into a *participant* in the creative act): in this song two lovers arrange a meeting in order that the third, the god of love, might himself appear with them at the appointed hour:

> *Pur che il terzo sia presente,*
> *E quel terzo sia l'Amor.*

> So that the third is also present,
> So that the third is Love.

III

L'Amór / che muove il Sóle / e l'altre stélle—"Love, which moves the Sun and other Stars . . . ." Here, in the concluding verse of Dante's *Paradise*, the images form a myth, and wisdom is taught by the music of the verse.

Let us analyze the musical structure of this melodic verse. Its three rhythmic waves are accented by the caesurae and in turn accent the words: *Amor*; *Sole*, *Stelle*; for it is on them that the ictus falls. As a result of this word arrangement, the radiant images of the god of Love, the Sun, and the Stars seem blinding. They are divided by the valleys of the rhythm, the indeterminate and dark *muove* (moves) and *altre* (other). Night yawns in the intervals between the radiant outlines of those three ideas. Music is made incarnate in a visual phenomenon; the Apollonian vision appears above the gloom of Dionysian disturbance: the Pythic dyad is undivided and unconfused. Thus, the starlit firmament is boundlessly and powerfully imprinted on the soul. The soul becomes the contemplator (epoptes) of the mysteries, but it is not deprived of the guidance of a teacher who could explain to the consciousness what it has contemplated. Some hierophant, standing above the soul, proclaims: "Wisdom! You see the movement of the radiant sphere, you hear its harmony: know then that this is Love. Love moves the Sun and other Stars."—The hierophant's holy word (*hieròs lógos*) is the word as *lógos*.

Thus, Dante is crowned with the threefold crown of melodious power. But this is not all that he achieves. The startled soul not only perceives, not only repeats the prophetic word: the soul finds within itself its own, complementary word, and out of its mysterious depths the soul painlessly gives birth to this word. The powerful magnet magnetizes the soul: it itself becomes a magnet. The universe is revealed within it. Whatever it sees above itself in the heavens is opened within it below. Love is within the soul: for it now loves. *Amor* . . .—this sound affirms the magnetic state of the living universe and also causes the soul's molecules to arrange themselves magnetically. And within the soul is the sun, and the stars, and the hum of the harmonious spheres, moved by the power of the Divine Mover. The soul sings its own melody of love in harmony with the cosmos, just as Beatrice's melody sang in the soul of the poet when he uttered his cosmic words. We must therefore analyze Dante's verse not only in its own right, as an object of pure aesthetics, but also in its relation to the subject, as the agent of heartfelt emotion and inner experience. This verse not only appears to be full of outer musical sweetness and inner musical energy, but it is also polyphonous, since it causes additional musical vibrations and awakens certain palpable overtones. This is why it is not only an artistically perfect verse but also a symbolic verse. This, then, is why it is divinely poetic. Moreover, the individual words of the verse are pronounced so powerfully in the given connection and given combinations that they themselves are symbols, and therefore the verse is composed from symbolic elements; thus the verse represents a synthetic judgment in which an active verb (moves the Sun and the Stars) is found for the symbol-subject (Love). Thus, we see before us a *mythopoetic* crowning of Symbolism. For myth is a synthetic judgment in which the predicate verb is attached to a subject-symbol. The holy word, *hieròs lógos*, turns into the word as *mythos*.

If, having described the effect of the concluding words of *The Divine Comedy*, we dared to evaluate it according to the religio-metaphysical hierarchy of values, we would have to call this effect theurgic. And—within the category of analysis sketched above, which is actually far from obligatory for the aesthetics of symbolic art—this example would serve to verify for us the hypothesized identity of true and supreme Symbolism and theurgy, an identity that has already been proclaimed on more than one occasion.

IV

Thus, I am not a Symbolist if I am unable to awaken through an imperceptible hint or influence incommunicable feelings in the listener's heart. These feelings are similar at times to primeval recollection ("and long in the world it suffered, full of a wondrous desire: the tedious songs of the earth could not replace the sounds of heaven"[2]), at times similar to a distant, vague presentiment, at times to the tremor felt at someone's familiar and desired approach. Moreover, we experience both this recollection and this presentiment or presence as an incomprehensible expansion of our personal makeup and empirically limited self-consciousness.

I am not a Symbolist if my words do not arouse in the listener a feeling of connection between his "I" and what he calls his "not-I," a connection between things that are empirically divided; if my words do not immediately convince him of the existence of hidden life where his reason did not suspect any life at all; if my words do not move in him an energy of love for what he had previously been unable to love because his love did not know how many mansions it had.

---

2   RB: From Lermontov's poem "The Angel" (1830); "it" refers to "the soul."

I am not a Symbolist if my words are equal to themselves, if they are not an echo of other sounds, about which, as of the Spirit, you know not whence they come and whither they go—and if they do not awaken an echo in the labyrinths of souls.

V

In this case, I am not a Symbolist—for my listener. For Symbolism denotes a relation, and a symbolic work cannot exist by itself, just as an object cannot exist removed from its subject.

Abstract aesthetic theory and formal poetics analyze the work of art in itself; therefore, they do not know Symbolism. One can speak of Symbolism only if one studies a work in its relation to the perceiving subject and the creative subject, understood as integral personalities. Hence, it follows that:

1. Symbolism lies outside of aesthetic categories.
2. Every work of art can be evaluated from the viewpoint of Symbolism.
3. Symbolism is tied to the integrity of the personality, both that of the artist himself and that of the person experiencing the artistic revelation.

It is obviously unthinkable that a Symbolist be a craftsman; it is similarly unthinkable that a Symbolist be an aesthete. Symbolism deals with man. Thus, it restores the word "poet" in its old meaning of poet as personality (*poetae nascuntur*)[3] in opposition to the common usage of our day, which tries to reduce this lofty name to the meaning of "an artist-versifier acknowledged as talented and skillful in his technical field."

VI

Is the symbolic element obligatory in the organic composition of a perfect creation? Must a work of art be effective symbolically in order to be called perfect?

The requirement of symbolic efficacy is no more obligatory than the demand of *ut pictura* or *dulcia sunto*....[4] What formal feature is ever absolutely

---

3   RB: "Poets are born [not made]"; a paraphrase of Cicero, *Pro Archia poeta oratio* [...].
4   RB: "Unto painting" and "let them be sweet" are phrases from Horace's poetic theory, given in their context in sec. 1.

necessary in order that a work be called artistic? Since such a feature has never been named, there cannot yet be a formal aesthetics.

But there are schools of thought. And each is distinguished by the particular, supraobligatory, so to speak, demands that it freely imposes upon itself, as the rule and vow of its artistic order. In this way, the symbolic school demands from itself more than other schools.

Clearly, the very same demands might also be satisfied unconsciously, without any rule or vow. Each work of art may be tested from the viewpoint of Symbolism.

Since Symbolism denotes the relation of the artistic object to a double subject (creative and perceiving), whether or not any particular work is symbolic depends to a large degree on our perception. For example, we can take symbolically Lermontov's words: "Out from under a mysterious, cold demimasque your voice sounded forth to me . . ."[5] although, in all likelihood, the author of these verses considered these words to be equal to themselves in their logical capacity and content, and he had in mind a mere meeting at a masquerade. On the other hand, by studying the relationship of a work to the integral personality of its creator, we can also establish its symbolic character independent of our own perception. In any case, the following confession of Lermontov appears to us to exemplify this:

> The word newborn
> Of flame and light
> Will meet no response
> Amidst worldly noise.[6]

One clearly sees the poet attempting to express an inner word by means of an outer word, and despairing of the accessibility of the latter to the perception of those who are listening; this perception, however, is necessary in order that the word-flame, word-light not be engulfed by darkness.

---

5   RB: The first lines of an untitled poem by Lermontov ("Iz-pod tainstvennoi, kholodnoi polumaski," 1842).
6   RB: From Lermontov's "There are kinds of speech whose meaning" ("Est' rechi—znachen'e. . . ," 1839).

Symbolism is magnetism. A magnet attracts only iron. Iron molecules are normally in a magnetized state. And whatever is attracted by a magnet becomes magnetized....

So, we Symbolists do not exist—if there are no Symbolists listening. For Symbolism is not only creative activity but also creative cooperation, not only the artistic objectification of the creative subject but also the creative subjectification of the artistic object.

"Is Symbolism dead?" our contemporaries ask. Some answer, "Of course it is dead!" It is for them to know whether Symbolism has died or them. We, however, the dead, bear witness by whispering to those feasting at our funeral repast that death does not exist.

[....]

Osip Mandelstam

The Morning of Acmeism (1913)

Translated by Jane Gary Harris

I

Given the immense emotional excitement associated with works of art, it is desirable that discussions of art display the greatest restraint. A work of art attracts the great majority only insofar as it illuminates the artist's world view. The artist, however, considers his world view a tool and an instrument, like a hammer in the hands of a stonemason, and his only reality is the work of art itself.

To exist is the artist's greatest pride. He desires no other paradise than existence, and when people speak to him of reality he only smiles bitterly, for he knows the infinitely more convincing reality of art. The spectacle of a mathematician who, without seeming to think about it, produces the square of some ten-digit number, fills us with a certain astonishment. But too often we fail to see that the poet raises a phenomenon to its tenth power, and the modest exterior of a work of art often deceives us with regard to the monstrously condensed reality contained within. In poetry this reality is the word as such. Right now, for instance, in expressing my thoughts as precisely as possible, but certainly not in a poetic manner, I am essentially speaking with my consciousness, not with the word. Deaf mutes can understand each other perfectly, and railroad signals perform a very complex function without recourse to the word. Thus, if one takes the sense and the content, everything else in the word must be regarded as a simple mechanical appendage that merely impedes the swift transmission of the thought. "The word as such" was born very slowly. Gradually, one after another, all the elements of the word were drawn into the concept of form. To this day the conscious sense, the Logos, is still taken erroneously and arbitrarily for the content. The Logos gains nothing from such an unnecessary honor. The Logos demands nothing more than to be considered on an equal footing with the other elements of the word. The Futurists, unable to cope with the conscious sense as creative material, frivolously threw it overboard and essentially repeated the crude mistake of their predecessors.

For the Acmeists the conscious sense of the word, the Logos, is just as magnificent a form as music is for the Symbolists.

And if, for the Futurists, the word as such is still down on its knees creeping, in Acmeism it has for the first time assumed a dignified upright position and entered the Stone Age of its existence.

II

The sharp edge of Acmeism is neither the stiletto nor the sting of Decadence. Acmeism is for those who, inspired by the spirit of building, do not like cowards renounce their own gravity, but joyously accept it in order to arouse and exploit the powers architecturally sleeping within. The architect says: I build, that indicates I am right. The consciousness of our rightness is dearer to us than anything else in poetry, and, rejecting the games of the Futurists, for whom there is no greater pleasure than catching a difficult word on the end of a crochet hook, we introduce the Gothic element into the relationship of words, just as Sebastian Bach established it in music.

What madman would agree to build if he did not believe in the reality of his material, the resistance of which he knew he must overcome? A cobblestone in the hands of an architect is transformed into substance, but a man is not born to build if he does not hear metaphysical proof in the sound of a chisel splitting rock. Vladimir Solovyov experienced a peculiar prophetic horror before gray Finnish boulders. The mute eloquence of the granite mass startled him like sorcery. But Tyutchev's stone, which "having rolled down the mountain, lay in the valley, torn loose itself, or loosened by a sentient hand," is the word. The voice of matter in this unexpected fall sounds like articulate speech. Only architecture can answer this challenge. Reverently the Acmeists raise this mysterious Tyutchevian stone and make it the foundation stone of their own building.

It was as if the stone thirsted after another existence. It revealed its own dynamic potential hidden within itself, as if it were begging admittance into the "grained arch" in order to participate in the joyous cooperative action of its fellows.

III

The Symbolists were poor stay-at-homes; they loved to travel, yet they felt unwell, uncomfortable in the cage of their own organisms or in that universal cage which Kant constructed with the aid of his categories.

Genuine piety before the three dimensions of space is the first condition of successful building: to regard the world neither as burden nor as an unfortunate accident, but as a God-given palace. Indeed, what can you say about an ungrateful guest who lives on his host, takes advantage of his hospitality, all the while despising him to the depths of his soul, thinking only of how to deceive him? Building is possible only in the name of the "three dimensions," for they are the conditions of all architecture. That is why the architect must be a good stay-at-home, and the Symbolists were poor architects. To build means to conquer emptiness, to hypnotize space. The handsome arrow of the Gothic belltower rages because its function is to stab the sky, to reproach it for its emptiness.

IV

We perceive what is particular in a man, that which makes him an individual, and we incorporate it into the far more significant concept of the organism. Acmeists share their love for the organism and for organization with the physiologically brilliant Middle Ages. In chasing after refinement the nineteenth century lost the secret of genuine complexity. What in the thirteenth century appeared to be the logical development of the concept of the organism—the Gothic cathedral—now has the esthetic effect of something monstrous: Notre Dame is the triumph of physiology, its Dionysian orgy. We do not want to distract ourselves with strolls through the "forest of symbols," because we have a dense more virgin forest—divine physiology, the infinite complexity, our own dark organism.

The Middle Ages, defining the specific gravity of man in its own way, sensed and acknowledged it for each individual regardless of his merits. The title of *maitre* was given readily and without hesitation. The humblest artisan, the lowest ranking cleric possessed the secret knowledge of his own true worth, of the devout dignity so characteristic of that epoch. Yes, Europe has passed through the labyrinth of fine open-work culture, when abstract being, completely unadorned personal existence, was valued as a heroic feat. From this stems the aristocratic intimacy uniting all people, which is so alien in spirit to the "equality and fraternity" of the French Revolution. There is no equality, there is no competition, there is only the complicity of all who conspire against emptiness and non-existence.

Love the existence of the thing more than the thing itself and your own existence more than yourself: that is Acmeism's highest commandment.

V

A=A: what a magnificent theme for poetry! Symbolism languished and yearned for the law of identity. Acmeism made it its slogan and proposed its adoption instead of the ambiguous *a realibus ad realiora*.[1]

The capacity for astonishment is the poet's greatest virtue. Yet how can we not be astonished by the law of identity, the most fruitful of all poetic laws? Whoever has experienced reverence and astonishment before this law is a true poet. Hence, having recognized the sovereignty of the law of identity, poetry receives, absolutely and unconditionally, lifelong feudal claims over all existence. Logic is the kingdom of the unexpected. To think logically is to be perpetually astonished. We have come to love the music of proof. Logical connection for us is not some popular song about a finch, but a choral symphony, so difficult and so inspired that the conductor must exert all his energy to keep the performers under his control.

---

1 *Author's note:* Vyacheslav Ivanov's formula. See his "Thoughts on Symbolism" in the volume *Furrows and Boundaries (Borozdy i mezhi)*. [*Eds.* Ivanov's essay is included in the present volume.]

How convincing the music of Bach! What power of proof! The artist must prove and prove endlessly. The artist worthy of his calling cannot accept anything on faith alone, that is too easy, too dull ... We cannot fly, we can ascend only those towers which we build ourselves.

VI

The Middle Ages are very close to us because they possessed to an extraordinary degree the sense of boundary and partition. They never confused different levels and treated the beyond with utmost restraint. A noble mixture of rationality and mysticism as well as a feeling for the world as a living equilibrium makes us kin to this epoch and encourages us to derive strength from work which arose on Romance soil around the year 1200. And we will prove our rightness in such a way that in answer to us the entire chain of cause and effect, from alpha to omega, will shudder. And we will learn to bear "more easily and freely the mobile fetters of existence."

Osip Mandelstam

The Word and Culture (1921)

Translated by Constance Link

Grass on the streets of Petersburg—the first sprouts of a virgin forest that will cover the site of modern cities. This bright, tender verdure, astonishing in its freshness, belongs to a new, inspired nature. Petersburg is truly the most advanced city in the world. Speed, the pace of the present, cannot be measured by subways or skyscrapers, but only by the cheerful grass thrusting itself forth from under city stones.

Our blood, our music, our State—all will be continued in the tender life of a new nature, a nature-Psyche. In this kingdom of the spirit without man every tree will be a dryad and every phenomenon will tell of its own metamorphosis.

Stop? Why? Who stops the sun as it rushes along its sparrow harness to its paternal home, possessed by the thirst for return? Is it not better to celebrate it with dithyrambs than to entreat it for a pittance?

> He did not understand anything,
> He was weak and shy, as children are,
> Strangers caught game and fish
> For him in nets.[1]

---

1   CL: From Pushkin's narrative poem *The Gypsies*, lines 194-97.

I thank you, "strangers," for your touching concern, for your tender care of the old world, which is no longer "of this world," which has given way to expectations and preparations for the coming metamorphosis:

> *Cum subit illius tristissima noctis imago,*
> *Quae mihi supremum tempus in urbe fuit,*
> *Cum repeto noctem, qua tot mihi cara reliquit,*
> *Labitur ex oculis nunc quoque gutta meis.*[2]

Yes, the old world is "not of this world," yet it is more alive than it ever was. Culture has become the Church. A separation of Church-Culture and the State has taken place. Secular life no longer concerns us. We no longer take a meal, but a sacrament, not a room, but a monastery cell, not clothes, but raiment. We have finally found inner freedom, true inner joy. We drink water in clay jugs like wine, and the sun is happier in a monastic refectory than in a restaurant. Apples, bread, potatoes—from now on they will quench not only physical but spiritual hunger. The Christian—and now every cultured person is a Christian—does not know mere physical hunger, mere spiritual nourishment. For him, the word is also flesh, and simple bread is a joy and a mystery.

Social differences and class antagonisms pale before the new division of people into friends and enemies of the word: literally, sheep and goats. I sense an almost physically unclean goat-breath emanating from the enemies of the word. Here the argument which emerges last in any serious disagreement is fully appropriate: my adversary smells bad.

The separation of Culture and the State is the most significant event of our revolution. The process of secularization of the State did not stop with the separation of Church and State as the French Revolution understood it. Our social upheaval has brought about a more profound secularization. Today the State has a unique relationship to culture that is best expressed by the term *tolerance*. But at the same time a new type of organic interrelationship is beginning to appear, one which connects the State with Culture in a way not unlike that

---

2   CL: Ovid's *Tristia*, Book 1, No. 3, lines 1-4, a literal translation being: "When I remember the fearful image of that night which marked my last moments in Rome, when I recall that night when I left so many precious things behind, even now tears flow from my eyes."

which once linked the appanage princes to the monasteries. The princes maintained monasteries for *counsel*. This explains everything. The isolation of the State insofar as cultural values are concerned makes it fully dependent on culture. Cultural values ornament the State, endowing it with color, form, and, if you will, even gender. Inscriptions on State buildings, tombs, and gateways insure the State against the ravages of time.

Poetry is the plough that turns up time in such a way that the abyssal strata of time, its black earth, appear on the surface. There are epochs, however, when mankind, not satisfied with the present, yearning like the ploughman for the abyssal strata of time, thirsts for the virgin soil of time. Revolution in art inevitably leads to Classicism, not because David reaped the harvest of Robespierre, but because that is what the earth desires.[3]

One often hears: that is good but it belongs to yesterday. But I say: yesterday has not yet been born. It has not yet really existed. I want Ovid, Pushkin, and Catullus to live once more, and I am not satisfied with the historical Ovid, Pushkin, and Catullus.

It is indeed astonishing that all are obsessed with poets and cannot tear themselves away from them. You would think that once they were read, that was that. Transcended, as they say now. Nothing could be farther from the truth. The silver trumpet of Catullus—*Ad claras Asiae volemus urbes*[4]—alarms and excites us more forcefully than any Futurist riddle. Such poetry does not exist in Russian. Yet it *must* exist in Russian. I chose a Latin line because it is clearly perceived by the Russian reader as a category of obligation: the imperative rings more vividly in it. Such an imperative characterizes all poetry that is Classical. Classical poetry is perceived as that which must be, not as that which has already been.

Thus, not a single poet has yet appeared. We are free from the burden of memories. On the other hand, we have so many rare presentiments: Pushkin, Ovid, Homer. When in the stillness of the night a lover gets tangled up in tender names and suddenly remembers that all this already was: the words and the hair and the rooster crowing outside his window, exactly as it had been in Ovid's *Tristia,* the profound joy of recurrence seizes him, a dizzying joy:

---

3 CL: Reference to Jacques Louis David's paintings of scenes from the French Revolution. [....]
4 CL: From Catullus' "Carmen No. XLVI." [....]

Like murky water, I drink the turbid air
Time is upturned by the plough, the rose is as the earth.[5]

Thus, the poet has no fear of recurrence and is easily intoxicated on Classical wine.

What is true of the single poet is true of all. There is no need to create poetic schools. There is no need to invent your own poetics.

The analytic method applied to the word, movement, and form is a completely legitimate and clever device. Recently, destruction has become a purely formal precondition of art. Disintegration, decay, decomposition—all this is still *decadence*. But the Decadents were Christian artists, the last Christian martyrs in their own way. The music of decay was for them the music of resurrection. Baudelaire's "Charogne"[6] is a lofty example of Christian despair. Conscious destruction of form is an entirely different matter. Painless Suprematism.[7] The denial of the appearance of things. Calculated suicide for the sake of curiosity. It is possible to take things apart, it is also possible to put them together: it might seem that form is being tested, but actually the spirit is rotting and decomposing. (Incidentally, having named Baudelaire, I would like to mention his significance as a kind of ascetic hero in the original Christian meaning of the word, *martyre*.)

The life of the word has entered a heroic era. The word is flesh and bread. It shares the fate of bread and flesh: suffering. People are hungry. The State is even hungrier. But there is something still hungrier: Time. Time wants to devour the State. The threat that Derzhavin scratched on his slate resounds like a clarion call. Whoever shall raise the word on high and confront time with it, as the priest displays the Eucharist, shall be a second Joshua of Nun. There is nothing hungrier than the contemporary State, and a hungry State is more terrifying than a hungry man. To show compassion for the State which denies the word shall be the contemporary poet's social obligation and heroic feat.

---

5   CL: See [Mandelstam's] poem [...] "Sisters—heaviness and tenderness" (1920).
6   CL: Baudelaire's *Les Fleurs du Mal* (1857) was extremely influential on the Symbolist movement in France, Russia, and elsewhere, in particular in providing examples of "decadent" themes. [....] "Une charogne" was one of Baudelaire's most popular poems.
7   CL: Suprematism in Russian painting paralleled the Futurist movement in Russian poetry. Suprematism was most closely connected with the names of the painters Kasimir Malevich (1878-1935) and Ivan Puni (1894-1956), both of whom were associated with the Futurists, in particular, Ego-Futurism. [....]

> Let's glorify the fateful yoke
> Which the leader of the people bears in tears,
> Let's glorify the twilight yoke of power,
> Its intolerable weight.
> Whoever has a heart must hear, O Time,
> How your ship sinks to the bottom...[8]

Do not demand from poetry any special substantiality, materiality, or concreteness. It is that very same revolutionary hunger. The doubt of Thomas. Why must you touch it with your fingers? But most important, why equate the word with the thing, with grass, with the object it designates?

Is the thing really the master of the word? The word is a Psyche. The living word does not designate an object, but freely chooses for its dwelling place, as it were, some objective significance, material thing, or beloved body. And the word wanders freely around the thing, like the soul around an abandoned, but not forgotten body.

What is said about materiality sounds slightly different when applied to imagery:

> *Prends l'eloquence et tords lui le cou!*[9]

Write imageless verses if you can, if you are able. A blind man recognizes a beloved face by barely touching it with seeing fingers, and tears of joy, the true joy of recognition, will fall from his eyes after a long separation. The poem lives through an inner image, that ringing mold of form which anticipates the written poem. There is not yet a single word, but the poem can already be heard. This is the sound of the inner image, this is the poet's ear touching it.

> Only the instant of recognition is sweet to us![10]

Today a kind of speaking in tongues is taking place. In sacred frenzy poets speak the language of all times, all cultures. Nothing is impossible. As the room

---

8   *CL*: Mandelstam's poem [...] "Twilight/Dawn of Freedom" written in May, 1918 [...].
9   *CL*: This is a reference to Stanza 6 of Verlain's "Art poétique." [....]
10 *CL*: See Mandelstam's poem [...] "Tristia" (1918).

of a dying man is open to everyone, so the door of the old world is flung wide open before the crowd. Suddenly everything becomes public property. Come and take your pick. Everything is accessible: all labyrinths, all secret recesses, all forbidden paths. The word has become not a sevenstop, but a thousand-stop flute, brought to life all at once by the breathing of the ages. The most striking thing about speaking in tongues is that the speaker does not know the language he is speaking. He talks in a completely unknown language. It seems to everyone, and to himself, that he speaking Greek or Chaldean. It is something like a complete reversal of erudition. Contemporary poetry, despite all its complexity and inner inventiveness, is naive:

Ecoutez la chanson grise . . .[11]

The modern poet-synthesizer, it seems to me, is not a Verhaeren, but a kind of Verlaine of culture. For him all the complexity of the old world is like that same Pushkinian flute. He sings of ideas, systems of knowledge, and State theories just as his predecessors sang of nightingales and roses. They say the cause of revolution is hunger in interplanetary space. Grain must be scattered through the ether.

Classical poetry is the poetry of revolution.

---

11 CL: [Another] reference to [. . .] Verlaine's "Art poétique." [. . . .]

Vasily Rozanov

From The Apocalypse of Our Times (1917)

Translated by James Edie

In a mysterious way Christianity came little by little to concern itself with "trifles." It answered the question of the earth and the moon by "the squares of distances." It resolved the caterpillar-cocoon-butterfly problem in an even less satisfactory manner by saying: "That's the way it is!" "Christian science" was ultimately reduced to twaddle, to positivism, to absurdity. "I have seen, I have heard, but I do not understand." "I see but I grasp nothing," and even "I have no opinion about it." Now the caterpillar, the cocoon, and the butterfly have an explanation, not in physiology but in cosmogony. Physiologically they are inexplicable, i.e., *inexpressible*. However, from the point of view of cosmogony, they are perfectly intelligible. Every living thing, absolutely everything which lives, participates thus in life, death, and resurrection.

The stages of the life of the insect represent the phases of universal *life*. The caterpillar: "We crawl, we eat, we are lifeless and immobile." "The cocoon" is the tomb and death, the tomb and vegetative life, the tomb and the *promise*. The butterfly is the "soul" plunged into the cosmic ether, flying, knowing only the sun and nectar, and nourishing itself only by plunging into the immense corollas of flowers. Christ said: "In the *future life* there will be no desire, neither will men give or be given in marriage." Yet the "butterfly" is the "future life" of the caterpillar, a life in which there is not only marriage but in which—in spite of the Gospel, in spite of the relative awkwardness of the caterpillar and the apparent death of the cocoon—the butterfly, which is wholly spiritualized and gives up eating entirely (it is stupefying! not only is its papilla not designed to eat with but it does not even have an intestine, at least in certain species), strange to say is in contact exclusively *with the sexual organs* of certain "beings which are strangers to it"—with the Tree of Life itself, so to speak, with incomprehensible, mysterious plants. This *je ne sais quoi* which appears to each butterfly is enormous, unfathomable. It is a forest, a garden. What does this mean? In a mysterious fashion the life of the butterfly shows us or predicts that our souls, too, beyond the cocoon-tomb, will taste of the nectar of two or of both divinities. For it is said that the Universe was created by Elo*him* (the dual for of the divine Name cited in the Biblical story of the Creation of the world) and not by Elo*ah* (singular). Thus there are *two* divinities and not one: "In the *image* and *likeness* of whom *God created man in the forms of man and woman.*"

The butterfly is the soul of the caterpillar. The soul alone, without extraneous elements. But this proves that the "soul" is not immaterial. It is tangible, visible; it *exists*, but *differently than in earthly existence*. How then? Oh, our dreams and our nocturnal visions are sometimes more real than our waking thoughts. The caterpillar and the butterfly demonstrate that on earth we do nothing but "eat," while "in the beyond" everything will be flight, movement, myrrh and incense.

The life *beyond the tomb* will be made of light and perfume. Precisely of something perceptible to the senses, physically odoriferous, of what gives off scent in a carnal and not in an incorporeal manner. We cannot say the words "temptations of this world" with a straight face. It is precisely in them that "the life of the future age" circulates, as flowing from the soul of things, from their entelechy. And that part of our face which was created to taste and to smell and which is, generally, the most beautiful and "celestial" part of our face, is beautiful only through the contours of the lips, the mouth and the nose. "What a monster is the man who has no lips or nose," or on whom they are mutilated or simple misshapen or ugly. What is most apocalyptic in us is our smile. The smile is the most apocalyptic of all.

> Joy, you are the sparks of heaven, you are divine.
> Girl of the Elysian fields ...

This is no allegory; it is a real, or more exactly a noumenal, truth. "It is good to be seduced" and "it is good to let oneself be tempted." He is good who "enters the world through temptation." He brings the edge of heaven to earth, which is rather dull by itself. A mysterious thing, the Gospel does not once mention scent, nothing odoriferous, aromatic, as if to emphasize its divergence from the flower of the Bible, the *Song of Songs*, that song of which a *starets* of the East once said: "The whole world is not worth the day which saw the creation of the *Song of Songs*." Thus the Gospel represents "this life" and the "future life" completely backward. The "ways" of life insofar as they are *physiological ways* are *the essential, the celestial* (the Throne of the *Apocalypse*); this is the "subject" which is "predicated."

As to the other "way of life," the "way of the spirit," this is an "adverb," the way of laziness, of aesthetics, of conversations ...

> And long has it languished in the world.

It is the terrestrial life of the caterpillar, who crawls and eats ...

> Filled with a marvelous desire ...

It is the butterfly which bathes in ether, in the sun's rays. In the rays of the same Sun which is there only to envelop, "with the stars and the moon," "the woman with child."

> The tiresome songs of the earth
> Cannot, for her, replace the songs of love. (Lermontov)

No "hell or gnashing of teeth" *there*, but nectar taken from flowers. After having borne the sufferings, the mud, the dung, and the "geophagy" of the caterpillar, the tomb and the semblance, but only the *semblance* of death, in the cocoon, the soul will rise from the coffin, and every soul, innocent or sinful, will live its ineffable "song of songs." It will be rendered unto each man according to his soul and his desire. Amen.

Fyodor Sologub

Poets' Demons (1907)

Translated by Sibelan Forrester

I
The Circle of Demons

I am a poet, and I want to speak about poets. More precisely, about their demons.

Of course, there are no demons. So what, perhaps there aren't any poets either? Whether there are, or there aren't—it's all the same. The only relevant thing is that I want to speak about these subjects.

The poet who speaks about poets finds himself in exclusively happy conditions. Given the poet's pleasant ability to be surprised at everything, to be ecstatic over everything and to take inspiration from all kinds of phenomena of life, the works of verse that a poet reads create in him an enchanting, agitating impression. For a poet someone else's poetry is always either completely dead, doesn't exist at all, or else it agitates and touches him to the extreme. If a person is capable of experiencing ecstasy before the dead play of demons of air and dust in the atmosphere, will he be someone who yawns over a splendid epic poem? Will he damn with faint praise the play of the creative spirit, be it even a "petty demon, one of the lowest ranking"?

To understand each grimace, to sweep up all these slight tremblings in the corners of the lips, to reflect every fleeting, momentary spark in yourself, to peer under the very last mask—that is a very refined pleasure, for which each of us feels such gratitude to another poet.

A very refined pleasure, though also a very dangerous one. Sometimes the arrow flies farther than the target—a thread spun too finely will snap too soon between the fingers of the spinner who twitches unexpectedly—honey that is sweet before it is poured out suddenly turns into a bitter dish.

Overly profound understanding collects treasures that no one scattered and reaps wheat that no one sowed, giving joy to the crafty ones who are always making fun of a person.

The poet is an inspired creator, a wonder-worker and a dreamer. He opens a strange book and works sorcery over it.

Self-setting tablecloth, spread yourself before me—treat me to a marvelous meal. I want subtle wines and nice-smelling victuals.

The cloth opens up—and the table is spread.

Sated and drunk, I rise from the wondrous feast, my head spins languorously—and one of the crafty ones titters uncleanly, and whispers in an insinuating and spiteful way:

"Your victuals are nothing but ashes and coals, your wine is red with bog canker, the vessels whose elegance dazzle you are stinking shards."

Look—he's right, the crafty one.

Well, and so what! You too are right, poet. You took pleasure—and no one can take those sweet moments away from you.

And say the creation of another poet was for you an ocean that overwhelmed the resounding of free waves on the black line of the shores. You passed above the ocean, you measured its immeasurable breadth with your steps, you measured its depth with fathoms—but you felt no shame at the ecstatic praises: wasn't it you who were the sun, reflecting its visage in the ocean?

Praise is the poet's work, ecstasy is his truth.

The poet's ecstasies are more worthy than the carping interpretation of the critic.

There was never a time in Russia when criticism did not carry out the shameful deed of damning literary reputations. Russian critics reached the point where in the imagination of the Russian people, still so simple-hearted, the word "criticism" itself came to mean the same thing as "name-calling." Lovers of disparaging expressions used to be and still are delighted to read critical articles, where the creative labor and bright inspiration of poets were assessed and still are assessed with a crude swagger, like a deed that is stupid and shameful.

"You'll hear the judgment of the fool and the laugh of the cold crowd."[1]

"What does it matter to us, whether you suffered or not!"

I read an article by Belinsky, the most sincere of the Russian critics, about the brilliant Baratynsky's poetry. What crudity! What an unadulterated lack of desire to understand!

But so what! The examples are uncountable.

In our days too, who among the critics now living has not in their literary careers spat on a greater or lesser number of poets whose names they themselves now pronounce with respect.

And sometimes criticism has awarded laurels that were either belated or unearned.

So it was and so it tends to be, because the critic approaches any literary phenomenon with a code of rules prepared in advance. And everything that is alive in poetry sneaks outside the frames of those rules.

The simple reader, who is neither a poet nor a critic, occupies a middle position in judging poets. He is not capable of delight at the beauties that still need to be magicked out of a dead mass of words; he is not capable of understanding what lies so deeply hidden beneath the images, the thing the poet perhaps doesn't put into his images, but that can be very subtly and accurately intended. For him this narrows the range of the beautiful and the wise in the poet.

But the reader has no use for literary rules on a pedantic foundation—what he seeks in a book is not illustration of his theories, but immediate pleasure. For him both the exacting demands of the critic and the dreamy ecstasies of the poet are replaced by accidental tendencies and affinities, arising from the experiences he has happened to have. If he too sometimes picks up, for amusement or for deeper thinking, the rusty iron cliché of the critic, he applies this toy to whatever he runs into and in any way he wishes.

---

1   *Eds*. A line from Pushkin's 1830 sonnet "To the Poet."

His praise and his reproof alike are unexpected and odd. He crowns with loud fame a dull graphomaniac who has made a profitable craft of prostituting high art, and he passes indifferently by Tyutchev, by Baratynsky, by Fet, by ...

I want to move beyond this triangle of incorrect attitudes. I don't want to feel ecstasies over anyone—I am oversated on both ecstasies and emotion, and I no longer want to taste tempting coals and sweet ashes simplemindedly.

"I find inspiration in myself"—and that's enough for me.

I won't insult anyone's creative intelligence with blasphemy. Everything in the realm of poetry is sacred for me. I recognize no canon of any kind, I use no theory to press the living tissue of poetic daydreaming.

I am spared the accidents of readers' taste by the very Demons of the poets, which already await me.

They stand around me in a wide circle, they have divided up the whole horizon and my whole atmosphere among themselves, they display to me the whole many-faced and many-voiced Irony of the living word. And each visage they show is the exact truth, and every one of their howls says Yes. They confirm the contradictory genuineness of the world.

What are they themselves?

The whole sphere of poetic creation is visibly divided into two parts, which tend toward one pole or the other.

One pole is the lyrical oblivion of the given world, rejection of its meager and boring two shores, its always flowing mundanity and always recurring everydayness, the eternal striving towards what does not exist. The daydream of building the marvelous palaces of the impossible, and of predicting what does not exist, incinerates everything that exists, that is manifest, with the fire of sweet song-singing. Everything that makes life rejoice is told: No.

In a smoke-filled and bespittled alehouse sits a bourgeois with his nose in the air; before him is a stein of beer and sausages. He is smoking a stinking cigar, listening to the drunken racket, and feeling blissful, floating in a Golden Dream. Nectar stands before him in a crystal goblet, and ambrosia on an embossed tray, and the blue smoke of aromatic incense curls before him. He himself is young and handsome, and his splendid head is framed in golden curls. He is a poet. He sits—and sings (i.e., composes verses). And what all do you find, there in his verses!

> "He celebrates, simple-hearted..."
> "The poet on the inspired lyre..."
> "Fly with your soul above the dust
> And gaze upon the angels' faces..."
> "You go into the world so it may hear the prophet,
> But in the world be grandiose and holy..."

He goes out into the world on the street, meets a maiden

> "with a rosy smile, like the first glow
> of the young day beyond the grove..."

To the eyes of a chance passerby and a sober man, it's simply a crude and untidy girl ... a woman ... perhaps not without vices ... perhaps, entirely vicious. But for the lyric poet with his head in the clouds she is the beautiful Dulcinea.

Of course the eternal exponent of the lyric attitude toward the world, Don Quixote, knew that Aldonsa was only Aldonsa, a simple peasant girl with vulgar habits and the narrow worldview of a limited creature. But what does he need with Aldonsa? And what is Aldonsa to him? There is no Aldonsa! He doesn't need Aldonsa. Aldonsa is an awkward accident, the momentary and momentarily lived-out caprice of the drunken Aisa. Aldonsa's image captivates her peasant suitors, who need a working housewife. Don Quixote—a lyric poet—an angel, who says to life an eternal No—must elevate another, a dear, eternal image above the momentary and accidental Aldonsa. What is given in crude experience is marvelously transformed—and above the crude Aldonsa arises the eternally beautiful Dulcinea del Toboso.

An incinerating No is said to crude experience, the world is Dulcineated through lyrical striving. This is the sphere of the Lyric, of poetry, the bright land of Dulcinea, which rejects the world,

> "From the flaming serpent
> Hiding her holy charms,
> Towards me leaned Dulcinea.
> She is mine, forever Mine."

I will not now depart into this land of the lyrical No. This land of the desired, the splendid, the harmonious has from time immemorial been the favorite place for all good and evil critics to stroll. No matter what masks the poets put onto hard-working and tubby Aldonsa—the mask of Aphrodite or the Medusa, of the Virgin Mary or Astarte, of the Beautiful Lady or the Whore of Babylon, of kind Lilith or crafty Eve, Tatiana or Zemfira, Tamara, the daughter of Gudal, or of the tsaritsa Tamara—all these bright, external, colorfully painted masks have long been familiar to every schoolchild.

Whereas I want to be submissive to the end. I am drawn now to that pole of poetry that eternally utters Yes to every expression of life. I will not start gathering the accidentally dear features into one captivating image—I will not say: "No, your skin does not smell of goat, and it isn't onion that wafts from your mouth—you are fresh and fragrant, like the Rose of Sharon, and your breath is sweeter than attar of Kashmir rose, and you yourself, Dulcinea, are the most beautiful of women."

Rather, I submissively admit: "Yes, you are Aldonsa."

To approach the phenomena of life submissively, to say Yes to it all, to accept and confirm everything that is phenomenal to the end, is a very difficult deed. It is difficult to go far along this path, because it is guarded by the Dragon of Eternal Contradiction.

But anyone who has come to cognize the great law of the equality of complete opposites will not fear the dragon, and will stride without flinching into the realm of eternal Irony.

Removing cover after cover, mask after mask, Irony reveals a visage behind the covers and the masks that is eternally dual, eternally contradictory, always and forever distorted. Behind the poets' angelic sweet-voicedness, behind the images of their golden dream, it exposes the great host of unsightly demons.

CRITICISM

Anna Akhmatova

Innokenty Annensky (1963)

Translated by Mary Ann Sporluk

I

Whereas Balmont and Bryusov brought what they had started to completion themselves (even though they continued to confuse provincial graphomaniacs for a long time), Annensky's work came alive with exceptional vigor in the next generation. And if he had not died so early, he would have seen his cloudbursts pour down onto the pages of Pasternak's books, his half-*zaum* "Dedu Lidu ladili" in Khlebnikov, his *rayoshnik* ("Balloons") appear in Mayakovsky, and so on. I don't mean to imply that they all imitated him. But he traveled so many paths at the same time! He had so much that was new in him that all innovators seemed related to him...

Boris Leonidovich Pasternak ... affirmed categorically that Annensky played a large role in his work...

Osip and I spoke about Annensky several times. He also spoke of Annensky with true piety.

I don't know whether Marina Tsvetaeva knew Annensky.

There is love and admiration for his Teacher in both Gumilyov's poetry and prose.

II

In recent times Innokenty Annensky's poetry has begun to resound especially strongly. I find this completely natural. Let us recall that Alexander Blok, citing lines from *Quiet Songs*, wrote to the author of *The Cypress Chest*: "This will be in my memory forever. Part of my soul has remained in this." I am convinced that Annensky should assume a place of honor in our poetry alongside Baratynsky, Tyutchev, and Fet.

... It is not because they imitated him that Annensky is the teacher of Pasternak, Mayakovsky, and Gumilyov—no ... these poets were already "contained" in Annensky. Let us recall, for instance, Annensky's poem from "Sideshow Trefoil":

> Buy my balloons, kind sirs!
> Hey, fox fur coat, if you have some to spare,
> Don't begrudge five little kopecks:
> I'll let them go right up to the sky—
> Two hours later, get an eyeful, with both your eyes!

Compare "Children's Balloons" with the verse of the young Mayakovsky, with his declamations in "Satyricon" that are filled with a lexicon that is markedly that of the common people.

If an inexperienced reader comes across:

> Chatterbox-bells
> Chatterbox-bells
> Clanked and clashed,
> The further, the more ...
> Clanked and clashed,
> Chatterbox-bells.
> Tin bells flew past,
> Added their jabber,
> Clattered, babbled,
> Clattered, blabbered,
> Quit their chatter.

he will think this is Velimir Khlebnikov's poetry. In the meantime I read Annensky's "Sleigh Bells." We shall not be mistaken if we say that "Sleigh Bells" cast the seed from which Khlebnikov's sonorous poetry later grew. The lavish Pasternakian cloudbursts already pour down on the pages of *The Cypress Chest*. The sources of Nikolai Gumilyov's poetry are not in the poems of the French Parnassians, as is usually thought, but in Annensky. I find my own "origin" in Annensky's poems. His work, in my view, is marked by a tragic element, by sincerity, and artistic integrity.

Innokenty Annensky

From "On Contemporary Lyrism" (1909)

Translated by Ronald E. Peterson

I

[....]

The new poetry?... That's no joke... just try to make some sense in that sea... no, it's not a sea... in that book depository of a bibliophile who is in no way squeamish... a week before a sale: endings, beginnings, middles... rarities and popular literature, the lives and leisures of Celadon.

It will be, I dare say, more practical to begin with those poets who have made the whole history of our Symbolism. Three names. We won't deal with the primary one, although he is the brightest. I have already said all, or almost all, that I could say about Balmont in another book.

And the main thing is that Balmont, and I hope this is clear to everyone, has already completed one very significant period in his work and as yet there is no second one beginning.

[....]

༄

[....]

Valery Bryusov is a Muscovite. He began publishing in 1892. The basic collection which contains everything that the poet retained from his previous poetry is called *Roads and Crossroads* (two volumes, the second appeared in 1908). It includes, for example, almost all of *Urbi et Orbi* (1903) and *Stephanos* (1906). The last book of poems (many of which are new) appeared in 1909 and is called *All Melodies*. It gives something of today, but signifies more of the future Bryusov, so we will use mainly it for this essay.

Bryusov's poetry is clothed in Parnassian robes, but at the same time it is full of attempts, trials, and accomplishments—and only a careless reader would fail to see how often these searches have been painful, difficult for the poet, and even agonizing. Bryusov's work is not something in which we can search for his personal experiences of life (as in Pushkin, Heine, or Stecchetti)—real or fantasized (it's all the same). No, Bryusov's poetry is an annal of unbroken apprenticeship and self-examination, but not of events—of work, not of life. Or, has all its personal side been concealed?

How Valery Bryusov has *lived*, however, doesn't matter.

The waters of Lake Malar, or an English keepsake, a date with a woman, or a childhood memory—all of these are only shadows for Bryusov—everything is a stage for future creation—at first, then evaluations and distillations. Valery Bryusov stores colors and tastes, what is his own and what is foreign, tenderness that has suddenly flared up, and even fatigue from concentrated work, and filters these in thoughts in order to clothe them, if they can be of use, with the metaphor and music of verse in the stillness of his laboratory—there, where his poetry passes through and real life is created. No one can show better than Valery Bryusov through the cold beauty of words and the delicate, often alarmed, waves of rhythms the whole *repugnant uselessness of life*, the whole trial of exacting passions.

[....]

I am afraid of resurrecting words from his preface to *Urbi et Orbi*; there are none preceding his second volume, *Roads and Crossroads*. But at that time Valery Bryusov still *imagined verses detached from poetry*.

For the *distant* future (I don't really believe that for a poet any sort of future has seemed exactly distant) he has seen verse in the capacity of a "perfect form of speech," displacing prose "most of all in philosophy." If he has been thinking such thoughts until now, that explains a lot, of course, in *All Melodies*, and even throws light on the title of the collection. And Valery Bryusov's apprenticeship, decadence, and pedantry are dated for us in this way by the given degree of his understanding of the world. Listen, Bryusov, can verse really be *speech*, i.e., a feature of everyday life?

Because it's really laughable to project a sort of hieratics of styles in the future with an academy in Cheboksary.[1]

Each field of knowledge seeks precisely to free itself from the way of the metaphor, from the mythological nets of speech—of course not for any refinement of style, but to escape into terminology, into silence, into writing, into the alphabet of the Morse Code. What will it do, tell me, with verse, this singing genius of myth, which assures it of Proteus' eternity and the immortality of a legend that is forever being created?

And who will need philosophy without a system, and even more, verse that has refused to be personal, irrational, divinely unexpected?

It is easier, however, to guess than to judge, and criticism is, I dare say, more *a priori* than an affirmation ... I protest against one thing in Bryusov's words—"doubtlessly," and it's good that he wrote this word six years ago and now, perhaps, he has already forgotten it!

In any case his verse bore, at one time, and not without reason, not only a philosophical dream but also a philosophical doctrine. Our elegies until now have tended toward "philosophicality." [....]

There are, however, poets in Russia for whom *philosophicality* has become a sort of integral part of their being. One cannot, of course, call their poetry *philosophy*. This is not the philosophical poetry of Sully-Prudhomme; the atmosphere in which the sparks of this poetry are born is necessary for such poets' creativity—it is densely saturated with mystical fog: there are particles of theosophical coke, of that most bourgeois aspect of the Anti-mortalists; it's possible to discover even some steam of Khlystic zeal in it—a mildewed page of Schopenhauer glimmers through it, the yellow cover of the Light of Asia—Zarathustra raved about the Apocalypse in this fog.

Oh, I am far from wanting to draw a caricature. I am speaking about *our soul*, about the *ailing and sensitive soul* of our times.

And you have already guessed that I am speaking about a poet and novelist, for whom the *Petty Demon* and "The Disappointed Bride" would be enough for his name to remain an immortal expression of the time, which we,

---

[1] *Eds.* Cheboksary, now capital city of the Chuvash Republic, is a port on the Volga River; its foreign-sounding name lets Annensky refer to the Russian provinces.

as does every other generation, tend to consider timeless because we have no perspective for that.

Fyodor Sologub is from Petersburg.

The last of his books of verse that I know of is referred to as his eighth one (published in 1908, Moscow).

Two things are most foreign to Sologub's poetry, as far as I have managed to learn: 1) spontaneity (although where are our Francis Jammeses? perhaps our sly Blok?), 2) inability or lack of desire to stand outside his verse. In this regard he is in striking contrast to Valery Bryusov who cannot—and I don't know if he even wants to—stand inside his verse, and also with Vyacheslav Ivanov, who even seems to boast that he can step back from his creations, to any distance he wants. (Try to find, for example, V. Ivanov in *Tantalus*. No, stop looking, he was never there.)

Sologub, no matter how strange it seems, is best characterized for me by his unity of these two opposingly formulated traits.

As a poet he can breathe only in his own atmosphere, but his *verses crystallize themselves;* he does not build them. [....]

Sologub is a whimsical and capricious poet, not at all an erudite pedant. There is more often even something revealing and pedagogically clear in his works.

But Sologub also has *word-tics*, and in garnishing his verse, they give it an individual color, like incorrect speech habits that *consequently* mark the speech of the majority of us.

People have found in Henri de Regnier's works recently exactly such word-tics—*or* and *mort*. Sologub abuses the words *ill* and *evil*. Everything is ill for him: children, lilies, dreams, and even valleys. Then Sologub the lyric poet has eccentricities in his perceptions. *Naked female legs,* for example, seem somehow especially affectionate and sinful in his verse—but they mainly seem immeasurably corporeal.

Sometimes sounds soothe Sologub. But he is not V. Ivanov, the visionary of the Middle Ages, who has experienced the Renaissance in order to become one of the most sensitive of our contemporaries. When V. Ivanov filters, mangles, and presses *words* for that faience mortar where he will prepare—as an alchemist—his *blinding Yes,* he first of all arouses an intellectual feeling, an interest, even an excitement, I dare say, for his knowledge and art. [....]

I omit the portrait of V. Ivanov (who made his debut with *Guiding Stars* in 1901 and then *Transparence* in 1904) from the space next to Bryusov and Sologub, since the collection, on the basis of which such a portrait could be done (*Cor Ardens*), has not appeared yet. But in speaking more about art, I will have much to say about V. Ivanov's poetry.

II

Symbolism in poetry is a child of the city. It is cultivated and grows, filling out creativity to the degree that life itself becomes more artificial and even fictive. Symbols are born where there are no myths yet, but where there is no longer any faith. Symbols can play spaciously between straight stone lines, in the noise of the street, in the magic of gas lamps, and the lunar decorations. They soon get accustomed not only to the anxiety of the stock market and of green cloth, but also to the fearsome routine of some Paris morgue, and even to the repugnant, because of their excessive lifelikeness, wax figures in a museum.

Symbols which are forever being created have nothing to do in that space where, eternally and calmly alternating to the fullest, the day darkens and the night melts; where groves are full of druids and satyrs, and brooks with nymphs, where Life and Death, Lightning or a Hurricane are already overgrown with metaphors of joy and anger, horror and conflict...

Therefore, Myth is free to propagate its own gods and demons there.

Call them what you want. It will doubtlessly seem to you that the *poetry of spaces,* reflecting this world finished once and for all, cannot and *should not add anything to it.*

Of course the city didn't start inspiring poets yesterday:

> The cast-iron design of your fences.
> The transparent twilight, the moonless luster
> Of your pensive nights.

Pushkin wrote not only "The Bronze Horseman" but also "The Queen of Spades." But there are probably two million people now living in Petersburg.

And Pushkin's Petersburg needs filling out, like the pictures of Alexander Benois. "Peter's creation" has become a legend, and this wonderful "city" is already somewhere over us with its coloring of tender and beautiful reflection. Now we dream of new symbols, we are besieged by still unformed and different agitations, because we have passed through Gogol, and Dostoevsky has tortured us.

Alexander Blok, for example, gives us a different, enigmatic, white night in a new way.

The first poet of the *contemporary* city, the city that is the father of symbols, was Baudelaire, after him came Verlaine, Arthur Rimbaud, Tristan Corbière, Rollinat, Verhaeren, just to name the major ones.

Paris was, however, God knows when, Lutetia. And sometimes the silhouette of a poet, in Martial's style, glimmers in its ironic temptation. What do we need the French for? There is still too much of the steppe, the Scythian love for space, in us. The Byzantine bucolic with its gardens, pastures, lady's tears, and gilded ornaments, is just a stratum—also ancient—over the Scythian soul.

And this is probably the deepest cultural layer of our soul.

The king of our poetry is Balmont, who before he managed to get tired of being in Mexico, under the same sun, and even under a bird in the same air, made an incursion against the stone houses, the free prisons for people. It was proud... Stuffed-shirts love and now declaim this Balmont, but how distant they are from our dear nomad of those years.

Bryusov penetrated the melancholy of the city even more intimately and magically, and he is the first—the new Orpheus—to make cobblestones cry.

> There will be light from the lamp in the window...
> I'll distinguish her earrings...
> Suddenly the quiet light will go out,
> *I'll sigh in response to it.*
> I'll wait till dawn in the square...
> She'll come out that door.
> There'll be a flower on her breast,
> A dark blue cornflower...

or this:

> And every night, regularly,
> I stand under a window.
> *And my heart is grateful*
> *That it sees your lamp.*

The special colors here are not exciting, but the city, another soul, wounded in another way, sorrowful and yielding in another way, excites us because it firmly knows its own market value.

Let another—the old, wise, greedy, alert soul of the poet—look into it, this still poor, this still new soul. But weren't they both tightly driven into the stone? And perhaps even borne by this stone? Balmont struggled with this city. He hated it. But there are exotic souls, who cannot be ruled in such a sense even by the stones that gave birth to them. The city is not in Ivanov's poems. I know of six lines dedicated to Paris, and a sonnet about stones with talons, that were dropped at one time on our Academy. In order to love the city, V. Ivanov needs the height of a bird's eye view, and in order to merge with its white night—a hieratic symbol. [....]

The more city life develops, the more souls themselves become inevitably crucified, adapting to the stones, museums and signboards.

The wonderful mosaics of icons, which no one prays to, the pretty river's waves (hiding repugnant death), love, grace, and beauty offstage in the golden powder and under the electric light; a secret at a spiritual seance—and freedom in red rags—these are the conditions among which the young poets grow up.

[....]

The champion of our young poets is undoubtedly Alexander Blok. He is, in the full sense of the word and without the slightest irony, the beauty of the rising poetry. What beauty?—rather, its enchantment. He is not only a real, born Symbolist, he is himself a symbol. His picture postcard features appear to us like those of an elegant androgyne, and his voice, coquettishly, intentionally dispassionate, white, hides of course the most tender and sensitive modulations.

An androgynous mask—but under it in the poetry itself lies the most brightly expressed male type of love, a love that can deceptively captivate, and when necessary, when a woman desires, can conquer and merrily fertilize.

But I especially like Blok when he is not speaking about love in his verse at all. For love somehow suits him less. I like him when he walks around love not with art—what is art?—but with a strange magic, one hint, one languorous gleam in his eyes, one barely audible, but already enchanting melody, where the word love is not included. [. . . .]

Now a direct transition from a poet who has fallen silent [Sergei Makovsky] to a singer who cannot stop. Although this new singer has not yet seen his thirtieth spring, Andrei Bely (the pseudonym of B. N. Bugaev, revealed by the author himself), has already published three collections of verse and two of them are quite large.

A richly gifted nature, Bely simply doesn't know which one of his muses will smile at him next. Kant is jealous of his poetry. Poetry of music. A bumpy road of an Indian symbol. Valery Bryusov wants to exchange staffs with him, and Zinaida Nikolaevna Gippius herself has resolved the theme of his Fourth Symphony. Criticism and the theory of creativity (articles about Symbolism) go along—on the side. And you admire that youthful-audacious building of a life. And sometimes it's scary for Andrei Bely. Lord, when does this person think? And when does he find time to burn and crush his creations?

My task is not concerned with Bely's Symphonies and other prose, but I somehow don't even understand his poems, although, God knows, I have studied them diligently. Much is likable ... but it's impossible not to see a certain perplexity in the poet, and then ... that unfortunate telegraphist with a wife, whose "side hurts ..." A vital, responsive, fiery heart, that tries so hard to get out that his tears boil (read "Through the Window of the Train" in *Ashes*, p. 21). You feel sorry for him, you like him as a person, but as a poet... sometimes it's a pity. [. . . .]

III

Among the concluding theses of the last chapter, one was missing. I thought that it would be more appropriate as the beginning of this third chapter, as a clamp between both of them. This is the thesis.

Lyrics by females are one of the achievements of that cultural labor which will be bequeathed by modernism to history.

Now we have women writing verse. Women work on the problems of Russian lyrism with the same unconquerable fervor that they devote to science. I think that this phenomenon is determined to a significant degree by the traits of that lyrism which I tried to characterize in the first chapter.

But for the explanation of this thought, we need to divert ourselves for a minute from contemporary times.

In older Russian poetry, when a song didn't yet have letters, there were two definite types of lyrism—one was masculine, the other feminine. We don't know the authors of these songs, the singers are all the same for us.

The authors are replaced for us so to say by lyric personae. This is the *he* and *she* that arc strictly isolated in their lyrical types. *He* is a conqueror of life. *She* only accepts life.

He threatens or steadfastly thinks; *he* sneers and sometimes repents. *She* only cries quietly and submissively; *she* affectionately remembers. A man's irony in a folk song often seems to be only suppressed spite. [....] Love more often goes from the freely lyrical sphere into the world of fortune-telling, wizardry, and love potions. Like a caress from the sun, she hides bashfully from song, and the spell-bound secret of love is closer to the folk soul than its beauty and joy.

Amorousness, like lyrism, like the written form, came to us from the West, together with books and assemblies.

But no one led love for a woman to adoration, to apotheosis, like Pushkin, in whom genius has so maddeningly beautifully combined the temperament of a black and the lyrical style of an Italian.

No one's genius passed more freely from revealing confessions (like the well-known piece of 19 January 1825) to almost mystical verse, at least in our perception, no longer sensitive to its conventionality:

> My soul has been awakened,
> And you have appeared again,
> Like a passing vision,
> Like a genius of pure beauty.

The woman "deified" by Pushkin ascended so high in his lyrics that her voice was no longer audible from there.

The "genius of pure beauty" has left a heavy trace on our literature.

How many Ophelias, how many mad, martyred women, how many pure, extremely beautiful women and girls have passed before us on the pages of novels, in lyric poems, and on the pavement—between *Evgeny Onegin* and the "Kreutzer Sonata," with its dishonored, its deformed conqueror of what probably seemed at one time to him the "genius of our beauty." I don't want to name those names, too close to our time, Artsybashev's *Sanin* and Andreev's *Anfisa*.

After Pushkin's period, a light current of George Sandism, let's say, passed through Russian lyrics.

He sang then:

> Give me a woman, a wild woman!

And *she* confessed:

> No fiery young rascal
> Has captured my inexperienced gaze;
> I met a Circassian in the mountains
> And from that time I gave myself to him.

But these voices have somehow not been sung to their fullest extent among us.

There is no longer a deified woman in contemporary poetry. The vicious circle of Pushkin's lyrics has been broken, most probably, forever.

Our chosen ones have different central tasks for lyricism, other justifications for life.

In Sologub's poetry the desire to believe in a metempsychosis is central, and this motif, combined with the perspicacious genius of the poet, is the source of deeply interesting and often captivating motifs.

Valery Bryusov seeks a magical secret in words and rhythms. And if he has not yet found the key that can master our hearts, then he has often compelled us to believe, together with him, that such a key is precisely in words...

V. Ivanov—a sharply imperative, almost categorical, mind—is hobbled by dualism, which the centuries of culture have imposed on him as a scholar with all its weight... As a poet, he has surrounded us with a forest of symbols and demands that we believe, with the same fervor that he himself would like to believe, in the proximity of the blossoming little meadow of myth. V. Ivanov's genius is proud, but it is almost an agonizing pride.

But Balmont? No, Balmont does not deify Her either. He loves only love, like he does the sun, air, freedom, not Her at all. Blok, the poet of the Beautiful Lady, has also strayed far from Pushkinianism, and even more from Turgenevism. His Lady dons captivating clothes, but she herself is only a symbol with, moreover, a philosophical hue.

But who then? The word-sculptor Makovsky, worn out by the melodious ease of his verse and the non-literary precision of what he expresses lyrically? No, irony has led him away from Pushkinianism. Gorodetsky, with the frightening breadth and sincerity of his confessions, or Andrei Bely, in the boundlessness of his horizons, gifts, ideas, beginnings—a responsive, tremulous, almost mirage-like, but after all, still a *future* person?

Or Kuzmin, tender, full of nuances, of the fearful beauty of his unjustified beliefs? I have not named all the names that are crowded in the hollow of my pen. But there are enough of them not only to justify female lyrism but also to demand its appearance.

Lyrics have become so individual and foreign to the commonplace, that it now *needs* types of female musicalities. Perhaps she will reveal even new lyric horizons to us, this woman, no longer an idol, condemned to silence, but our comrade in shared, free, and endlessly varied work on Russian lyrics.

Two completely defined women's names naturally open our examination. Do we need to guess them? Zinaida Gippius and Allegro-Poliksena Solovyova. Z. N. Gippius is a poetess of the first calling. All the fifteen-year history of our lyrical modernism is in her works. I don't want, however, treating the theme of my article pedantically, to condemn myself to an analysis of Gippius' latest poems.

Her *Collected Poems*, 1904, remains the canonical collection. I like this book for its melodious abstractness. [....] Gippius' abstractness is not schematic at all in its essence, more exactly, her anxiety, or what is unsaid, or the agonizing swaying of a pendulum in her heart, always shows through in her diagrams. [....]

I perceive all the confessions in Gippius' book, no matter how much they might seem to contradict each other at times, as lyrically sincere; there is in them, for me at least, a certain absolute instantaneousness, a certain persistent, burning need to convey rhythmically the "full feeling of each minute," and their force and charm are in this. [....]

Gippius' favorite guise is indifference, apathy, and fatigue. [....] Her symbols are spiders, leeches, stopped clocks, Charon's boat, a stony sky, "heavy waters ... like lead," thoughts that are gray birds. It doesn't matter for Gippius that the world has so many sounds, that it is so grossly varicolored! [....]

The poetess has not only arranged her pieces in a book that consists of letters alone with great tact, but she has also not given it one of the names that lyric poets so often think up to decorate their collected verse: *Collected Poems*—and that's all. For Z. Gippius, as far as I have understood her "prayers," the external beauty of impressions does not exist as something of worth by itself; all this obtrusive glimmering, shining, covering—and falling snow, lamplight, and a "thorny, gloomy orchard"—these things only keep her from praying, in my opinion. But, alas, there is nothing for her to pray about, there is nothing *above* her—and that is why it is so frightening for her, a lyrical person, in her life—and what would she pray to—in a word, that which she so painfully knows: *It must be (debet esse).*

For Z. Gippius there is only an immeasurable *I* in her lyrics, not her *I* of course, not Ego at all. It is the world and it is God; in it and only in it is the whole horror of fatal dualism; in it is all the justification of our doomed thought; in it is all the beauty of Z. Gippius' lyrism. [....]

Among all the types of our lyricism, I don't know any braver, even audacious, lyricism than that of Z. Gippius. But her thoughts and feelings are so serious, her lyric reflections are so absolutely true, and the consuming and decaying irony of our old soul are so foreign to her, that the male mask of this amazing lyrism (Z. Gippius always writes about herself exclusively in the masculine gender) has hardly fooled even one attentive reader [....]

Without any special effort, I could find among masculine lyrism parallels to the feminine type mentioned. But it would be cheerless work. If the reader wants, he or she can do it. Hardly anyone will want to ... I will limit myself to indicating the most characteristic features of the dissimilarity between *oní* and *oné* (male and female lyric poets).

The women are more *intimate,* and despite their *tenderness,* they are more *audacious* because their lyrism is almost always more *typical* than the masculine type. But the men have cut down more of the forest and are still busy with the brushwood around themselves. They are more persistent ... for now. Then they reflect life certainly more sensitively because life lies on them as a heavier yoke—the men are more responsible for life.

The female lyric poet suffers more softly. The male lyric poet grieves more deeply and with more concentration.

ALEXANDER BLOK

In Memory of Vrubel (1916)

Translated by Sibelan Forrester

The life and illness of a brilliant artist have passed by us unnoticeably. For the world there remain marvelous colors and fanciful drawings that were snatched from Eternity. For a few—strange stories about Vrubel's earthly visions. For a narrow circle of people—a small waxen face in a coffin with a work-worn forehead and lips tightly compressed. How short is the bridge into the future! A few more decades—and the memory will weaken: only the works and the legend that had already formed in the artist's lifetime will remain.

Vrubel lived simply, the way we all live; for all his passion for events, there weren't enough events in the world for him, and events penetrated into his inner world—the fate of the contemporary artist; the more accurately the earth's crust is divided into cells, the deeper the gods of fire and light who move us go away under the ground.

It may be that in his temperament Vrubel was no less than Velasquez or the legendary heroes similar to him; the little bit that I happened to hear about him is more like a fairytale than like ordinary life. It's all so simple and, it seems, trivial—but at the same time a green branch of legend is woven into every page of his life; this is also confirmed by the detailed biography, written somehow with old-fashioned nobility and simplicity (A. P. Ivanov writes just the way the old masters were written about—and indeed, how can you do otherwise? Life, when united with legend, is already hagiography.)

Here is a page from the "legend of Vrubel," now already fairly lengthy: they say he repainted the head of the Demon as many as forty times; once someone who happened to catch him at work saw a head of indescribable beauty. Vrubel later erased this head and repainted—*spoiled* it, as the words of the legend would have it; these words force one to testify that the work we see in the Tretyakov Gallery is but a weak recollection of what was created at some moment that was lost and somehow seized by the memory of only one person.

The result is lost—and that is all; perhaps a miniscule piece of the face's pearly gleam has fallen away from some part of the face: but this could also be the work of time. To us, artists, that is unimportant—it almost makes no difference; for more important than anything is the fact that creative energy was spent, lightning flashed, a genius was born. The rest is due either to an error of the master's hand as it shook (and can't the hand of even the greatest master shake?), or else to the power of time—which destroys without missing its mark. Let the public lament about mistakes and about time, but we, artists who have the Golden Age "in our pockets," to whom it is more vital that Venus has been *found* in the marble than that her statue *exists*, ought not to mourn. Creation would be fruitless if the result of the creation depended on that barbarian, time, or the barbarian person.

Here is a tile from the mosaic of Vrubel's legend; there is the head of the Demon, here—the turn of the apostle's body in *The Descent of the Holy Spirit*, and there again—a story about some Englishwoman from a *café chantant*, and again, and again; Vrubel's dreams, his delirium, his conversations, his repentance ... All shattered for us, scattered; we still do not see those worlds that he saw as a whole, and therefore our lot—for some of us—is to laugh, for others—to feel a tremor, pronouncing the impoverished word "genius."

What is a "genius?" Thus we speculate every day and every night, and we dream; and every day and every night a dull wind comes flying from those other worlds, bearing snatches of whispers and words in an unknown language; we still are not able to hear the main thing. It may be that he who could make out a whole phrase through the wind, compose the words and write them down, is a genius; we know but a few such noted-down phrases, and they all mean approximately one and the same thing. Both on Mount Sinai, and in the bright room of the Most Pure Virgin, and in the studio of a great artist the words ring out: "Seek the Promised Land." He who has heard it cannot fail to obey, whether he is fated to die on the frontier, or to see his son crucified on the cross, or to burn up on the bonfire of his own inspiration. He keeps moving—because the "boring songs of the earth" can no longer replace the "sounds of the heavens." He goes farther and farther away, while we, who remain behind, lose sight of him, lose the thread of his life, in order for the following generations, who have ascended above us, to acquire it, once it has turned scarlet around their own youthful, curly heads.

We lost the thread of Vrubel's life not at all when he "went mad," but much earlier: when he was creating his life's dream—The Demon.

An unheard-of sunset has gilded the unheard-of dark blue-lilac mountains. This is only our name for those three predominating colors, for which there is still "no name" and which serve only as a sign (a symbol) of what the Fallen One hides within him: "And evil had begun to bore him." The colossus of Lermontov's thought is contained in the colossus of Vrubel's three colors.

The Fallen One no longer has a body—but he once had one, a monstrously beautiful one. The young man is in the forgetfulness of "Boredom," as if rendered powerless by some kind of worldwide embraces; the wringing hands, the extended wings; and the old wind pours and pours gold into the dark blue valleys: that is all that remains. Somewhere below, noticeable only to him, flickers, perhaps, the unneeded chador of the earthly Tamara who has departed.

> He resembled a clear evening—
> Neither day, nor night, nor gloom, nor light.

The dark-blue twilight of night rises from below and takes its time in submerging the gold and pearl. Something different is already flickering in this battle of gold and blueness; the heart of a prophet opens within the artist. Solitary in the universe, not understood by anyone, he summons the Demon himself, in order to enchant the night with the clarity of his sorrowful eyes, the marvelous light of his visage, the peacock gleam of his wings—with his divine boredom, at last. And the gold burns without burning up: not for nothing was Vrubel's teacher the golden Giovanni Bellini.

A fallen angel and an artist-exorcist: it is frightening to be with them, to see the unheard-of worlds and to lie down in the mountains. But measured times and deadlines come only *from there*; for now, we have no other means but art. Artists, like the heralds in ancient tragedies, come to us from there, into settled life, with the stamp of madness and fate on their visages.

Vrubel came with a face that was mad but blissful. He is a herald, his news is that the gold of an ancient evening is scattered in a dark-blue lilac worldwide night. His Demon and Lermontov's Demon are symbols of our times:

> Neither day, nor night, nor gloom, nor light.

We, like fallen angels of a clear evening, must enchant the night. The artist lost his reason, he was drowned by the night of art, then later—the night of death. He moved because "the sounds of the heavens" cannot be forgotten. It is he who once painted a head of unheard-of beauty; it may be, the one that did not come out right in Leonardo's *The Last Supper*.

Yes, he should be in the same Paradise of which he sang.

> He sang of the bliss of sinless spirits
> In the groves of the gardens of paradise.
> He sang of the great God, and his praise
> Was not counterfeit.

Kornei Chukovsky

Chertova kukla (The Devil's Doll): *A Novel by Z. N. Gippius* (1911)

Translated by Sibelan Forrester

I

If you don't love the world,
If there's no fire in the world,
Then you don't love me either.

                        Z. Gippius

You're with a woman you don't love. And everything around you is bad, uncomfortable. The stone stairs, the wind. You've gotten bored with her—"if I could just get loose!"—and start longing for the cemetery, with feelings *à la* Sologub ... You're just being contrary. It's that same *mania contradicens* that Bryusov speaks of in his "Republic of the Southern Cross." I love death and I hate immortality. I love death and I hate happiness. I love hate, I hate love.

I hate happiness,
I can't stand joy.
Etc. etc. etc.

II

Everything in this contrariness is full of a stubbornly unshifting monotony. What is it? Coquetry? Bravado? A Nietzschean Khlestakov mood? A pose?

In your poetry I keep on reading:

- Humble pride.
- The madness of wisdom.
- Resurrected death.
- Diurnal night.
- Boiling iciness.
- Faithful treachery.
- Snowy fire.

How monotonous and impoverished. As if it's been manufactured by machine in whole batches, by the dozen. You keep fabricating more and more:

- Where the beginning is, there is the end.
- All that's above is also below.
- We, the humble, are shamelessly silent.
- I'm frightened when there's no fear in my soul.

There are some of your typical utterances. Each one bears your trademark. And it's characteristic: when you find yourself on the shore of Lethe, the river of forgetfulness, you immediately say to yourself: "There's no forgetfulness even to the splash of Lethe."

What is all this? "The humility of shamelessness," "the original end," "passionate dispassion"—what's going on with you? Is it just verbal masturbation, a *façon de parler*, or a genuine deep feeling?

I think it's both things. But there is more of the genuine, deep feeling. I'm sure that fundamentally everything here is genuine; perhaps a few words are off key and false, but the lyric, you know, never lies. And it's precisely in your lyrics, in their very tone and rhythm, that I hear, besides all the words, the same complexity and mixed feelings that your words tirelessly try to express: "crucify" and "hosanna" together, ecstasy and weariness; you speak in words what is beyond words—with all the electricity of your poetry, with every nerve of your verse. You not only tell about yourself, but at least for a moment you infect us just a tiny bit with yourself, and under the power of your poetry we naturally feel for a moment that truth is deceptive and that death is sweet. The lyric cannot lie; it's speech from one soul to another. The fireworks of aphorisms are powerless here—and the little bells of jingling words. And indeed what power of persuasion, what sincerity and pathos are needed to imbue others with such feelings, which are alien and "inverted" for almost every human soul, in order to convey, to depict (if only distantly!) such a distorted, tangled, complicated soul as yours!

> "You, miseriette, don't lurk on guard for me"

> You bring close two opposite desires,
> You rest on entangled knots,
> You seek mixedupness, meetingness, palpating.

You long for simplicity, your complexity is burdensome to you. "Pitiful, death-dealing and rude is all that is complex." "I flee from bitterly complex pain...." "And from entangled knots".... In splendid sonnets you prove (and you absolutely must prove!) that one should live "like a child," be "joyful and simple"— "I'll be merry and simple, as long as I live"—but, of course, those are pointless daydreams—so far "the tangler" has kept you entangled.

You often turn to God with prayers, for example. But your prayers are inside out too:

> I pray to Thee for the Devil,
> Lord! He too is Thy creation.

Both blasphemy and prayer at once. And people shouldn't think that this is demonism. Here we have that very same *mania contradicens*, the play of antigenetic feelings:

> "I can't submit to God, if I love God."

Submission and challenge at once.

> "But I'll give you humility, it is the lot of slaves."
> "I won't hand over my soul to the weakness of humility."
> "Humility is the most mortal sin."
> "Humili-wisdom will ruin us etc., etc."

You can't do it differently; it's the nature of your depraved heart. And having once said, "I love myself, like God," you expect mercy from God for your arrogance:

> "Lord, bless my rebellions and my arrogance."

In rebellion and arrogance—sanctity; in prayer—blasphemy; in pride—love; here too you are forthright and stubborn.

III

And now the most important thing.

After all, seeing white in black and black in white means seeing only grey.

Going forward and backward at once means standing in place.

Loving and hating at once means being indifferent.

And therefore all your lyric poetry is a lyric of greyness, stagnation and indifference. It's from your books that I first learned: stagnation too has its pathos, and indifference has its lyricism.

"I love no one. I know nothing. I only sleep." You are already saying nothing but "All is as it is."

> "I live without life, not suffering."
> "I live dully, slowly."
> "I live without thought and without will, without ecstasy and sorrows."
> "Without struggle and without effort I go down to the bottom."
> "There's cobweb on my eyes; it's soft, grey, adhesive."

Even at an insanely exciting moment—in October of 1905[1]—even then you felt:

> Intoxicated—and bored,
> Good—and I don't care.

Dream, stagnating, stupefaction of the soul, infernal boredom and torment—these are your constant topics, and how many images you find for them, what melodies and rhythms. Here you are an incomparable artist. And your curses of this stagnant, and terrible, and stupefied dead soul are inexhaustible:

> "In its conscienceless and pathetic lowness, it's grey as dust, like the ashes of the earth, and I am dying from that closeness, from its indivisibility from me.
>
> "It is rough, it is stinging, it is cold, it is a serpent. I am all wounded by its repellently burning, articulated scales.
>
> "O, if I felt a sharp sting! It's sluggish, dull, quiet. So heavy, so wilted. And there's no access to her, she's deaf."[2]

Not the soul, but some kind of petty demon [*nedotykomka*]. There's no life in it, it's a corpse: you yourself see that clearly and tormentingly. "My soul is a dead hawk. Like a dead hawk it lies in the dust, abandoning itself dully to the power of the earth." "And this dead thing ... is my soul ..."

And how else can it be? A person who doesn't care about anything, both crucify and hosanna; for whom yes and no are equally sacred, whose love has been killed by hate, passion by dispassion, faith by lack of faith—that person has a dead soul, and no Chichikov will look at it twice. And all your poems are requiems, funeral songs for your dead soul.

> A heavy cold is in my soul.
> I bend to the earth, I meld with it.
> And both are dead—she and I.

---

1 *Eds.* The height of the 1905 Revolution.
2 *Eds.* See the translation of Gippius's poem "She" in this volume.

Every feeling, barely born, is slain at once by its "counter-feeling," is reduced to zero, to emptiness. For if God's truth is God's deception, then there's no pride and no humility, but again just some kind of pit. And if, as you say, your soul is a snowy fire, then there's neither snow nor fire: the snow's melted and the fire's gone out, and again it's non-being, *nihil*.

Perhaps I'm oversimplifying this all too much, but fundamentally it is indubitably so.

Until now we never had nihilism in Russia. Even Smerdiakov, even he couldn't bear it, he went right off and hanged himself. You are the first and only nihilist in Russia. The greatest poet of nihilism. A brilliant poet of emptiness. Until now, it seems, we'd never known such a devastated soul.

You hymn nothing. With every poem you say, "I have nothing in my soul." Nothing, nothing, nothing:

"Neither firmness, nor tenderness, nor cheerfulness on the road."
"Neither pain nor happiness, nor fear, nor peace."
"Neither laziness, nor knowledge, nor the strength to be people."

You count up your zeroes, total up the account: emptiness. And isn't that why your poems are thingless, colorless? For their topic is nonbeing, rejection of what exists; and isn't that why individual words in them are like symbols of non-being:

Bloodless.
Growthless.
Rainbowless.
Powerless.
Loveless.
Griefless.
Fireless.
Stringless.
Thankless.

There are a great many of these words in your poems. Not a rainbow, but rainbowlessness; not fire, but firelessness; not power, but powerlessness nourish your poems. Something that does not exist is a lack, an absence, a minus, a detriment—lifelessness and desirelessness.

> "Isn't it better in quiet pitilessness to fall asleep, as the steppe feather-grass sleeps?"

To die—to fall asleep. Not to be. Quiet, forgetting, *Mara*, sleep. Lullaby, lullaby! "Close your empty fleshly eyes and rot quickly, dead man. There is no morning, no days, there are only nights . . . The end . . ." And emptiness! "A desert sphere in an empty desert, like the understanding of the Devil." But what flowers and bows you use to decorate—emptiness! The most lifeless and traditional of your poems has this for a name: "None." In these verses non-being speaks of itself:

> "The One who created me offended me, I cry because I don't exist."

Zero cries about being zero! Someone comes up to it, wants to help, but it repeats its own idea:

> "Why do you come up to me, knowing that I will never exist—and don't now?"

Who, besides you, could sing this song about someone who will not sing—and sleep so movingly, with such tender elegance:

> O why do you disturb me?
> I do not need your path.
> You can't do anything for me:
> The one who isn't cannot be
> saved . . .
> You lay down your soul for me—
> While I'll remain to drink my garland.
> It's God who didn't let me—
> be?
> (Female).

Never yet has non-being been manifest in so charming a form and spoken such nice words! Like Ophelia, twisting a garland by the stream—Nothing has turned its purest, most poetic visage towards you. But often it appears to you in another, a repellent mask—of the petty demon, the Nedotykomka, a devil—and asks you to let it sponge off you: "an eternal companion" of all manner of stagnation, somnolence, limpness:

"First of all I disturbed myself with everything: I wanted this, I dreamed of that . . . But with him my house . . . not so much came to life, but stretched out like a layer of fluff."

"Unhappily-fortunately, both tenderly sleepy and dark . . . With the little devil I feel sweetly bored . . . A bairn, an old man—does it matter?"

"He's so funny, soft, flimsy, he kept sticking, sticking—and stuck on."

He hasn't unstuck to this day. A spirit of uncomplainingness, firelessness, lovelessness, rainbowlessness, gracelessness, grieflessness—a thousand variously significant "withouts" that devastate and slay the soul.

"And both of us became the same thing. I'm already not *with* him—I'm in him, in him! I myself smell doggy in bad weather, and I lick my fur before the fire."

IV

But to whom do I write these lines? To Zinaida Gippius, "the famous decadent poet?" To her alone? Is she the only one who has been pawed by this lousy devil of anxiouslessness? The spirit of non-being, the spirit of stagnation and emptiness, the nasty little anathema of *Nullus*, doesn't it play with us and our souls? Now we're all the devil's dolls! "You're dead meat, a rotting stinker," each of us could say to himself. Gippius hates the dead meat in her more and more as she goes on, her "dull, wilted, grey, dead" soul.

She is languishing, and from the first line to the last her poems are some kind of wordless, stupefied sobbing. And she has already reached the point where she has consigned herself to anathema and written about herself the harshest, most spiteful book about herself, giving it this very title: *The Devil's Doll*.

This book has just come out (Moskovskoe knigoizdatel'stvo, 1911), and it appears to be a contemporary novel, the most ordinary Boborykin, but in essence it is the author's savage reprisal against herself.

The author intended to depict a hero of our time. Who is this hero? Sanin?[3] If you like, Sanin too, but "corrected and expanded." Sanin lacked a multitude of the traits that are so indicative of our contemporary age. Where do we see Azef[4] in Sanin? Where do we see the decadents in him? Where are the reactionaries? And there, Gippius has resolved to write the kind of Sanin who contains all of that—and to show what a devil's doll is, a demonic delusion, a living dead man. The topic is excellent, the conception is the grandest, but the more I got into reading it the more I was struck: but this is the poet herself, the "well-known decadent" Zinaida Gippius, it's her own blood brother, and she hates him just the way we hate our own close relatives!

He's the incarnation of precisely that grieflessness, lovelessness, gracelessness that Gippius always expressed so virtuosically. Just like her, he is

> Intoxicated—and bored,
> Good—and I don't care.

He's also a hero of non-being, stagnancy, deadness. "Perhaps he doesn't exist at all, but it only seems that he does," someone in the novel says about him, and the author herself in the foreword indicates, "I wanted to gather, to focus the traits of spiritual deadness in a single person."

The hero has "a dead face—as if it had never been alive."

And everything around him is dead too: "a lightless, unbounded space"—"external blackness, external death." He senses the emptiness of this desert, and if he were a poet, he would have written what Z. Gippius wrote so well:

> A desert sphere, in the empty wilderness...
> Despair! Despair!

He systematically kills God in himself, stamps out all kinds of, as they say, inspirations. She in this Sahara of hers eternally wants at least to sow something, to plant, to start nurturing "at least some kind, at least a poor little God," and calls, longing:

---

3   *Eds*. Hero of Mikhail Artsybashev's 1907 novel of the same name.
4   *Eds*: Evno Azef (1869-1918), a double agent who was both a socialist revolutionary and plotter of assassinations, and a spy for the Tsarist secret police.

> Oh Lord, my Lord, Sun, where art Thou?
> Save a captive soul!

And she waits for some kind of sacramental "deadlines," some kind of reincarnation: "I sleep, submissive to my dormition, but I look for the resurrection of eternal truth" and almost, as much as she can, believes: "everything will be different," whereas he coddles precisely this deathliness in himself, he is victorious, he sticks out his chest and laughs like an eyeless skull.

"Oh unbeloved, I don't know why, but I await your love, I wish for you to love!"

It's unnatural. Improbable. You wanted to hit, but there you are kissing. Pushing away, you lure it closer. What kind of strange love—inside-out. And this always happens with you—in all your loving feelings. We, for example, the rest of us, we wither and wilt when passion is unrequited. While you, on the other hand, you are almost jolly.

"So what, my Svetlana, if you don't love me," those are your true words. "Oh, so what if I don't see you, the deeper I love ... Undivided love is dearer to me than all joys ..." And when our passion fades, we, all the rest of us, how we grieve then! The eternal elegiac quality of dying, burning-out passion! Here too you are *à rebours*: neither sorrow nor pain:

"I was not sad, I was not pained. —I thought of how my soul felt free ..." And it's come to the point where the betrayal of your beloved, humiliation, an insult to passion is your highest triumph. We, the others, are jealous and tormented, we cripple our competitors, our confidants, while with you ... here is your song of a betrayed girl:

> Not me he loves—but her, her,
> Yet I'm not jealous,
> I know my happiness
> And, suffering, I'm triumphant.

An unheard-of "song of triumphant love!" Who out of millions of lovers for thousands and thousands of years would have sung a song like that! The young woman "knows happiness," when her lover caresses another!! What a strange, perverted heart!

I'm not even speaking of the fact that it's dear to you, of how you take care that your love will without fail be hopeless:

"We measure the power of love—by impossibility alone. —I will not give up my joy to anyone . . . Loving, we are not melded . . ."

At one point in my childhood I thought the residents of the antipodes were the same kind of people that we are, only with everything backwards. That ice burns them, and they use fire to put out water. The plaintiffs judge the judges, and everyone dreams of death, of disease, of famine as if that is the greatest blessing.

Now that I've read your books, these *Collected Poems of Z. N. Gippius* of yours, I see that my daydream is no dream. Such a tribe, indubitably, exists, and it is a tribe related to us. There among you this must be the usual thing, among you it must be the "norm" to speak and feel such things:

> "All joys are tedious . . ."
> "I love my despair so boundless . . ."
> "I welcome my defeat . . ." (Z. N. Gippius, *Sobranie stikhov*, vols. I and II).

It must be that your favorite words are truisms there: "the weight of happiness," "Joy of suffering," and it must be that everyone is pierced by these rare sensations of yours: "In the ultimate cruelty—there is an abyss of tenderness: and in God's truth—God's deception."

And if I somehow by chance read you writing that grief, for example, was burdensome, while joy was sweet, I would be quite astonished at that, as if at the most outlandish paradox. For you, the everyday is a paradox. Love without hate and cheerfulness without grief are inaccessible to you, I think. You write about death, for example, with a smile and tenderness:

"O, why am I fated to love you irresistibly? —The heart is always glad at the ending, as at death."

"The heart is strangely cheered by wordlessness and death—I greet death with a mad delight and I don't need the torment of immortality!"

So they won't think this is a cult of death, with all her soul, Gippius "follows it, as if it's some kind of monstrous insect"—with fear and disgust—stamps on it, waves it away, defends herself—carries on a protracted, dull struggle with it, and that comprises the charm and poignancy of her poetry.

Meanwhile her hero, carrying on as a satiric, gleams with self-satisfaction: for him everything's a bowl of cherries—the most contemporary of the contemporary!—he's a worse Gippius, a caricature of her, her little demon, Gippius without the lyrics, Gippius without complexity, without longing, without spiritual convolutions, but Gippius all the same; agreed, there's much in her that is not in him, but everything that's in him is in her!

V

Everyone is panning this new novel by Z. N. Gippius, yet at the same time it's very good. It has only one flaw: it hasn't been written yet. It's not a novel, but a kind of sketch of a novel, a blueprint—just as there are blueprints of buildings, machines. Everything is marked out excellently: the pipes, and the roof, and the windows—but it still has to be built, you need iron and wood. However, even that is worthy of praise. Perhaps "a stonemason, a stonemason in a white apron" will turn up and make it real, complete it all.

BUT—and here's the main misfortune in all these sketches and lazy outlines that comprise the novel—the same stagnancy, the same indifference. There's no chaos of any kind. The novel is a philippic; the author wants to curse, to hate, but every page says: who cares, the hell with it, I don't care.

That petty demon of indifference and undisturbedness—you should chase him away when you write a social novel! You have people shooting themselves, dying, committing atrocities, while it's as if you are humming:

> Live, people, play, children...
> Below, barely audibly, the stream rustles
> While I'm rocking in an airy net,
> Equally distant from earth and heaven.

The poems are wonderful, but if your hero of non-being were a gifted poet, these verses would absolutely have been his.

Nikolai Gumilyov

Reviews of Works by Blok, Klyuev, Balmont, and Others (1912)

Translated by Sibelan Forrester

Alexander Blok. *Nocturnal Hours. A Fourth Collection of Poems.* (Musaget) Price: 1 ruble.

N. Klyuev. *The Chime of Pines.* (Znamenskii & K** M. S. K.) Price: 60 kopecks.

K. D. Balmont. *Complete Collected Poems.* Vol. 8. *The Green Garden.* (Scorpio). Price: 1 ruble 50 kopecks.

Paul Verlaine. *Collected Poems.* Trans. Valery Bryusov. (Scorpio) Price: 2 rubles. Paul Verlaine. *Notes of a Widower.* (Halcyon) Price: 1 ruble.

M. G. Veselkova-Kil'shtet. *Songs of a Forgotten Estate.* Price: 1 ruble.

Vadim Shershenevich. *Spring/Vernal Thaw Holes.* Price: 60 kopecks.

I. Genigin. *Poems.* Price: 45 kopecks.

Two sphinxes stand before Alexander Blok; they force him to "sing and weep" with their unsolved riddles: Russia and his own soul. The former is Nekrasovian, the latter—Lermontovian. And often, very often Blok shows them to us combined in one, organically inseparable. Impossible? But wasn't it Lermontov who wrote "The Song of the Merchant Kalashnikov"?

From Nekrasov's vows to love the fatherland with grief and rage Blok has taken only the first. For example, in the poem "Beyond the Grave" he begins severely, accusingly:

> He was only a fashionable scribbler,
> Only the author of blasphemous words...

but he immediately adds:

> But the dead man is related to the people's soul:
> It sacredly honors every purpose...

Or in the poem "To the Homeland," after the magnificently terrible lines:

> Over the Black Sea, over the White Sea
> In black nights and white days
> A torpid face is visible,
> Tatar eyes cast flames...

Pacifying lines follow immediately, in the same rhythm, with three adjectives standing in a row:

> Quiet, drawn-out, red dawn
> Every night above your becoming...

This shift from indignation without relationship to a deed or a call, but to harmony (let it be bought at the price of new pain—the pain is melodious), towards a Schillerian, I would say, beauty, is typical of the Germanic current in Blok's work. We face not Ilya Muromets, not Alyosha Popovich, but a different guest, a glorious knight from overseas, some kind of Dyuk Stepanovich. And he doesn't love Russia as his mother, but as his wife, whom he finds when the time is right. In his Lohengrinian longing Blok truly knows of nothing that is not beautiful, that is base, to which he could say, finally, a masculine "No!" And perhaps he wants that, he seeks it?

But one moment—and even the topic of the forgotten train station sobs for him like the most resonant violin:

> The traincars passed in their usual line,
> They clanked and screeched,
> The yellow and dark-blue ones were silent,
> In the green ones people cried and sang...

In Blok's purely lyric verses and avowals there is a Lermontovian calm and sadness, but here too a characteristic difference as well: instead of the dear arrogance of the little Hussar, he has the noble thoughtfulness of a Mikael Kramer. Besides that, one more feature strikes one in his work that is unlike not only Lermontov, but of all Russian poetry in general, and that is his moralism. Turning up in its original form of not wishing evil to another, this moralism lends Blok's poetry the impression of some particular, once again Schillerian, humanity.

> For her mother is not waiting for her by the door
> With a candle, in ancient alarm.
> For the poor husband behind the thick shutter
> Will not be jealous of her...

He develops this almost at the moment of embracing and falls in love with the woman for her "youthful scorn" for his desire. Blok knows like no one else how to combine the two topics in one, not setting them up as opposites, but combining them chemically. In "Italian Verses"—a grandiose and bright past and "a certain wind, singing through black velvet of future life," in "Kulikovo Field"—the Tatar invasion and the story of a warrior of the Russian host who is in love. This approach opens to us infinite horizons in the field of poetry.

In general, Blok is one of the miracle-workers of Russian verse. It is hard to find an analogy to the rhythmic perfection of verses such as "The reed-pipe began singing" or "Today I don't remember." As a stylist, he does not avoid ordinarily pretty words; he knows how to bring out their original enchantment.

> Valentina, a star, day-dreaming,
> How your nightingales are singing...

And his great service to Russian poetry is that he has cast off the yoke of exact rhyme, found that rhyme depends on the acceleration of the verse, its assonances, scattered in evenly rhymed stanzas, and indeed not only the assonances, but also simply slant rhymes ("plecho"—"ni o chem," "vesti"—"strasti"), always have in mind some especially subtle effect and always achieve it.

This winter brought lovers of poetry an unexpected and precious gift. I speak of the book by N. Klyuev, a poet almost unpublished before this. In him we encounter an already completely mature poet, a continuer of the traditions of the Pushkin era. His verse is full in sound, clear and imbued with content. Such a dubious device as placing the complement before the subject is completely in place with him, and it lends his verses a dignified weightiness and expressiveness. Inexactness of rhymes can also not disconcert anyone because, as always in great poetry, the center of gravity lies not in the rhymes but in the words inside the line. But in compensation such lexical inventions as "vlastiokaia" [power-eyed] or "mnogoochit" [many-eyed] make one proudly recall similar experiments by Yazykov.

The pathos of Klyuev's poetry is rare, exceptional—it is the pathos of one who has found [what he seeks].

> Unreachable the depth of death,
> And the rivers of life are swift-flowing—
> But there is a magical wine
> To prolong the enchanting eternally...

He says this in one of the first poems, and his whole book proves that he has drunk deep of this wine. Drunk deep, and the vaults of paradise opened to him, the shores of another land and, exuding blood and flame, a six-winged Archangel. Enlightened, he came to love the earth in a new way, both the tatters of sea-foam, and the chime of pine trees in a forested vagabond wilderness, and even the gold-embroidered sarafans of girls coming of age or the belts of bonny lads from Solovki, racers and daredevils. But...

> Only one thing is lacking
> For the soul in its exilic vale:

> That the meadows' spaces, the waters' bosom
> Not give voice with a moan of pain...
>
> And in order for man not to endeavor
> To snatch the crown of the Creator,
> For the fact that, put to shame forever,
> I forfeited bright paradise...

Doesn't this sound like: Glory to God in the highest, and peace on earth, and good will to men? The Slavic sensation of a bright equality of all people and the Byzantine consciousness of a golden hierarchy at the thought of God. Here, with the apparent violation of this purely Russian harmony, the poet lives through grief and rage for the first time. Now he dreams terrible dreams:

> The twilight only grows more blue.
> The brume enwraps the river—
> My father, wearing a noose on his neck,
> Will come and sit down by the fireplace.

Now he knows that cultured society is only "the day off of a deaf, rumbling wave that's lost its strength." But the Russian spirit is strong, it always finds the path to the light. The poem "A Voice from the People" sounds the leitmotif of the whole book. To take the place of an outlived culture that has led us to a longing godlessness and purposeless anger, people come who can say of themselves: "We are the stormclouds before the sunrise, the dewy dawns of spring—in every form and moment is our demanding father... our waters are wonder-working and fire many-eyed." What then will these fair-haired warriors do with us, the dark, the blindly arrogant and blindly cruel? What punishment will they subject us to?

Here is their answer:

> We're like the currents of underground rivers,
> We invisibly flow up to you
> And in a boundless kiss
> We run together our brotherly souls.

One notes in Klyuev's work the possibility of a truly great epos.

K. Balmont is a riddle that eternally troubles us. Here he writes a book, then a second, then a third, in which there's not a single comprehensible image, not a single genuinely poetic page, but only all these "hundredringingnesses" and "self-immolations" and other such Balmontisms in a wild bacchanalian rush. The critics take up their pens in order to announce "the end of Balmont"—they love dealing the *coup de grace*. And then suddenly he publishes a poem, and one that's not just magnificent but amazing, that stays in your ears for weeks—in the theater, and in a cab, and in the evening before you fall asleep. Then it begins to seem that perhaps the "self-immolation" is splendid as well, and "Adam the arche-red," and that only your own lack of sensitivity prevents you from understanding it. But months go by, and regardless of all the efforts you make the Balmontisms don't get dearer, and then you start again running up against the strange thought that even a very major poet can write very bad poems. But it's still frightening...

By the way, these fears should not touch on the reader, and, when speaking of Balmont a critic is always at risk of putting his foot in his mouth. In "The Green Garden" there is such an amazingly wonderful poem—"Starfaced."

> His face was like the Sun at that hour when the Sun's at the zenith,
> His eyes were like stars—just before they fall from the skies.

and further:

> "I'm the first," he spake, "and the last"—and the thunders answered resoundingly,
> "The hour of harvest," said the Star-eyed. "Ready your sickles. Amen."
> In a faithful crowd we arose, in the sky fissures showed scarlet,
> And golden heptaconstellations led us to the bounds of the deserts.

Balmont has infused *The Green Garden* (Words of Osculation) with the songs and sayings of the Khlyst sect. Many of the poems are simply imitations.

Their genuine religious fragrance, of course, has been aired out by Balmont, who never could distinguish heavenliness from airiness. But there are stanzas in which their typical naivety is wonderfully conveyed, for example in a poem about the tree of paradise:

> But the most evil thing about it
> Is that it has a prohibition,
> O fatal tree,
> You sow rebellion . . .
> or craftiness:
> We not by the law,
> We by grace
> After gazing at the icon,
> Will lie down on the bed . . . .

and, finally, wildly energetic expressions:

> I consign it to damnation,
> I consign it to tremnation,
> To quatramnation I consign it.

Paul Verlaine has had a strange fate. The previous generation, rather suddenly after long inattention, declared him their teacher; his name was a slogan, his poems were avidly read. Even now graying Symbolists, such as René Gille, having generously forgotten former squabbles, dedicate whole monographs to him. But the young generation in France, their most brilliant representatives, stubbornly have no desire to think about him. This is so in Russia as well. Of the modernists, only Bryusov, Annensky and Sologub have translated him. The young keep silent. This fact may have many explanations. For example: Symbolism at its origin had a great deal in common with Romanticism, broadened, deepened and ennobled. Whereas Verlaine seemed a direct continuer of Villon, so dear to the Romantics. He was sincere, apt to fall in love, freely elegant, pious and debauched—in actual fact a fascinating figure, when people's store of merry and thoughtless energy is unspent by their slumberous fathers, the Parnassians or the tongue-tied poets of our own

1880s. But young people do not have such a rich inheritance, though the habit of merry-making remains, and here they are choosing their favorites more strictly, demanding broad ideas and worthy realization, conscious and fertile efforts, and not puerile enthusiasm, but rather the sacred fire of Prometheus. Verlaine, apparently, did not have that. His poetry is a lyrical intermezzo, precious as a human document and characteristic of the epoch, but that is all. Valery Bryusov's book gives a full representation of Verlaine as a poet. Perfect knowledge of all his poetry has allowed the translator to take advantage of Verlaine's own vocabulary in those places where an exact translation would make no sense. Many stanzas, even poems compete with the original in enchantment. The translations from *Romances sans paroles* are especially successful. The introduction supplied with the book has an exhaustive character.

A splendid supplement to Bryusov's book for a fuller acquaintance with Verlaine is *Notes of a Widower*, published by "Halcyon." Verlaine is no less captivating as a prose writer than he is as a poet. A series of the wittiest paradoxes, unexpected images and moments of purely French aristocratic gentility, scattered through the whole book, make it absorbing to read.

Mme. Veselkova-Kil'shtet's poetry has one indubitable strong point: its theme. It is an elegant idea to devote a whole book to the poetry of forgotten estates, so movingly helpless, scattered throughout great and frightening Russia. The author has both knowledge of and love for her theme. There are whole successful poems, excellent individual stanzas.

For example, a young woman pining in the poem "Patience":

> For something to do I lay out cards,
> And he follows. King and ace . . .
> Ah, my heart! your king's in the garden,
> And to him in vain I make haste.

But the book's lack of purely literary aims, of any even slightly interesting artistic devices, makes an unpleasant impression. The stamp of dilettantism, albeit intelligent, albeit talented, lies indelibly upon it.

Vadim Shershenevich is entirely under the impression of Balmont's poetry. But perhaps this is the most natural path for a young poet. His poems have no limpness, no lack of taste, but neither is there power or novelty. With his book he has announced only that he exists, and one may accept this fact without a disparaging grimace. But he must still show what he is as a poet.

How often people take an abundance of thought, richness and diversity of impressions for poetic talent. It is precisely in its absence that these very qualities prevent a person from becoming even a competent versifier. He gets mixed up in periods, violates the most immutable laws of poetry, falls into tastelessness, into illiteracy, and all in order to express more exactly a thought or a feeling that is dear to him. Such is Ivan Genigin. Only a great acquisition of culture would be able to prove to him that he is not a poet. But that is what he lacks.

NIKOLAI GUMILYOV

Review of Akhmatova's Beads (1914)

Translated by Robert T. Whittaker, Jr.

In Anna Akhmatova's *Beads*, on the contrary, the ideological aspect is thought out least of all. The poetess has not "created herself," has not put in the center of her experiences some sort of external fact by which to unify them. She does not address herself to something known or understandable to herself alone, and this distinguishes her from the Symbolists. But on the other hand, her themes frequently are not exhausted by the limits of a given poem; much in them seems insubstantial because it remains unproven. As with the majority of young poets, in Anna Akhmatova one frequently meets the words: pain, sorrow, death. This youthful pessimism, so natural and therefore so beautiful, has until now been the property of "pen testers," and, it seems, in Akhmatova's verse for the first time it has taken its place in poetry. Everyone has wondered, I think, at the magnitude of youth's capacity and willingness to suffer. Laws and objects of the real world suddenly assume the place of former ones now pierced through by a dream in whose fulfillment he believed: the poet cannot help but see that they are self-sufficiently beautiful, and he is incapable of comprehending himself among them, of coordinating the rhythm of his spirit with their rhythm. But the force of life and love is so powerful in him that he begins to love his orphanhood itself and achieves the beauty of pain and death. Later, when an "inadvertent joy" begins to appear to his spirit, tired of being ever in one and the same condition, he shall feel that man can joyously comprehend all aspects of the world, and from the ugly duckling which he appeared to himself in his own eyes, he shall become a swan, as in Andersen's fairy tale.

To those people who are not fated to achieve such a transformation, or to those who possess a feline memory, which attaches itself to all passed stages of its spirit, Akhmatova's book will seem exciting and valuable. In it a series of beings, mute until now, acquire a voice—women in love, cunning, dreamy, and rapturous, at last speak their own genuine, and at the same time artistically compelling language. That bond with the world about which I spoke above, and which is the lot of every genuine poet, has almost been achieved by Akhmatova, because she knows the joy of perceiving the external and knows how to transmit this joy to us.

> Tightly her dry lips are shut,
> Three thousand candles flame hot.
> Princess Eudoxie thus lay
> On a sapphire and scented brocade.
>
> And tearless, a mother bent low;
> Prayed for her blind little boy,
> And a voicelessly thrashing hysteric
> Strained to gulp air with her lips.
>
> A dark-eyed and humpbacked old man,
> Come from a far southern land,
> As if at the gate of paradise,
> To the darkening step has pressed close.

Here I turn to that which is most significant in Akhmatova's poetry, to her stylistics: she almost never explains; she shows. This is achieved both by a carefully considered and original choice of images, as well as (and this is most important) by their detailed elaboration. Epithets defining the value of the object (such as beautiful, ugly, happy, wretched, and so on) occur rarely. This value is suggested by the description of an image and by the interrelationship of images. Akhmatova has many devices for this. I shall indicate a few of them: the conjunction of an adjective defining color with an adjective defining form:

> ... And the dark green ivy
> Thickly entwined the high window.

Or:

> ... There a raspberry sun
> Over disheveled grey smoke ...[1]

Repetition in two successive lines which doubles our attention to the image:
Or:

> ... Tell me how they kiss you,
> Tell me how you kiss them.
> ... In snowy branches to black jackdaws,
> To black jackdaws refuge give.

Transformation of an adjective into a substantive:

> ... The orchestra is playing [something] gay ...

and so forth.

There are many definitions of color in Akhmatova's verse, and most frequently of yellow and grey, until now very rare in poetry. And perhaps as confirmation of the nonaccidental nature of her taste, the majority of her epithets emphasize in particular the poverty and paleness of objects: a threadbare rug, worn-down heels, a faded flag, etc. In order to love the world, Akhmatova must see it as nice and as simple.

Akhmatova's rhythmics serve as a magnificent support to her stylistics. Paeans and pauses help her to single out the most necessary word in the line, and in the whole book I did not find a single example of a stress falling on an unstressed word, or vice versa, a word stressed in meaning but without a

---

1 *Eds.* See Akhmatova's poem "I went to visit the poet ...," included in this volume.

stress. Were someone to take upon himself the task of examining the collection of any contemporary poet from this point of view, he would become convinced that usually the case is quite different. A faintness and brokenness of breathing is characteristic of Akhmatova's rhythmics. The tetrametric strophe (in which almost the whole book is written) is too long for her. Her periods most frequently encompass two lines, sometimes three, even occasionally one. The causal relation with which she attempts to replace the rhythmical unity of the strophe for the most part does not achieve its goal. The poetess must elaborate upon her strophe if she wishes to master composition. A single spontaneous transport cannot serve as a basis for composition. This is why Akhmatova as yet knows only the consecutiveness of a logically developed thought or the consecutiveness in which objects appear in her field of vision. This does not constitute a shortcoming of her verse, but it cuts off before her the path to achieving many virtues.

Compared to *Evening* (*Vecher*), published two years ago, *Beads* represents a great step forward. Her verse has become firmer, the content of each line—more solid, the choice of words—sparingly chaste, and, what is best of all, the incoherence of thought has vanished, that incoherence so characteristic of *Evening* and comprising more a psychological curiosity than a poetic quality.

Mikhail Kuzmin

Foreword to Evening by Anna Akhmatova (1912)

Translated by Sibelan Forrester

In Alexandria there was a society whose members, in order to enjoy life more sharply and intensely, considered themselves condemned to death. For them every day, every hour was the hour before death. Although the way time was spent before death in the given society came down to endless orgies, it seems to us that the very thought of a pre-death sharpening of receptivity and sensitivity of the epidermis and of feeling is more than justified. Poets especially should have a sharp memory of love and eyes wide open at the whole dear, joyful and sorrowful world, in order to gaze their fill at it and to drink it every minute for the last time. You yourself know that in minutes of extreme danger, when death is near, in one brief second we recollect more than our memory could present in a long hour of the spirit's everyday state.

And these recollections do not go logically, and not as a whole, but run one after the other in a sharp and burning wave, from which things will gleam: first long-forgotten eyes, then a cloud in a spring sky, then someone's blue dress, then the voice of a passerby, a stranger to you. These details, these *concrete* fragments of our life torment and disturb us more than we had expected and, as if they had nothing to do with the matter at hand, precisely and dependably lead us to those minutes, to those places, where we loved, wept, laughed and suffered—where we lived.

You can love things, the way collectors or people emotionally apt to become attached to things love them, or as sentimental souvenirs, but that is not at all the sense of a connection, incomprehensible and inevitable, that opens up to us in a first sorrowful, then triumphant ecstasy, as described above.

It seems to us that, unlike other lovers of things, Anna Akhmatova possesses the ability to understand and love things precisely in their incomprehensible connection with the minutes of experience. Often she exactly and definitely recalls some object (a glove on the table, a cloud like a squirrel-skin in the sky, the yellow light of candles in the bedroom, a three-cornered hat in the park of Tsarskoe Selo), which it would seem has nothing to do with the whole poem, thrown away and forgotten, but precisely because of that mention we feel a more palpable sting, a more delightful poison. Without that squirrel-skin, the whole poem perhaps would lack that fragile piercingness that it possesses. We do not wish to say that things always have such a particular significance for the author; often they are nothing more than sentimental souvenirs or the transfer of feelings from a person to things that belong to him. We say this not to reproach the young poet, because that is already quite a lot—to make the reader begin to daydream, and to cry, and to feel angry with himself at the same time, if only by means of sentimental emotionality— but we especially value her first understanding of the sharp and incomprehensible meaning of things, which is not that often encountered. And it seems to us that Anna Akhmatova has that heightened emotionality for which members of the society that considered itself condemned to death were striving.

By this we do not mean to say that her thoughts and moods are always related to death, but they have that kind of intensity and sharpness. Let us suppose that she does not belong among the especially cheerful poets, but is always compassionate.

It seems to us that she is alien to mannerism, which if she has any of it is somewhat similar to the mannerism of Laforgue, that is of a capricious child used to being listened to and admired. Among the very young poets, understandably, there are others who strive toward a subtle and, we might say, fragile poetry, but while some of them seek it in describing objects that are generally considered to be fine: Sèvres cups, tapestries, fireplaces, harlequins, knights and madonnas (Ehrenburg), others in an unusually refined analysis of ostentatiously baroque experiences (Mandelstam), a third group in ironizing description of an intimate, somewhat demonstratively prosaic life (Marina Tsvetaeva)—it seems to us that Anna Akhmatova's poetry produces the impression of being sharp and fragile because her own perceptions are that way; the only thing the poet adds of herself is the manneredness, pleasant to our taste, à la Laforgue.

Vyacheslav Ivanov once expressed the thought that original poets are the first to show their own manner, which they subsequently reject for their "personae," which in turn is sacrificed to their own style. From the fact that in the case at hand the poet already has a manner, one may easily conclude that this is an original poet and that a new female voice, distinct from others and audible, regardless of the evident weakness of tone, which seems to be desirable to its owner, has joined the choir of Russian poets.

We are not writing criticism, and our role is a very modest one: only to say the name and, as it were, to introduce the new arrival. We may hint slightly at her ancestry, indicate a few objects and express our guesses, as we have done. Thus, ladies and gentlemen, a new, young poet, but one who already has what is required to become genuine, comes to us. And her name is—Anna Akhmatova.

Osip Mandelstam

Review of Igor Severyanin's The Thunder-Seething Goblet (1913)

Translated by Constance Link

Igor Severyanin. *The Thunder-Seething Goblet (Gromokipiashchii kubok)*. Poems. Introduction by Fyodor Sologub. Moscow: "Grif" Publishing House, 1913.

As a poet Igor Severyanin is defined chiefly by the shortcomings of his poetry. His use of monstrous neologisms and foreign words, which apparently hold an exotic fascination for the author, produces a sense of gaudiness. Insensitive to the laws of the Russian language and unable to hear how a word grows and matures, he prefers words that have fallen into disuse, or that were never part of the language, to living words. He often sees beauty in an image of "urbanity." Nevertheless, Igor Severyanin is a poet by virtue of his simple rapture and his dry *joie de vivre*. His verse resembles a grasshopper in its powerful musculature. Having hopelessly confused all cultures, the poet is sometimes able to give charming forms to the chaos that reigns in his imagination. It is impossible to write verses that are "just good." If Severyanin's "I" is difficult to grasp, that does not mean that it does not exist. He is able to be unique only in his superficial displays, from which we must draw our own conclusions about his profundity.

Osip Mandelstam

On Contemporary Poetry: Almanac of the Muses
(1916)

Translated by Jane Gary Harris

"On Contemporary Poetry: *Almanac of the Muses*" (Almanakh muz). Petrograd: Felana, 1916.

An almanac containing works by twenty-five contemporary poets has just been published. On this occasion it would be fitting to speak of the high level of technical competence in contemporary poetry, to point out how nowadays everyone is capable of writing poetry, and to bemoan the fact that today's poetry is artificial and dead. However, I shall do nothing of the kind: why do critics so love to indulge in melancholy lamentations every time they see a batch of poems? It takes very little to attain "a high level" in their eyes, yet in their sweeping condemnation of artificiality they avoid the task (often beyond their strength) of analyzing the complexities of art. It would be beneficial to explain what "progress" in poetry is, so as to end, once and for all, these hypocritical complaints by indifferent outsiders about the seeming impoverishment of poetry, as if poetry were congealed in some concept of "Alexandrine perfection." There is no such thing as a "high level" of contemporary poetry in comparison to the poetry of the past. Most poems today are simply bad, as most poems have always been bad. Bad poems have their own hierarchy and, if you like, even perfect themselves rushing after good poems, reworking and distorting them in their own peculiar fashion. Nowadays people write bad poetry in a new way—that is the only difference! And, indeed, what kind of progress can there possibly be in poetry in the sense of improvement? How absurd—progress in art! Did Pushkin really perfect Derzhavin, that is, annul him in some way? No one writes odes in the style of Derzhavin or Lomonosov today, despite all our "victories." In retrospect, it is possible to imagine that the course of poetry is an uninterrupted, irretrievable loss. The lost secrets are as numerous as the innovations. All talk of progress in art is rendered meaningless by these lost secrets: the proportions of the matchless Stradivarius or the formulas of the paints used by the ancient icon painters.

Almanac of the Muses contains some extremely diverse contributions—good and bad poems are represented. To speak of some average level of achievement is impossible since the contributors to this collection are as distant from each other as the stars in the sky. The older generation of poets is represented by Valery Bryusov and Vyacheslav Ivanov, whose poems are already capable of arousing the noble lament that no one writes like that anymore. There is a kind of satiety in Ivanov's poems: we know beforehand all that they contain! Obviously, the poet has attained such sublimity, when he is able to touch the cithara even as he drowses, barely fingering its strings.

> But to me the visible faces of Spring
> Are as sorrowful as forgotten dreams.

Valery Bryusov is energetic by nature even in the weakest of his poems. Two of Bryusov's poems included in the *Almanac of the Muses* belong to his most unpleasant manner and revive that dreadful literary vanity which, fortunately, has receded into the past along with the epoch which engendered it. An immodest apotheosis of versification bursts through the rather pallid landscape:

> His vision is eternally woven into stanzas . . .

And in another:

> Birches in their splendid mantles
> Hastily lower their heads
> Before the prophetic Magus.

We can no longer astonish anyone with the "prophetic Magus." The tawdry mantle of pseudo-Symbolism has completely faded, lost all its form, and justifiably evokes a merry smirk from the younger poets.

Kuzmin's classicism is captivating. How sweet it is to read a classical poet living in our midst, to experience a Goethean blend of "form" and "content," to be persuaded that the soul is not a substance made of metaphysical cotton, but rather the carefree, gentle Psyche. Kuzmin's poems not only lend themselves easily to memorization, but also to recall, as it were (the impression of recollection after the very first reading), and they float up to the surface as if out of oblivion (Classicism):

> Surely, the seraphim are as cold
> To each other in paradise.

Kuzmin's clarism, however, has its dangerous aspect. It seems that such magnificent weather as that evoked in his poetry, especially in the later poems, does not exist at all.

Akhmatova's combination of the subtlest psychologism (Annensky's school) with song-like harmony astonishes our sense of hearing because we are accustomed to associating the song with a certain spiritual simplicity, if not spiritual poverty. The psychological design in Akhmatova's songs is as natural as the veins in a maple leaf:

> While in the Bible a red maple leaf
> Is left to mark the Song of Songs.

However, the poems in the *Almanac* contain little that is characteristic of the "new" Akhmatova. They are still very pointed and epigrammatic, while the poet has already entered a new phase.

Akhmatova's most recent poetry indicates a propensity for hieratic significance, religious simplicity and solemnity: I would say that the *wife* has taken the place of the woman. Remember: "meek, dressed as a beggar, but with the majestic bearing of a regal wife." The voice of renunciation grows ever stronger in Akhmatova's verse, and at the present moment her poetry is close to becoming a major symbol of Russia's grandeur.

Vladimir Mayakovsky

V. V. Khlebnikov (1922)

Obituary note

Translated by Sibelan Forrester

Viktor Vladimirovich Khlebnikov has died.

Khlebnikov's poetic fame is incomparably less than his significance.

Out of the mere hundred people who read him, fifty simply called him a graphomaniac, forty tried to read him for pleasure and were surprised when that didn't work, and only ten (Futurist poets, the philologists of "OPOYAZ") knew and loved this Columbus of new poetic continents, which we now inhabit and cultivate.

Khlebnikov is not a poet for consumption. He's impossible to read. Khlebnikov is a poet for the producer. Khlebnikov has no long poems. The completion of his published things is a fiction. The semblance of completion was more often than not the work of his friends. Out of the heap of rough drafts he had thrown away we chose the ones that struck us as the most valuable and had them published. Not rarely the tail of one draft would get glued onto another one's head, putting Khlebnikov in a cheerful quandary. You couldn't let him proofread, he'd cross everything out, entirely, producing a completely new text.

When he brought something for publication, Khlebnikov would usually say, "If anything's wrong, redo it." When he was reading his work he would sometimes stop halfway through a word and just indicate, "well, and so on." That "and so on" contains all of Khlebnikov: he would assign a poetic task, suggest a solution, but as for using that solution in a practical way—he simply handed that over to others.

Khlebnikov's bibliography is comprised by his brilliant verbal constructions. His bibliography is an example for poets and a reproach to writers on the make.

Khlebnikov and the Word

For so-called new poetry (our most recent), especially for the Symbolists, the word is material for writing verses (the expression of feelings and thoughts); its material, building, resistance, treatment were unknowns. They groped the material unconsciously and without consistency. Alliterative accidents of similar words were passed off as internal soldering, as an indivisible genetic bond. The stagnant form of a word was honored as eternal; they would try to put it on things that had outgrown the word.

For Khlebnikov the word is an independent force, the organizing material of feelings and thoughts. Hence his delving into roots, into the origins of the word, into the time when a name corresponded to the thing. The time when, perhaps, a dozen words with the same root arose, and new ones appeared as cases of the root (declension of the root according to Khlebnikov), for example, "byk" (bull) is the one who beats, "bok" (side) is the place that is beaten (by the bull). "Lys" (bald or treeless) is the thing that became "les" (a forest); "los" (moose) and "lis" (fox)—the ones who live in the forest.

Khlebnikov's lines—

> *Lesa lysy.*
> *Lesa obezlosili. Lesa obezlisili.*
> [The forests are bald.
> The forests are mooseless. The forests are foxless]—

can't be torn apart—they're an iron chain.

But see how this falls apart by itself:

> *"Chuzhdyi charam chernyi cheln"*
> [The black canoe alien to charms]

Balmont

The word in the sense in which it's used now is a chance word, needed for some kind of exercise. But the precise word should calibrate every shade of thought.

Khlebnikov created a whole "periodic table of the word." Taking a word with undeveloped, unknown forms, comparing it with a developed word, he demonstrated the necessity and inevitability of new words appearing.

If the developed word "plyas" [dance] produces "plyasunya" [woman dancer]—then the development of aviation, "let" [flight] should give "letunya" [woman flier]. If we have "krestiny" for the day one is christened, then the day one flies should be "letiny." Needless to say, there's not even a trace of cheap Slavophilism with its "mokrostup" [dampstep]; it doesn't matter if the word "letunya" isn't needed now, doesn't take root now—Khlebnikov gives only the method of correct word creation.

Khlebnikov the Master of Verse

I said above that Khlebnikov has no completed works. In his last piece, "Zangezi," for example, you clearly feel two different variants that were printed together. Khlebnikov should be taken in the excerpts that best resolve the poetic assignment.

In all Khlebnikov's things, what strikes the eye is his unprecedented mastery. Not only could Khlebnikov write a poem quickly upon request (all day his head was working only on poetry), but he could give a piece the most unusual form. For example, he has a very long poem composed of palindromes:

>
> *Koni, Topot. Inok.*   [Stallions, Stamping. A Monk.]
> *No ne rech', a cheren on.* [But not speech, whereas he's black.]
> etc.

But this, of course, is only conscious joking—from overfullness. Playing jokes didn't really interest Khlebnikov, as he never made things either to show off or to sell.

Philological work led Khlebnikov to verses that develop the lyrical theme with a single word.

The very well-known poem "Incantation by Laughter," published in 1909, is equally loved by poets, innovators, and parodists and critics:

> Oh, start laughing, laughers,
> Who laugh with laughings,
> Who laughalot laughily,
> Oh, laugh yourself out outlaughingly laughter
> Of laughter laughmen[1]
>   etc.

Here a single word gives both "smeievo" [laughia], the country of laughter, and the crafty "smeunchiki" [laughleters], and "smekhachi" [laughmen]—strongmen.

What verbal poverty we see if we compare Balmont, who tried to construct a verse similarly on the single word "love":

> Love, love, love, love,
> Love insanely, love the love
>   etc.

A tautology. Impoverishment of the word. And this for the most complex definitions of love! Once Khlebnikov handed in to be printed six pages produced from the root "lyub" (love). It couldn't be printed because the provincial typography didn't have enough of the letter "L."

Khlebnikov moved on from naked word-creation to its application in a practical task, let's say the description of a grasshopper:

> Little-winging goldwritten of slenderest tendons,
> A grasshopper in the truckbed of its belly laden
> Overmuch various greens and beliefs.
> Peen-peen-peen—the sensifer bangity-banged.
> Oh unwaiter of the evening glow!

---

1   *Eds*. See also Paul Schmidt's translation of this poem in this volume.

> Oh unwaited!
> Englow!

And finally the classic:

> By the well
> The water so wanted
> To split apart,
> So that in the bit of swamp
> With a bit of gilt
> Reins would be reflected.
> Racing, like a narrow snake,
> The current so wanted
> The bit of water so wanted
> To run away and scatter,
> So that at the price of work achieved
> Her black-eyed footwear
> Would grow greener.
> Whisper, whimper, languishing moan,
> The dark shade of shame,
> Hut windows on three sides,
> The dark shade of shame.

I'm misspeaking: I'm citing the poem from memory, I could be mistaken in the details, and I'm not at all trying to trace all of Khlebnikov in this tiny sketch.

One more thing: I'm intentionally not lingering on Khlebnikov's most enormous fantastic-historical works, because it's basically poetry.

Khlebnikov's Life

Khlebnikov is described best of all by his own words:

> Today I will set out anew
> There—to life, to trade, to the market,
> And I'll lead a troop of songs
> Into a duel with the surf of the market.

I knew Khlebnikov for twelve years. He would often come to Moscow, and then, except in the most recent months, we'd see him every day.

I was struck by Khlebnikov's work. His empty room was always piled up with notebooks, sheets and scraps of paper, written in his tiny handwriting. If something didn't happen to make the publication of some collection happen around that time, and if no one pulled a printable page out of the heap—Khlebnikov would stuff the manuscripts into pillowcases, when he traveled he'd sleep on the pillow, and then he'd lose the pillow.

Khlebnikov traveled a lot. No one understood either the reasons or the timing of his trips. Three or so years ago I managed with great difficulty to arrange paid publication of his manuscripts (Khlebnikov had passed on to me a small folder of very mixed-up manuscripts that Jakobson had taken to Prague after writing a wonderful article about Khlebnikov, the only one until now). The day before he was going to receive permission to print and the money, which he knew about, I ran into him on Teatral'ny Square holding a little suitcase.

"Where are you going?"

"South, it's spring!"

And off he went.

He left on the roof of a train car; he traveled for two years, advanced and retreated with our army in Persia, had typhus after typhus. He came back that winter in a train car of epileptics, overstrained and robbed of everything, wearing nothing but a hospital gown.

Khlebnikov came back without a single line. Of his verses from that time, I know only a bit about hunger that was printed in some Crimean newspaper or other and the two most amazing manuscripts that he had sent earlier—*Ladomir* and *A Scratch on the Sky*.

Ladomir was submitted to the State publishing house, but it didn't get published. Was Khlebnikov really capable of breaking a wall with his forehead?

In practice, Khlebnikov was a most disorganized person. Gorodetsky's eulogy of Khlebnikov ascribed an almost organizational talent to the poet: the creation of Futurism, printing "A Slap in the Face of Public Taste," etc. And that is completely wrong. Both *A Trap for Judges* (1908), with Khlebnikov's first poems, and the "Slap" were organized by David Burlyuk. And we had to pull Khlebnikov in almost by force to everything that followed. Of course, a lack of practicality is repellent if it's the caprice of a rich man, but with Khlebnikov, who rarely had even a pair of pants of his own (to say nothing about "rations"), the self-denial took on the character of real heroism, martyrdom for the sake of a poetic idea.

Everyone who knew Khlebnikov loved him. But it was the love of healthy people for a healthy, most educated, most witty poet. He had no family members capable of dedicatedly taking care of him, at all. Illness made Khlebnikov demanding. When he saw that people weren't giving him their attention, Khlebnikov would get suspicious. An accidental harsh phrase, even if it didn't refer to him, would be blown up into not recognizing his poetry, into poetic disrespect for him.

In the name of preserving the correct literary perspective I consider it my duty to print in black and white in my own name and, I have no doubt, in the names of my friends, the poets Aseev, Burlyuk, Kruchonykh, Kamensky, Pasternak, that we considered and consider Khlebnikov one of our poetic teachers and the most magnificent and most honest knight in our poetic struggle.

After Khlebnikov's death, articles about him appeared in various journals and newspapers, full of sympathy. I read them with disgust. When, finally, will we see the end of the comedy of posthumous healings?! Where were the people who are writing now when the living Khlebnikov, spat on by the critics, was walking around Russia alive? I know living people, maybe, who are not equal to Khlebnikov, but who are threatened by a similar end. Give up, finally, on the homage of centenary jubilees, the reverence of posthumous editions! Articles to the living! Bread to the living! Paper to the living!

Sofia Parnok
(Andrei Polyanin)

In Quest of a Path for Art (1913)

Translated by Sibelan Forrester

Those moments in a person's fate that represent real happenings in his family circle become events of greater or lesser significance in the evaluation of a dispassionate observer. N. Gumilyov and S. Gorodetsky's announcement of "Acmeism" or "Adamism," "a new direction," supposedly bound "to take the place of Symbolism"—in a circle of persons entitled "the Poets' Guild," to the extent that it constitutes a happening—will appear in the historian's eyes as a chance event, notable (if at all) as an illustration of the spiritual inertia that has so sharply marked the last decade of our poetry.[1] For the time being "Acmeism" or "Adamism" exists in the form of an idea, insufficiently thought through and felt through, in the imagination of its inventors; it exists in the form of a new coinage for lovers of all sorts of novelty, and it also vainly strives to exist in the form of an aesthetic theory on the pages of the journal *Apollon*, in the truly impoverished critical and prophetic attempts of N. Gumilyov and S. Gorodetsky.[2] It is indicative that the "new direction,"

---

1 *Author's note*: The italics in all quotations are ours [A. P.].
2 *Author's note*: Nikolai Gumilyov—"Nasledie simvolizma i akmeizma" [The heritage of Symbolism and Acmeism]. Sergei Gorodetsky—"Nekotorye techeniia v sovremennoi russkoi poèzii" [Some Currents/Tendencies in Contemporary Russian Poetry]. *Apollon*, 1913, No. 1.

which is by no means pragmatically determined, was fated to come into the world precisely in the form of a "theory." This theory, its prophets are convinced, is supposedly already realized in the "new school's" writing. However, so far there have been no Acmeistic works up either in the "monthly journal of verse and criticism," *Hyperborea*, nor in the various other editions of the "Poets' Guild"—the core of the "new movement." And so, in our era of many wonders, it has come to pass that a child was born before its mother. We pass over those pages by N. Gumilyov and S. Gorodetsky that are devoted to "criticism" of Symbolism, if one can call it criticism, this vain babble of "thinkers" who haven't even managed to reach an agreement in their understanding of Symbolism: these earthbound attempts have been duly evaluated in an extensive article by Valery Bryusov.[3] We will limit ourselves to a mere survey of Acmeism's fundamental principles.

After Symbolism, which "having filled the world with correspondences," "turned it into a phantom," after all sorts of "refusal to accept," the world "is irrevocably accepted by Acmeism, in all the wholeness of its beauties and uglinesses." In this world, "irrevocably accepted" anew, "a rose has once again become beautiful in itself," the same way "a putrescence," "a crust of waste" that has grown on the pole where a criminal sits, is beautiful in itself. The "new Adams" look at the life around them as if it were newly created, full of a "new" care "to rename the names of the world and by so doing to summon all creatures out of damp twilight into the transparent air." (Though isn't the creative process of artists of all ages founded on this "new" striving—calling images out from "damp twilight into the transparent air"?) "The uncognizable" also hides "in the damp twilight," however, but since it is "by the very meaning of the word" not cognizable, it is not subject to discussion. An Acmeist, by the way, is not forbidden to "depict the soul in those moments when it trembles, approaching the Other," but then it is *supposed* "only to twitch." Such are the principles of Acmeist theory and politics.

The new Adams' entry into Russian contemporaneity so lacks historical preparation that it produces a truly carnivalesque impression, especially when we recognize at the head of the procession the versifier N. Gumilyov, such a haughtily civilized *monsieur* Adam, and Anna Akhmatova, whom S.

---

3   Valery Bryusov. "Novye techeniia v russkoi poèzii" [New Currents/Tendencies in Russian Poetry]. *Russkaia mysl'* [Russian Thought] 1913, No. 4.

Gorodetsky simple-heartedly presents as a new Eve. Out of "damp twilight into the transparent air," Eve summons what is fit to be subjected to "women's eyes." There are the "little whip," "the glove," "the old sachet," etc. summoned by Anna Akhmatova. We have not yet forgotten Gumilyov's *Romantic Flowers*, *Pearls* and *Foreign Sky*; Anna Akhmatova's *Evening* is also memorable to us. By what miracle have these thoroughly Europeanized writers turned into "somewhat sylvan animals"? It's true, N. Gumilyov asserts that "it's harder to be an Acmeist than a Symbolist," "but the new movement's principle is always to pursue the path of greatest resistance." Isn't that because N. Gumilyov is trying to reforge himself from a pure-blooded Parnassian into an Acmeist? For now the Acmeists' victories come down to permitting "the fetters of meter by way of syllables, ever freer stress placement," of writing poems "by a newly thought-out syllabic system of versification." But what victories await the new Adams, when they are taken for realization of the strict demand of Acmeism: "to guess every hour what the following hour will be for us" (the Acmeists), "for our cause, for the whole world, and to hasten its" (i.e., the hour's) "approach"? Has the "new school" also thought through a system of training in the art of prophecy? (And by the way, why shouldn't the founders of a "Poets' Guild" also organize a "Prophets' Guild"?) And, finally, when will the Acmeists learn to "guess" what ineffable system they should use to create in such a way that a rose, in their depiction, will remain splendid *in itself* as such, "and not in its posited resemblances" to something else? At the same time it must differ from the Realist's rose "in that chemical synthesis that alloys the phenomenon with the poet, which no one, *even the very best realist*, can even dream of?"

But our article's goal is not at all to unmask the newly minted thinkers' lack of experience at thinking; if we have lingered on evaluating the "new direction," then that is not at all due to the interest that the names of the new Adams arouse: with the exception of S. Gorodetsky, a talented though undependable poet, they are all mediocre versifiers, nothing more. We are occupied with evaluation of Acmeism only insomuch as we are concerned with the question of "literary movements" in general, their relationship to the single path of art.

The aesthetic principle, like the religious principle, has its roots in the human psyche; it leads the spirit to search for unshakable norms during the catastrophic and contemplative moments of life. Like the history of religion, it shows us the evolving principle of a subject's disinterested relationship to an object. Therefore it's natural that, in seeking a path for art, the seeker will look toward history, just as a traveler, to figure out where he is, consults a geographical map to find the line of the path he has been following. In the field of literature, so-called "literary schools" serve as mileposts for the researcher on the path of theoretical thought, indicating moments in history when one or another aesthetic view decisively comes to outweigh others. But a "literary school," like any military organization that fights under a certain banner, takes on the defense of positions that were won in one way or another, but not the surrender of those positions in the name of truth (for truth is invisible to eyes that are blinded by other torches). Therefore, the significance of the literary schools' activity, in quest of a path for art, comes down to the role of religious sects, which elevate this or that theological prejudice as the basis of their credo. A seeker of religious truth goes past the sects to the great founders of religions, who brought revelations to the world. And the seeker who thirsts for aesthetic wisdom, after rejecting the crooked curve of "literary movements," should go speedily toward the undimmed source of aesthetic experience, to the priceless models of theoretical insight that great artists leave to us. Here, in the documents of various epochs, documents that speak in various languages, he will perceive an unusual, marvelous unity of thought. Reading into the letters, diaries, articles and notes of world-class geniuses, the seeker moves from German philosophy, lit by an eternal noon, to brilliant France, returns to the fiery dawn of our own homeland—and notices with intoxication that over all the world a single sun is shining in a single sky.

Verily, if you give serious thought to the fact that so-called "Realism as a theory of art," in all its monstrous naïveté, could have flowered in Russia half a century ago; that so-called Symbolism had to march against it with fanfares; and that in our own day, finally, "Acmeism" could arise, "a new school" that has taken up arms against the symbol, as if the symbol had been invented by the Symbolists—if you think hard about the fact that all this took place *after Pushkin*, after Pushkin, whose image is the essence of art told in words—how can you avoid falling into dejected confusion? And frankly, the talent of memory is a trait of the aristocratic soul, and there is no feature more characteristic of ordinary souls than their happy ability to forget. They don't know how to remember and, not knowing how to remember, they don't know how to pay respect. The history of the aesthetic quests of "literary schools" makes this clear to us.

A restless sense that somewhere those mysterious "means of poetic activity" are to be found, and not at all contained in mindlessly conscientious representation of the external world. The extent to which the "lovers of nature" practiced their approach moved the Symbolists to undertake a pilgrimage into the internal world, into their own souls, towards creation *out of themselves*. And now—has much time passed?—a "new school" is already accusing its own "worthy father," Symbolism, of "foregrounding purely literary tasks: free verse, more unusual and neglected meter, and metaphor elevated above all." True, this reproach sounds excessive on the lips of an Acmeist, who seeks "the means of poetic activity" in breaking apart "the fetters of meter by permission of syllables" and so on, i.e., who is preoccupied with the very same "purely literary tasks"; but, no matter how flighty the accuser, alas, his accusation is not without foundation. He is wrong in one thing only: "Purely literary tasks" were not the Symbolists' goal, and it was quite unexpected for the Symbolists, it seems to us, that they wound up in the "foreground." The history of this catastrophe is as follows. Having elevated digging poetic matter *out of oneself* into a principle, the Symbolists lost sight of the facts that: 1) there is no content that will not run dry, and one must keep a tireless eye on one's goblet lest, one fine day, one find it empty; 2) the lees that settle to the bottom are not always the noble remnant of an old wine, 3) not every drop, even from an overflowing vessel, is precious. The Symbolist dug down into himself with a net woven not by strict artistic principle, but by a self-satisfied and uncomprehending hand, and that is why his net filled up with small fry that were not worth catching. The Symbolists deserve to be accused of making a cult of "purely literary tasks" because every form, if not justified by the content, is no more than fulfillment of a literary task, and the work of Symbolist lyric poets was full of examples of form unjustified by content. Symbolism lifted the edge of the curtain that had been lowered over the secret of "poetic activity" and once again seduced literature with the dream of the spirit realm, the cradle of creativity, and so Symbolism as a theory of art is worthy of every respect, but what is incomparably more significant for us is that its fate serves us as a truly tragic lesson. If the image of Pushkin, as a perfect sculpture incarnating the features of the artistic ideal, tells us what a creator should strive for, the ruins of Symbolism speak no less eloquently of the mortal dangers that lie on the path of the artist.

But what kind of path is it, and, if a school of creators could be imagined, then what should be the principle of that education? What should an artist study first and foremost? The answer to that question may be formulated succinctly: the artist should first of all study the endless creative process. To create one's own soul, to search for and reveal the elevated values in the chaos of one's own ego, to build up and destroy in the name of that same building—the artist should first of all study unending spiritual life. What kind of criterion should guide the creator in choosing artistic material from within? What should be embodied in the word, the line, the sound, and what should not be? Nature gives the artist an example of creative wisdom: when does she command the spring bud to open, to unfurl in a moist leaf? When ripeness crowds the green bundle unbearably, *at the last moment*. A creator should measure the value of his ideas by the power of that last moment.

It would be a miracle if these lines "delivered" even one youthful talent from "the evil one." The guesses and pondering of great aesthetic wisdom were uttered not in mere words, but out of "flame and light," and if we permit ourselves here to utter our thought where it agrees with the chosen ones that's only because we want to remind recent poetry, exhausted in the pathless wilderness, that it has a paternal home and a priceless heritage from its forebears. But will all the "teaching about art" create even one poet? The heart beats, untaught by anything, and no teaching has ever created a living, beating heart.

VASILY ROZANOV

On Symbolists and Decadents (1901)
(from *Religiia i kul'tura*, St. Petersburg)

Translated by Joel Stern

The terms "Symbolism and Decadence" imply a new type not so much of poetry as of poetic art, a type that is vastly dissimilar in form and content to all previous kinds of literary endeavor. Having arisen only 10-12 years ago, the Symbolist movement has spread with extraordinary rapidity throughout all the countries of the civilized world, obviously finding a well-prepared soil and conditions favorable for its acceptance everywhere. As specimens of this type of art let us cite two or three poems:

> Corpses illuminated by gas!
> Scarlet ribbon on the sinful bride!
> Oh, shall we go to the window and kiss!
> Do you see how pale the faces of the dead are?
> This is a hospital where children are in mourning...
> These are oleanders on the ice...
> This is the jacket of romances without words.
> Darling, the moon cannot be seen through the window.
> Our souls are the flower in your boutonniere.
>
> *(V. Darov)*

In a somewhat more lively meter:

> The shadow of uncreated creations
> Flickers in sleep,
> Like the laminae of latania
> On the enameled wall.
> Violet-colored hands
> On the enameled wall
> Sleepily draw sounds
> In the sonorously sounding depths,
> They grow like spangles
> In the azure moonlight;
> The denuded moon rises
> In the azure moonlight;
> Sounds soar sleepily,
> Sounds snuggle up to me,
> Secrets of uncreated creations
> Snuggle up to me caressingly,
> And the shadow of latania flickers
> On the enameled wall.
>
> *(Russian Symbolists,* Book II)

The two poems cited above are Russian, of native origin; here is a poem by Maeterlinck:

> My soul is sick all day,
> My soul is sick from parting,
> My soul is struggling with silence,
> My eyes encounter the shadow,
> I see the phantoms of longings;
> A half-forgotten track leads
> The dogs of secret desire
> Into the depths of forgetful forests,
> Packs of lilac-colored fantasies race along,
> And yellow arrows—reproaches—
> Slay the deer of mendacious dreams.

> Alas, alas! Everywhere desires,
> Everywhere returning dreams,
> And the breathing is too blue . . .
> On the heart the moon's visage grows dim.

What is indisputable and understandable about the content of Symbolism is its general tendency toward eroticism. The god as old as Mother Nature, driven once and for all, so it seemed, from the civic poetry of the 1850s-1870s, broke into a sphere that has always belonged to him and that he has loved since time immemorial, but in a strange and mutilated, in a shamelessly bare form:

> Oh, wondrously tender and passionate disease!
> In you lie my whole life and dear ideal!
> You clasped me in your star-like embrace
> like a mold clasps the earth,
> like rust the battle-wearied dagger!
> You gave me freedom, I am dread and great
> Not with bilious rudeness, nor strength, nor knowledge;
> Covered with ulcers is my panic-stricken tongue,
> And I can infect with my breath alone
> Vestal virgins, old men, helpless children;
> I can reward all with the naked disease.
> I despise life, Nature, and people,
> I laugh at anguish, at grief and tears.
>   (Emel Yanov-Kokhansky)

And also in the following poem, which is extraordinarily hideous even in form:

> Do not enter, you out there!
> Do I not have white legs?
> Do I not have arms that entwine?
> Do not enter, you out there!
> I shall go mad and grow weak
> Behind the sable canopy.
> I shall twine my serpentine arms,

> I shall touch my bare shoulders,
> I shall kiss thy swarthy eyes....
> Do not enter!..
>
> (A. Dobrolyubov)

This same motif stands out distinctly in prose as well:

> What art thou imploring, Bright One? Is it not undivined eyes thou cravest, or the bated breath of passion? Is it not a smile dressed in tears, or the dewy soul of youth?
>
> I shall give thee a virginal body, shameless, bold, legs, intoxicating lips.... Thou hast approached the morning couch, Stern One.
>
> Am I not young? Serpentine arms will intertwine. The pale white night will grow pale from my embraces and will leave the chamber through the window, into the open.
>
> Bright One! I am comfortable.... I am hurt, Bright One! The white night gazeth at thee with fathomless eyes. It doth not leave. Like a widow, the night is sad.... Like a hired mourner, it weepeth. It weepeth over the cemetery morning. I am afraid, Bright One!
>
> (A. Dobrolyubov)

Here Eros is no longer dressed in poetry, no longer hidden or obscured; all the meaning, all the beauty, all the endless torments and joys from which the act of love proceeds, and which (connected with a different kind of poetry and concerns) follow from this act—all that is discarded here; the very face of the beloved person is discarded; this new "poetry" throws a cover upon it, as though it were the face of a patient on the operating table, lest its expression of suffering, horror, and entreaty interfere with something "vitally important" to be carried out here, around it, but without any attention to it. A woman—not only without form but always without name—usually figures in this "poetry," in which the head of the depicted object plays almost as trifling a role as is played by the head of the depicting subject; as we can see, for example, in the following poem (classic in its brevity) whose content is exhausted in one line:

> Oh, cover your pale legs! (Bryusov)

Here the viewpoint on man and, it seems, on all human relations, i.e., on life itself, is not revealed from above, does not come from the face, and is not imbued with meaning, but rises from somewhere below, from the legs, and is imbued with sensations and desires that have nothing in common with meaning.

II

The birthplace of Symbolism and Decadence is, as is well known, France; and for virtually the first time in its history, in this new "poetry," it has come forth not as the expounder of others' ideas and aspirations, but as the guide and mentor in a certain new kind of "tastes." The homeland of Marquis de Sade has clearly shown, at last, what it indisputably excels in among all the civilized nationalities, and it has nothing at all to learn from them in this regard. Suddenly, but with quite unexpected vigor, it expressed where its interests really lay, at a time when it was seemingly embroiled in political, religious, economic, and other controversies, before the eyes of a thrilled and often delighted world. Art is more sensitive than anything else to the future; it discloses more clearly than anything else the innermost workings of our soul. About four years ago, in the so-called "artistic" section of a French exhibition in Moscow, ingenuous Russians, had they been perspicacious enough, could already have read the "Decadence" conveyed—not in leg-obsessed poems devoid of rhyme, meter, and sense—but in a number of paintings without accessories, without settings, without the light of day or night, without garments, but with the invariable depiction of the female body, insofar as it is revealed from the direction of the heels. It made a strange impression on you, just as you were crossing the threshold of the gallery, to see a long row of canvases in which there was a complete absence of any other subjects: Nature was not portrayed, nor the sea, nor mountains, nor the sun, nor flowers, nor street views, nor domestic scenes, but only female figures stretched up in almost the same manner, with "thighs" and other details, with revoltingly pinched faces that stretched up, as it were, before the painters' "artistic imagination."[1] Obviously, for these artists history has died; and even in their favorite "subjects" the face, name, past, and future of man have died; and out of this dead silence, out of this dark non-existence

---

1   *Author's note:* It was related at the exhibition that the sovereign, Alexander III, who visited the exhibition, went to the artistic section first, but no sooner had he reached the door and glanced into the hall than he turned back, not wishing to see that "French art."

protruded—just as for the Decadents of our own day—nothing but "pale legs," the fixed idea of their morbidly disposed imagination.

But the absence of faces, not only intelligent-looking, expressive faces, but simply handsome or young and fresh ones, was not the main peculiarity of this gallery of naked bodies. What struck you here was the labored imagination of these artists, which strove yet failed to express more and more of the sphere of "nakedness." Thus, I remember one painting that portrayed the ocean depths, into which a sunbeam fell; on a closer examination you noticed that some horned shell, stretching upwards and entwining itself with the swirling waters, rose to meet this beam, embraced and absorbed it; on a still closer examination you noticed, with a certain surprise and disgust, that this was not the ocean depths, nor the contorted forms of a seashell reaching upwards, but a convulsively contorted, transparent female body wrapping itself around the beam.

One does not have to be a philosopher of human culture to guess, from looking at this painting, what the literature of the country must have been like during these years. Unfortunately, I have not had the occasion to read anything by Maupassant or Zola, but here is an excerpt from the former's work, as it was presented in a critical article about him (Miss N. L.: "Guy de Maupassant," in *The Russian Herald,* Nov. 1894); here we already enter the sphere of Decadence, although this page was written long before the appearance of this famous "school":

> .... Love, passionate love, is possible only when you do not see the object of your love. To see is to understand, to understand is to despise. You should love a woman drunkenly, as if you were drunk with wine; so drunkenly, that you no longer taste what it is you are drinking. And drink, drink, drink, without catching your breath, day and night.

This (writes the reviewer) is the entry which the hero of the short story made in his diary *before* his marriage; *after* his marriage he continues the diary:

> In marrying her I submitted to the unconscious attraction that drives you to a woman. She is now my wife. While I was only yearning for her in my soul, she seemed to be the embodiment of my unrealizable dream, which was about to come true. But as soon as I clasped her in my embrace I saw in her only a tool that Nature used to defeat my expectations.
> Did she (i.e., my wife) defeat them? No. But she has become hateful to me, so hateful that I cannot touch her without feeling indescribable revulsion of a higher order, revulsion toward sexual union in general, which is so

loathsome that beings *of a higher organization* should conceal this shameful act and speak about it only in a whisper, blushingly . . . .

I can no longer bear the sight of my wife when she comes up to me, embraces me, beckoning with a smile or glance. Only recently it seemed to me that her kiss would transport me to heaven! Once, for a short time, she was ill with a fever, and I could smell in her breath the light, subtle, almost imperceptible odor of decay; I was horror-struck!

Oh, frail body, enchanting living dung! Oh, moving, thinking, speaking, laughing decay, so rosy, seductive, and beautiful, yet so deceptive as the soul itself!

We sense behind these words a degree of physical enervation that precludes the possibility of real intimacy; and this enervation, as we can see from the brief passage above, results not from lavish expenditure of lavish energies, but from the exhausting work of the imagination on "subjects" of a certain type, long before they come near and become accessible *in re*.[2] And so a walking corpse, who believes, however, that he belongs to a race of "more highly organized" beings (see above) continues in the same *Diary:*

> . . . I love flowers like living creatures. I spend days and nights in a greenhouse, where I hide them, just as women in a harem are hidden. I have a greenhouse where no one intrudes except the gardener and me.
>
> I enter it as though it were a place of secret delights. In a high glass gallery I pass first of all between rows of crown-shaped flowers, which rise in steps from the ground to the roof. They send me the first kiss.
>
> These flowers, which decorate the antechamber of my mysterious harem, are my modest servant girls. Pretty and coquettish, they welcome me with a burst of their splendor and fragrance. Occupying eight steps on one side and eight steps on the other, they are so massed together that they appear to be gardens descending from both sides down to my feet. My heart beats excitedly, my eyes light with passion on seeing them, my blood rushes, and my hands tremble with desire to seize them. But I walk on. At the end of this gallery three closed doors are visible. I can choose. I have three harems.

Most often (continues the critic) he goes to the orchids:

> They quiver on their little stalks as if they were going to fly away. Will they fly to me? No, my soul will fly to them and soar above them—the soul of a mysterious male tormented by love.

---

2   *Eds. In re*: Latin for "in reality."

.... Flowers, flowers—in Nature only flowers give forth such wondrous fragrances—these vivid or pale flowers, whose soft hues make my heart beat so wildly and mist my eyes! They are so lovely and tender, so sensitive, half-open, more seductive than a woman's mouth; they are hollow, with pouting, jagged, fleshy lips that are strewn with the germs of life, which arouse in each of them a specific aroma. They, alone in all of Nature, multiply without shame to their inviolate (?) race, diffusing the wondrous scent of their love and their caresses, the fragrance of incomparable flesh that is full of ineffable charm and endowed with an unusual abundance of forms and colors and with the intoxicating allurement of the most diverse aromas.

(*The Russian Herald,* 94 [November] pp. 269-271)

This wedding flight, as it were, to flowers secluded in a greenhouse-harem recalls an analogous event that actually took place in the ancient world, when a certain Greek, inflamed with a similar passion for a marble statue, became so frenzied that once he secretly defiled it. History remembered that event, and the story of it has come down to us; obviously, the pagan Greeks were so astounded by it that they could not pass over it in silence, and not only in conversation and in the public square but also in books; now the imagination of a Christian writer falls to the depths of a similar brutishness, and even lower—to the depths of inanimate Nature, but he not only falls there, he generalizes and legitimizes his fall, couching it in the beauty of literary forms; and finally, he sings a hymn to it to the rapt attention of the "critics" of every land and to the pleasure of an innumerable throng of listeners and readers— only not without detriment to his own health, unfortunately. That, however, is not the main issue.

These fragments from *The Diary,* in their two sections—manlike and animal —represent a vividly expressed cadence of man and his imagination. Before its author got to flowers with fleshy, pouting lips "strewn with the germs of life," while he still preserved a certain semblance of humanity and had not yet fled the society of man, his imagination was active too, and it obeyed the same Law as that obeyed by the imagination of those "artists" of the brush who brought their works to show to the Moscow bigwigs: the same absence of details and accessories; the same absence of a *face* on the subject; the same disregard of history; the same ignorance of Nature; there was neither the bustle of the city nor scenes of family life; neither the family's past nor its present *needs* and *hopes,* hopes of having children, for example. The stern Roman "*Matrimonium liberorum quaerendorum causa*"[3] has died; so too the Biblical "Be fruitful and multiply, fill the earth and possess it," and the evangelical "What therefore God hath joined together let no man put asunder." Man has died and only his pants remain. Straightaway after this the degree of fall is even greater: in painting we saw this cadence in the portrayal of a seashell-woman who absorbed a sunbeam into her body; in belles-lettres—in the guise of a "mystic male" fluttering above womanlike flowers. In both cases the hideous has fallen to the absurd, and we feel no surprise and see nothing new when we read after *that* prose the following lines:

> The denuded moon rises
> In the azure moonlight;
> Sounds soar sleepily,
> Sounds snuggle up to me . . .

Or:

> Corpses illuminated by gas!
> Scarlet ribbon on the sinful bride!
> Oh, shall we go to the window and kiss!

And finally:

> My soul is sick all day,
> My soul is sick from parting,
> My soul is struggling with silence,
> My eyes encounter the shadow.

All these are nothing but "orchids" quivering on their little stalks, as if they were going to fly away. "Will they fly to me? No, my soul will fly to them and soar above them, the soul of a mystic male tormented by love."

Thus, Symbolism and Decadence are not a *separate new* school, which arose in France and spread throughout all of Europe: they represent the end and culmination of a certain other school whose links were very extensive

---

3   *Eds.* Latin: Marriage concluded for the cause of children.

and whose roots go back to the beginning of the modern age. Symbolism, easily deduced from Maupassant, can also be deduced from Zola, Flaubert, and Balzac, from *Ultra-realism* as the antithesis of the previous *Ultra-idealism* (Romanticism and "renascent" Classicism). It is precisely this element of *ultra*—the result of *ultra* manifested in life itself, in its mores, ideas, proclivities, and aspirations—that has wormed into literature and remained there ever since, expressing itself, finally, in such a hideous phenomenon as Decadence and Symbolism. The *ultra* without its referent, exaggeration without the exaggerated object, preciosity of form conjoined with total disappearance of content, and "poetry" devoid of rhyme, meter, and sense—that is what constitutes Decadence.

III

The great self-limitation practiced by man for ten centuries yielded, between the fourteenth and seventeenth centuries, the whole flower of the so-called "Renaissance." The root, usually, does not resemble the fruit in appearance, but there is an undeniable connection between the root's strength and juiciness and the beauty and taste of the fruit. The Middle Ages, it seems, have nothing in common with the Renaissance and are opposite to it in every way; nonetheless, all the abundance and ebullience of human energies during the Renaissance were based not at all on the supposedly "renascent" classical world, nor on the imitated Plato and Virgil, nor on manuscripts torn from the basements of old monasteries, but precisely on those monasteries, on those stern Franciscans and cruel Dominicans, on Saints Bonaventure, Anselm of Canterbury, and Bernard of Clairvaux. The Middle Ages were a great repository of human energies: in the medieval man's asceticism, self-abnegation, and contempt for his own beauty, his own energies, and his own mind, these energies, this heart, and this mind were stored up until the right time. The Renaissance was the epoch of the discovery of this trove: the thin layer of soil covering it was suddenly thrown aside, and to the amazement of following centuries dazzling, incalculable treasures glittered there; yesterday's pauper and wretched beggar, who only knew how to stand on crossroads and bellow psalms in an inharmonious voice, suddenly started to bloom with poetry, strength, beauty, and intelligence. Whence came all this? From the ancient world, which had exhausted its vital powers? From moldy parchments? But did Plato really write his dialogues with the same keen enjoyment with which Marsilio Ficino annotated them? And did the Romans, when reading the Greeks, really experience the same emotions as Petrarch, when, for ignorance of Greek, he could only move his precious manuscripts from place to place, kiss them now and then, and gaze sadly at their incomprehensible text? All these manuscripts, in convenient and accurate editions, lie before us too: why don't they lead us to a "renascence" among *us*? Why didn't the Greeks bring about a "renascence" in Rome? And why didn't Greco-Roman literature produce anything similar to the Italian Renaissance in Gaul and Africa from the second to the fourth century? The secret of the Renaissance of the fourteenth-fifteenth centuries does not lie in ancient literature: this literature was only the spade that threw the soil off the treasures buried underneath; the secret lies in the treasures themselves; in the fact that between the fourth and fourteenth centuries, under the influence of the strict ascetic ideal of mortifying the flesh and restraining the impulses of his spirit, man only stored up his energies and expended nothing. During this great thousand-year silence his soul matured for *The Divine Comedy*; during this forced closing of eyes to the world—an interesting, albeit sinful world—Galileo was maturing, Copernicus, and the school of careful experimentation founded by Bacon; during the struggle with the Moors the talents of Velasquez and Murillo were forged; and in the prayers of the thousand years leading up to the sixteenth century the Madonna images of that century were drawn, images to which we are able to pray but which no one is able to imitate.

From the fourteenth to the nineteenth century we have merely been expending the incalculable treasures discovered then and using up the great supply of energies gathered up to that time. Hence, modern history is the antithesis of the Middle Ages; man no longer wants to keep silent about himself: he hastens to express to others every slightest feeling and every new thought he may have through the medium of colors or sounds and, without fail, by means of the printing press. One might say that just as man studiously effaced himself up to the fourteenth century, so he becomes garrulous once he crosses into that century and all the succeeding ones. Not only what is wise, not only what is noble, but also what is ridiculous, stupid, and hideous in himself he couches in poetry and prose, sets to music, and would very much like, but he is unable, to express in marble and to fix within architectural lines. It is remarkable that architecture—that kind of impersonal art, that form of creation in which the creator is merged with his epoch and people, in which he does not rise above them, nor set apart his own *I* on their background—declines, as soon as we enter modern history, and not once during this period does it rise to the sublime or the beautiful.

Architecture is too selfless a form of art, and furthermore, modern man is absolutely at a loss how, by what means, he might be able to feel selfless. He is becoming more and more unaccustomed to praying: prayer is the turning of the soul to God; his soul, however, turns only to itself. Everything that constrains and constricts him, that hinders the independent display of his own *I*—be this *I* base or noble, profound or shallow—becomes insufferable for him; in the sixteenth century he throws off the Church, saying "*I* am the Church"; in the eighteenth century he throws off the State, saying "*I* am the State"; he proclaims the rights of this *I* (revolution); he poeticizes the depths of this *I* ("Faust" and "Werther," Byron); he says that the whole world too is but the reflection of this *I* (the philosophy of German idealism)—until this *I*, extolled, bedecked, and protected by legislation, on the ruins of all the great unifying institutions: Church, State, and Family—defines itself, towards the end of the nineteenth century, in this unexpectedly brief, yet expressive wish:

Oh, cover your pale legs!

From the exclamation point closing the line and from the empty margins surrounding it we conclude that on this page a certain "subject" has fully expressed all of his inner content.

IV

The religion of this *I*, the poetry of this *I,* and the philosophy of the same *I* that from Poggio and Felelfo to Byron and Goethe produced a number of works astonishing for their profundity and brilliance have finally exhausted its content; and in the poetry of Decadence we see the rapid falling away of the empty shell of this *I*. We remarked previously about the exaggeration without the exaggerated object, and about the precious style without the subject of this preciosity, which characterize this poetry—this is so in regard to its form; in regard to its content Decadence is above all hopeless egoism. The world, as an object of love, of interest, even as the object of indignation *or* contempt, has disappeared from this "poetry"; the world has disappeared, not only as an object exciting some reaction in this vapid *I*, but also as a spectator and Possible judge of this *I*; it is not even *present:*

> These are oleanders on the ice,
> This is the jacket of romances without words.

That is what has remained of the world in the uncertain, unloving, and incurious recollection of the ravaged and fallen *I*. One can scarcely find a proper noun in all this literature—the name of a city, or the designation of the locality and hour: before the empty *I* pass purely abstract visions, which do not catch onto any existing reality and do not contain anything of the real world, except isolated words, names of objects, and fragments of scenes that alternate capriciously; among these scenes, objects, and words seized by an uncertain recollection from the world of reality and rushing on without purpose or sense occur thoughts, lost and abandoned, as it were, thoughts without development and even without any necessary connection:

> I see the phantoms of longings;
> A half-forgotten track leads
> *The dogs of secret desire*
> Into the depths of forgetful forests,
> Packs of lilac-colored fantasies race along,
> *And yellow arrows—reproaches—*
> Slay the deer of mendacious dreams.

The italicized lines are thoughts interjected, as it were, into scenes of reality to which they have no relation; these very scenes, however, are not reality but fragments of a recollection about it, a recollection that is not very firm, little necessary in itself, and, it seems, little necessary to the person recollecting. We observe in this torrent of incoherence a lack of regularity in the subject himself; the *I* has fallen to pieces after struggling for three centuries against the great objective institutions and dissolving them with its subjectivism and rejecting in them any law that was sacred and binding on itself.

There is no reason to think that Decadence—obviously an historical phenomenon of great inevitability and significance—has confined itself to poetry; we should expect in the more or less distant future the Decadence of philosophy and finally the Decadence of morality, politics, and forms of communal life. To a certain extent Nietzsche can already be considered the Decadent of human thought—at least to the extent that Maupassant, in certain "final touches" of his art, can be considered the Decadent of human emotion. Like Maupassant, Nietzsche ended in madness; and in Nietzsche, just as in Maupassant, the cult of the *I* loses all restraining limits: the world, history, and the human being with his toils and legitimate demands have disappeared equally from the works of both; both were "mystic males" to a considerable degree, only one of them preferred to "flutter" above "quivering orchids," whereas the other liked to sit inside a cave or upon a mountaintop and proclaim a new religion to mankind in his capacity as the reborn "Zarathustra." The religion of the "superman," he explained. But all of them, including Maupassant, were already "supermen" in that they had absolutely no need of mankind and mankind had absolutely no need of them. On this new type of *nisus formativus*[4] of human culture, so to speak, we should expect to see great oddities, great hideousness, and perhaps great calamities and dangers.

A few more words on Decadence: we can genetically connect with very delicate threads the senseless and hideous Symbolism of our day with such an intellectually deep and resplendently beautiful creation as "Faust." They both expressed and still do express the notion of "free humanity," only in one this notion lies at the source of its vibrant energy, while in the other it has reached the end and is depleted of energy. But the essence of "freedom" and "humanity" is equally the main and characteristic feature of both. What is more, the second part of *Faust*, which proceeds from the same subjective spirit as the first part, but only when the creative energies of this spirit are exhausted, displays all the features of Symbolism and Decadence, but only in the structure of the whole, the parts of which are just as incoherent and fancifully joined together as the lines of Symbolist poems. In *Faust* we already find a few "enameled latania ... ." We mean to say that Symbolism and

---

4   *Eds.* Latin: a striving or impulse towards procreation.

Decadence—the negative attitude to which is indisputable to everyone except the "participants"—are genetically connected with everything brilliant and sublime created by the "unbound personality" during this period of time, from the Renaissance up to the development of electrical engineering; contrariwise, the border which they cannot cross is laid down where man understood that he was always "bound." The great continent of history, the continent of real deeds, practical needs, and more than all that, of *received* religion and the *established* Church—that is whose shore this stinking monster can never crawl into, that is where we are fleeing to from it, that is where man can always save himself. Where the monastery wall rises *this* surge of the faithless waves of history—no matter how strong it may become and how far it may spread around—will stop and fall back.

Vladimir Solovyov

Reviews of Russian Symbolists (1894)

Translated by Ronald E. Peterson

1st Issue. Valery Bryusov and A. L. Miropolsky (Moscow, 1894, 44pp.)

This notebook has undoubted merits: it does not burden the reader with its dimensions and partly entertains with its contents. The pleasure begins with the epigraph, taken by Valery Bryusov from the French decadent Stéphane Mallarmé:

> Une dentelle s'abolit
> Dans le doute du jeu supreme.
>
> [Lace is abolished
> In the doubt of the highest game.]

And here is Bryusov's Russian "prologue":

> Pink colors die down
> In the pale sheen of the moon;

Tales about spring's suffering
Freeze in the ice floes.
From the end to the beginning
Dreams are wrapped in mourning,
And their garlands are twined
With the silence of its coloring.
The roses of harmonies don't bloom.
In the flowerbeds of emptiness
Under the rays of a young daydream.
But through the windows of incoherent dreams,
Scattered daydreams
Won't see diamond stars.

The words, "the roses of harmonies in the flowerbeds of emptiness," and "windows of incoherent dreams" can be seen as at least symbolic, but they are also a rather true definition of this type of poetry. However, actual Russian "Symbolism" is represented rather weakly in this little collection. Except for the poems directly designated as translations, of the remaining poems, a good half are clearly inspired by other poets, and not even Symbolist poets at that. The one, for example, that begins with the lines:

She and I met accidentally
And I shyly dreamed about her,

and ends:

There's an old tale that was once
Condemned to be young forever.

undoubtedly came from Heine, although they are transplanted in the "flower bed of emptiness." The following:

An indistinct dream climbs the steps
It slightly opens the door of the moment—

an involuntary parody of Fet. His poems without verbs have inspired:

> Starry, passionless sky,—

but are we to take such a lack of successful imitating as originality?

> The stars gently whispered—

is a free translation from Heine.

> Boy your little head—

idem.

And here is a poem which I would have equal difficulty calling original or imitative:

> Little eyes sparkling with tears
> And little lips, pitifully pursed,
> And little cheeks burn with caresses
> And curls mussed and tangled—etc.

In any case, is it really Symbolism to enumerate, in diminutive forms the different parts of the human organism, and even ones that are familiar to everybody?

I have a different type of objection to Mr. Valery Bryusov's "conclusion":

> Golden fairies
> In a satin garden!
> When will I find
> The icy avenues?
> Silvery splashes of
> Infatuated naiads,
> Where are the jealous boards
> That will block your way.
> Lit by fire,
> The dusk has frozen
> Over the flight of fancies.

> Beyond the gloom of curtains
> There are funeral urns,
> And an azure vault of
> Deceitful stars doesn't wait.

Despite the "icy avenues in a satin garden," the subject of these verses is as clear as it is reprehensible. Attracted by a "flight of fancies," the author peeked into wooden bathing cabins, where persons of the female gender whom he calls "fairies" and "naiads" were bathing. But is it possible to smooth over such vile acts with magnificent words? And this is what Symbolism leads to in conclusion! We will hope at least that the "jealous boards" were up to their task. In the opposite case, the "golden fairies" would have had to pour water on our shameless Symbolist with the "incomprehensible vases," which are called wash tubs by common folk who use them to wash their legs in bathing cabins.

It is impossible to pronounce a general judgment of Mr. Valery Bryusov without knowing his age. If he is no more than fourteen, then he could become a rather good versifier, or maybe not. If this person is a grownup, then of course all literary hopes are out of place. I have nothing to say about Mr. Miropolsky. Of the ten small pages that belong to him, eight are taken up by prose fragments. But reading decadent prose is a task greater than my powers. The "flowerbeds of emptiness" would be tolerable only when the "roses of harmonies" are growing in them.

2nd Issue. Pub. by V. A. Maslov (Moscow, 1894)

The species of beings called Russian Symbolists has as its chief feature extremely quick reproduction. Just last summer there were only two, now there are a whole ten. Here are their names in alphabetical order: A. Branin, Valery Bryusov, V. Darov, Erl. Martov, A. L. Miropolsky, N. Novich, K. Sozontov, Z. Fuchs, and two more, one of whom is concealed under the letter M, and the other under three asterisks. I would be prepared to think that this species reproduces by arbitrary conception (*generatio aequivoca*), but such a hypothesis will hardly be accepted by exact science. Russian Symbolism, however, is enriched for now more by melodious names than melodious works. In the second issue, a total of eighteen original poems have been included; with ten authors that comes out to one and a fraction apiece (1.8 or

1 and 4/5). The reader will agree that my critical method for now is distinguished by its strongly scientific character, which leads to completely indisputable results. I would like to keep the same method for evaluating the qualitative merits of the Russian Symbolists, but this is much more difficult; you cannot get by with just arithmetic here. It is necessary to establish common principles or norms of artistic activity and check the given work by the postulates that come out of them.

Unfortunately, this solely scientific method has one inconvenience: it would demand many years of study for me and it would have to be presented by me in many volumes, but what is required of me is a little review of a little notebook with verse of problematic merit. I'll have to reject the scientific method, but on the other hand, I would not want to be subjected to a justified reproach for being subjectively arbitrary and tendentious. However, is there not really any middle path between strict science and personal impression? There is, no doubt. Without ascending to unconditional principles, it is possible to take the intention of a criticized author or artist, instead of a personal opinion, as the norm for judging. Thus, for example, when a painter personally writes: "Behold—a lion!" on his picture—while anyone can see that a poorly drawn dog is there, and the painter's intention to depict a lion has, in his realization, been limited to the yellow color of dog's fur, then every witness to this failure, without falling into subjectivism, can call the picture unsatisfactory. For, independent of personal opinions, it is clear from the essence of things that neither a yellow color nor a poor drawing are sufficient by themselves to make a dog a lion. This method of judging, based on the objective difference between the two mammals, I call a relatively scientific method. Its application to Russian Symbolists is made easier because they have seen to finding the most definite form for expressing their intentions. In the introduction, Mr. Bryusov explains that the poetry which he and his comrades serve is the poetry of hints. Following our relatively scientific method, we will see how representative of the poetry of hints the poems of the Russian Symbolists really are.

> The strings rust
> Under a damp hand,
> Dreams grow mute
> And are covered with gloom.

This is the beginning and concluding stanza of a little poem by Mr. Miropolsky, which opens this anthology. Here, reference is made, with exaggerated clarity, to that sad and hardly interesting fact that the guitarist depicted by the author suffers from a well-known pathological phenomenon. There are no hints and there is no poetry here. The first verse, "the strings rust," contains another reference, but again a clear reference, not a hint, to Mr. Miropolsky's low level of literacy.

The second poem, "I am waiting," consists almost entirely of repeating two verses: "A resounding heart beats within my breast," and "My dear friend, come, come!" What is unclear here, where are the hints? It's easier to notice an excessive desire for clarity here, for the poet explains that his heart beats in his breast—so that no one thinks that it beats in his head or his abdominal cavity.

Mr. Valery Bryusov, the same one who described his reprehensible peeking in women's bathing cabins in the first issue of Russian Symbolists, now depicts his own bathing. This is of course harmless, but the bad thing is that Mr. Bryusov says such words about his own bath that clearly, without any hints, demonstrate the author's not completely normal mood. We warned him that the indulgence of base passions, even under the guise of Symbolism, will not lead to a good end. Alas! Our premonitions have come true earlier than expected! Judge for yourself:

> The midnight moisture in the silvery dust
> Intoxicates tired daydreams with rest,
> And in the supple silence of a river sarcophagus
> A great man hears no slander.

To call a river a sarcophagus, and oneself a great man—this is a quite clear sign (and not just a hint) of a sick condition.

> The corpse of a woman, rotting and putrid,
> The great steppe, a cast iron sky...
> And a long moment, resurrected by mockery,
> Rises with reproaching laughter.
> A diamond dream... A burnt sketch above...
> And aroma, and tears, and dew...
> The rotting and putrid corpse is abandoned
> And a raven has pecked out its eyes.

In this poem, signed by Z. Fuchs (we will hope that the Z. stands for Zakhar not Zinaida), it's possible, I think, to find a hint, only not a poetic one, but a hint that three councillors in the Tambov assembly were, perhaps, not quite correct in their opinion, that they should direct it not to peasants who had not finished their grammar school, but to certain versifiers who call themselves Symbolists. However—

> *In jene Sphären wag' ich nicht zu streben...*[1]

I think that Mr. Fuchs has sufficiently punished himself by appearing in print with such a work. Nevertheless the impression produced by the poem of this Symbolist is so strong that I do not have enough spiritual calm for a relatively scientific analysis of further Symbolist pearls. And our Symbolists announce three forthcoming new editions on the last page, one of which is called *Les chefs d'oeuvre*. We will postpone final judgment until the appearance of these "chefs d'oeuvre," but now for the sake of fairness we will note that in the notebook discussed there is one poem that reminds us of real poetry:

> Child, look! there at the end of the avenue
> The bushes of nighttime beauty are spread...
> The fairies of the spring night have taken their image...
>   You did not understand my melancholy!
>
> The ray of the sun from dawn to night
> Pours passionate spells on the sleepy flowers...
> In vain he tries to look them in the eye just once...
>   You don't understand my melancholy!
>
> In the evening, hiding behind the mountain
> With the burning melancholy of a deceived dream,
> Powerless, he sees them kissing the moon...
>   You'll understand my melancholy, for sure!

---

1   *Eds.* "I dare not aspire to those spheres." A quote from *Faust*.

***Russian Symbolists.*—Summer, 1895. (Moscow, 1895, 52pp.)**
In the preface to this new issue, the young sportsmen who call themselves "Russian Symbolists" have "found it necessary to explain their attitude" toward the critics. In the opinion of Mr. Bryusov and Co., the majority of their critics were completely unprepared for this important task, and those who were prepared turned out to be malefactors. Such is the reviewer for *Vestnik Evropy*. "The reviews of Vladimir Solovyov," the Symbolists write, "aroused some interest in their time. Serious remarks actually pop up in them (e.g., about the imitativeness of many of Mr. Bryusov's poems in the first issue), but Mr. Vl. Solovyov was carried away by the desire to amuse the public, which led him to a number of witticisms of doubtful value and to a deliberate distortion of the sense of the poems. We say 'deliberate': Mr. Vl. Solovyov, of course, should easily catch the poet's most delicate hints because he has himself written Symbolist poems, as for example, 'Why words...' (*Vestnik Evropy*, 1892, No. 10)."

Why, however, are the Symbolists so sure that this poem—whether Symbolist or not—belongs to the author of the reviews. The poem is signed "Vladimir Solovyov," but the reviews are designated by the letters Vl. S., which could perhaps stand for Vladislav Syrokomlya or Vlasy Semyonov. I do not have to answer for Mr. Vladimir Solovyov and the accusation of his printing a Symbolist poem in *Vestnik Evropy*. But the accusation that I deliberately distorted the sense of the poems of Mr. Bryusov and Co., I, Vlasy Semyonov, have to explain that even if I were inspired by hell's own spite, even then it would be impossible for me to distort the sense of those poems—because of the complete lack of sense in them. With their new issue, the Symbolists have placed this matter beyond all doubt. Well, just let someone try to distort the sense of such a work:

> The shadow of uncreated creations
> Sways in a dream
> Like fans of latanias
> On an enamel wall.
> Violet hands
> On an enamel wall
> Outline sounds sleepily
> In ringing-sonorous silence.
> And transparent kiosks
> In ringing-sonorous depths

> Grow up like sparkles
> In the azure moonlight,
> The naked moon rises
> In the azure moonlight;
> Sounds flutter sleepily
> Sound caress me,
> Secrets of created creations
> Caress me with a caress
> And the shadow of latanias quivers
> On an enamel wall.

If I wrote that it is not only indecent for a naked moon to rise in the azure moonlight, but also completely impossible, since the moon (*mesyats*) and the moon (*luna*) are two names for one and the same thing, then would that really be a "deliberate distortion of the sense?"

Well then, take this "chef d'oeuvre":

> The heart's ray from the silver of agitation
> Rises over the space of hoar frost,
> And, shaking, sounds the crystal of lightning
> And it floats, splashed with foam.
> It floats... like a moaning pouring
> It beckons the ice of the stars from the abyss...
> A star sleeps, distant in the proud calm,
> A star twinkles and sleeps.

Or another:

> Colonnades of songs hung in the air,
> And the crystal of accord rings like a fountain,
> White masses in the azure
> And a matte granite in the rays of mist died down.
> The glow of languors beats like foam in thoughts,
> Dear features flash like lightning,
> Resonant bridges bent over like an arch,

Bright garlands entwined the facades,
The aromatic gleam of Carrara's marble...
And serenades resound victoriously and disappear,
And an inspired splash spreads an echo.

Some Symbolists lessen the difficulty of writing senseless poems with a rather successful device: having written one line, they then turn it inside out—and a new one appears:

Over the dark ravine,
The ravine dark,
Like an immodest picture,
A picture immodest,
Hung mists,
Mists hung,
Like deceits,
Deceits without thought,
Without thought or connection
In a passionless story.
In a story passionless,
In a story obscure,
Where the pale colors
Of a sad ending
Are sad like the tales
Of a homeland distant.

And here is a poem in which there is neither sense nor rhyme—as if it were written to illustrate the phrase—*ni rime, ni raison* [neither rhyme nor reason]:

Cadavers, lit by gas!
A vermillion ribbon on a sinful bride!
Oh! we're going to the window to kiss!
Do you see how pale the dead people's faces are?
This is a hospital, where children are in mourning...
This is oleanders on ice...

> This is the cover of Romances without words
> The moon isn't visible through the windows, dear.
> Our souls are a flower in your boutonniere.

The Symbolists rebuke people for being carried away by the desire to amuse the public, but they can see that this enthusiasm only leads me to simply reproducing their own pearls.

I should note that one poem in this collection has a clear, indisputable sense. It's very short—just one line:

> Oh, cover your pale legs.

For complete clarity, I would say, "For otherwise you'll catch cold," should be added, but even without this, the advice of Mr. Bryusov, evidently directed to a person suffering from anemia, is the most intelligent work of all Symbolist literature, not only Russian, but foreign as well. Of the examples of poems translated for the present issue, the following masterpiece by the famous Maeterlinck deserves attention:

> My soul has been ill all day,
> My soul is sick of farewells.
> My soul is struggling with silence.
> My eyes meet a shadow
> And under the knout of reminiscences
> I see the specters of desire.
> A half-forgotten track leads
> Dogs of secret desire.
> In the depths of forgetful forests
> Packs of lilac dreams rush by,
> And yellow arrows—reproaches—
> Punish the deer of false dreams.
> Alas, Alas! desires are everywhere
> Returned dreams are everywhere,
> And breath is too blue...
> The image of the moon on the heart grows dim.

Perhaps "a dog of secret desire has barked in the heart" of another stern reader long ago—exactly that desire that authors and translators of such poems would, in the future, write not only "under the knout of reminiscences" but also "under the recollection of the knout . . ." But my own critical pack is more distinguished by "friskiness" than by "spite," and the "blue breath" evoked in me the orange desire to the lilac composition of yellow verse, and the multicolored peacock of vainglory prompts me to share with the public three examples of my gris-de-perl, vert-de-mer and feuille-morte inspiration. Now at least Mr. Bryusov and Co. have the real right to accuse me of printing Symbolist poems.

    I.
Vertical horizons
In chocolate skies,
Like half-mirror dreams
In laurel-cherry forests.
The specter of a fire-breathing ice floe
Has died out in the bright twilight,
And a hyacinth Pegasus stands,
Not hearing me.
Immanent mandragoras
Rustled in the rushes,
And rough-decadent
Doggerel in wilting ears.

    II.
Above the green hill,
Above the hill green,
Above the couple in love,
Above the in love couple,
A star shines at noon,
At noon it shines,
Although no one ever
Notices this star.
But a wavy mist,

But a mist wavy,
From a radiant land it,
From a land radiant,
It slips through between the clouds,
Above a dry wave,
A motionless flyer
And even with a dual moon.

III.

In the skies church chandeliers burn
And below—darkness.
Did you go to him, or didn't you go?
Say yourself!
But don't tease the hyena of suspicion,
The mice of melancholy!
Don't look at how the leopards of vengeance
Sharpen their teeth!
And don't call the owl of wisdom
In this night!
Donkeys of patience and elephants of meditation
Ran away.
You alone have given birth to a crocodile
With your fate here.
Let the chandeliers burn in the sky
In the grave there is—darkness.

Marina Tsvetaeva

Downpour of Light: Poetry of Eternal Courage (1922)

Translated by Angela Livingstone

Before me is a book by Pasternak, *My Sister—Life*. In its khaki dustcover, recalling at once the free distributions of the South and the scanty alms of the North, bleak and boorish and covered in a kind of funereal bruising, it could be an undertaker's catalogue or the last gamble of some croaking publisher. But only once did I see it like that: in the first moment of getting it, before I'd time to open it. Since then it hasn't been closed. My guest of two days, I carry it with me round all the spaces of Berlin: the classic Linden, the magical Underground (no accidents, while it's in my hands!), I've been taking it to the Zoo (to get acquainted), I take it to dinner at my boarding-house, and—finally—I wake at the first ray of sun with it lying wide open on my chest. So, not two days—two years! I've the right of long acquaintance to say a few words about it.

Pasternak. Who is Pasternak? ("Son of the artist"—I'll leave that out.) Not quite an Imagist, not quite... Anyway, one of the new ones... Ah, yes, Ehrenburg is strenuously proclaiming him. Yes, but you know Ehrenburg with his there and back rebellion!... And it seems he hasn't even any books to his name...

Yes, ladies and gentlemen, this is his first book (1917)—and isn't it telling that in our time, when a book that ought to be written in 1927 is already squandered in 1917, Pasternak's book, written in 1917, arrives five years late. And what a book! As if he'd deliberately let everyone else say all they had to say, then at the very last moment, with a gesture of bewilderment, he takes a notebook from his pocket: "Well actually I . . . though I can't guarantee anything . . ." Pasternak, let me be your guarantor to the West—for the moment—till your "Life" appears here. I declare I'll vouch for it with all my non-demonstrable assets. Not because you need it, but from sheer cupidity: it's a precious thing to take part in such a destiny!

I'm reading Pasternak's poems for the first time. (I have heard them, orally, from Ehrenburg, but thanks to the rebellion that is in me too—no, the gods forgot to drop the gift of all-embracing love into my cradle!—thanks to an age-old jealousy, a total inability to love in twos, I quietly dug my heels in: "Maybe they're even works of genius, but I'll do without them.") With Pasternak himself I've no more than a nodding acquaintance: three or four fleeting encounters. Almost wordless ones, as I never want anything new to happen. I heard him once, with other poets, in the Polytechnic Museum. He spoke in a toneless voice and forgot nearly all the lines. The way he was out of his element on the stage reminded me strongly of Blok. There was an impression of painful concentration, one wanted to give him a push, like a carriage that won't go—"Get a *move* on . . ."—and as not a single word came across (just mutterings, like some bear waking up), one kept thinking impatiently: "Lord, why does he torment himself and us like this!"

Pasternak's outward being is splendid: there's something in his face of both the Arab and the Arab's horse—alert, watchful, listening, ready to break into a run at any moment! His eyes' enormous sideways glance, again horse-like, wild and shy. (An orb, not an eye.) An impression of always listening to something, incessantly watching, then suddenly he'll burst out into speech—usually with something primordial, as if a rock had spoken or an oak. When he speaks (in conversation) it's as if he were breaking an immemorial silence. And not only in conversation—I can say the same of his verse, and with far more experience to back me. Pasternak doesn't live in his words, as a tree doesn't live in its obvious foliage but in its root (a secret). Beneath the whole book—like some vast passage beneath the Kremlin—lies a silence.

> Silence, you are the best thing
> Of all that I have heard . . .

As much a book of silences as of chirpings.

Now, before I speak of his book (this series of blows and rebounds), a word about the wires which carry the voice—his poetic gift. I think: this gift must be enormous, since the enormous essence comes over whole. The gift is clearly equal to the essence—a very rare case, a miracle, for nearly every book by a poet makes us sigh: "With *such* potentialities . . .", or (immeasurably less often): "Well, at least *something* gets across . . ." No, God spared Pasternak this, and Pasternak spared us. He is unique and indivisible. His verse is the formula of his essence. The divine case of "couldn't be done any other way." Wherever there may be a dominance of "form" over "content," or of "content" over "form," no essence ever set foot. And you can't copy him: only garments can be copied. You'd have to be born as another him.

Of the demonstrable treasures in Pasternak (rhythms, meters, and so on) others will speak in their turn—and doubtless with no less feeling than I when I speak of the *non*-demonstrable treasures.

That is the job of poetry specialists. My specialty is Life.

My Sister—Life! The first thing I did, when I'd borne it all from the first blow to the last, was spread my arms out wide, so that the joints all cracked. I was caught in it as in a downpour.

Downpour: the whole sky onto my head, plumb-down, pouring vertically and pouring slantingly—a drench, a draught, a quarrel of rays of light with rays of rain—and you don't count here: once you're caught in it, grow!

A downpour of light.

Pasternak is a major poet, at the moment bigger than any other: most present poets *have been*, some *are*, he alone *will be*. For in reality he isn't yet: a babbling, a chirping, a clashing—he is all Tomorrow!—the choking cry of a baby, and this baby is the World. A choking. A gasping. Pasternak doesn't speak, he hasn't time to finish speaking, he's wholly exploding—as if there weren't room in his chest: a-ah! He doesn't yet know our words; it all seems to come from an island, childhood, the Garden of Eden, and it doesn't make sense—and knocks you over. At three this is common and is called "a child," at twenty-three it is uncommon and is called "a poet." (Oh, equality, equality! How many God had to rob, even down to the seventh generation, just to create one Pasternak like this!)

Forgetting himself, beside himself, he'll sometimes wake up suddenly, and thrusting his head through the winter-window (into life, with a small "l")—but wonder of wonders! instead of the three-year-old's illumined dome it's the crankish cap of the Marburg philosophers—in a sleepy voice, from his garret heights, he'll call down into the yard to the children:

> Tell my, my dears, what
> Millennium is it out there?

You can be sure he won't hear the answer. Let me return to Pasternak's childlikeness. It isn't that Pasternak is a child (for then he would grow up not into dawns but into forty-year-old repose, the lot of all earthborn children!), not: Pasternak is an infant, but: the world is an infant within him. Pasternak belongs more to the very first day of creation—the first rivers, first dawns, first storms. He is created *before* Adam.

I'm afraid, too, that my helpless effusions may convey only one thing: Pasternak's gaiety. Gaiety. Let me think. Yes, the gaiety of an explosion, an avalanche, a stab, the sheerest discharging of all vital fibers and forces, a kind of white-heat which you might—from a distance—take to be just a white page.

I'm still thinking: what is *not* in Pasternak? (For if everything were in him he'd be life, and then he himself would not be. Only through a "no" can we fix the existence of a "yes"; something distinct.) I listen for an answer: the spirit of gravity! Gravity is for him only a new form of action, something to be thrown off. You'll more likely see him hurling down an avalanche than sitting somewhere in a snowbound hut watching over its deadly thud. He will never wait for death: far too impatient and eager, he'll throw himself into it, head-first, chest-first, everything first that persists and outstrips. Pasternak cannot be robbed. Beethoven's "Durch Leiden—Freuden."[1]

The book is dedicated to Lermontov. (To a brother?) The illumined to the darkened. A natural gravitation: the general pull toward the precipice: precipitate. Pasternak and Lermontov. Related yet thrusting apart, like two wings.

Pasternak is the most penetrable poet, and hence the most penetrating. Everything beats into him. (Evidently, there's justice even in inequality: thanks to you, a unique poet, more than one human dome is delivered from celestial thunders!) A blow—a rebound. And this rebound's thousand-fold lightning speed: the thousandmound echo of all his Caucasuses. No time to understand? (Which is why, most often in the first second, but often at the last as well, there is bewilderment: "What? What's going on?" "Nothing! It's gone!")

Pasternak is all wide-open—eyes, nostrils, ears, lips, arms. Before him there was nothing. Doors all swing off their hinges: into Life! Nonetheless, more than anyone else he needs to be opened up. (A Poetry of Intentions.) Thus you understand Pasternak in spite of Pasternak, by following some latest track, the latest of all. Lightning-like, he is lightning to all experience-burdened skies. (A storm is the sky's only exhalation, as the sky is the storm's only chance of *being*, its sole arena!)

Sometimes he is knocked down: life's pressure through the suddenly flung-open door is stronger than his stubborn brow. Then he falls—in bliss—on his back, and is more effective in his knocked-down state than all jockeys and couriers from Poetry, panting this very moment in full gallop over the barriers.[2]

---

1 Eds. "Through suffering—delights."
2 *Author's note:* The following two facts turned up at the last moment: (1) *My Sister—Life* is *not* his first book; (2) the title of his first book is neither more nor less than *Over the Barriers*. In any event, in *My Sister—Life* this barrier has been—taken.

A flash of illumination: why, he's simply the beloved of the gods. No, a more luminous illumination: not simply, and not the beloved! The *unbeloved*, one of those youths who once heaped Pelion on Ossa.

Pasternak is spendthrift. An outflow of light. An inexhaustible outflow of light. In him is made manifest the law of the year of famine: Waste, and you won't want. So we are not anxious for *him*, but we may reflect, about *ourselves*, being confronted with his essence: "Who is able to contain this, let him contain it."

Enough choking. Now for a sober and sensible attempt. (No need to worry: he will still be there in the clearest light of day!) By the way, a word on the element of light in Pasternak's poetry. Photo-graphy (light-writing), I would call it. A poet of *lightnesses* (as there are, for instance, poets of darknesses.) Light. Eternal courage. Light in space, light in movement, gaps (draughts) of light, explosions of light—very banquetings of light. He is flooded and whelmed. Not just with the sun, but with all that radiates—and for Pasternak everything gives off rays.

And so, having worked my way out at last from the dreamy eddies of commentary—out into reality, onto the sober shoal of propositions and quotations!

1. Pasternak and everyday life.
2. Pasternak and day.
3. Pasternak and rain.

Pasternak and Everyday Life

Byt ["everyday life"]. A heavy word. Almost like *byk* ["bull"]. I can only bear it when it's followed by "of nomads." *Byt* is an oak, and under the oak (around it) a bench, and on the bench a grandfather who was yesterday a grandson, and a grandson who will tomorrow be a grandfather. Solid, stifling, ineluctable. You almost forget that the oak, as a tree sacred to Zeus, is honored more often than others by Zeus' favor, lightning. And it's just when we are completely forgetting this that there come to our rescue, at the very last second, like lightning striking our oaken brows—Byron, Heine, Pasternak.

The first thing to strike us in Pasternak's verse, an unbroken chain of first things, is everyday life. Its abundance, its detail, its—"prosiness." Tokens not just of the day, but of the hour!

I fling the book open—"To the Memory of the Demon."

> A yard or so from the window,
> Plucking the woolen threads of a burnous,
> He swore by the ice of steep places:
> Sleep on, my girl, but I . . . return as avalanche!

Further, in the poem "My Sister—Life":

> That in the thunder eyes and lawns are lilac,
> And the horizon breathes moist mignonette,
> Or that in May when you in transit scan
> Timetables on a branch-line to Kamyshin . . .

(I'm giving the accompanying lines on purpose, to establish the context.)

Further, about a fence:

> Unforgettable the more
> For dust distending it,
> For wind uncasing spore
> To cast about on burdocks.

About the wind:

> Wind attempts to raise
> The rose's head, requested

Thereto by lips, hair, shoes,
Familiar names and hemlines.

About a house in the country:

Still the woods are ours, for porch;
Moon's fire behind the pines, for stove;
And like an apron hanging out, fresh laundered,
A thundercloud that mutters, drying out.

About the steppe:

Mist from all quarters is a sea about us
As thistle-patches check us, catch at socks . . .

Just a moment! "The choice of words—it's all for the sake of repeating the 'ch' . . ." But ladies and gentlemen, has none of you ever had burrs biting into your socks? Especially in childhood when we're all in short clothes. True, it isn't "burr" here but "thistle-patch." But isn't "thistle-patch" better? (For its rapacity, tenacity and wolfishness?)

Further:

In the gutters
Like sleeves of damp shirts
Branches went limp . . .

From the same poem:

In the powder stillness
Sodden, like an overcoat . . .

(This poem is "A Still More Sultry Dawn." My fingers itch to quote it in full, just as they do to tear to bits all these thoughts on the subject and send *My Sister— Life* herself around the bookstalls of the West. Alas, I've not enough hands!)

Further:

> The mills have the look of a fishing-village:
> Grizzled nets, corvettes...

Then, in the tea-room:

> Even in the nights they flow,
> Flies off dozens, pairs and portions,
> Off the wild convolvulus,
> Off the poet's turbid book,
> Like delirium from the pen...

Approaching Kiev by train:

> Approaching Kiev—sands
> And spattered tea
> Dried on to hot temples
> Burning through all the classes...

(Tea that has already turned into sweat, and dried. A Poetry of Intentions! "Burning through all the classes"—third-class carriages are hottest of all! This quatrain contains all the Soviet "hunt for bread.")

"At Home":

> The turban slips from the sun:
> Time for renewing towels
> (One soaks in the pit of a pail).
>
> In town—the discoursing of membranes,
> Shuffle of flowerbeds and dolls...

Then, on the eyelids of a sleeping woman:

> Dear and deathly apron,
> And the pulsing temple . . .
> Sleep on, Queen of Sparta,
> It is early still, still damp . . .

(The eyelid: an apron to protect a feast from dust, the magnificent feast of the eye!) Then, in the poem "Summer":

> The small rain stamped its feet at the doors.
> There came up a smell of wine-corks.
> So smelled the dust. And such was the smell of the weeds.
> And if you look into it closely
> That was the smell of all the gentry's screeds
> About equality and brotherhood.

(Smell of young wine: of storms! Isn't the whole of the *Serment du Jeu de Paume*[3] in this?)

And now, ladies and gentlemen, the final quotation, which seems to contain the whole solution to Pasternak and everyday life:

> When, towards the well-head rushes
> The whirlwind, anguish, pausing in mid-passage
> The storm applauds our household management
> —What more do you ask for?

Why nothing! It seems not even God has the right to ask more from a storm!

Now let us think it over. The presence of everyday life seems proved. Now, what shall we do with it? Or rather, what does Pasternak do with it and what does it do with him? First of all, he sees it clearly: he'll grasp it and let it go. Everyday life, to Pasternak, is like the earth to a footstep: a moment's restraint and a pulling away. In his work (check by the quotations) it's almost always in movement: a windmill, a carriage, the vagrant smell of fermenting wine, the

---

3   *Eds.* French: the Tennis Court Oath.

discourse of membranes, the shuffling of flower-beds, spattered tea—I'm not having to hunt for examples! Check for yourselves. In his poems even sleep is in movement—a pulsing temple!

Everyday life as inertia, as furniture, as an oak (a dining-room of oak, as advertised, which poets so often repanel in Paul and Catherine rosewood), everyday life as an oak won't be found here at all. His everyday life is in the open air. Not settled, but in the saddle.

Now about the prosiness. There's a lot to say here—it's bursting out! But I'll give way to what's bursting out even more strongly: Pasternak himself:

> He sees his neighbors celebrating weddings,
> How they get roaring drunk and sleep it off,
> How they call common roe—that pickled frogspawn—
> Once ritually treated, caviare.
>
> And how life like the pearl of a jest by Watteau
> They can contrive to cram into a snuff box
> And are a scourge to him, perhaps, because
> All the time that they contort and crook,
>
> Through the lickspittle lies of sniggering comfort
> While, like the drones they are, they creep and crawl...

Pasternak's prosaic quality, besides being a natural clear-sightednes, is Life's holy rebuff to aestheticism—the axe to the snuffbox. Most priceless of all. Where, in the whole length of these 136 pages, will you find a single aestheticizing comma? He is as free of the common poetical stock of "moons" and "swoons" as he is to the "oh so distinctive" tooth-picks of aestheticism. This double vulgarity misses him by a hundred-mile loop. He is human—*durch*. Nothing but life, and every means to it the best. And it is not the Watteau snuffbox he stamps on, this infant Titan of everyday life, but the kind of life that will fit into a snuffbox.

Pasternak and Mayakovsky. No, Pasternak is more formidable. His "Afterword" alone completely eclipses all Mayakovsky's 150 millions.

Look at the end:

> And all that was breathed to the age's ravines,
> All the dark of the botanic vestry,
> Wafts over the typhoid yearning of a mattress,
> Thrusts out, chaos of herbage, spurting.

This is—Retribution! Chaos of herbage smothering the rotting mattress of aestheticism!

What's a decree and a bayonet—to the Ganges!

For Pasternak everyday life is a curb, it's no more than an earthly token (a tie) of holding back (holding out).

For the immemorial lure of such souls—undoubtedly—in all their radiance, is: Perdition.

Pasternak and Day

Not cosmic day which is heralded by dawn, not broad daylight which makes everything clear, but the element of day (light).

There is another day—evil (because blind), effective (because blind), irresponsible (because blind); tribute to our transience, day as tribute—today. Endurable only because yesterday it was tomorrow and tomorrow it will be yesterday: from transience to forever: under eyelids.

The summer day of 1917 is hot, aglare under the tramp of the stumbling front. How did Pasternak meet this avalanche of avalanches—Revolution? There are few definite signs of 1917 in this book; but if we listen with vigilance, take up the faintest hints—some three, or four, or five such signs.

Let's start. In the poem "The Model":

> All years that were erewhile
> One year like this outdoes.
>
> All lived it dry, half-starved,
> And in the struggle hardened.
> And none cared that the prodigy
> Of life was one hour long.

Then, in the poem "Break up":

> It, where the eye was used to yield
> To the small mercies of the droughty steppe,
> Now, muffled in mist, arose,
> Haystack of revolution!

And further on, in the same poem:

> And the air of the steppe is stirred.
> It takes the scent, it drinks the air
> Of soldiers' mutinies and summer lightnings.
> It freezes in its tracks, it is become all ears.
> It lies full length, then hears the summons: Turn!

(Doesn't he mean himself?)

Again, in the poem "The Militiaman's Whistle" (needless to say, omitting the militiaman):

> ... behind the fence
> The north of villainy grows grey ...

Three more lines from the poem "A Sultry Night":

> In the unparented, insomniac
> Damp and universal vast
> A volley of groans broke loose from standing posts ...

I'd interpret the poem to Kerensky, "Spring Rain"—with these amazing lines:

> In whom was that heart where all the blood in him fast
> Gushed to glory, sucked back out of the cheeks ...

—as the magic the word "enthusiasm" works upon youth, not at all as a political preference.

That's all.

One thing is clear from these conjectures: Pasternak didn't hide form the Revolution in any of the intelligentsia's cellars. (No cellar in the Revolution—only an open square and a field!) He did have an encounter with it. He saw it for the first time—somewhere far off—in a mirage—as a haystack rearing wildly in the wind, he heard it—in the groaning flight of the roads. It gave itself to him (reached him), like everything in his life—through nature.

Pasternak's word about the Revolution, no less than the Revolution's word about itself, is yet to come. In the summer of 1917, he walked in step with it, listening.

Pasternak and Rain

Dozhd' ["rain"]. What first springs to mind, in the fellowship of assonances? *Dazhd'* ["grant"]. And with "grant"—naturally—"God."

God grant—what?—Rain! The very name of the Slavonic sun contains a prayer for rain. More, rain is somehow already granted in it. How amicable! How succinct! (Your teachers, Pasternak!) And, turning our brow to the past decade, which of us has written nature? I don't want to stir up names (tear myself away and think about others), but—at a lightning glance—no one, ladies and gentlemen. A lot has been written (above all by Akhmatova) about oneself in nature, eclipsing nature so naturally (when the poet's Akhmatova!); about nature in ourselves (becoming like it, likening it), about happenings in nature, its separate countenances and seasons; but, however amazingly, all wrote *about* it, no one wrote *it* itself: point blank.

> But here's Pasternak. And a wondering starts: who is really writing whom?

Clue: penetrability. He lets the leaf, the ray, pierce him so deeply that he is no longer he, but a leaf, a ray. Rebirth. Miracle. From the Lermontov avalanche to the Lebedyan burdock, everything is present, nothing's left out, nothing missed. But the rain fell in love with Pasternak more passionately than the grasses, dawns and blizzards. (And how it be-rained the poet—the whole book swims!) And this isn't the sparse little rain of autumn! Not drizzling, but driving; not pedestrian—equestrian!

We'll begin.

> My sister, life! Today in the flooding over
> Shattered in spring rain on us all . . .

Further, "The Weeping Garden" (astounding from the first line to the last; I'm biting my fingers, being forced to pull it to pieces):

> Appalling! it drips and listens—is it
> Alone in the world or (now it presses
> Lace-like, a twig on the window-pane)
> Does it have witnesses? . . .

> . . . No sound. No hint of espionage,
> Assured all's empty, it takes up
> Its old affairs, it sheets athwart
> The roof, brims over gutters, and across.

(I stress: it's the loneliness of the rain, not that of the man being rained on!)

Next, "The Mirror":

> Thus after rain the slugs crawl journeying
> Like eyes of garden effigies.
> Water lisps in the ear . . .

And here is something wholly enchanting:

> Drops weigh as collar-studs, the garden
> Dazzles like a stretch of waters,
> All besplotched and all bespattered
> With a million bluish tears . . .

Further, in the poem "Rain":

> Come spin, as mulberry worm,
> Beat at the window pane,
> Come swathe, come swaddle yet,
> Thicken the murk again...
>
> ...And now come run, as if
> A hundred guitars made moan,
> To know the lime-washed, dim
> Saint-Gothard, garden-adorned.

Further (my fingers will be gnawed to bits!):

> From calyx onto calyx sliding
> It has slipped athwart a pair of them—in both
> Like an immense drop formed of agate
> It is hung up, and dazzles there, and trembles.
>
> Let the wind, that breathes past meadowsweet,
> Flatten it out, that drop, and worry it,
> It's whole, and does not break apart but, twinned,
> The couple that it is still drink and kiss.

Next, the opening of the poem "Spring Rain":

> It laughed at the bird-cherry, sobbing, wetted
> Lacquer of landaus, tremor of the trees...

Further ("Earth's Sicknesses"):

> And here's the downpour. Brilliance of hydrophobia,
> Vortex, flecks of a rabid saliva...

A quatrain from the poem "Our Storm":

> Still at the waterbutts they drink the storm
> From the sweet bonnets of profusion.
> The clover is as tossed and crimson
> As claret-colored splotches of house painters.

A few pages later:

> The rain will pierce the wing with pellets...

Further (opening of the poem "Sultry Night," one of the most ineffable in the book):

> A spattering came, but one that did not bend
> Even the grasses in the thunder's sack.
> Only the dust swallowed the rain in pellets,
> Iron in powder, speck on quiet speck.
>
> The village hoped for no alleviation,
> The poppy-head was deep as fainting is...

And—let's just list them:

> Hard behind in an unseeing scurry
> Some slant drops fled...

> ...A thin rain wrapped
> The cornfield in a quiet treading-across...

> Spatter of rain. Light-footedly
> Clouds moved over a dusty market square...

> Rain rushed down, a solid fence...

> With adder and with lemon
> Leafage is asperged...

> ... rain in the brain-cells
> Roared, not echoing back as thought.

(That's why it is *rain* [life!], and not thoughts on the subject!) And on the last page of the book:

> ... in the rain each leaf
> Tears loose for the steppe ...

Ladies and gentlemen, now you know about Pasternak and rain. The same thing happens with dew, leaves, dawn, earth, grass ... By the way, note the striking absence of the animal kingdom in Pasternak's nature—not a tusk, not a horn. Only some scales slide by. Even birds are rare. As if for him the creation of the world stopped on the fourth day—yet to be grasped, yet to be thought through.

But let's return to the grass; or rather, let us stride after the poet

> ... into the dark, past the wicker-fence,
> Into the steppe and the smell of sleepy drugs ...

(mint, chamomile, sage).

Sage? Yes, ladies and gentlemen, sage. The poet, like God, or a child, or a beggar, doesn't disdain anything. And isn't this *their* horror—God's, or the child's, the beggar's?

> ... crossing the road and passing behind the fence
> Is not to be done but you tread the frame of the world ...

Responsibility for every step, a trembling warning: "Don't disturb!", and what vast—inescapable—awareness of power! If the poet hadn't already said this of God, I'd say it of the poet himself: he's the one "to whom nothing is bauble..." Tokens of the earth, his poem of genius "The Great God of Details":

> You ask, who stablishes
> That August be a power?

> To whom nothing is bauble,
> Who goes about to staple
> Light leaves to the maple,
> And since Ecclesiastes
> Has never left his station,
> Working the alabaster?
>
> You ask, who stablishes
> That asters taste, and peonies,
> Agonies, come September?
> That the meager leaf of broom
> From grey of caryatids
> Came down upon dank flags of
> Infirmaries of the fall?
> You ask, who stablishes?
>
> The omnipotent God of details,
> The omnipotent God of love,
> Of Hedwigas, Yagailos . . .

No questions in Pasternak, only answers. "If I've given this answer, then somebody somewhere must have asked the question; maybe I did in my sleep last night, maybe I'll ask it in my sleep tomorrow." The whole book is an affirmation, for everyone and everything: I am! Yet how little directly about himself. Beside himself . . .

Pasternak and thought. Does he think? No? Is thought there? Yes. But beyond the gesture of his will. Thought is what works in him, digs out subterranean burrows till suddenly—in an explosion of light—it bursts to the outside. Revelation. Illumination. (From within.)

> But we shall die with all the suffocation
> Of these investigations in our breast . . .

Perhaps in this couplet is the chief tragedy of all Pasternak's kind: the impossibility of spending himself—income tragically exceeds expenditure.

> Gardens and garden-ponds and palisades,
> And, seething in white lamentations,
> The world's whole frame, are but the types of passion,
> The kinds of it man's heart accumulates.

And more helplessly and simply:

> Where shall I put this happiness of mine?
> In verses? In a rigorous eight-line stanza?

(And still they say "the poor in spirit!")

> It seems this moment is the time
> For every coiled-down spring to fly apart.

> Where? In what places? Or in what
> Wildly envisaged region?
> The most I know is, in the drought, in thunder,
> July, a storm impending—this I know...

(What else but an illumination?)

And the last:

> How drowsy living is,
> And openings-up, how sleepless!

Pasternak, when do you sleep?
 I'm stopping. In despair. I've said nothing. Nothing—about nothing—for before me is Life, and I haven't the words.

> And only the wind can bind
> What breaks into life and breaks in the prism
> And is glad to play in tears.

This is not a review: it's an attempt to get out, so as not to choke. The only one of my contemporaries for whom my lungs have not sufficed.

One doesn't write of contemporaries like this. I repent. It's solely the zeal of the Trade. Not to surrender to the first glib pen, in some fifty years, this my heartfelt hymn of praise. Ladies and gentlemen, this book is for everyone. And everyone ought to know it. This book is for the soul what Mayakovsky is for the body: a release in action. Not merely healing—like those slumberous grasses of his—but wonder-working. Read it trustingly, without resistance and with utter meekness: it will either sweep you away or it will save you! A simple miracle of trust: go as a tree, a dog, a child, into the rain!

And no one will want to shoot himself, and no one will want to shoot at others . . .

> Suddenly there was a sense
> Of people being discharged from a thousand hospitals!

Maximilian Voloshin

The Horoscope of Cherubina de Gabriak (1909)

Translated by Sibelan Forrester

Once upon a time the fairies would gather around newborn princesses and put their gifts into the cradle, gifts that were, in essence, no more than wishes. We—the critics—also gather over the cradles of newborn poets. But more often we love to play the role of the wicked fairy and predict the moment when their talent will be pricked on the spindle and fall into a deep sleep. Meanwhile, our words have a genuine power. People will believe what we say about a poet. They'll remember what we cite from his verses. One should be very careful and cautious with newborns.

Now we are standing over the cradle of a new poet. This one is a foundling in Russian poetry. Someone, no one knows who, left a willow basket on Apollo's terrace. The babe is swaddled in linen of fine batiste with embroidered crests, with a motto from Toledo: "*Sin miedo*" [without fear]. A sprig of heather lies at its head, dedicated to Saturn, and a bouquet of "*capillaires*," called "Venus's tears."

A note with a black border and rapid, sharp-pointed feminine script says: "Cherubina de Gabriak. Née 1877. Catholique."

Apollo adopts the new poet. We, as Astrologer assigned to the temple, are tasked with casting the horoscope of Cherubina de Gabriak. We will strive, following the rules of the regal science, to establish its elements.

Two planets define the individuality of this poet: deathly pale Saturn and the shepherds' green evening star—Venus, whose morning hypostasis is named Lucifer.

Their combination above the cradle of the newborn speaks of a charming character, passionate and tragic. Venus is beauty. Saturn is fate. Venus opens the blinding flashes of love; Saturn traces out an inexorable life path.

Venus is a witness to generosity, a welcoming and expansive character; Saturn tightens a ring of pride, gives the character a moroseness that can be broken open only by a passionate, always tragic gesture.

"The line of Saturn is deep," Cherubina de Gabriak says of herself... "But I myself chose the agate's gloom, the hand of evening leads me along the flames of sunset into the constellation of Sleep. Our narrow path, our difficult feat of passion is woven by the longing of brume and of gleam."

A different young woman, also born under the conjunction of Venus and Saturn—the heroine of Villiers de l'Isle-Adam's *Axel*—says of herself:

"All the caresses of other women are not worth my cruelness! I am the gloomiest of young women. It seems to me that I remember how I once tempted angels. Alas! Flowers and children die in my shadow. I know pleasures in which every hope perishes."

The French letter that the unknown mother wrote to recommend her child to Apollo was closed by a black seal with the grievous and threatening motto, "*Vae victis*!" [woe to the vanquished]. It recalls the "Too late!" on the signet ring of Barbey d'Aurevilly.

Villiers de l'Isle-Adam, Barbey d'Aurevilly—these are the names that will help define the sign of the historical Zodiac of Cherubina de Gabriak. They are two stars from the constellation that does not rise but sets over the night horizon of European thought and soon ceases to be visible in our latitudes. We would not want to call it by the name of "Romanticism," which is shallower and overly broad. Cherubina de Gabriak calls it "the Constellation of Sleep." Let's leave it with this name.

At one time this constellation stood at the zenith of the Sky of Europe, and a magnificent knightly culture flowered with its currents, its sign the sword in the form of a cross. Its age-old decline began long ago. Now, when it rises on autumn nights for a few brief hours over the surge of the agitated sea, its gleam is no less grandiose and terrible than the gleam of Orion. The people born under it now are like black diamonds: they are sorrowful, dark and dazzling. They harbor a love for death, they are drawn to the sunset of coruscating Sleep—below the line of the visible horizon. ("I'm bitter and death-dealing, like almond—more tender than Death, more deceptive and bitter.") They hear the beat of invisible birds' dark wings over their heads, and in their souls the sound of a funeral bell tolls ceaselessly: "Too late!" They live amid contemporary people just as Villiers de l'Isle-Adam does, "in a non-existent tower that faces the setting of the Heraldic Sun." They are the possessors of fabulous treasures that have lost their value; they are the masters of thrones and crowns that no longer exist on earth. Their souls are oppressed by consciousness of the fruitlessness of all the splendors they clutch in their hands—

> My longing shall never see
> A crown's gleam, nor a throne's purple.
> And on my maidenly hand
> Is the unneeded ring of Solomon.

It is not hard to define the countries with which they are linked by the Zodiac sign. They are the Latin lands of the Catholic world: Spain and France. In the East—Persia and Palestine. In the physical body, it rules the centers of thought and feeling—the heart and head.

The conjunction of this declining constellation with rising Venus and rising Saturn lends this fate an unusually gloomy radiance ("And the black Angel, my protector, stands with a blazing sword").

It speaks of a hopeless and inexorable love, of Satanic pride and proximity to the underworld. Those born under this conjunction are distinguished by beauty, pallor of the face, a particular gleam of the eyes. They are of medium height. Slender and flexible. Their hair is dark, but with a reddish tinge. Imperious. Capricious. Given to unexpected actions.

Such are the paths the constellations and planets ordain for the creativity of Cherubina de Gabriak. But let's not forget that they determine the worldly spheres of creativity and the age-old motivations of life. All that has been said pertains to this sphere and does not touch at all on either the talent of the given poet or his power, nor his significance. Those born under this conjunction smolder so much within themselves that they can lack the sphere of artistic creativity completely. Fortunately, this cannot be said of Cherubina de Gabriak.

No matter how dubious are horoscopes cast for poets, it can be verified that Cherubina de Gabriak's poems contain qualities that are precious and rare: temperament, character, and passion. We are beguiled by the passion of Lermontov. We value Balmont's temperament and Bryusov's character, but these features are not what we are used to in a woman-poet, and they make our heads spin a bit. For the last few years young poets have so overwhelmed us with their flawless poems, fastened up with every button of their shining rhymes, that this fluent speech with its circumlocutions, and sometimes its mistakes, seems new to us and especially winning.

This handsome and genuine gesture of knightliness ("Thou, who hadst crimsoned thy sword with blood, bent meekly the plumes of thy helmet before the shine of slender tapers at the entrance of Bethlehem's cave"), this accent of frenetic Catholicism in the hymn of St. Ignatius Loyola, is unusual for Russian verse. This "flower of the heavenly seraphim"—"Flores de Serafinos"—of St. Theresa, this image of the paladin the holy Virgin dreams of (" ... And the daydream of God's mother") conveys us to Spain in the seventeenth century, where asceticism and voluptuousness fuse into a single mystical halo.

Faith sometimes rises to such a height that it has no fear of making contact with blasphemy. Let us recall Barbey d'Aurevilly's great comment: "For our Lord Jesus Christ it was great good fortune that he was God. As a person he lacked character." Thus speaks a man about a man. Let us not be surprised that Cherubina de Gabriak, following the example of St. Theresa, speaks of Christ as a woman speaks of a man:

> These hands, like pliant grapes,
> All gleam in precious rings.
> But the sharp nails have left
> Barely visible signs on them.

Her utterances sound so haughty and so uncontemporary, just as if some kind of ancient soul were speaking through her lips. And we find strange confirmation of this in the poem dedicated to Her "who died in 1781"—a woman who perished in religious madness from a blasphemous and criminal love for "the Lad from Nazareth."

> An alien daydream dwells in me,
> The dream of a girl who has died.
> And the visage of the Christ from the cross
> Glances, threatening madness,
> And His dark lips are wrathful.

> He hasn't forgotten that he once saw
> In a similar face's features
> The trace of passion heavier than lead
> And for the lad from Nazareth
> An impulse and dread unceasing.

> And my voice sings out like a flame,
> Hiding the fumes of its love,
> In my eyes is her bonfire,
> And I wait to take the banner of madness—
> The ultimate gift of her sin.

In Cherubina de Gabriak's poetry one often hears a struggle with this ancient soul that has not yet died out in her. She first compares herself to the fiery blossom of a fern that flowers only once, begs to be picked, to yield to her amorous corruption, then recalls the "White Jordan, the whiteness of the heavenly flower." She does not yet know which path to choose: the path of the "Rose and Cross," or the incinerating path of earthly fire, "path of the madness of all hopes—the fatal path of overweening pride: it holds the flame of fiery hopes (accepted as redemption by the knights of the Temple) and the dolor of the abandoned desert"; she does not know what to write in the gilded field of her shield—"The convolvulus of the gloom, or the Roses of the Temple? The bronze seal of Tubal or the acacia of Hiram?"; the passionate path of the sons of Cain ("it seems to me that I remember how I once tempted Angels") or the priestly path of the builder of the Temple of Solomon, on whose grave, as a symbol of "consecration," an acacia grew.

But the poetry of Cherubina de Gabriak is not limited to these profound, so to speak fundamental, starry experiences.

Consciousness of the unneededness of her dream and her exile often sounds in her verses ("... And alone once again in the steppes of an alien land, and there is no one like me around... Why are the wrists of my hands so gentle, so refined the name Cherubina?").

Sometimes the realities of life present themselves to her in the form of Cinderella's evanescent dream:

> In the morning the ballroom talk subsides...
> I'm alone... The cricket sings...
> On my foot there is a crystal
> > Slipper.
>
> The path bequeathed to me since childhood—
> To live by one vanished dream.
> The paltry inheritance of glory...
> > Outside the window.
>
> Millions of strangers' shadows,
> A long row of grey buildings,
> And the rags of Cinderella—
> > Are my outfit.

Along with this she gives her external, real-life visage of a purely worldly young woman, who hides bitterness under a mask of irony:

> The dark-lilac violets
> You bring me every day;
> O, how naively pathetic they are,
> The blooms of your infatuation.
>
> > Your blinded mind can't understand,
> > The teaching of elegant love
> > And a smile of boredom slightly
> > Distorts my delicate mouth.

> My perfume, like old-fashioned poison,
> So sweetly intoxicated you.
> But with a single weary glance
> I slay the unneeded flowers.

But much more often this irony, characteristic of her worldly gesture, gives way to a weary capriciousness:

> Even the sonnets of Ronsard
> Did not unlock my sadness.
> Everything the poets have said,
> I've known it long by heart.

> You won't drive away the gloom of grief
> With the sign of the holy cross.
> And the princess in exile
> Has lost even her jesters . . .

Or through irony comes sincere, profound sadness, as for example in this little "Lai" (Cherubina de Gabriak likes the rare and closed forms of old-fashioned poems, such as the "rondeau," the "lai," and various systems of interweaving and repeating lines, for example in her poem "Golden branch," but she never underlines her intentions, using these refined forms easily and freely, as her own natural language). This "Lai" in its compressed lines contains a whole complex psychological epic and can serve as a model of the astonishing mastery of Cherubina de Gabriak:

> The flutes and cymbals
> In the gleam of the ballroom
> Through the gloom;
> Let the goblets chime,
> Let my eyes be weary—
> I'll understand it . . .
> The corals of your lips
> Are so madly scarlet . . .
> What's the point?

These traits give a lifelike completeness to her image. Without them, it would remain overly abstract, almost a literary formula.

These are the data from the horoscope; these are the data of talent. What sort of gift should we, the fairy-critics, lay in the cradle of this foundling poet in Apollo's temple? We feel that she has need of only one—a golden, uncertain and joyless gift: fame.

We lay it in the cradle of Cherubina de Gabriak.

MEMOIRS

Anna Akhmatova

Reminiscences of Alexander Blok (1955)

Translated by Ronald Meyer

In Petersburg in the fall of 1913, on the day when Verhaeren's arrival in Russia was celebrated in some restaurant, a large, private reception (for students only) was held at the Bestuzhev Institute. One of the organizers was thoughtful enough to invite me. I was supposed to pay tribute to Verhaeren, whom I dearly loved, not for his celebrated urbanism, but for the short poem "On the Little Wooden Bridge at the End of the World."

But after I pictured to myself the splendor of a celebration in a Petersburg restaurant, which for some reason always resembled a wake with its tailcoats, good champagne, and the bad French and toasts, I opted for the students.

The lady patronesses, who had devoted their whole lives to the struggle for equal rights for women, came to this reception as well. One of them, the writer Ariadna Vladimirovna Tyrkova-Vergezhskaya, who had known me since childhood, said to me after my reading: "Anichka has won equality for herself."

I met Blok in the greenroom.

I asked him why he was not taking part in the Verhaeren celebration at the restaurant. The poet answered with a winning directness: "Because they'll ask me to speak and I don't speak French."

A student came up to us with a list and said that I would read after Blok. I begged him: "Alexander Alexandrovich, I cannot read after you." He—with a reproach in his voice—replied: "Anna Andreyevna, we are not tenors." He was Russia's most famous poet of the period. For the previous two years I had been reading my poetry fairly often at the Poets' Guild, at the Society of Lovers of the Artistic Word and at Vyacheslav Ivanov's Tower, but this was completely different.

If the theatrical stage is capable of hiding a person, then reading alone on stage can mercilessly expose him. The stage is similar to an executioner's block. Perhaps, I experienced that for the first time then. The audience begins to look like a many-headed hydra to the performer. It's very difficult to command the hall—Zoshchenko was a genius at that. And Pasternak was good on stage as well.

Nobody knew me and when I came out there was a cry of "Who's that?" Blok had advised me to read "We Are All Carousers Here."[1] I started to resist: "They laugh when I read 'I put on a tight skirt.'" He replied: "They laugh too when I read 'And the drunkards with their rabbit eyes.'"[2]

I think that it was at some literary evening or other, not that one, when Blok returned to the greenroom, after listening to Igor Severyanin read, and said: "He has a voice like a sleazy lawyer." On one of the last Sundays of 1913 I brought Blok copies of his books so that he would inscribe them for me. In each one he simply wrote: "To Akhmatova From Blok." (Here is *Verses on a Beautiful Lady*.) But in the third volume he wrote out his madrigal dedicated to me: "Beauty is frightening, they'll tell you."[3] I have never had the Spanish shawl in which Blok portrays me, but at the time Blok was mad about Carmen and made a Spaniard out of me, too. And it goes without saying that I never wore a red rose in my hair. It is not accidental that this poem is written in the Spanish stanzaic form known as the romancero. At our last meeting, back-stage at the Bolshoi Dramatic Theater in 1921, Blok came up to me and asked: "But where is your Spanish shawl?" Those were the last words that I ever heard him say.

---

1   *Eds.* Included in this volume as "All of us here are hookers and hustlers..."
2   *Eds.* From his poem "Stranger," included in this volume.
3   *Eds.* Included in this volume as "'Beauty is frightening,' they will tell you..."

The one time that I visited Blok at his home, I mentioned in passing that the poet Benedikt Livshitz had been complaining that he, Blok, interfered with his writing just by his very being. Blok did not break out into laughter, but replied completely seriously: "I understand that. Leo Tolstoy interferes with my writing."

In the summer of 1914 I was at my mother's in Darnitsa, near Kiev. In early July I set off for home, to the village of Slepnyovo, by way of Moscow. In Moscow I got on the first mail train that came along. I was smoking on the open platform. Somewhere near an empty platform the engine slowed down and they threw on a bag of mail. Suddenly Blok appeared before my amazed eyes. I shout, "Alexander Alexandrovich!" He looks around and since he was not only a great poet but also a master of the tactful question, he asks: "Who are you traveling with?" I manage to answer: "I'm alone." And the train pulls out.

Today, fifty-one years later, I open Blok's *Notebook* and under July 9, 1914, I read: "Mother and I went to look over the sanatorium near Podsolnechnaya.—A demon is teasing me.—Anna Akhmatova riding a mail train."

Blok writes elsewhere that Delmas, Yelizaveta Kuzmina-Karavayeva, and I had worn him out with our telephone calls. I think I can shed some light on this.

I had called Blok. Alexander Alexandrovich with his typical straightforwardness and habit of thinking out loud asked me, "You probably are calling because Ariadna Vladimirovna Tyrkova told you what I said about you." Dying of curiosity, I went to Ariadna Vladimirovna's on one of her at-home days and asked her what Blok had said. But she was implacable. "Anichka, I never tell one of my guests what others say about him."

Blok's *Notebook* offers small gifts by wresting dates from the depths of oblivion and returning them to half-forgotten events. Once again I see the burning wooden St. Isaac's Bridge as it floats out to the mouth of the Neva, and my companion and I watch this unprecedented sight with horror. And this day has a date, as recorded by Blok: July 11, 1916.

And once again after the Revolution (January 21, 1921), in a theater cafeteria I meet an emaciated Blok with crazed eyes, who says to me: "Everybody meets here as if they were in the other world."

And here the three of us (Blok, Gumilyov, and myself) are having dinner (August 5, 1914) at the Tsarskoe Selo train station during the first days of the war (Gumilyov is in a soldier's uniform). Blok then was making the rounds of the recruits' families in order to offer them assistance. When the two of us were left alone, Kolya said, "Can it really be that he will be sent to the front? That's the same thing as roasting nightingales."

And a quarter of a century later in that very same Dramatic Theater—an evening to commemorate Blok (1946)—I read the poem that I had just written:[4]

> He was right—again the street lamp, the drug store,
> The Neva, silence, granite . . .
> Like a monument to the century's beginning,
> There this man stands—
> When he, bidding farewell
> To Pushkin House, waved his hand
> And accepted mortal weariness
> As undeserved peace.

---

4   *Eds*. Included in this volume as "The poet was right: once again . . ."

Anna Akhmatova

From "Osip Mandelstam" (1964)[1]

Translated by Anna Lisa Crone and Ronald Meyer

[....]
    Mandelstam was one of the most brilliant conversationalists. He didn't just listen to himself and answer himself, which is what almost everyone does nowadays. In conversation he was polite, quick to react, and always original. I never heard him repeat himself or "play the same old record." He learned foreign languages with unusual ease. He could recite pages of *The Divine Comedy* in Italian. Shortly before his death he asked Nadya to teach him English, which he didn't know at all. The way he spoke about poetry was stunning: he was passionate and sometimes monstrously unfair, about Blok, for instance. He said of Pasternak: "I think about him so much that it makes me tired" and "I'm sure he hasn't read a single line of mine." And about Marina: "I am anti-Tsvetaeva."
    Osip was at home with music, and this is a very rare trait. What he feared most was becoming mute, he called it asphyxia. He was horror-struck when it seized him and he would think up absurd reasons to explain the disaster. A second and frequent disappointment was his readers. He always thought that the wrong kind of reader liked his poetry. He knew and remembered other

---

[1] *Eds.* Because this text has been heavily excerpted, we have not marked some instances where text was excised from the original publication.

people's poetry well, would often become fascinated by a single line, and easily memorized what was read to him.

[....]

I met Osip Mandelstam at Vyacheslav Ivanov's Tower in the spring of 1911. He was a wiry boy then, with a lily of the valley in his lapel, his head thrown way back, with fiery eyes and lashes that reached almost halfway down his cheeks. The second time I saw him was at the Tolstoys' on Old Nevsky. He didn't recognize me, and Alexei Nikolayevich [Tolstoy] began to ask him what Gumilyov's wife looked like. Mandelstam gestured with his hands to show what a big hat I wore. I got frightened that something irreparable would happen and introduced myself.

That was my first Mandelstam, the author of the green *Stone* (published by Acme) with the inscription: "To Anna Akhmatova—flashes of consciousness in the forgetfulness of days. Respectfully, the Author."

With his peculiarly charming self-irony Osip liked to tell the story of how an old Jew, the owner of the print shop where *Stone* was printed, congratulated him on the book's publication, shook his hand, and said: "Your writing will only get better and better, young man."

[....]

Naturally, we would run into each other everywhere in the 1910s: in editorial offices, at the homes of acquaintances, at *The Hyperborean* on Friday, that is, at Lozinsky's, at The Stray Dog, where Lozinsky, by the way, introduced me to Mayakovsky. Once at the Dog, when everyone was eating loudly and the dishes were clanking, Mayakovsky took it into his head to recite poetry. Osip went over to him and said: "Mayakovsky, stop reciting poems. You're not a Romanian orchestra." I witnessed this in 1912 or 1913. The sharp-witted Mayakovsky was at a loss how to respond and he later told the whole story to Khardzhiev very amusingly. We would likewise meet at the Academy of Poetry (The Society of Zealots of the Artistic Word), where Vyacheslav Ivanov was king, and at the meetings of the Poets' Guild, which was hostile to the Academy. Mandelstam very soon became concertmaster at the Guild. It was then that he wrote the enigmatic (and not very successful) poem "A black angel in the snow." Nadya claims that it refers to me.

[....]

A souvenir of Mandelstam's visit to Petersburg in 1920, in addition to his amazing poems to Olga Arbenina, are the lively posters of the period (faded, like Napoleonic banners) announcing evenings of poetry, where the name of Mandelstam stands alongside Nikolai Gumilyov and Alexander Blok. The old Petersburg signboards were still all in place, but behind them there was nothing but dust, darkness, and yawning emptiness. Typhus, hunger, execution by firing squad, dark apartments, damp wood, and people swollen beyond recognition. You could pick a large bouquet of wildflowers in Gostiny Dvor. The famous Petersburg wooden pavement was rotting. The smell of chocolate still wafted from the basement windows of Kraft. All the cemeteries had been pillaged. The city had not just changed, it had turned into its exact opposite. But people still loved poetry (mainly the young people) almost the same way as they do now, that is, in 1964.

[....]

Mandelstam greeted the Revolution as a fully-formed and well-known poet, albeit in a limited circle.

He was totally absorbed by the events taking place.

Mandelstam was one of the first to write poems on civic themes. The Revolution was a tremendous event for him, and the word "the people" *(narod)* appears in his poetry for a reason.

Mandelstam would often come to take me out for rides in a horse-drawn cab past the incredible potholes of the revolutionary winter, amidst the celebrated bonfires that burned almost until May, and we would listen to the gunfire wafting from who knows where. That's how we would drive to readings at the Academy of Arts, where they held benefits for the wounded and where we both read several times. Osip was also with me at Butomo Nazareva's concert at the Conservatory when she sang Schubert ("They sang Schubert to us...").

All the poems Mandelstam addressed to me date from this period.

In the summer of 1924 Osip Mandelstam brought his young wife to meet me (Fontanka, 2). Nadyusha was what the French call *laide mais charmante* [homely but charming]. My friendship with Nadyusha began then and continues to this day.

Osip's love for Nadya was extraordinary and unbelievable. When she had her appendix taken out in Kiev, he didn't leave the hospital, but stayed the whole time in the hospital porter's room. He wouldn't let her out of his sight, didn't let her work, was insanely jealous, and asked her advice on every word in his poems. In general, I have never seen anything like it in my life. The letters that have survived from Mandelstam to his wife fully confirm my impression.

[....]

In the fall of 1933 Mandelstam finally received an apartment (which he immortalized in verse), two rooms, a fifth-floor walkup (no gas stove or tub) on Nashchokin Lane ("The apartment is as quiet as paper").[2] It seemed his wandering life had come to an end. There for the first time Osip had books, mainly old editions of Italian poets (Dante, Petrarch).

In actual fact nothing had ended. He constantly had to be phoning somewhere, waiting for something, hoping for something. And nothing ever worked out.

[....]

Though the times were relatively vegetarian, the shadow of misfortune and doom hovered over that house. Once we were walking down Prechistenka (February 1934); I don't remember what we were talking about. We turned onto Gogol Boulevard and Osip said," I'm ready for death." Twenty-eight years have gone by and I recall that moment every time I pass that spot.

[....]

In a word, there was nothing for them to live on—some semitranslations, semi-reviews, semi-promises. His pension was barely enough to pay for the apartment and his ration. By this time Mandelstam's physical appearance had changed drastically. He had put on weight, turned gray, and had trouble breathing. He looked like an old man (he was forty-two years old), but his eyes sparkled as before. His poetry got better and better, and his prose did too.

A few days ago I was reading *The Noise of Time* (I hadn't opened the book since 1928) and I made an unexpected discovery. In addition to his sublime and original poetic achievements, he also managed to be the last chronicler of Petersburg. He is precise, lucid, objective, and unique. In his book those streets, half-forgotten and much maligned, come to life in all their freshness of the 1890s and 1900s. They'll say that he wrote it five whole years after the Revolution, in 1923, that he was out of touch with the times, but absence is

---

2   *Eds.* See the poem "Flat" in this volume.

the best cure for forgetting (I'll explain later). The best way to forget something forever is to see it every day.

Sometimes this prose reads like a commentary to his poetry, but Mandelstam never presents himself as a poet, and if you didn't know his poetry, you'd never guess that this was a poet's prose. Everything he wrote about in *The Noise of Time* lay very deep within him. He never spoke about it and was a bit put off by the *World of Art* infatuation with old (and not so old) Petersburg.

This prose, so unprecedented and forgotten, is only now beginning to find its reader. Yet, on the other hand, I constantly hear, mainly from young people who are crazy about it, that there has never been prose like this in all of the twentieth century. (The so-called *Fourth Prose*.)

On May 13, 1934 he was arrested. On the same day, after a torrent of telegrams and phone calls, I left Leningrad (where shortly before he had had his confrontation with Alexei Tolstoy) for the Mandelstams.

Yagoda himself had signed the order for Mandelstam's arrest. The search of the apartment lasted all night. They looked for poems, they walked on manuscripts that had been thrown out onto the floor from the small suitcase. We all sat in one room. It was very quiet. You could hear someone playing a ukulele next door at Kirsanov's. An investigator unearthed "Wolf" in my presence ("For the sake of the future's trumpeting heroics") and showed it to Osip. He nodded silently. He kissed me as he was leaving. They took him away at 7:00 a.m. It was completely light outside. Nadya set off for her brother's and I went to the Chulkovs on Smolensk Boulevard, No. 8, and we agreed to meet somewhere. We returned home together, cleaned up the apartment, and sat down to breakfast. Again there was a knock on the door, it was them again, another search. Yevgeny Khazin said: "If they come again they'll take you with them."

Early in the morning fifteen days later, they called Nadya and suggested that if she wanted to accompany her husband she should be at Kazan Station that evening.

[....]

It's striking that space, breadth, and a deep breathing appeared in Mandelstam's verse precisely in Voronezh, when he was not free at all.

> When I get my breath back, you can hear
> In my voice the earth, my last weapon...

After I returned from the Mandelstams, I wrote my poem "Voronezh." Here is the ending:

> And in the disgraced poet's room
> Fear and the Muse stand guard in turn.
> And there is a night,
> Which knows no dawn. (*The Flight of Time*, 1965)

Osip wrote of himself in Voronezh: "I am an expectant person by nature. That makes it all the harder for me here."

In Voronezh they employed not altogether aboveboard tactics to force Osip into giving a lecture about Acmeism. We should not forget what he said in 1937: "I do not disown the living or the dead." Asked to define Acmeism, he answered: "Nostalgia for world culture."

An eccentric? Of course, he was. For instance, he threw out a young poet who came to complain that he wasn't getting published. The embarrassed youth descended the stairs, while Osip shouted at him from the upper landing: "Did they publish André Chénier? Or Sappho? Or Jesus Christ?"

[. . . .]

Was he an eccentric? But that's hardly the point. Why do memoirists of a certain ilk (Shatsky, E. Mindlin, S. Makovsky, G. Ivanov, Benedikt Livshitz) so carefully and lovingly collect and preserve all kinds of gossip and nonsense, which basically presents a philistine view of the poet, instead of bowing their heads before so great and incomparable a phenomenon as the birth of a poet, whose very first poems amaze us with their perfection and which seemingly come forth out of nowhere.

Mandelstam has no teacher. That is something worth thinking about. I don't know a similar case in all of world poetry. We know Pushkin's and Blok's sources, but who can show us the source of this divine new harmony, which we call the poetry of Osip Mandelstam?

Zinaida Gippius

Bryusov (1925)

(*excerpt from the book* Living Faces)

Translated by Sibelan Forrester

Naturally, given his ruling passion, Bryusov did not and could not love any kind of art. But even if he "considered it necessary" to recognize the old artists, to study them, even to "venerate" them—he nonetheless despised all his contemporaries, writers (as well as non-writers, by the way), completely and absolutely, making no distinctions. However, his natural quick-wittedness allowed him to develop a particular flexibility, a surprising subtlety, in his relationships with people. Even a person who was far from stupid would emerge from a discussion with Bryusov convinced that Bryusov really did despise everyone—everyone but him. Of course it is a kind of flattery, and an especially refined one, to badmouth everyone while talking with someone else. And Bryusov never "let it hang out": he only just very slightly, not openly but intelligibly, rejected the one he was talking about in a few condescendingly unkind words. Meanwhile the person he was talking with, unwittingly flattered by Bryusov's "trust," would already have started to feel that he was Bryusov's co-conspirator. [. . . .]

Bryusov had no competitor in the refinement of his *external* understanding of poetry. His gift for "style" and form (isn't it terrible that now he has lost even that!) permitted him "jests" such as the publication of a whole volume of poems written as if by a woman, under the mysterious pseudonym "Nelly." It was, of course, just Bryusov, cold towards eroticism (and therefore cynical), naturally lacking content. But thanks to his external mastery he was cleverly masked.

He had absolutely no *inner* taste and sensitivity for poetry, which would presume at least some kind of *love* for poetry. I had many occasions to be convinced of this. Here is one.

Someone sent a youthful poet to me: little, dark, hunched over, so modest, so bashful that when he read it was barely audible, and his hands got damp and cold. We hadn't heard anything about him before, I forget who sent him to me (maybe he came by himself), I have great faith in youthful poets. His poems were far from perfect, yet—all the same, it seemed to me, without a doubt, that he was not one of the ones you wind up having to listen to by the dozens every day.

I decided that the boy was not without abilities, and I offered (for the first time in my life, it seems, without being asked) to get his poems printed somewhere: in *Russian Thought* perhaps; I'd send them to Bryusov.

The answer didn't come very soon, and even came, by the way, in a letter about something else. The answer was mocking, careless and a bit crude: as for your young poet "with abilities," then I have too great an abundance of that sort of youth with just the same or even greater abilities in Moscow too. I recommend against printing this . . . There was more in the same vein, if not worse.

However, the youth turned out to be, and unusually soon, a *poet*, in any case recognized as such by everyone, including even his precision of form, the aspect of talent of Bryusov's type. It was O. Mandelstam.

VLADISLAV KHODASEVICH

The End of Renata (1928)

Translated by Sibelan Forrester

On the eve of February 23, 1928, in Paris, in a beggarly section of a beggarly neighborhood, Nina Ivanovna Petrovskaya turned on the gas and committed suicide. On that occasion the newspaper notices referred to her as a writer. But a title like that, somehow, does not entirely suit her. To tell the truth, what she wrote was insignificant both in quantity and in quality. She did not know how, and—the main thing—didn't at all want to "waste" the small gift she possessed on literature. However, from 1903 to 1909 she played an important part in the life of literary Moscow. Her personality influenced circumstances and events that would seem to have no connection with her at all. However, before telling her story, I must touch on what they call the spirit of the epoch. Without this, Nina Petrovskaya's story is incomprehensible, and also uninteresting.

The Symbolists didn't want to separate the writer from the person, the literary biography from the personal one. Symbolism aimed to be not only an artistic school, a literary movement. It constantly strove to become a method of both art and life, and in that was its most profound, perhaps unincarnatable truth, but in essence its whole history flowed in constant striving towards this truth. It was a series of attempts, at times truly heroic ones, to find the alloy of life and creativity, a sort of philosopher's stone of art. Symbolism persistently sought a genius in its milieu who would know how to fuse life and creativity into one. We know now that no such genius appeared; the formula was never discovered. In fact the history of Symbolism turned into a history of broken lives, while it was as if their creativity was not fully incarnated: a part of the creative energy and part of the internal experience was incarnated in writings, while another part was not fully incarnated, departed into life, the way electricity flows away without sufficient insulation.

The percentage of this "energy flow" was different in various situations. The "person" and the "writer" struggled for dominance within each personality. Sometimes one would be victorious, sometimes the other. The victory most often fell to that side of the personality that was more gifted, stronger, more capable of life. If a literary talent turned out to be stronger—"the writer" would conquer "the person." If the talent for living turned out stronger than the literary talent—literary creation would retreat into the background, would be suppressed by creativity of another, "real life" order. It seems strange at first glance, but in essence it followed that at this time and amid these people the "gift of writing" and the "gift of living" were valued almost in equal amounts.

In the first edition of *Let's Be Like the Sun*, Balmont wrote in the dedication, among other things: "To Modest Durnov, an artist who made a poem of his personality." These were not at all empty words then. They are stamped with the spirit of the age. Modest Durnov, an artist and versifier, passed without a trace in *art*. A few weak poems, a few not-so-great book covers and illustrations—and that was it. But legends formed about his life, about his personality. An artist who created "a poem" in his life, not his art, was a lawful phenomenon at the time. And Modest Durnov was not alone. There were many like him—Nina Petrovskaya among them. Her literary gift was not great. Her gift for living was immeasurably greater.

> From this poor and accidental life
> I made a tremor without end.

—she would have had every right to say that about herself. From her life she made an endless thrill in truth, from her creative gift—nothing. She created a "poem from her life" more skillfully and more decisively than others. I have to add: and a poem was a created about her, herself. But that part is yet to come.

Nina hid her age; I think she was born around 1880. We got acquainted in 1902. When I met her she was already a beginning writer. It seems she was a government employee's daughter. She had graduated from the *gimnazia*, then dental courses. She was engaged to one man, then she married another. Her youthful years had been accompanied by drama, which she did not like to recollect. She didn't like to remember her early youth in general, before the start of the "literary epoch" in her life. The past struck her as impoverished, pathetic. She had found herself only after she showed up among the Symbolists and decadents, in the *Scorpio* and *Grif* circle.

Yes, here she lived a special life, not at all like her previous life. Maybe it wasn't like anything else at all. Here they were trying to turn art into reality, and reality into art. The events of everyday real life, combined with the lack of clarity, the tenuous outlines by which these people sketched reality, were never lived through as *only* and *simply* life; they immediately became part of the inner world and a part of creation. And the inverse: something that someone had written became real, a life event for everyone. In this manner, both reality and literature were as it were created by the common, at times feuding, but united (even in their feuds) forces of everyone who took part in this unusual life, in this "Symbolist dimension." It seems to have been a genuine case of collective creativity.

They lived in frenetic tension, in constant excitement, in aggravation, in a fever. They lived on several planes at once. In the end, they were most complicatedly entangled in a common web of loves and hatreds, personal and literary. Soon Nina Petrovskaya had become one of the central knots, one of the main nodes in that web.

I can't "sketch her natural character," as a memoirist should. Blok, who came to town in 1904 to get acquainted with the Moscow Symbolists, described her in a letter to his mother: "Very sweet, fairly intelligent." Definitions like that don't cover anything. I knew Nina Petrovskaya for twenty-six years, I saw her good and bad, accommodating and stubborn, cowardly and brave, obedient and headstrong, truthful and lying. One thing never changed: both in kindness and in spite, and in truth and in lies—always, in everything, she wanted to reach the end, the limit, fullness, and she demanded the same thing from other people. Her motto could have been "All or nothing." That's what ruined her. But it wasn't something born in her: it was inoculated by the epoch.

I spoke above of the effort to alloy life and creation as the truth of Symbolism. That remains its truth, though not its truth alone. It is an eternal truth, just most deeply and brightly lived through by Symbolism. But it also led to the great error of Symbolism, its mortal sin. Having declared a cult of personality, Symbolism assigned it no tasks besides "self-development." It demanded that this development should be completed; but how, in the name of what and in what direction—it did not indicate, didn't want to indicate, and indeed didn't know how to. For each person who entered the order (and in a certain sense Symbolism was an order), it demanded nothing but an unceasing burning, a movement it didn't matter for what purpose. All paths were open with only one obligation—to go as fast and as far as possible. This was the sole, fundamental dogma. One could worship both God and the Devil. It was permitted to be obsessed by whatever you wanted: all that was required was *complete obsession*.

Hence: the feverish pursuit of emotions, regardless of what kind. All "experiences" were considered riches, as long as they were many and powerful. This in turn led to the indifferent attitude towards their consistency and worthwhileness. "The personality" became a coin jar of experiences, a sack to pour the piled up emotions in without selection—the "moments," in Bryusov's expression: "We gather moments, ruining them."

The ultimate consequence of this emotional hoarding was the most profound emptiness. The covetous knights of Symbolism were dying of spiritual hunger—on sacks of piled-up "experiences." But this was in fact the final consequence. The nearer one, which had begun to be felt long before, almost right away, was something different: the unceasing striving to reconstruct thought, life, relationships, even one's own very customs in accordance with the imperative of the next "experience" pulled the Symbolists into unceasing acting for themselves—into playing out one's own life as if it were a theater of fervid improvisations. They knew that they were playing—but the playing became life. The penalties were not theatrical. "I'm bleeding cranberry juice!" Blok's clown shouted. But sometimes the cranberry juice turned out to be real blood.

Decadence, decadency, it is a relative concept: a decline is defined in relation to an original elevation. Therefore when applied to the art of the early Symbolists the term decadence made no sense: this art in and of itself was no kind of decline, relative to the past. But those sins that grew up and developed *within* Symbolism itself—in relation to it they were a decadence, a decline. Symbolism, it seems, was born with this poison in its blood. To various extents it ran in all the Symbolists. To a certain extent (or at a certain time) each one was a decadent. Nina Petrovskaya (and she was not the only one) accepted only decadence from Symbolism. She immediately wanted to *play* her own life—and in this essentially false task she remained truthful, honest to the end. She was a true victim of decadence.

For the Symbolist or the decadent, love opened the straightest and shortest access to an inexhaustible trove of emotions. It was enough to be in love for a person to be supplied with all the subjects of prime lyrical necessity: Passion, Despair, Triumph, Madness, Vice, Sin, Hatred and so forth. Therefore everyone was always in love: if not in actual fact, then they at least persuaded themselves that they were as if in love; they would fan the least spark of anything resembling love with all their might. Not for nothing were there even such things as "love of love."

A genuine feeling has degrees from eternal love to a fleeting infatuation. The very concept of "infatuation" was repellent to the Symbolists. They were *obligated* to extract the maximum emotional possibilities from each love. According to their moral and aesthetic codex, each love was supposed to be fateful, eternal. They sought the superlative degree in everything. If making a love "eternal" didn't work out, one could fall out of love. But each fall out of love and new falling in love had to go along with the most profound upheavals, internal tragedies and even new coloring of one's whole worldview. That was in essence why it was all being done.

Love and all the emotions proceeding from it were supposed to be experienced in extreme intensity and fullness, without half-shades and chance admixtures, without hateful psychologisms. The Symbolists wanted to nourish themselves on the most full-bodied essences of feeling. A genuine feeling is personal, concrete, unrepeatable. A made-up or inflated one lacks those qualities. It turns into its own abstraction, into an idea about a feeling. That's why it was so often written with a capital letter

Nina Petrovskaya was not pretty. But in 1903 she was young—and that's a lot. She was "fairly intelligent," as Blok said, was "unexpected," as they would have said if she had lived a century earlier. The main thing was that she was very good at "picking up the tone." She became the object of loves at once.

The first to fall in love with her was a poet who fell in love with everyone without exception. He offered her a headlong and incinerating love. There was no possible way to refuse: she was moved both by flattered self-regard (the poet was becoming famous), and by fear of seeming provincial, and by the main thing: she had already accepted the idea of "moments." It was time to begin "experiencing." She persuaded herself that she was also in love. The first affair flashed and burned out, leaving an unpleasant residue in her soul—something like a hangover. Nina decided to "purify her soul," which was in fact already somewhat defiled by the poet's "orgiasm." She renounced "Sin," put on a black dress, repented. In fact, repenting was the right thing to do. But this was more an "experience of repentance" than genuine repentance.

In 1904 Andrei Bely was still very young, with golden curls and blue eyes, and charming to the highest degree. The backstreet newspapers cackled over his poems and prose, which struck people with their novelty, impertinence, and sometimes with flashes of genuine brilliance. How and why his brilliance was eventually wasted is another question. At the time no one could foresee this misfortune.

People went into raptures over him. In his presence it was as if everything instantly changed, realigned or was illuminated with his radiance. And in fact he really was radiant. Even the people who envied him seemed to be a little bit in love with him. Even Bryusov would sometimes fall under his charm. The all-round rapture, of course, was also picked up by Nina Petrovskaya. Soon it moved into being smitten, then into love.

O, if in those times they had been able to love simply, in the name of the one you loved, and in your own name! But it had to be love in the name of some kind of abstraction and against the abstraction's background. Nina was obliged to love Andrei Bely in any case in the name of his mystical vocation, in which she forced herself to believe, as did he. And he was supposed to appear before her in no other way than in the gleam of his ... I don't want to say counterfeit, but his Symbolist radiance. She decked out the lesser truth, her human, simply human love, in the garb of an immeasurably greater truth. A black string of rosary beads appeared on Nina Petrovskaya's black dress, and a black cross. Andrei Bely was wearing a cross of just the same kind ...

O, if he had just fallen out of love, simply cheated on her! But he didn't fall out of love, he "fled from temptation." He ran away from Nina, so that her overly earthly love would not smirch his pure raiment. He fled from her in order to shine more dazzlingly for another, whose name and patronymic and even mother's name were so arranged that it was Symbolistically obvious: she was the harbinger of the Woman clothed in the Sun. Meanwhile his friends, lisping and bowlegged mystics, came to visit Nina—to reproach her, to rebuke and offend her:

"Madam, you all but defiled our prophet! You are stealing the knights of the Eternal Feminine! You're playing a very dubious role! You are inspired by the Beast that emerged from the abyss."

Thus they played with words, distorting their meanings, distorting lives. Afterwards they distorted the life of the Woman dressed in the Sun herself, and of her husband, one of the most precious Russian poets.

Meanwhile Nina wound up abandoned as well as insulted. It's only too easy to understand that, like many abandoned women, she wanted simultaneously to get revenge on Bely and get him back. But the whole story, once it had fallen into the "Symbolist dimension," continued its development in the same place.

In autumn of 1904 I once happened to say to Bryusov that I saw many good things in Nina.

"What do you mean?" he snapped. "What, that she's a good housekeeper?"

He made a point of not noticing her. But he changed at once when her break with Bely became obvious, because in his position he couldn't remain neutral.

He was the representative of demonism. He was expected to "languish and gnash his teeth" before the Woman clothed in the Sun. Therefore, Nina, her competitor, now turned from a "good housekeeper" into something more significant, took on a demonic aura. He offered her an alliance—against Bely. The alliance was immediately anchored by mutual love. Once again it's all very understandable and true to life: things like this often happen. It's understandable that Bryusov fell in love with her, in his way, understandable that she unwittingly sought consolation in him, to soothe her wounded pride, and to "get revenge" on Bely through union with him.

At that time Bryusov was interested in occultism, spiritualism, black magic—most likely not believing in all of it for real, but believing in the exercises themselves as a gesture that expressed a certain movement of the soul. I think Nina had just the same attitude to it. She can't have believed that her magical experiments, directed by Bryusov, would in fact restore Bely's love for her. But she experienced it as a genuine alliance with the devil. She wanted to believe in her own witchery. She was a hysteric, and perhaps that was especially attractive to Bryusov: he happened to know from the latest scholarly sources (he always respected scholarship) that in "the great age of witchcraft" hysterical women were considered, and considered themselves to be, witches. If "in the light of science" the witches of the sixteenth century turned out to be hysterics, then in the twentieth century it was worth Bryusov's trying to turn a hysteric into a witch.

However, not trusting too much in magic, Nina tried to take refuge in other means. In spring of 1905, Bely was giving a lecture in the small auditorium of the Polytechnic Museum. During the intermission Nina Petrovskaya went over to him and shot a Browning at close range. The revolver misfired; it was immediately taken from her hands. It's remarkable that she never made a second attempt. Once she told me (much later), "Never mind him. To tell the truth, I already killed him there, in the Museum."

I wasn't at all surprised at this "to tell the truth"—that's how mixed up, how confused reality and imagination were in people's consciousness.

What had become the center of life for Nina was for Bryusov the next in a series of "moments." When he had extracted all the emotions that ensued from the given situation, he was drawn to the pen. He depicted the whole story in his novel *Fiery Angel*, with a certain unoriginality, representing Andrei Bely as Count Heinrich, Nina Petrovskaya as Renata, and himself under the name of Ruprecht.[1]

In the novel Bryusov cut apart all the knots of relationship between the characters. He thought up a denouement and wrote "the end" under the story of Renata before the real-life collision that formed the basis of the novel had been resolved in reality. Nina Petrovskaya, for whom on the contrary the affair was dragging out hopelessly, did not die with Renata's death. What was still life for Nina had turned into a worn-out plot for Bryusov. It was burdensome for him to keep endlessly experiencing the same old chapters. He started to distance himself from Nina more and more. He started up new love affairs, less tragic ones. He started devoting more time to literary matters and all sorts of congresses, which he was always very keen on. He was in part even drawn to the home hearth (he was married).

For Nina this was a new blow. In essence, by this time (and it was already around 1906) her sufferings over Bely had dulled, gone quiet. But she had embraced the role of Renata. Now she faced a terrible danger—losing Bryusov too. She tried several times to resort to the time-tested method of many women; she tried to keep Bryusov by awakening his jealousy. These fleeting affairs (with "passersby," as she expressed it) made her feel disgust and despair. She scorned and insulted the "passersby." But it was all for nothing. Bryusov was cooling. Sometimes he tried to exploit her infidelities in order to break with her completely. Nina moved from one extreme to another, first loving Bryusov, then hating him. But in every extreme she gave herself to despair. She would lie on the couch for two days straight, without food or sleep, covering her head with a black shawl, and cry. It seems that her encounters with Bryusov would pass in an equally difficult atmosphere. Sometimes she would be

---

1   *Author's note*: In 1934, in Moscow, a little book of Bryusov's selected poems came out from the publisher Academia. The appendix gives "Materials for a biography," put together by his widow, who confirms that *The Fiery Angel* was based on an actual "episode."

overcome by attacks of fury. She would break furniture, smash objects, throwing them "like boulders from a catapult," as *The Fiery Angel* describes a similar scene.

She resorted in vain to cards, then to wine. Finally, already in spring of 1908, she tried morphine. Then she got Bryusov addicted to morphine, and that was her true, though unwitting revenge. In autumn of 1909 she became gravely ill from the morphine, and she almost died. When she had recovered somewhat it was decided that she would go abroad, "into exile" in her words. Bryusov and I saw her off at the station. She was going away forever. She knew she would never see Bryusov again. She was leaving still half-sick, with a doctor to attend her. It was November of 1911. She had lived through seven years of earlier Moscow sufferings. She was leaving now for new ones, which were fated to last another sixteen years.

I don't know her wanderings abroad in detail. I know that from Italy she traveled to Warsaw, then to Paris. Here, in 1913 it seems, she once jumped out a hotel window onto Boulevard Saint-Michel. She broke her leg, which didn't heal well, and she wound up lame.

The war found her in Rome, where she stayed until autumn of 1922 in horrifying poverty, first in spasms of despair, then in bouts of resignation, which would give way to even more tempestuous despair. She lived by begging, asked for alms, sewed underwear for soldiers, wrote screenplays for a film actress, then starved again. She drank. Sometimes she would reach very deep degrees of decline. She converted to Catholicism. "My new and secret name, written somewhere in the indelible rolls of San Pietro, is Renata," she wrote to me.

She came to hate Bryusov. "I was smothering from spiteful happiness that *he* can't reach me now, that now others are suffering. As far as I know—what kind of others—he'd already finished off L'vova before . . . I was living, taking revenge on him with each movement, with each movement of thought."

She came here, to Paris, in spring of 1927, after five years of a beggarly existence in Berlin. She arrived without a penny to her name. She turned out to have a fair number of friends here. They helped her as well as they could and, it seems, sometimes more than they could. Sometimes they managed to find work for her, but she was unable to work any more. In eternal drunkenness, without losing her reason, she already had one foot in the grave.

In Blok's diary, on November 6, 1911, there's a strange entry:

Nina Ivanovna Petrovskaya is "dying."

Blok had received this news from Moscow, but why did he write the word "dying" in quotation marks?

At that point Nina really was dying: this was the illness before her departure from Russia, which I spoke of above. But Blok put the word "dying" in quotation marks because he heard the news with an attitude of ironic distrust. He knew that Nina Petrovskaya had been constantly promising to die, to kill herself, ever since 1906. She lived with the unending thought of death for twenty-two years. Sometimes she would joke about herself:

> Ustiushkin's mother
> Was preparing to die.
> She didn't actually die:
> She just killed time.

Now I'm looking over her letters. February 26, 1925: "It seems that I can't manage any more." April 7, 1925: "You probably think I've died? Not yet." June 8, 1927: "I swear to you, there's no other way out." September 12, 1927: "Just a little longer, and I won't need any more places, any kind of work." September 14, 1927: "This time I should be dying soon."

This is in her more recent letters. I don't have the older ones at hand. But it was always the same thing—in letters, and in conversations.

What kept her back? I think I know what.

Nina's life was a lyrical improvisation, in which, just measuring it against similar improvisations by other characters, she strove to create something integral—"a poem from her personality." The end of the personality, just like the end of a poem about it, is death. In essence, the poem was finished in 1906, the same year that the plot of *The Fiery Angel* breaks off. After that both in Moscow and in her foreign wanderings Nina lived through a protracted, tormenting, terrible, but unnecessary epilogue that lacked any development. Nina wasn't afraid of breaking it off, but she couldn't. The sense of an artist, who was creating life like a poem, whispered to her that the end should be connected with some other final event, with the snap of some one other thread that attached her to life. Finally that event took place.

From 1908, following her mother's death, she was the guardian of her younger sister Nadya, a creature who was both mentally and physically undeveloped (some kind of childhood accident had happened to her: she'd been scalded with boiling water). She was not an idiot, but she was distinguished by a kind of extreme quietness, humility. She was unbearably pathetic and attached to her older sister to the point where she forgot about herself. Of course, she had no kind of life of her own. In 1909, as she left Russia, Nina took her along, and from then on Nina shared the miseries of life abroad with her. This was the sole and final being who still had a real connection with Nina and who connected Nina to life.

All autumn of 1927 Nadya was ill, as quietly and uncomplainingly as she had lived. She died just as quietly, on January 13, 1928, of stomach cancer. Nina went to the mortuary hospital where Nadya was a patient. She pricked her sister's little corpse with a safety pin, and then with the same pin—her own hand: she wanted to infect herself with post-mortem poison, to die *the same* death. However, her hand healed after at first swelling up.

At that time Nina would sometimes visit me. Once she stayed with me for three days. She spoke with me in that strange language of the 1900s, which had once connected us, was common to us, but which I had since then almost lost the ability to understand.

Nadya's death wrote the final phrase of the extended epilogue. A month and change later, with her own death, Nina Petrovskaya added the final period.

Versailles, 1928.

BENEDIKT LIVSHITZ

From The One-and-a-Half-Eyed Archer (1933)

Translated by John E. Bowlt

[On first reading Khlebnikov's manuscripts]:

I soon sensed that I was being separated from my planet and that I was already observing it as an outsider.

What I experienced in that first moment was not like being lifted up in an aeroplane and losing contact with the earth.

There was no flight of inspiration.

No liberty.

On the contrary, the whole of my being was rooted to the spot by an apocalyptic terror.

If the dolomites, the porphyries and the slates of the Caucasus mountains had suddenly come to life before my eyes and, gnashing their teeth with the flora and fauna of the mesozoic era, had approached me from all sides, they could not have made any greater impression on me.

Because I saw language *come alive* with my very own eyes.

The breath of the primordial word wafted into my face.

And I realized that I had been born dumb.

The whole of Dal[1] with its countless locutions floated amidst the raging elements like a tiny island.

The elements swamped it, turned roots upwards the petrified linguistic strata—whose strata which we had come to regard as firm ground.

Dal, so immense and impenetrable, suddenly became cozy and familiar. You could come to grips with him. Indeed, he lay in the same historical stratum as I and was entirely commensurable with my linguistic consciousness.

But this minute script on accounting paper ruined all my speech patterns, chucked me into a wordless space, condemned me to dumbness. I experienced the fury of a social misfit and out of a sense of self-survival was prepared to repudiate Khlebnikov.

Of course, this was only my first impulse.

I stood face to face with an extraordinary phenomenon.

[. . . .]

In the pictorial and poetical iconography of the "King of Time" there exists a notable tendency to depict him as a bird. In his immutable grey suit—whose cloth was so tangled up that it had taken the form of his body and had turned into plumage—he really did resemble a pensive stork. [. . . .] And that head, sunken between his shoulders, gave him an air of extreme absentmindedness which aroused one's mischievous desire to prod him with a finger, to pinch him, to see what would happen.

Aware of his own "celestial" significance, he moved in an orbit and at a speed which he had selected, and he did not attempt to adapt this movement to any chance encounters. If, in the field of history, nothing attracted him more than the consistency of events expressed in numbers, in his personal life he allowed chance to intrude upon his own, Khlebnikovian fate with condescension and arrogance. [. . . .]

Today I write "genius" without hesitation . . .

---

1   *Eds.* Vladimir Dal's magisterial *Explanatory Dictionary of the Great Russian Language.*

Irina Odoevtseva

From On the Banks of the Neva (1967)

Translated by Sibelan Forrester

G umilyov's first lecture at the Tenishchev School was scheduled for five. But I was there an hour early, to get a seat near the front.

The auditorium gradually filled up with a wide variety of people. The audience at the first lectures is completely different from the audience afterwards. The better part were listeners of an advanced age, even a very advanced age. Some fine ladies, some bearded members of the intelligentsia, intermixed with proletarians in red ties. Soon they all dropped out and, without having received what they sought from "The Living Word," moved to other courses.

There were a great many courses at that time—from basket-weaving and chicken-farming to the study of Egyptian and Sanskrit inscriptions. You could study anything you wanted to—and for free.

Five o'clock arrived. Then quarter past, then five-thirty. The audience began to show unmistakable signs of impatience—coughing and stamping their feet.

Vsevolodsky had already jumped up on stage twice to announce that the lecture would, absolutely would be taking place:

"Nikolai Stepanovich Gumilyov has already left his house and he'll be here right now, right now. Don't leave! Here you have a warm place to sit. Here it's warm and light. And comfortable. But on the street it's cold and windy, rainy. The devil knows what's going on outside. And at home too, you also have no heat and no light. Nothing but a smoky lamp," he went on persuasively. "Don't leave!"

But the audience, not heeding his persuasions, began to dribble out little by little. My neighbor on the left, a nervous lady with a pince-nez trembling on her nose, loudly left the auditorium, giving me a mocking nod:

"And you, what, you're staying? You plan to hibernate here all winter?"

My neighbor on the right, a university student, answered her in a reasonable way:

"We've waited so long, we can wait a little longer. Especially because there's nowhere to rush off to. At least, not for me."

"Or for me," I repeat like an echo.

I really was ready to wait until morning.

Vsevolodsky, busting his gut, tried to keep the audience from leaving. "Nikolai Stepanovich will be here any moment! You'll be sorry you didn't hear Gumilyov's first lecture!"

"He'll appear any second!"

And Gumilyov really did appear.

He "appeared," instead of walking in. It was a strange phenomenon. There was something theatrical in it, even something occult. Or, more accurately, it was the manifestation of a being from another planet. And everyone felt it—a surprised whisper rolled through the rows.

And fell silent.

On the stage, after slipping in through a side door, stood Gumilyov. Tall, narrow-shouldered, in a deerskin coat with a white pattern on the hem, which flapped around his long, skinny legs. His deerskin hat with earflaps and his bright African briefcase gave him an even more unusual appearance.

He stood motionless, looking straight in front of him. For a minute? Perhaps more, perhaps less. But it seemed like a long time to me. Painfully long. Then he moved towards the speaker's table right by the footlights, sat down, carefully put his bright briefcase on the table and only then lifted his deerskin hat with earflaps off his head, using both hands—like a bishop's mitre—and installed it on the briefcase.

He did all this slowly, very slowly, clearly counting on the effect.

"Ladies and gentlemen," he began in a ringing voice that rose into the heavens, "I presume that most of you are poets. Or, rather, you consider yourselves poets. But I fear that, once you've heard my lecture, you'll be very much shaken in that certainty of yours.

"Poetry is not at all what you think, and what you write and consider to be poetry has hardly even a distant relationship to it.

"Poetry is a science just like, say, mathematics. Not only is it impossible to become a poet (with the very rare exception of geniuses, who of course don't count) without studying it completely, but you can't even be a person who can understand, who can value poems."

Gumilyov spoke solemnly, smoothly and peremptorily. I listened with distrust and bewilderment and looked at him.

So that's what he's like. And I hadn't even known that a poet could be so little like a poet. Blok (his picture hung in my room) is what a poet should be like. And Lermontov, and Akhmatova...

Out of naivety, I thought that you could always recognize a poet.

I looked confusedly at Gumilyov.

A sharp disappointment—Gumilyov was the first poet, the first live poet, I had seen and heard, and he was so not like a poet!

Meanwhile, I was listening to him badly. I sat in some kind of mindless stupefaction. I saw, but I didn't hear. Or rather, I heard, but I didn't understand.

It was hard for me to concentrate on the complicated theory of poetry that Gumilyov was developing. The words slipped past my consciousness, break up into sounds.

And they didn't mean anything.

So that's what he's like, Gumilyov? It was hard to imagine a more unattractive, more peculiar person. Everything in him was peculiar and peculiarly unattractive. An elongated head, as if it had been pulled upward, with an inordinately high, flat forehead. Hair of an indeterminate color, in a buzz cut. Thin eyebrows, as if moth-eaten. Under heavy eyelids, completely flat eyes.

An ashen-grey color to his face. Narrow pale lips. He also smiled in a completely peculiar way. There was something piteous and at the same time crafty in his smile. Something Asiatic. Something of the "metallic idol," with which he compared himself in a poem:

> I'm here like a metallic idol
> Amid the playthings of porcelain.

But it was only much later that I saw his smile. That day he didn't smile even once.

Although he resembled a "metallic idol" even now... He sat overly straight, lifting his head high up. His narrow hands with long straight fingers, like bamboo rods, were crossed on the table. One leg crossed over the other. He maintained complete immobility. It seemed as if he didn't even blink. Only the pale lips stirred on his frozen face.

And suddenly he sharply changed his position. He put his left foot forward. Straight at the audience.

"What's he doing sticking the hole in the sole of his shoe right into our noses? How rude!" my neighbor the student whispers.

I shush him.

But he really did have a hole in the sole of his shoe. A hole not in the middle, but on the edge. And half the heel was worn down, as if cut off with a knife. That meant Gumilyov had a crooked, clumsy gait. And that didn't suit a poet at all either.

He continued speaking solemnly and verbosely. I continued gazing at him without looking away.

And it started to seem to me a bit as if his slanted flat eyes were shining with a particular mysterious gleam.

I understood that it was about him, of course about him, that Akhmatova had written:

> And the eyes of mysterious, dark visages
> Took a glance at me...

For she had been his wife. She had been in love with him.

And now I already saw a completely different Gumilyov. Perhaps still unattractive, but enchanting. He really did have an icon's face—flat, as in the ancient icons, and the same kind of bifurcated, riddling look. If he had been Akhmatova's husband, then perhaps he was "like a poet" after all? Only I hadn't been able to see it at first.

Gumilyov finished. He lifted his head and gave the audience an expectant look.

"He's waiting for us to applaud," whispered my neighbor the student.

"Perhaps someone would like to ask me a question?" the ringing, solemn voice spoke out again.

Silence in reply. Silence that lasted a long time. Clearly—there was nothing to ask about.

And suddenly, from one of the back rows, a ringing, mockingly nervy question: "And where can a person read all these subtleties?"

Gumilyov lowered his heavy eyelids and thought a bit; then, as if he had thought over every side of the answer, he pompously pronounced:

"You can't read 'these subtleties' anywhere at all. But in order to prepare for an understanding of these, as you were so good as to express it, subtleties, I recommend that you read the eleven volumes of natural philosophy by Titus Lucretius Carus."

My neighbor the student snorted indignantly.

"What does natural philosophy have to do with this?"

But Gumilyov's answer had clearly produced the desired impression. No one else had the nerve to ask a question.

After waiting a little bit, Gumilyov stood up and, facing the audience, put his deerskin hat on his head like a crown. Then he turned and slowly picked up his bright African briefcase off the table and slowly processed toward the side door.

Now I saw that his walk really was uneven, but that didn't interfere with its solemnity.

"A pea-green clown! A circus trickster!" people said indignantly behind me. "He's dressed up as a Samoyed native and putting on an act!"

"What arrogance, what disrespect for the audience! No professor would permit himself..." my neighbor the student was boiling over.

"I feel personally offended," a grey-haired lady clucked. "How dare he? Who is he, just imagine?"

"Yes, we've witnessed a genuine African hunter. He's lying about all of it, probably. He looks just like an office worker and never did visit Africa ... Malarkey!"

That was the last thing I heard. I was running into the wind so as not to hear the repulsive offended voices as they condemned the poet. I wasn't with them, I was with him, even if he wasn't what I had expected...

Many months later, when I had already become "Odoevtseva, my pupil," as Gumilyov would call me with pride, he admitted to me with a laugh what a torment that ill-fated lecture, the first one in his life, had been for him.

"What it was! Ah, Lord, what it was! Lunacharsky suggested that I teach a course on poetry and lead a practical workshop at "The Living Word." I was glad to agree right away. Of course! My long-cherished wish had come true—to educate not only real readers, but perhaps even real poets. I went home in the happiest mood. That night, I woke up and suddenly saw myself on the stage—all those eyes looking at me, all those ears listening to me—and I went cold with fear. It's hard to believe, but it's true. I lay awake there until morning.

"That night I started to suffer from insomnia. If you only knew what I suffered! I was ready to run to Lunacharsky and resign, to explain that I'd made a mistake, that I couldn't ... But pride stopped me. A week before the lecture I stopped eating. I rehearsed my lecture in front of the mirror. I learned it by heart.

"The last couple of days I prayed that I'd get sick, break my leg, that the Tenishchev School would burn down—everything, everything you can imagine, just to get free from that nightmare.

"I left my house the way people go to be executed. But I couldn't make myself go into the entrance of the Tenishchev School. I kept walking back and forth with the consciousness that I was perishing. That's why I was so late.

"On the stage I didn't see anything or understand anything, from fear. I was afraid of tripping, falling, or missing the chair when I sat down and landing on the floor. That would have been something to see!

"I brought the lecture with me and wanted to read it from the manuscript. But I had absent-mindedly put my hat on my briefcase and I didn't have the strength to move it to another place.

"Oh, Lord, what a horror it was! When I started speaking, it got much better. My memory didn't let me down. But then my damn knee started twitching. And how! Worse and worse. I had to stretch out my leg so it wouldn't start jumping. Horrible! I don't know, I don't remember how I managed to finish. I was conscious of only one thing; that I had disgraced myself forever. And I decided on the spot that the next day I'd leave for Bezhetsk, that I couldn't remain in Petersburg after such a disgrace.

"And why on earth did I blab about the eleven volumes of natural philosophy? From fear and shame, it must be. In a complete stupor."

"But you had such an unbelievably self-confident, pompous tone and look," I say.

Gumilyov rocked with laughter.

"I went overboard out of a feeling of self-preservation. Like that eccentric, you remember, who:

> Hanged himself entirely in the attic
> Out of a sense of self-preservation.

"No it's true, what all that looked like most of all was suicide. An utter catastrophe. The most dreadful day of my life.

"When I got home, I made a vow to myself never to give lectures again." He spreads his arms. "And, as you see, I didn't keep the vow. But now, when I often have two lectures a day, it doesn't even occur to me to worry.

"And what, I ask, was I so deathly afraid of?"

[....]

Winter of 1919-1920. A very cold, very hungry, very black winter.

Every day I come back alone from the Institute of the Living Word late in the evening. Along completely deserted, dark—"just poke your eye out"—frightening streets. Robbery had become an everyday phenomenon. With the arrival of twilight, people were getting robbed all over. In utter silence, in the utter silence I would sometimes hear the sound of footsteps from a person walking ahead of me. I would try to get closer to him. It didn't even occur to me that any second now a flashlight could light up and I'd hear the terrible, "Off with your fur coat!"—my cat-skin coat with the ermine collar. I was very fond of it. Not the way you're fond of a thing, but as if it were a living creature, and I called it "Murzik."

Gumilyov liked Murzik as well. Sometimes in the morning, dropping by to see me unexpectedly, Gumilyov would suggest, "Should we take Murzik out for a walk in the snow? He must be bored up there on the hanger."

I always agreed gladly.

Passing by a church, Gumilyov always paused, took off his deerskin hat with the earflaps, and zealously blessed himself with a wide sign of the cross, "to make enemies fear." Precisely "blessed himself with the sign of the cross," he didn't just simply cross himself.

Passersby would look at him with surprise. Some would flinch away to one side. Some would laugh. It really was an astonishing spectacle. Gumilyov, long, narrow-shouldered, in a wide coat with a white pattern along the hem, which flapped like a skirt around his thin legs, with his hat off in the freezing cold, in front of a church, could seem not only strange, but ridiculous.

But to have the nerve in those days to underline one's belonging to a persecuted "cult" so sharply—you had to have civic courage.

Gumilyov had more civic courage than is necessary. No less than he had thoughtlessness.

Once at a poetry evening with men from the Baltic fleet, reading his African poems, he declaimed especially loudly and distinctly:

> I gave to him a Belgian pistol
> And a picture of my sovereign.

A rumble of protest ran around the auditorium. A few sailors jumped up. Gumilyov continued reading calmly and loudly, as if he hadn't noticed, not deigning to pay attention to the indignant listeners.

When he finished his poem, he crossed his arms on his chest and calmly looked around the hall with his slanted eyes, waiting for the applause.

Gumilyov waited and looked at the sailors, the sailors looked at him.

And suddenly the applause burst out, thundered, roared.

It was clear to everyone: Gumilyov had won. He hadn't ever been applauded like this here.

"There was a minute when I even started to feel scared," he told me, as we were coming back from the reading. "After all some comrade sailor, 'the pride and glory of the red fleet,' could have pulled out his un-Belgian pistol and taken a shot at me, the way he'd shoot at the 'picture of my sovereign.' And, notice, without any unpleasant repercussions for himself. In a revolutionary outburst, so to speak."

I had been sitting in the front row between two of the Baltic fleet sailors. And I was so frightened that my hands and feet went cold in spite of the heat in the hall. But I hadn't thought that Gumilyov would be scared too.

"Even very scared," Gumilyov confirmed. "How could I not be? Only an idiot doesn't see danger and fear it. Bravery and fearlessness aren't synonyms. You can't avoid fearing what's frightening. But it's essential to know how to overcome fear, and the main thing is not to show that you're afraid. That's the way I conquered them today. And it's such a pleasant feeling. As if I'd been to Africa hunting lions. I haven't felt so light and so good for a long time."

Yes, Gumilyov was pleased. But a "rumor" started going around in the city, like smoke driven by the wind, about "Gumilyov's counterrevolutionary performance." Meeting on the street, two citizens who "weren't yet slaughtered" would whisper to each other, looking around timidly:

"Did you hear? That Gumilyov! He went and declared to the sailors from the stage, 'I'm a monarchist, true to my sovereign, and I carry his portrait close to my heart.' Good for him, even if he is a poet!"

That rumor, perhaps, reached ears for which it was ill-suited. The conclusion—that Gumilyov was a monarchist and an active counterrevolutionary—was made, perhaps, some time before Gumilyov was arrested.

BORIS PASTERNAK

On Vladimir Mayakovsky (1931)
(*from* Safe Conduct)

Translated by Christopher Barnes

[....]
Our first meeting took place in the inhibited atmosphere of group prejudices. Long before that, in the way that one poet shows off another, Yulian Anisimov had shown me his verses printed in *The Judges' Hatchery*. But that was in the epigone circle called "Lirika." The epigones were not ashamed of their sympathies, and in their circle Mayakovsky was discovered as a phenomenon of promising proximity, like a colossus.

On the other hand, in the innovatory "Tsentrifuga" group of which I soon formed part (this was in the spring of 1914), I learned that Shershenevich, Bolshakov and Mayakovsky were our enemies and that a deadly earnest confrontation was in store. I was not in the least surprised at the prospect of a quarrel with the man who had already astonished me and whom from a distance I found increasingly attractive. That was all there was to the innovators' originality. All winter the birth of "Tsentrifuga" was accompanied by endless rows. All winter I was aware of doing nothing but playing a game of group discipline, and all I had done was sacrifice both taste and conscience to it. Now I prepared once again to betray anything and everything when the time came. But on this occasion I overestimated myself.

It was a hot day in late May, and we were already sitting in a teashop on the Arbat when the three men just mentioned staged a noisy, youthful entrance from the street. They handed their hats to the attendant without toning down their conversation, which up till now had been outdinned by tramcars and cart-horses, they approached us with relaxed dignity. They had beautiful voices—this marked the beginning of what later became the declamatory manner in poetry. Their dress was elegant, whereas ours was slovenly. Our adversaries' position was in every way superior to our own.

It all hinged on the fact that they had once provoked us, we had answered even more rudely, and now the whole matter had to be cleared up. Whilst Bobrov wrangled with Shershenevich, I watched Mayakovsky without taking my eyes off him. I believe it was the first time I saw him at such close quarters.

His open letter "e" instead of "a" was an actor's trait which rocked his diction like a piece of sheet iron. His deliberate brusqueness could easily be imagined as the hallmark of other professions and situations. He was not alone in this striking manner. His companions sat next to him. One of them played the dandy as he did. The other, like him, was a genuine poet. Yet these similarities did not diminish the exceptional quality of Mayakovsky but only emphasized it. Instead of playing one game, he played all of them at once. And instead of playing roles, Mayakovsky on the contrary played at life itself. This much could be sensed at first glance without any thought of his eventual fate. And it was this that riveted one's attention and also scared one.

Although any person can be seen at full height when he walks or stands, whenever Mayakovsky appeared it seemed miraculous and everyone turned in his direction. What was natural in his case appeared to be supernatural. The reason for this was not his stature, but a more general elusive quality. To a greater extent than with other people, his being was there in his personal manifestation. He contained within him all the expression and finality which are lacked by the majority, who emerge from the murk of their half-brewed intentions and barren conjectures—and then only do so when particularly jolted. He seemed to exist as on the day after completing some immense spiritual life that had been lived through already in reserve for all future occasions, and everyone now encountered him wreathed in its irreversible consequences. He would sit down on a chair as though mounting a motorbike. He bent forward, cut and quickly swallowed his Wiener Schnitzel. He played cards with sidelong glance and never a turn of the head. He walked majestically along the Kuznetsky and dully intoned through his nose some particularly profound snatches of his own and other people's verse, like extracts from the liturgy. He scowled, he grew, he travelled and he gave public recitations. And just as behind the upright stance of a speeding skater, always in the background one seemed to glimpse some day of Mayakovsky's own, preceding all others, on which he had taken that amazing run-up which set him so unconstrainedly and massively erect. Behind his bearing one had a vision of something akin to a decision which had been put into effect and whose consequences could not be revoked. This decision was the fact of his own genius. And at some point he was so astonished on encountering it that it had prescribed a theme for him for all time, and he surrendered the whole of himself to its embodiment without mercy or hesitation.

But he was still young. The forms which this theme was to take still lay ahead of him. Yet the theme itself was an insatiable one and brooked no delay. So, as an initial gesture of deference to it he was obliged to anticipate his own future, and when realized in the first person such self-preemption is an act of posing. From these poses—natural in the highest realm of self-expression as everyday rules of propriety—he selected one of outward integrity, which is the hardest pose for an artist to maintain and the noblest one vis à vis his friends and those close to him. And he maintained this pose with such perfection that it is now almost impossible to describe what lay behind it.

But the mainspring of his brashness was a farouche timidity, and his pretense of willpower covered up a lack of will, phenomenally suspicious and prone to a quite gratuitous gloom. And just as deceptive was the function of his yellow blouse. He used it not to campaign against jackets worn by the middle classes, but to combat the black velvet of talent within him, whose dark-browed saccharine forms began to outrage him earlier than they would less gifted men. For nobody knew like him the utter vulgarity of a natural fire that is not gradually roused to fury by cold water. No one knew as he did that the passion which suffices to continue the race is insufficient for creativity, since the latter requires the passion needed to continue the race's *image*—i.e., a passion which inwardly resembles any human passions and one whose novelty has the semblance of a new divine promise.

Suddenly the discussions came to an end. The enemies we were meant to annihilate went away undefeated. And in fact the terms of the truce that had been concluded were humiliating for us.

Meanwhile it had grown dark outside and a drizzle had begun falling. After our foes had left, the teashop was drearily empty. One began noticing the flies, half-eaten cakes and glasses blinded with hot milk. But no thunderstorm came. The sun struck sweetly at the pavement snared in a network of fine mauve spots. It was the May of nineteen fourteen. The reverses of history were so very close. Yet who spared them a thought? The crass city was aflame with foil and enamel as in *The Golden Cockerel*. The lacquered greenery of poplars glistened. For the last time colors had that poisonous herbal quality which they were soon to part with forever. I was crazy about Mayakovsky and already missing him. Need I add that the people I betrayed were not at all the ones I intended?

Chance brought us together the following day beneath the awning of the Greek coffee-house. The great yellow boulevard lay flat outspread between the Pushkin monument and Nikitskaya Street. Lean, long-tongued dogs yawned and stretched themselves and settled their muzzles comfortably on their front paws. Nannies in garrulous pairs prattled on, constantly carping and lamenting at this and that. Butterflies folded their wings for a few moments, dissolving in the heat, then suddenly they spread themselves, drawn sideways by irregular ripples in the sultry air. A little girl in white and probably wringing wet hung suspended in the air, whipping herself about the heels with the swishing circles of a skipping-rope.

I caught sight of Mayakovsky from a distance and pointed him out to Loks. He was with Khodasevich playing heads or tails. Then Khodasevich got up, paid off his gambling debt, walked from under the awning and set off towards Strastnoy Boulevard. Mayakovsky was left sitting alone at his table. Loks and I went in a greeted him and fell into conversation. After a short while he offered to recite one or two poems for us.

The poplars glowed green. The lime-trees were a dryish green. Driven into a fury by fleas, the dozing dogs kept springing up on all four paws, calling on heaven to witness their moral impotence against brute force, then they would roll back on to the sand in an exasperated torpor. On the now renamed Brest Railway Line locomotives sounded raucous whistles, and all around people were cutting hair and shaving, baking and frying, trading and travelling—all of them totally unaware.

It was his tragedy *Vladimir Mayakovsky*, which had then just appeared. I listened with bated breath, my whole heart seized in rapture and completely forgetting myself. I had never heard anything like it before. Everything was there in it—the boulevard, the dogs, the poplars and the butterflies, the barbers, bakers, tailors and locomotives. Why bother to quote from it? We can all remember that sultry, mysterious and summery text, which is now available to everyone in its tenth edition.

Far away in the distance locomotives roared like bulls. In the laryngeal territory of his art there was that same absolute distance as on earth. Here was an unfathomable inspiration without which there is no originality; here, opening up at any point in life in any direction, was that infinity without which poetry is no more than a misunderstanding that merely needs to be clarified.

And how simple it all was! Art was called tragedy—the right name for it. And the tragedy was called *Vladimir Mayakovsky*. The title concealed a simple discovery of genius—that a poet is not the author, but the subject of a lyricism addressing itself to the world in the first person. The title was not the name of the author, but the surname of the contents.

As I left the boulevard that day, I carried the whole of him away with me and took him into my life. But he was gigantic. Parted from him there was no way of retaining him. And I kept losing him. Then he would remind me of himself—with poems called "Cloud in Trousers," "The Backbone Flute," "War and the Universe" and "Man." And what was eroded away in the intervals between was so immense that extraordinarily immense reminders were required. And such they were. Each of the stages I have mentioned caught me unprepared. Each time he had grown beyond recognition and was completely born anew, as on the first occasion. It was impossible to get accustomed to him. What was it about him that was so unusual?

He was endowed with some qualities that were relatively permanent. And my enthusiasm too was fairly constant. It was always ready for him. This being the case, it might seem that the process of growing accustomed to him need not have proceeded in such leaps, but that was how it was. While he continued to exist creatively I spent four years trying to get used to him, but I failed. And then I did so in the space of two and a quarter hours, the time required to read and examine his uncreative "150,000,000." After that I languished in this acclimatized state for more than ten years. Then, all at once, the condition cleared and left me with tears in my eyes as he again reminded me of himself "at the top of his voice" as once he used to do, but this time from beyond the grave.

What one failed to grow accustomed to was not Mayakovsky himself but the world which he held in his hands and which, when the fancy hit, he could either set in motion or bring to a standstill. I shall never understand what he gained by demagnetizing his magnet, after which, though still outwardly preserving its appearance, the horseshoe that once used the "feet of his lines" to make any imagination stand on end or attract any weights failed to stir so much as a grain of sand. In all history there can hardly be another example of a man advancing so far in a new experience and then so completely rejecting it, at the very hour he himself predicted and just at a time when this experience could have fulfilled such a vital need, albeit at the price of discomforts. Outwardly so logical yet inwardly hollow and unspontaneous, his place in the Revolution will always remain a mystery to me.

It was impossible to get accustomed to the Vladimir Mayakovsky of his tragedy, to the surname of its contents, to the poet eternally contained within poetry, to a potential realized only by the strongest, and not merely the so-called "interesting personality."

[....]

In what I have written so far I have described my own perception of Mayakovsky. But there is no love without scars and sacrifice. I have already described what Mayakovsky was like as he entered my life. It remains for me to recount how my life changed in consequence, and I shall now fill in this gap.

I returned home from the boulevard that day utterly shaken and unable to think what to do next. I felt that I was totally bereft of talent. But that was only half the trouble. I also felt a sort of guilt before him and could not make sense of it. Had I been younger, I would have given up literature. But my age prevented that. After so many transformations I had not the resolve to change course a fourth time.

Something else happened instead. The age and influences we shared established a kinship between Mayakovsky and myself. We had certain similar features in common. I noticed this and I realized that if I did not do something they would become more frequent in future. I had to protect him from their vulgarity. Unable to put a name to it, I resolved to renounce the thing which gave rise to them. I renounced the romantic manner. And hence came the non-romantic poetics of *Over the Barriers*.

But the romantic manner which I henceforth forbade myself concealed a whole way of viewing life. It was a conception of life as the life of a poet. It came down to us from the Symbolists, and the Symbolists adopted it from the Romantics, chiefly the Germans.

This conception of life had a hold on Blok, although only for a certain time. In the form that came naturally to him it failed to satisfy him. He was obliged either to intensify it or else to abandon it. And in fact he parted company with the idea. It was Mayakovsky and Esenin who intensified it.

The poet who posits himself as life's measure and pays for this with his life has a romantic conception of life which is overwhelmingly brilliant and irrefutable in its symbolism—i.e., in everything about its imagery which has any bearing on Orphism and Christianity. In this sense something permanent is embodied in the life of Mayakovsky and in the fate of Esenin—a fate which defies all adjectives and self-destructively pleads to be registered and disappears in the realm of myth.

But outside the legend this romantic scheme is a false one. The poet on whom it is founded is inconceivable without non-poets to set him off. Because this poet is not a living person absorbed by moral perception, he is a visual biographical emblem which requires a background to make his contours visible. Unlike Passion plays, which need a heaven in order be heard, this drama needs the evil of mediocrity in order to be seen, as the romantic always needs the philistine and with the disappearance of bourgeois mentality loses half its content.

The concept of biography as spectacle was characteristic of my age, and I shared it together with everyone else. I parted company with it at a stage when it was still a mild option with the Symbolists and before it presupposed any heroics or smelt of blood. I escaped from it first of all unconsciously, by renouncing the romantic devices which were upon it. But, secondly, I also consciously avoided it as a piece of glamour that ill-suited me, because by confining myself to craftsman—I was afraid of any poeticizing which might put me in a false or inappropriate position.

And when *My Sister—Life* appeared, in which some totally uncontemporary aspects of poetry found expression which were revealed to me the summer of the Revolution, the name of the force that produced the book became a matter of complete indifference to me, because it was a force immensely greater than myself or the poetic conceptions surrounding me.

[....]

In public registry offices there is no equipment for measuring truthfulness and no X-ray test for sincerity. In order for a record to be valid, nothing is needed but the firm hand which makes the entry. And then no doubts or disputes can arise.

Before he dies, the poet writes a last message in his own hand, leaving a legacy of treasure to the world as patent evidence. He measures his own sincerity and X-rays it with a speed that permits no alteration ... and then people all around start discussing, doubting and making comparisons!

They compare that last message with earlier examples, whereas it is comparable only with him alone and with the whole of his previous existence. People make conjectures about his feelings and are unaware that it is possible to love not just in a space of days (albeit for eternity) but (albeit not forever) with the entire accumulated force of the past.

There are two expressions which have long been marked by an equal banality: "man of genius" and "woman of beauty." How much they have in common!

From childhood she is constricted in her movements. She is lovely and realizes it early on in life. What we commonly call God's good earth is the only entity with which she can be completely herself, because with others she cannot take one step without causing hurt or else being hurt herself. When still a young girl she goes out of the house. What does she have in mind? She already receives letters via a mail-box. Only two or three friends are let into her secrets. All this is already here. So let us suppose she is going out to keep some tryst . . . .

She goes out of the gate. She would like the evening to notice her. She would like the heart of the air to be wrung for her and the stars to pick up something of her story. She would like the same renown enjoyed by trees and fences and all things on earth when they exist not in the mind but in the open air. Yet if one ascribed such wishes to her she would simply laugh and deny any such thought. But she has a distant cousin in this world, a person of immensely ordinary habit, who is there in order to know her better than she can know herself and ultimately to answer for her. She has a healthy love of healthy nature and is unaware that she constantly expects the universe to reciprocate this feeling.

It is springtime, a spring evening, old women sit out on the benches, and there are low fences and shaggy white willows. The sky is winegreen, weakly infused and pale. Here is her homeland, here are dust and dry, splintering voices. The sounds fall dry as woodchip, and their splinters fill the smooth hot silence. A man comes along the road to meet her—the very man it would be natural for her to meet. In her joy she keeps on telling him that she has come out just in order to meet him. Partly she is right. Who after all is not to some degree dust and homeland and a quiet spring evening? She forgets why she came out, but her feet remember. He and she walk together and the further they go the more people they encounter. And since she loves her companion with all her heart, her feet cause her more than a little distress. But they still carry her onwards, and the two of them can hardly keep pace with one another. But the road leads them unexpectedly to a wider space where it seems less crowded and where they might pause for breath and look around. Yet often at this very moment her distant cousin makes his own way there and they meet. And whatever happens now, it is all the same. All the same, some blissfully perfect "I am thou" binds them with every tie this world can conceive. And proudly, youthfully and wearily it stamps one profile on another like on a medal.

The beginning of April surprised Moscow in a white stupor of returning winter. On the seventh it began to thaw again, and on the fourteenth when Mayakovsky shot himself not everyone was yet used to the novelty of spring.

When I heard of the tragedy I summoned Olga Sillova to the scene. Something suggested to me that this shock might provide an outlet for her own grief. Between eleven and twelve the circle of waves caused by the shot was still spreading outwards. The news shook telephones, shrouded faces in pallor and sent people rushing to Lubyansky Passage, through the courtyard and into the house. There folk from the town and other tenants were already perched all the way up the staircase, huddled and weeping, hurled and splattered against the walls by the flattening force of the event. Yakov Chernyak and Romadin, who were first to tell me of the tragedy, came up to me. Zhenya [Pasternak's first wife] was with them. As I caught sight of her my cheeks started twitching convulsively. She was weeping as she told me to hurry upstairs. But at that moment they carried the body down past us on a stretcher, completely covered. Everyone rushed downstairs and blocked the exit, so that by the time we our way out, the ambulance was already driving out through the gateway. We followed after it and went to Gendrikov Lane.

Life outside the gates pursued its course and was indifferent as some folk wrongly claim. There still remained the concern of the asphalt courtyard, forever a participant in such dramas. The weak-legged air of spring wandered through the rubbery mud as though still learning to walk. Cockerels and children proclaimed their presence for all to hear. Their voices carried strangely in the early spring, despite the busy rattling of the town.

Slowly the tramcar made its way up Shvivaya Hill. There is a place there where first the right-hand and then the left-hand pavement approach so close below the window that you seize the strap as you involuntarily sway and bow down over Moscow. It is as though one were stooping to assist an old woman who has slipped, since the town suddenly drops on all fours, dolefully sheds watchmakers and cobblers, and raises and rearranges a few rooftops and belfries before suddenly standing up, shaking out its skirt-hem and launching the tramcar down a level and quite ordinary street.

This time its movements were such an obvious excerpt from the man who had shot himself, they so strongly recalled a vital part of his essence, that I quivered all over and the famous phone call from the "Cloud" thundered inside me as though someone was speaking it loudly right next to me. I stood in the gangway next to Sillova and bent over to remind her of those eight lines, but . . .

"And I sense that my 'I' is too small for me . . ."

My lips shaped the phrase like gloved fingers, but in my agitation I could not pronounce a single word.

Two empty cars stood by the gateway at the end of Gendrikov Lane. They were surrounded by a small inquisitive gathering. In the hall and dining-room people stood and sat. Some wore hats while others were bareheaded. He was lying further away, in the study. The door leading from the hall to Lili's room was open and on the threshold Aseev stood weeping with his head pressed against the door-frame. In there, over by the window, Kirsanov quivered finely as he sobbed in silence, his head drawn into his shoulders.

Even here the damp mist of mourning was interrupted by low murmurs of anxious conversation—just as after a requiem service thick as jam the first whispered words are so dry that they seem to come from beneath the floorboards and reek of mice. During one such interruption the concierge came cautiously into the room with a chisel slotted in his boot-top. Taking out the winter window-frame, he slowly and noiselessly opened the casement. Anyone outside without a coat must have shuddered with cold, and the sparrows and children kept rallying one another with inconsequent cries.

Someone tiptoed out from the room where the dead man lay and quietly asked whether a telegram had been sent to Lili. L. A. G. answered that it had. Zhenya took me to one side and commented how courageously L. A. was bearing the awful burden of the tragedy. She burst into tears. I squeezed her hand firmly.

The apparent unconcern of a boundless world came pouring in at the window. Across the sky, as though between earth and sea, grey trees stood and guarded the boundary. As I looked at the boughs covered in a fluster of buds I tried to picture far away beyond them that improbable city of London where the telegram had gone. Soon someone over there would be bound to give a cry, stretch out their arms towards us and fall down in a faint: My throat tightened. I decided to go back into his room in order this time to weep my fill.

He lay on his side with his face to the wall, sullen, tall, covered by a sheet up to his chin, and with his mouth half-open like someone asleep. Proudly turned away from everyone, even as he lay there, even in this sleep he stubbornly strained to get away and escape. His face reminded one of the time when he once described himself as a "handsome twenty-two-year old," for death had ossified a facial attitude that scarcely ever falls into its clutches. It was an expression with which people begin their life, not one with which they end it. His face was pouting and indignant.

Then there was a movement in the hall. The dead man's younger sister, Olga Vladimirovna, had turned up at the apartment independently of his mother and elder sister, who were already there, silently grieving among the crowd. Her entry was noisy and demanding. Her voice floated into the room ahead of her. As she came up the stairs alone, she was talking loudly to someone, obviously addressing her brother. Then she actually appeared, walking past everyone as if they were so much rubbish, and as she reached her brother's door she threw up her hands and stopped.

"Volodya!" she screamed, and her voice rang through the entire house. A moment passed. "He won't speak!" she shouted even louder. "He won't say anything! He won't answer! Volodya! Volodya! How horrible!" She began to collapse. They caught her and quickly tried to bring her round. But she had hardly come to herself when she greedily moved towards the body and hastily renewed her unquenched dialogue, sitting at his feet. I finally burst into the fit of weeping for which I had been longing.

It had been impossible to weep like this at the scene of the event where a herd-like sense of drama was quickly ousted by the fresh-fired fact. The asphalt yard there had stunk of deified inevitability, like saltpetre, which means that it reeked of a false urban fatalism that was founded on apelike mimicry and viewed life as a series of amenable, recordable sensations. They had been sobbing out there too, but only because the stricken throat and its animal sixth sense had reproduced the convulsions of apartment blocks, fire-escapes, a revolver case, and all the other things that made one sick with despair and vomit murder. His sister was the first person to weep for him of her own will and choice, as people weep for something great, and to the sound of her words, like a roaring organ accompaniment, one could weep insatiably and expansively.

She continued unrelenting. "They wanted a Bath-house!" Mayakovsky's own indignant voice could be heard strangely transposed to his sister's contralto. "They wanted it as funny as possible! And they had a good laugh! 'Called him out on stage!' ... And look what was happening to him! ... Why didn't you come to us, Volodya?" she wailed on, sobbing. Then she took a grip on herself and made an impulsive move to sit closer to him. "Do you remember? Can you remember, Volodya dear?" she suddenly reminded him, almost as though he were alive. And she began to recite:

> And I sense that my 'I' is too small for me.
> Someone stubbornly tries to break out of me,
> Hallo!

Who is speaking? Mother?
Mother! Your son is splendidly ill.
Mother! His heart is on fire.
Tell his sisters Lyuda and Olya.
Now he's nowhere to go.

When I went there in the evening he was already lying in his coffin. The faces that had filled the room during the day were now replaced by others. It was fairly quiet. Hardly anyone was weeping now.

Suddenly down below the window I imagined I could see his life, belonging now entirely to the past. It stretched away obliquely from the window in the form of a quiet road planted with trees like Povarskaya Street. And the first thing on that road, right by the wall, was our Soviet State—this impossible, unprecedented State of ours, bursting in upon the centuries and taken up by them for ever after. It stood right below. One could have called and reached out one's hand to it. In tangibility and extraordinariness it somehow resembled the dead man. So striking was the link between them both, they could have seemed like twins.

And then it also occurred to me quite spontaneously that in fact this man had been the only citizen of our State. Others had struggled, sacrificed their lives and created things, or else they had endured and been perplexed, but still they had all been natives of a past epoch and despite their differences they were relatives and kinsmen of that age. Only this man had had the climatic newness of the times flowing in veins. And the whole of him was strange with the strange features of the epoch, half of which had still to be realized. I began recalling traits of his character and his independence, utterly unique in many ways. And all of these were explained by his adjustment to conditions which, though implicit in our age, had not yet assumed a relevance to the present. Since childhood he was the spoilt favorite of a future that yielded to him quite early on and seemingly with no great effort.

MAXIMILIAN VOLOSHIN

From a review of Kuzmin's Alexandrian Songs (1906)

Translated by Sibelan Forrester

[....] When you meet Kuzmin for the first time, you want to ask him, "Tell me frankly, how old are you?" but you don't have the nerve, fearing that you'll get this answer: "Two thousand years old."

Without a doubt, he's young and, reasoning common-sensically, he can't be older than thirty, but there is something so ancient in his outer appearance that the thought appears: couldn't he be one of the Egyptian mummies who through some kind of sorcery had recovered his life and memory? Only he's not a mummy from ancient Egypt. You often encounter faces like his in the portraits of El-Fayum, which, since they were discovered quite recently, awoke such interest in European scholars, as they gave the first conception of the character of faces of the Alexandrine epoch. Kuzmin has the same kind of enormous black eyes, the same kind of smooth black beard, which sharply frames his pale, waxen face, the same kind of thin moustache that flows over his upper lip without hiding it.

He's short in height, narrow-shouldered and flexible in his body, like a woman.

He has a splendid Greek profile, a finely modeled and boldly sculpted skull, a forehead in one line with his nose and a deep, bold indentation separating his nose from his upper lip and passing into the fine bow of his lips.

You may see such a profile in depictions of Pericles and on the bust of Diomedes.

But the character of indubitable antique genuineness gives Kuzmin's face a particular violation of proportions which is encountered only on Greek vases: his eye is very deep-set and low in relationship to the bridge of his nose, as if somewhat moved onto his cheek, if you look at him in profile.

His mouth almost always reveals his upper teeth somewhat, and that gives his face the character of decrepitude that is so striking in it.

It cannot be doubted that he died in Alexandria as a young and handsome man and was very inexpertly embalmed. But the time he spent in the grave can be sensed in him, as on the resurrected Lazarus in Dierx's poem.

OTHER PROSE WORKS

INNOKENTY ANNENSKY

Letter to Alexander Blok (1907)

Translated by Sibelan Forrester

June 18, 1907
Tsarskoe Selo
in Èderman's house

Dear Alexander Alexandrovich,

I have read "Snow Mask" and read it once more. There are marvelous lines, stanzas and pieces. Others I still have not made sense of and will I make sense of them, i.e., will I be able to understand the possibility of survival? The unruly rhythmic quality evades me. I try to read, I recall your reading—I put the book down on my knees...

"Infatuation" is hellishly difficult, but

> a green spot of light
> In the smoldering crystal...

a marvelous symbol of the exhaustion of dawn.
  I thank you, dear poet.

Your I. Annensky

I'm sending this letter with a delay, was waiting to get your address.
  I. Annensk. [sic]

INNOKENTY ANNENSKY

Letter to Maximilian Voloshin (1909)

Translated by Sibelan Forrester

March 6, 1909

Dear Maximilian Alexandrovich,

Yes, you'll be alone. Get used to burning like a candle that burglars forgot as they went down into the cellar, and one that flares up, and flickers, and spills wax on the stone step, and casts light only on zigzags—mice, perhaps Apollonianly ghostly ones at that, You are condemned to an ungrateful role, perhaps, at least for the next few years. For you have a school... you have not only luminaries, but all kinds of brown spots of grass, tangled by Night, that have yet to awaken... know that they are the *word* and that nothing, *besides the word*, will allow *them*, the luminaries, not to exist, that their beauty, and lapidarity, and urgency, and melancholy all spring from there. And do many people really understand what the word is—among us? Why, hardly anyone. Three of us, and maybe I've miscounted. By the way, I may be mistaken, Sergei Konstant[inovich] and you see farther ahead than I, dejected as I am by the past. But you know, among us too of late, oof! how many are there of those who tend the word and, if you please, are ready to talk about a *cult of the word*. But they don't understand that the most *terrible* and *powerful* word, i.e., the most *mysterious*—perhaps precisely the word—is *quotidian*. What did

Vyacheslav Ivanov alone do with the Russian public? He scared everyone south of the Moscow River to death. Worse than Arthur Rimbaud. We understand him, we feel good and aren't scared; we're even interested ... it's great that way. But how would a mere woman feel? Do you like Charles Cro??? There's a poet: do-re-mi-fa-so-la-ti-do ... Remember? That's what we need—i.e., *we* in the broad sense of the word—we the readers of Russia. Perhaps that's the very bridge that, perhaps only as a mirage, but will nevertheless be cast across—well, for half an hour, say—is that really too little?—from the millennial Ironic Lutecia to us in lip-sucking Palestine.

Your I. Annensky

Futurist Manifestos (1912, 1913)

Translated by Boris Dralyuk

A Slap in the Face of Public Taste (1912)

To the readers of our New First Unexpected.

We alone are the *face* of *our* Time. Through us the horn of time blows in the art of the word.

The past is too tight. The Academy and Pushkin are less intelligible than hieroglyphics.

Throw Pushkin, Dostoevsky, Tolstoy, etc., etc. overboard from the Ship of Modernity.

He who does not forget his *first* love will not recognize his last.

Who, trustingly, would turn his last love toward Balmont's perfumed lechery? Is this the reflection of today's virile soul?

Who, faintheartedly, would fear tearing from warrior Bryusov's black tuxedo the paper armorplate? Or does the dawn of unknown beauties shine from it?

Wash Your hands which have touched the filthy slime of the books written by those countless Leonid Andreevs.

All those Maxim Gorkys, Kuprins, Bloks, Sologubs, Remizovs, Averchenkos, Chornys, Kuzmins, Bunins, etc. need only a dacha on the river. Such is the reward fate gives tailors.

From the heights of skyscrapers we gave at their insignificance!...

We *order* that the poets' *rights* be revered:

1. To enlarge the *scope* of the poet's vocabulary with arbitrary and derivative words (Word-novelty).
2. To feel an insurmountable hatred for the language existing before their time.
3. To push with horror off their proud brow the Wreath of cheap fame that You have made from bathhouse switches.
4. To stand on the rock of the word "we" amidst the sea of boos and outrage.

And if *for the time being* the filthy stigmas of Your "Common sense" and "good taste" are still present in our lines, these same lines *for the first time* already glimmer with the Summer Lightning of the New Coming Beauty of the Self-sufficient (self-centered) Word.

D. BURLYUK, ALEXEI KRUCHONYKH, V. MAYAKOVSKY, VICTOR KHLEBNIKOV

(Untitled)

From *A Trap for Judges*, 2 (1913)

Finding the principles stated below fully expressed in the first issue of A Trap for Judges and having already given impetus to the much-discussed and wealthy (if only in the sense of Metzl & Co.) Futurists, WE nonetheless believe that we have traveled this path through and, leaving its reworking to those who do not have any new tasks, we now use a certain form of orthography in order to focus public attention on the new tasks already arising before us.

We first brought to the fore the new principles of creativity which were clear to us in the following order:

1. We ceased to regard word formation and word pronunciation according to grammatical rules, since we have begun to see in letters only *vectors of speech*. We loosened up syntax.

2. We started to endow words with content on the basis of their graphic and *phonic characteristics*.
3. Through us the role of prefixes and suffixes was fully realized.
4. In the name of the freedom of individual caprice, we reject normal orthography.
5. We modify nouns not only with adjectives (as was usual before us), but also with other parts of speech, as well as with individual letters and numbers:
    a. considering as an inseparable part of the work its corrections and the graphic flourishes of creative expectation.
    b. considering handwriting a component of the poetic impulse.
    c. and therefore, having published in Moscow "hand-lettered" (autographic) books.
6. We abolished punctuation marks, which for the first time brought to the fore the role of the verbal mass and made it perceivable.
7. We understand vowels as time and space (a characteristic of thrust), and consonants as color, sound, smell.
8. We shattered rhythms. Khlebnikov gave status to the poetic meter of the living conversational word. We stopped looking for meters in textbooks; every motion generates for the poet a new free rhythm.
9. The front rhyme (David Burlyuk), as well as the middle and the inverse rhyme (Mayakovsky), have been worked out by us.
10. The richness of a poet's lexicon is its justification.
11. We believe the word to be a creator of myth; in dying, the word gives birth to myth, and vice versa.
12. We are enthralled by new themes: superfluousness, meaninglessness, and the secret of powerful insignificance are celebrated by us.
13. We despise glory; we know feelings which had no life before us.

We are the new people of a new life.

DAVID BURLYUK, ELENA GURO, NICHOLAS BURLYUK, VLADIMIR MAYAKOVSKY, KATHERINE NIZEN, VICTOR KHLEBNIKOV, BENEDIKT LIVSHITZ, A. KRUCHONYKH

[The Word as Such] (1913)

In 1908 *A Trap for Judges, 1* was in preparation. Part of the works (of the Cubo-Futurists) ended up in that miscellany, part in The Studio of the Impressionists. In both collections, V. Khlebnikov, the Burlyuks, S. Miasoedov, and others outlined a new aesthetic direction: the word was being developed as such.

From then on a poem could consist of *a single word*, and merely by skillful variation of that word, all the fullness and expressiveness of the artistic image could be achieved.

However the expressiveness was of a different kind—an artistic work was perceived and critiqued (or at least was intuitively felt) simply as word.

The work of art is the art of the word.

As an inevitable consequence, tendentiousness and bookishness of all kinds were eliminated from literary works.

A closeness to the passionlessly passionate machine.

The Italians inhaled the Russian air and started producing crib notes on art, word-for-word translations.

They made no verbal artifacts until 1912 (the year their big collection was issued), or later.

That's understandable: the Italians relied on tendentiousness. Like Pushkin's little devil, they sang praises to Modernity and carried it on their shoulders, but instead of preaching modernity they should have jumped on its back and sped off, they should have delivered it as the sum of their works.

After all, preaching which does not result from art itself is wood painted to look like iron. Who would trust such a lance? The Italians turned out to be vociferous braggarts, but taciturn artist-writhers.

They ask us about the ideal, about pathos? It's not a question of hooliganism, or of heroic deeds, or of being a fanatic or a monk. All Talmuds are equally destructive to the wordwright, what constantly remains with him is only the word as (such) itself.

A. KRUCHONYKH, V. KHLEBNIKOV

OSIP MANDELSTAM

Letters to Vyacheslav Ivanov (1909)

Translated by Constance Link

To V. I. Ivanov [A postcard. Postmark: Pavlovsk, St. Petersburg, June 20, 1909]

My dear and greatly esteemed Vyacheslav Ivanovich

Wherever my letter finds you, I beg one thing of you. Let me know your address, and also if and when you will be in Switzerland. Until our departure abroad I am living with my family at Tsarskoe Selo without ever going out. Your seeds have been implanted deep in my soul, and I am frightened looking at their enormous sprouts.

    I rejoice in the hope of meeting you somewhere this summer.

                      From the almost ruined by you but repaired,
                                        Osip Mandelstam
[in the corner, written at a slant: St. Petersburg, Kolomenskaya 5]

To V. I. Ivanov [August 13/26, 1909]

                    Kurhaus de Territet et Sanitorium
                    l'Abri
                  Montreux-Territet

Dear Vyacheslav Ivanovich!

First allow me a few reflections on your book.[1] It seems impossible to dispute—it is captivating and destined to win hearts.

When a person steps under the vaults of Notre Dame does he really ponder the truth of Catholicism, and does he not become Catholic merely by virtue of being under those vaults?

Your book is magnificent in the beauty of its great architectural creations and astronomical systems. Every true poet would write just as you did if he could write books on the basis of the precise and immutable laws of his work.

You are the most incomprehensible and, in the everyday sense of the word, the obscurest poet of our time, precisely because you are, as is no one else, faithful to your nature, having consciously entrusted yourself to it. However, it seems to me that your book is too—how shall I say it?—too circular, without any angles. No matter which direction one approaches it from, it is impossible to cause injury to it or to oneself, since it has no sharp edges.

Even the tragedy in it is not an angle because you give it your consent.

Even the ecstasy is not dangerous because you foresee its outcome. And your book is fanned only by the breathing of the Cosmos, which imparts to it a charm it shares with Zarathustra and which compensates for the astronomical circularity of your system, which you yourself flaunt in the best parts of the book, and even flaunt persistently. Your book has something else in common with Zarathustra: each word in it fulfills its destiny with ardent hatred and each sincerely hates its place and its neighbors.

Excuse me for this outpouring...

I spent two weeks in Beatenburg but then decided to spend a few weeks in a sanitarium and went to Montreux.

Here I observe a strange contrast: the sacred quiet of the sanitarium, interrupted by the dinner gong, and the call to evening roulette in the casino: *faites vos jeux messieurs!—remarques messieurs! rien ne va plus!*—the shouts of the croupiers, full of symbolic horror. I have a strange taste: I love the patches of electric light on Lake Leman, the deferential lackeys, the noiseless flight of the elevator, the marble vestibule of the hotel, and the Englishwomen who play Mozart in a half-darkened salon for an audience of two or three official listeners.

---

1   JGH & CL: Probably *By the Stars* (*Po zvedzam*) (1909).

I love bourgeois, European comfort and am attached to it not only physically, but also emotionally.

Perhaps my poor health is to blame for this? But I never ask myself whether it is good or bad.

I would also like to tell you the following:

There is one place in your book where two great perspectives open up, as if from the rational solution of the postulate about the two parallel geometries—Euclid's and Lobachevsky's. This is the amazingly penetrating image where the man who refused to dance covers his face with his hands and leaves the circle of dancers.

Have our friends already gathered in St. Petersburg?

What is *Apollon* doing?[2] And *Island*?[3]

How I long to see one of our poet friends, or even one of our poets with whom I am not acquainted. Do you know what, V. I.? Write to me (I know you will answer me, but what if you suddenly don't?) when someone goes abroad. Perhaps somehow I will see someone, and to see you I am ready to travel a very great distance if necessary. One more request. If you have an extra copy, a completely extra copy of *Guiding Stars*, could it not somehow find its way into my careful hands? . . .

Tell me also, V. I., what kind of lyric poets there are in Germany these days. Besides Dehmel, I do not know of a single one. The Germans likewise do not know—but all the same there must be lyric poets.

I kiss you affectionately, V. I., and am grateful to you, I myself do not know for what, which is the best kind of gratitude.

Osip Mandelstam

P.S. I am sending some poems. Do whatever you want with them—whatever I want—whatever you can.

No. 4. To V. I. Ivanov [Postcard. Heidelberg, October 13/26, 1909]

Dear Vyacheslav Ivanovich!

If you want to write me and are not answering me for some extraneous reason, write me all the same.

---

2   *JGH & CL*: Periodical founded in 1909 by Gumilyov and Sergei Makovsky.
3   *JGH & CL*: Literary magazine edited by A. N. Tolstoy and Gumilyov.

There are many things I want to tell you, but I can't. I'm not up to it.

Love,
Osip Mandelstam

No. 5. To V. I. Ivanov [Postcard. Heidelberg, October 22/November 4, 1909]

Dear, as before, Vyacheslav Ivanovich!

I cannot help sending you my lyrical quests and achievements. Just as I am obliged to you for the former, so the latter also belong to you by right although you, perhaps, are not even aware of it.

Yours,
Osip Mandelstam

VIKTOR SHKLOVSKY

Quote about the Stray Dog cabaret (no date)

Translated by John E. Bowlt

We weren't the ones who did the drinking in the *Dog*. We were the others.

NADEZHDA TÈFFI

The Demonic Woman (1913)

Translated by Sibelan Forrester

A demonic woman differs from an ordinary woman, first and foremost, in her way of dressing. She wears a black velvet cassock, a chain on her forehead, a bracelet on her ankle, a ring with an empty compartment "for potassium cyanide, which they'll send her by next Tuesday without fail," a stiletto tucked in her collar, rosary beads on her elbow and a picture of Oscar Wilde in her left garter.

She also wears the ordinary elements of a lady's toilette, just not in the places where you would expect them to be. So, for instance, the demonic woman permits herself to wear a belt only on her head, an earring on her forehead or on her necklace, a ring on her thumb, a watch on her ankle.

At the table the demonic woman eats nothing. She never eats anything, ever.

"What's the point?"

The demonic woman can occupy the most varied positions in society, but most often she's an actress.

Sometimes just a divorcée.

But she always has some kind of secret, some kind of laceration or separation that can't be spoken of, which no one knows or should know.

"What's the point?"

Her eyebrows are raised in tragic commas, her eyes half-lowered.

To the gentleman who is accompanying her after a ball, and who is carrying on a languid conversation about aesthetic eroticism from the point of view of the erotic aesthete, she suddenly says, with a twitch of every plume on her hat, "Let's go to church, my dear, let's go to church, quickly, quickly, quickly. I want to pray and sob before the sunrise."

The church is locked at night.

The gracious gentleman suggests sobbing right there on the church porch, but "she" is already extinguished. She knows that she is damned, that there is no salvation, and she submissively lowers her head, sticking her nose into her fur scarf.

"What's the point?"

The demonic woman always feels drawn to literature.

And often she secretly writes novellas and poems in prose.

She doesn't read them to anyone.

"What's the point?"

But she mentions in passing that the well-known critic Alexander Alexeevich, who got hold of her manuscript at the risk of his life, read it and then sobbed all night and even prayed, it seems—actually, probably not that last bit. And two writers are predicting a great future for her, if she would just agree to publish her works. But the public would never be able to understand them, and she won't show them to the mob.

"What's the point?"

But at night, when she's alone, she opens her writing desk, gets out the conscientiously typed pages, and spends a long time erasing the censorious words, "Reject," "Reject and return."

"I saw a light in your window at five in the morning."

"Yes, I was working."

"You'll wear yourself out! My dear! Take care of yourself for us!"

"What's the point?"

Seated at a table laden with tasty things, she lowers her eyes, attracted with irresistible power by the suckling pig in aspic.

"Marya Nikolaevna," her neighbor, a simple, not demonic woman, with earrings in her ears and a bracelet on her wrist, says to the hostess, "Marya Nikolaevna, please pass me some wine."

The demonic one covers her eyes with her hand and starts to speak hysterically: "Wine! Wine! Give me some wine, I want to drink! I'm going to drink! I drank yesterday! I drank two days ago, and tomorrow ... yes, tomorrow I'll drink too! I want, I want, I want some wine!"

To be honest, what is so tragic about a lady having a bit to drink three days in a row? But the demonic woman can make things come out in a way that makes your hair stand on end.

"She's drinking."

"So mysterious!"

"And tomorrow she's going to drink too, she says ..."

An ordinary woman starts eating, says, "Marya Nikolaevna, if you would, please give me a piece of herring. I like the onion."

The demonic one opens her eyes wide and, gazing into space, cries out, "Herring? Yes, yes, give me some herring, I want to eat herring, I want to, I want to. Is that onion? Yes, yes, give me some onion, give me a lot of everything, everything, herring, onion, I want to eat, I want banality, quickly ... more ... more, look everybody ... I'm eating herring!"

In essence, what has happened?

Just that her appetite kicked up and she wanted something salty! But what an effect!

"Did you hear? Did you hear?"

"She shouldn't be left alone tonight."

"Or else she'll probably shoot herself with that potassium cyanide that they're bringing her on Tuesday ..."

There are unpleasant and ugly minutes in life, when an ordinary woman, fixing her eyes fully on the shelf unit, crumples a handkerchief in her hands and says in a trembling voice:

"I don't need it for long, honestly ... only a bit ... twenty-five rubles. I hope I'll be able ... that next week or in January ..."

The demonic woman will sit down with her chest lying on the table, lean her chin on both hands, and look straight into your soul with mysterious, half-closed eyes. "Why am I looking at you? I'll tell you. Listen to me, look at me ... I want—do you hear?—I want you to give me, right now—do you hear?—right now, twenty-five rubles. I want you to. Do you hear?—I want you to. For you, no one but you, to give nothing but twenty-five rubles, to no one but me. I want you to! I'm a terrrrrrible creature! ... Now go ... go ... Don't turn around, go away quickly, quickly ... Ha-ha-ha!"

The hysterical laugh is supposed to shake her whole being, even both beings—his and hers.

"Quickly ... quickly, without turning around ... go away forever, for your whole life, for your whole life ... Ha-ha-ha!"

And he is "shaken" in his whole being and doesn't even realize that she's just snagged twenty-five rubles from him without saying she'll pay it back.

"You know, she was so strange today ... mysterious. She told me not to turn around."

"Yes. One senses a secret here."

"Perhaps ... she's in love with me ..."

"!"

"Secret!"

THEMATIC INDEX

Readers interested in particular traits or issues can use this index to choose which poets they want most to read—both in this collection, and in wider exploration of their work. Poets in parentheses are less closely related to the movement or topic than others listed for that keyword.

Acmeism (Adamism): xliv– xlviii, 110, 290-293, 330, 332, 409–412, 482
Akhmatova 410-411, 478; Gorodetsky xlvii, 409; Gumilyov xlvii, 409-411; Mandelstam xlvii, 329-332, 478, 482; Narbut xlvii; (Annensky, Kuzmin, Voloshin) xlvii, 110
Androgyny
Bely 69; Blok 359-360; Gippius 69
Anthroposophy
Bely (Voloshin), xlv, 38
Art: Mayakovsky, Voloshin, xliv, xlviii, xlix, liii–liv, 111, 117, 133, 141, 182, 232, 237, 252–254, 256–257, 259–291, 293, 306, 311–312, 314–319, 323, 325–327, 329, 336–337, 346, 357, 360, 369, 399–400, 411–419, 426, 428, 483, 486–487, 489, 512, 530
Astrology: Bely, Bryusov, Pasternak, Tsvetaeva, Voloshin, xlv

Avant-Garde
Aseev xlix; Khlebnikov xlix, lvii; Kruchonykh xlix, 107; Lifshitz 245-246; Mayakovsky xvi, xlix, lvii, 147-148; Pasternak xlix; Severyanin xlix
Bisexuality: Gippius, Ivanov, Tsvetaeva (Voloshin), xxxix
Catholicism, catholic 466-467
Khodasevich 94; Petrovskaya 494; (Ivanov, Mandelstam) 532
Classicism, classical, classics x, xvi-xvii, xlv, 252, 275, 298, 322, 336, 424
Annensky 22; Ivanov xxxix, 80,; Kuzmin xl, 401; Mandelstam 130, 334-339; Merezhkovsky 166; Parnok 171
Decadence, decadent: xliv, lii, 270, 286, 287, 330, 337, 415-429, 487, 489
Bryusov lii, 58, 354, 420, 430, 433; Gippius lii, 377-378; Sologub lii, 198
Drama (play): x, xlvii, 252, 261, 272, 319, 514, 517, 519
Blok 45, 267, 110; Gippius 68; Ivanov 259, 267; Khlebnikov 83-84; Mayakovsky xviii, 147-148, 164, 512; Sologub 198; Solovyov, Vladimir 204; Tsvetaeva, 211
Early Death
Blok liv, 45; Gumilyov liv, 74-75; Guro 120-121; Khlebnikov liv; Klyuev lv; Lokhvitskaya 120; Mandelstam lv; (Kuzmin, Parnok, Tsvetaeva) lv
Emigration, émigrés xlii, liii, lvii, 199
Adamovich 246; Balmont xlii, 33; Gippius 166; Ivanov, Vyacheslav 81; Khodasevich liv, 94; Merezhkovsky 166; Severyanin liv, 190; Teffi 246; Tsvetaeva xlii, liv; (Bely), xlii, 39, 94, 246
Exile 14, 68, 168, 170, 469, 494
Balmont 32; Klyuev 101; Mandelstam 127; Shkapskaya xlii, 193; Voloshin 237
Female Pseudonyms
Bryusov 484
Feminine, feminist lii-liii, 5, 68, 314, 361, 365, 464, 491
Lokhvitskaya 121
Folklore, folk traditions, folktale xlvi, 248, 361
Aseev 28; Khlebnikov 28, 83; (Tsvetaeva)
Futurism, futurist, futuristic xxxviii, xlii–xlvi, xlviii, lii, 211, 245-246, 290, 330, 336, 337n7, 527-530
Burlyuk xlviii; Guro lin3, 120; Khlebnikov xlviii- xlix, lii, lvii, 83, 402, 407; Kruchonykh xlix, 107; Mayakovsky xlviii- xlix, lvii, 147-148, 160; Severyanin xlix, 190; (Aseev, Esenin, Pasternak) xlix, 28, 176

Gay xxxix

Klyuev 101; Kuzmin 110

Judaism, Jewish xxxix, 204, 208, 246

Mandelstam xxxix, 126, 146, 478; Parnok xxxix, 171; (Pasternak, Khodasevich) xxxix, 94, 176

Lesbian xxxix, 171

Parnok xxxix, 171

Male Pseudonyms

Gippius 68; Parnok xxxv, 171

Moscow l, li, liv, 94, 210, 419, 422, 484-485, 487, 494-495, 516-517, 529

Akhmatova 475; Aseev 28; Balmont 32; Bely l, 38-39; Bryusov 58-59, 493n1; Esenin 64; Ivanov 80-81; Khlebnikov 83, 407; Khodasevich 94; Kruchonykh 107; Lokhvitskaya 120; Mayakovsky xlviii, 147, 156, 516; Parnok 172; Pasternak 176-177, 516–517; Shkapskaya 193; Solovyov 205; Tsvetaeva 210–211, 220, 229; Voloshin 237–238

Motherhood 197

Music, musicality, musicians x, xviii, xxxviii, xlii, xlv, liii-liv, 120, 128, 151, 159, 248, 271, 280, 297-298, 300, 312, 317, 322-324, 330, 332-334, 337, 360, 363, 425, 477

Akhmatova 19; Annensky 24; Balmont 33; Bely 338; Khodasevich 97, 99; Kuzmin 81, 110; Parnok 172; Pasternak 176, 185; Tsvetaeva 219, 233; (Blok, Bryusov, Esenin, Mandelstam, Voloshin) 62, 64, 354, 477

Orthodoxy Russian lii, 126

Kuzmin xl; Parnok 171; Pasternak 176; Solovyov 204

Philosophy, philosopher xiii, xxxviii-xl, xliii, xlv, xlviii, liii, 74, 81, 246, 249, 253, 255, 257-258, 265-267, 269, 278, 280, 282, 297-298, 301-302, 354-355, 363, 412, 420, 426, 428, 446, 486

Bely 38; Gippius 68, 166; Gumilev 74, 503, 505; Merezhkovsky lii, 166-167, 253; Pasternak 176, 446; Solovyov 204-205,

Posters, poster art xlix, 479

Mayakovsky 148, 479

Provinces, provincial 198, 350, 355n1, 405, 490

Pseudonym xxxv, xxxix, 3, 68, 171, 484

Akhmatova 5; Bely 3, 38, 360; Severyanin xlix; Teffi 120

Religion (Christianity, conversion, Judaism, Orthodoxy, Hellenic) xiii, xxxviii-xxxix, xlv, lii, 68, 94, 246, 253, 255, 259–262, 266, 296, 298-303, 309-316, 319, 335, 337, 340, 411-412, 415, 422, 424, 428–429, 468, 514

Akhmatova 401; Balmont 388; Bely 259–262; Blok 266; Gippius 68; Ivanov 80, 259, 266, 296n2, 299n6; Klyuev 101; Kuzmin xl, 110; Mandelstam xxxix, 126, 335; Merezhkovsky lii, 166, 253, 262, 316; Parnok 171; Pasternak xxxix, 176; Solovyov xlv, 204, 208, 262

Sex, sexuality x, xxxiii-xl, xlv, lii, 6, 57, 253, 301, 341, 420

Gippius 68; Kuzmin li, 110; Merezhkovsky 166; Parnok li; Shkapskaya 193; Tsvetaeva li

St. Petersburg/Petrograd xliii, l, 38, 245-246, 334, 357-358, 473, 479-481, 505

Akhmatova 5, 18-19, 473; Annensky 22; Bely xliii, 38-39; Blok 18, 44-45, 479; Esenin 64; Gippius 68, 72; Gumilyov 74, 479; Ivanov l, 80; Khlebnikov 83; Kuzmin 110; Lokhvitskaya 120; Mandelstam 126, 138-139, 334, 479-480, 531, 533; Merezhkovsky 166; Parnok 171; Severyanin 190; Shkapskaya 193; Sologub 198, 356; Solovyov 205

Suicide lii, 199, 337, 505

Balmont 32; Esenin liv-lv, 64; Mayakovsky liv-lv, 148; Petrovskaya 485; Tsvetaeva lv, 211

Symbolism, Symbolist xlii, xliii– xlviii, l-liv, 80, 94, 101, 110, 120, 126, 205, 210, 251–268, 283, 286, 290–292, 304–305, 309–315, 317–321, 323, 325–328, 330-332, 353, 357-360, 388, 401, 403, 409–413, 415-419, 423–424, 428, 430–441, 485–491, 514

Balmont 32, 353, 358, 486; Bely 38, 315, 360, 491; Blok liv, 38, 44-45, 315, 358, 487; Bryusov 38, 58-59, 267, 353, 430-435, 437; Gippius 38, 68-69, 315; Gumilyov 74; Ivanov 80, 263, 267, 357; Merezhkovsky 38, 68, 166; Sologub 198, 315, 356; Solovyov 126, 437

Theosophy: Bely (Voloshin), xlv, 292

Translation, translator xi-xxi, xli-xlix, lvii–lviii, 4, 44, 67, 81, 127, 198, 245–246, 297, 321, 335, 388-389, 431–432, 440-441, 480, 530

Akhmatova 6; Annensky 388; Balmont liii, 33; Bryusov 58-59, 388, 440; Gumilyov 74; Ivanov xlv, 300n7; Mandelshtam liii, 126; Mayakovsky 148; Merezhkovsky 166-167; Parnok 171; Pasternak 177, 186; Sologub 388; Tsvetaeva 211

Women writers/poets, issues xxxix, li–lii, lv, 4–5, 22, 121, 300, 316-317, 347-348, 361–363, 365, 435, 467-469, 473, 484, 492–493, 536-538
Akhmatova xxi, lin3, 5, 392, 401, 411; Gippius lin3, 68, 363; Guro lin3; Lokhvitskaya lin3, 121; Parnok li, 171–172; Shkapskaya 193; Tsvetaeva li, 171

Index of Poem Titles and First Lines (Russian)

NOTE: Where the original titles are in Latin, French, etc., and written in the Latin alphabet, we have put them as close as possible to where they would fit in the Russian alphabet rather than in a separate section of this index.

А все-таки (Mayakovsky), 155
А вы? (Mayakovsky), 149
Адам (Gumilyov), 76
Айя-София (Mandelstam), 129
Альпийский рог (Ivanov), 81
Анне Ахматовой (Pasternak), 180
Ах, уста, целованные столькими (Kuzmin), 114
Баллада (Сижу, освещаемый сверху) (Khodasevich), 98
Балтрушайтису (Voloshin), 238
Безглагольность (Balmont), 33
Бессонница. Гомер. Тугие паруса (Mandelstam), 131
Бо-бэ-о-би пелись губы (Khlebnikov), 85
Борису Пастернаку (Рас-стояние: Версты, мили . . .) (Tsvetaeva), 234
Будем как Солнце! (Balmont), 34
Было тело мое без входа (Shkapskaya), 194

Index of Poem Titles and First Lines (Russian)

В моем незнанье — так много веры (Lokhvitskaya), 122
В огромном городе моем — ночь (Tsvetaeva), 219
В Петербурге мы сойдемся снова (Mandelstam), 138
В полоборота, о печаль (Mandelstam), 130
В толпе (Parnok), 175
Весна (Pasternak), 178
Вещи (Lokhvitskaya), 125
Взорваль (Kruchonykh), 108
Владимир Соловьев (Bely), 39
Владимиру Владимировичу Маяковскому (Khlebnikov), 86
Во всем мне хочется дойти (Pasternak), 187
Волга (Aseev), 29
Вооруженный зреньем узких ос (Mandelstam), 144
Восхищенной и восхищённой (Tsvetaeva), 224
Вот дароносица, как золотое солнце (Mandelstam), 136
Все круче, все круче (Tsvetaeva), 226
Все мы бражники здесь, блудницы (Akhmatova), xx, 8
Вся в лазури сегодня явилась (Solovyov), 205
Второе крещение (Blok), 50
Вы! (Mayakovsky), 156
Вывескам (Mayakovsky), 149
Галка-староверка ходит в черной ряске (Klyuev), 104
Гамлет (Pasternak), 186
Где волк воскликнул кровью (Khlebnikov), 88
Где слог найду, чтоб описать прогулку (Kuzmin), 113
Гибель от женщины. Вот знак (Tsvetaeva), 213
Гимн Солнцу (Bely), 42
Гроза моментальная навек (Pasternak), 180
Да, говорят, что это нужно было (Shkapskaya), 194
Да с этой львиною (Tsvetaeva), 216
Двенадцать (Blok), 54
Девушка пела в церковном хоре (Blok), 47
Для того ль тебя носила (Akhmatova), 13
Добрые чувства побеждают время и пространство ... (Kuzmin), 116
Дочь Иаира (Annensky), 25
Душа (Khodasevich), 98
Дым от костра струею сизой (Blok), 51
Есть иволги в лесах и гласных долгота (Mandelstam), 130
Ex Oriente Lux (Solovyov), 206
Жираф (Gumilyov), 75

Заклинание (Gippius), 71
Заклинание (Lokhvitskaya), 123
Заклятие смехом (Khlebnikov), 86
Зангези (Khlebnikov), 91
Зеленый леший — бух лесиный (Khlebnikov), 87
Избрав свой путь, я шествую спокойно (Lokhvitskaya), 124
Изгнанники (Merezhkovsky), 168
Каждый стих — дитя любви (Tsvetaeva), 223
Как белый камень в глубине колодца (Akhmatova), 11
Как недобитое крыло (Kuzmin), 118
Как царство белого снега (Bryusov), 59
Канун Благовещенья (Tsvetaeva), 214
Квартира (Mandelstam), 141
Кинжал (Bryusov), 61
Красота страшна, вам скажут (Blok), 53
Кузнечик (Khlebnikov), 85
Ленинград (Mandelstam), 139
Лиличка! (Mayakovsky), 157
Лотова жена (Akhmatova), 15
Любви начало было летом (Klyuev), 102
Люблю говорить слова (Khodasevich), 95
Людовику XVII (Shkapskaya), 196
Маяковскому (Tsvetaeva), 225
Молюсь оконному лучу (Akhmatova), 6
Morituri (Merezhkovsky), 167
Мудры старики да дети (Kuzmin), 116
Мы живем, под собою не чуя страны (Mandelstam), 140
Мы — плененные звери (Sologub), 199
Мы чураемся и чаруемся (Khlebnikov), 84
На назначенное свидание (Tsvetaeva), 231
На шее мелких четок ряд (Akhmatova), 9
Настанет день — печальный, говорят (Tsvetaeva), 220
Насытив очи наготою (Sologub), 201
Нате! (Mayakovsky), 154
Наш марш (Mayakovsky), 161
Не знаю, зачем упрекают меня (Lokhvitskaya), 121
Не напрасно мы читали богословов (Kuzmin), 111
Не с теми я, кто бросил землю (Akhmatova), 14
Не снись мне так часто, крохотка (Shkapskaya), 195
Незнакомка (Blok), 48

Неколебимой истине (Bryusov), 60
Неподражаемо лжет жизнь (Tsvetaeva), 228
Нивы сжаты, рощи голы (Esenin), 65
Ночь. Улица. Фонарь. Аптека (Blok), 52
О, знал бы я, что так бывает (Pasternak), 182
О, ризы вечера, багряно-золотые (Klyuev), 103
О, эта женская Голгофа (Shkapskaya), 195
Обвела мне глаза кольцом (Tsvetaeva), 217
Обезьяна (Khodasevich), 96
Обманите меня... но совсем, навсегда (Voloshin), 238
Ожившая фреска (Pasternak), 184
Он прав — опять фонарь, аптека (Akhmatova), 18
Она (Gippius), 72
Орган (Parnok), 174
Осень (Balmont), 37
Отрада (Gippius), 69
Памяти Марины Цветаевой (Pasternak), 182
Пепел. Россия. Отчаяние (Bely), 41
Песня офитов (Solovyov), 206
Песня последней встречи (Akhmatova), 7
Под лаской плюшевого пледа (Tsvetaeva), 212
После концерта (Annensky), 23
Поэма без героя (Akhmatova), 19
Поэту (Annensky), 26
Поэту (Bryusov), 62
Приказ по армии искусств (Mayakovsky), 159
Прокрасться (Tsvetaeva), 232
Пролетарка, пролетарий, заходите в планетарий (Mayakovsky), 162
Психея (Tsvetaeva), 223
Рассвет на рельсах (Tsvetaeva), 229
Рас-стояние: версты, мили... (Tsvetaeva), 234
Расчет случаен и неверен (Shkapskaya), 197
Рельсы (Tsvetaeva), 233
Requiem (Akhmatova), 6, 17
Руки — и вкруг (Tsvetaeva), 227
Руки люблю (Tsvetaeva), 221
Сафические строфы (Parnok), 172
Сегодня праздник (Kuzmin), 112
Сегодня строгою боярыней Бориса Годунова (Khlebnikov), 90
Servus — Reginae (Blok), 45

Сестра моя—Жизнь и сегодня в разливе (Pasternak), 179
Сестры — тяжесть и нежность — одинаковы ваши приметы (Mandelstam), 137
Silentium (Mandelstam), 128
Сквозь туман едва заметный (Sologub), 202
Слово (Gumilyov), 78
Смычок и струны (Annensky), 24
Снег (Gippius), 70
Солнце (Bely), 40
Соломинка (Mandelstam), 132
Стекла стынут от холода (Kuzmin), 115
Сумерки свободы (Mandelstam), 135
Так на других берегах, у другого певучего моря (Parnok), 173
Татлин, тайновидец лопастей (Khlebnikov), 89
Темный ангел (Merezhkovsky), 169
Тот город, мной любимый с детства (Akhmatova), 16
3 стихотворения (Kruchonykh), 109
Tristia (Mandelstam), 133
Ты горишь над высокой горою (Blok), 46
Уводили тебя на рассвете (from *Requiem*) (Akhmatova), 17
Укротитель зверей (Gumilyov), 77
Февраль. Достать чернил и плакать! (Pasternak), 177
Холодный ветер от лагуны (Blok), 52
Чернозем (Mandelstam), 143
Юность (Klyuev), 105
Я (Mayakovsky), 150
Я был один в моем раю (Sologub), 200
Я в этот мир пришел, чтоб видеть Солнце (Balmont), 35
Я, гений Игорь-Северянин (Severyanin), 191
Я—изысканность русской медлительной речи (Balmont), 36
Я последний поэт деревни (Esenin), 66
Я пришла к поэту в гости (Akhmatova), 10
Я скажу это начерно, шепотом (Mandelstam), 144
Я слышу иволги всегда печальный голос (Akhmatova), 12
Я тебя отвоюю у всех земель, у всех небес (Tsvetaeva), 222

Index of Poem Titles and First Lines (English)

Adam (Adam, humiliated Adam) (Gumilyov), 76
After sating my eyes with the nudity (Sologub), 201
After the Concert (The sky has cast its blackness down onto the path) (Annensky), 23
All of us here are hookers and hustlers (Akhmatova), xxv, 8
Alpine Horn,The (In mountains far away I met a shepherd) (Amidst the silent hills I met a shepherd) (Ivanov) 81, 321
And Yet (The street's sunk like the nose of a syphilitic) (Mayakovsky), 155
Animal Tamer (Once more I tread a path I know by heart) (Gumilyov), 77
Appointment (I'll be late for the meeting) (Tsvetaeva), 231
Armed with the eyesight of thin-waisted wasps (Mandelstam). 144
Ash. Russia. Despair (Bely), 41
At my neck, small rosary beads (Akhmatova), 9
Autumn (Autumn. Dead space. Deepening sorrowful distances) (Balmont), 37
Ballad (I sit, illuminated from above) (Khodasevich), 98
Beneath the plush plaid's sweet caresses (Tsvetaeva), 212
"Beauty is frightening," they will tell you (Blok), 53
Beyond the Grave (He was only a fashionable scribbler) (Blok), 383
Black Earth (Too black, too much indulged, living in clover) (Mandelstam), 143
Bo-beh-óh-bee is the lipsong (Khlebnikov), 85

Bow and strings (What heavy, dark delirium!) (Annensky), 24
But with that leonine (Tsvetaeva), 216
By the well (Khlebnikov), 406
Chatterbox-bells (Annensky), 351
Children and old folk are wise (Kuzmin), 116
The Church Organ (I remember a solemn voice) (Parnok), 174
The city I have loved since childhood (Akhmatova), 16
The cold has frozen windowpanes (Kuzmin), 115
A cold wind blows from the lagoon (Blok), 52
Curse (Gouge yourselves out, disobedient spirits) (Gippius), 71
Dagger (Bryusov), 61
Dark Angel (Oh, dark angel of loneliness) (Merezhkovsky), 169
The Daughter of Jairus (Annensky), 25
Dawn on the Rails (Before the new day's rise) (Tsvetaeva), 229
The day will come—a sad one, people say (Tsvetaeva), 220
Delight (My friend, I am not tormented by doubt) (Gippius), 69
A deep-blue crevice (Aseev), 30
Dis-tances: miles, versts... (Tsvetaeva), 234
Don't come into my dreams so often (Shkapskaya), 195
Eve of the Annunciation (Tsvetaeva), 214
Every poem is a love-child (Tsvetaeva), 223
Ex Oriente Lux ("Light and strength come from the East!") (Solovyov), 206
Exiles (There's joy in the fact that people hated) (Merezhkovsky), 168
Fields are cut, the groves are bare, The (Esenin), 65
The fire is flowing away in smoke (Blok), 51
Flat (Mandelstam), 141
Flawlessly, matchlessly life lies (Tsvetaeva), 228
Fool me... but fully, forever (Voloshin), 238
Fresco Come to Life (Again the shells were falling) (Pasternak), 184
Giraffe (Gumilyov), 75
A goblin grabbles in the greeny forest (Khlebnikov), 87
Golden fairies (Bryusov), 432
Grasshopper (Glitter-letter wing-winker) (Khlebnikov), 85
The Great God of Details (You ask, who stablishes) (Pasternak), 460-461
Hagia Sophia (Mandelstam), 129
Half-turned, o sorrow (Mandelstam), 130
Hamlet (The noise subsides. I walk onto the stage) (Pasternak), 186
Hands that I so love (Tsvetaeva), 221
Hands up—and jump, from Earthly Signs (Tsvetaeva), 227
Harder and harder (Tsvetaeva), 226

Index of Poem Titles and First Lines (English) 553

Heaviness, tenderness—sisters—your marks are the same (Mandelstam), 137
Held captured and enraptured deeply (Tsvetaeva), 224
"Hey!" the wolf cries out in blood (Khlebnikov), 88
Holl roll shil (Kruchonykh), 109
Hymn to the Sun (Let blind men say our lyres have fallen silent) (Bely), 42
I am the last country poet (Esenin), 66
I am the refinement of Russian sluggish utterance (Balmont), 36
I came into this world to see the Sun (Balmont), 35
I don't know why they're reproaching me (Lokhvitskaya), 121
I have something I cherish (Kuzmin), 116
I hear the oriole's voice (Akhmatova), 12
I love to utter words (Khodasevich), 95
I pray to the light in the window (Akhmatova), 6
I, the genius Igor-Severyanin (Severyanin), 191
I think I can summon up words (Pasternak), 180
I was alone in my paradise (Sologub), 200
I went to visit the poet (Akhmatova), 10
I'll be late for the meeting (Tsvetaeva), 231
I'll conquer you from any land and from any sky (Tsvetaeva), 222
I'll say it in draft in a wisper (Mandelstam), 144
If I had known that this is what happens (Pasternak), 182
In everything I want to reach (Pasternak), 187
In Memory of Marina Tsvetaeva (Pasternak), 182
In my unknowing—there's so much faith (Lokhvitskaya), 122
In Petersburg we'll meet again (Mandelstam), 138
In the Crowd (You came in as thousands would come in) (Parnok), 175
Incantation (Lokhvitskaya), 123
Incantation by Laughter (Hlaha! Uthlofan, lauflings!) (Oh, start laughing, laughers) (Khlebnikov), 86, 405
Insomnia. Homer. The right-rigged sails (Mandelstam), 131
It's enveloped my eyes with (Tsvetaeva), 217
It's February. Grab the ink and weep (Pasternak), 177
Just for this I used to carry you (Akhmatova), 13
Kind Feelings Conquer Time and Space (Kuzmin), 116
Leningrad (I have come back to my city, so known my very being weeps) (Mandelstam), 139
Let us praise the twilight of freedom (Mandelstam), 135
Let's be like the Sun! (Balmont), 34
Like a kingdom of whitest snow (Bryusov), 59
Like a wing, a wing shot through (Kuzmin), 118

Lilichka! (Tobacco smoke's etched out the air) (Mayakovsky), 157
Lot's Wife (Akhmatova), 15
Me (All along the sidewalks) (Mayakovsky), 150, 519
A memory is in me (Akhmatova), 11
The Monkey (There was a heatwave. The woods were burning. Time) (Khodasevich), 96
Morituri (We're endlessly alone) (Merezhkovsky), 167
My enormous city is full of night (Tsvetaeva), 219
My body was lacking an entrance (Shkapskaya), 194
My sister, Life, is today overflowing (Pasternak), 179, 449, 457
My Soul (My soul's like a full moon) (Khodasevich), 98
My tsaritsa appeared to me (Solovyov), 205
Night. A street light, a drugstore (Blok), 52
No, not with those who left their land (Akhmatova), 14
Not for nothing did we read the theologians (from Alexandrian Songs) (Kuzmin), 111
O, my prophetic soul! (Tyutchev), 306
Oh, cover your pale legs! (Bryusov), 418, 426, 440
Oh, lips, kissed by so many (Kuzmin), 114
Oh, raiment of evening, scarlet-golden (Klyuev), 103
Oh, this female Golgotha! (Shkapskaya), 195
Old Believer jackdaw goes round in a black cassock (Klyuev), 104
Order to the Arts Army (They fiddle, the oldies' brigades) (Mayakovsky), 159
Orgiastic madness in wine (Sologub), 299
Our March (Beat the squares with rebellion's tread) (Mayakovsky), 161
Pink colors die down (Bryusov), 431-432
The poet was right: once again (He was right—again the street lamp, the drug store)
(Akhmatova), 18, 476
Poem without a Hero (Akhmatova), lv, 6, 19
Proletarianess, proletarian, Stop into the Planetarium (Mayakovsky), 162
Provisionally, then, and secretive (Mandelstam), 145
Psyche (I'm neither an imposter nor a guest) (Tsvetaeva), 223
Rails (The bed of a railway cutting) (Tsvetaeva), 233
Rain (Come spin, as mulberry worm) (Pasternak), 458
The reckoning's chancy and slipshod (Shkapskaya), 197
Sadness / of fire (Kruchonykh), 108
Sapphic Strophes (If I catch the song of the Aeolian lyre) (Parnok), 172
Second Christening (Blok), 50
Servus—Reginae (Don't send for me. No need to call) (Blok), 45

Shadow of uncreated creations, The (Bryusov), 416, 423, 437
She (In her unscrupulous and wretched nastiness) (Gippius), 72
Silentium (She has yet to be born) (Mandelstam), 128
So on other shores, by another singing sea (Parnok), 173
Solominka (Mandelstam), 132
Song of Our Last Meeting (Akhmatova), 7
Song of the Ophites (We make a bouquet of red roses) (Solovyov), 206
Snow (Once more it falls, so marvelously silent) (Gippius), 70
Spring (How many sticky buds, how many candle ends) (Pasternak), 178
The start of love was the summer (Klyuev), 102
Stranger (Above the restaurants, at night) (Blok), 48
Starfaced (His face was like the Sun) (Balmont), 387
Sultry Night (A spattering came, but one that did not bend) (Pasternak), 455-456
The Sun (The heart's ignited by the sun) (Bely), 40
Swan (Tyutchev), 308
Take It! (In another hour, out of the foyer) (Mayakovsky), 154
Tatlin! Poet of propellers (Khlebnikov), 89
That bully Zhiguli (Aseev), 30
That's enough: don't wait, don't expect (Bely), 41
Then afterwards summertime waved goodbye (Pasternak), 180
There is a certain hour of universal silence (Tyutchev), 307
There are kinds of speech whose meaning (Lermontov), 327
There are orioles in the forests and the only real mesure (Mandelstam), 130
There: the Eucharist, a gold sun (Mandelstam), 136
They are the bright blue stilland (Khlebnikov), 91
They took you at dawn, I remember (Akhmatova), 17
Things (The daytime nightmare of unceasing boredom) (Lokhvitskaya), 125
The Third Thrust (Kuzmin), 118
3 poems (Kruchonykh), 109
Through a barely visible mist (Sologub), 202
Thunderstorm for a Moment Forever (Pasternak), 180
Tightly her dry lips are shut (Akhmatova), 392
To Anna Akhmatova (Pasternak), 53, 181
To B. Pasternak (Tsvetaeva), 234
To Baltrushaitis (I'm drawn to your lines not by novelty) (Voloshin), 238
To Louis XVII (The people's fury once again) (Shkapskaya), 196
To Mayakovsky (High above cross and trumpet) (Tsvetaeva), 225
To Shop Signs (Read those iron books!) (Mayakovsky), 149
To Sneak Through (It may be that a better way) (Tsvetaeva), 232

To the Poet (In the separate trace of rays) (Annensky), 26
To the Poet9 You must be as proud as any banner) (Bryusov), 62
To Vladimir Vladimirovich Mayakovsky (Three V's, three M's, three words) (Khlebnikov), 86
To Z. N. Gippius (I have long disbelieved in) (Bryusov), 60
Today's a holiday (Kuzmin), 112
Tristia (I've studied well the art of separation) (Mandelstam), 133
Twelve, The (Blok), 54
Twilight of Freedom, The (Mandelstam), 135
Unbending as Boris Godunov's boyarina (Khlebnikov), 90
Verblessness (Balmont), 33
Vertical horizons (Solovyov), 441
Vladimir Solovyov (We choked on everyday vulgarity) (Bely), 39
Voice from the People, A (Klyuev), 386
Volga, The (Here the waves have set out loiterousy) (Aseev), 29
We are all carousers and loose women here (Akhmatova), xxi
We are beasts in a cage (Sologub), 199
We are heavy-drinkers and whores (Akhmatova,) xxii
We chant and enchant (Khlebnikov), 84
We live without feeling beneath us firm ground (Mandelstam), 140
We're all drunkards here, and harlots 9Akhmatova), xxiii
We're harlots here and carousers (Akhmatova), xxiv
Weeping Garden, The (Appalling! it drips and listens—is it) (Pasternak), 457
What about You? (I splintered the landscape of midday) (Mayakovsky), 149
Where shall I find the style to describe a stroll (Kuzmin), 113
With my path chosen, I walk on calmly (Lokhvitskaya), 124
Whoever breathes you, o god, He is a wing! (Ivanov), 296
Woman will be your downfall. There's—the mark (Tsvetaeva), 213
Word, The (God had bowed his face one day to look) (Gumilyov), 78
Yes, they say that it was necessary (Shkapskaya), 194
You! (You, wallowing in orgy after orgy) (Mayakovsky), 156
You burn bright above a high mountain (Blok), 46
You have come to Russia out of nowhere (Akhmatova) 19
A young girl sang in a cathedral choir (Blok), 47
Youth (My red tie is first rate) (Klyuev), 105
Zangezi (Khlebnikov), 91, 404

www.ingramcontent.com/pod-product-compliance
Lightning Source LLC
Chambersburg PA
CBHW051551230426
43668CB00013B/1817